P9-CSE-107

THE MERMAID SERIES.

EDITED BY HAVELOCK ELLIS.

THE BEST PLAYS OF THE OLD DRAMATISTS.

THOMAS MIDDLETON

II.

MOLL FRITH
The Roaring Girl.

The Best Plays of the Old Dramatists.

THOMAS MIDDLETON

Edited by Havelock Ellis.

" I lie and dream of your full Mermaid wine "—*Beaumont.*

II.

UNEXPURGATED EDITION.

LONDON:

VIZETELLY & CO., 16 HENRIETTA STREET,

COVENT GARDEN.

1890.

Republished

Scholarly Press, Inc., 22929 Industrial Drive East
St. Clair Shores, Michigan 48080

WILLIAM MADISON RANDALL LIBRARY UNC AT WILMINGTON

Library of Congress Catalog Card Number: 70-8060
ISBN 0-403-00123-4

" What things have we seen
Done at the Mermaid ! heard words that have been
So nimble, and so full of subtle flame,
As if that every one from whence they came
Had meant to put his whole wit in a jest,
And had resolved to live a fool the rest
Of his dull life."

Master Francis Beaumont to Ben Jonson.

" Souls of Poets dead and gone
What Elysium have ye known,
Happy field or mossy cavern,
Choicer than the Mermaid Tavern?"

Keats.

**Paper used in this edition is
a fine acid-free, permanent/durable paper
of the type commonly referred to as
"300-year" paper**

PR2712
.E5
1969
v.2

CONTENTS.

87143

PREFACE.

IDDLETON wrote the comedy of *The Roaring Girl* in conjunction with Dekker. The play is chiefly the work of Middleton, but we detect Dekker's hand in occasional fantastic or imaginative passages, as well as by the copious knowledge of thieves and their slang which somewhat deforms the concluding scenes. To that tender-hearted poet we probably owe much of the charity shed over the central figure in this delightful play. Mary Frith, commonly called Moll Cut-purse, was a noted character of the period, and her reputation was none of the best. She was about twenty-five years old at the time that she gave her name to this play, and only a few months later she had to do penance at Paul's Cross.[1] But this is not the Moll that our dramatists saw. She is strong and courageous, indeed, a " goodly personable creature," and her sword

---

[1] See the brief Memoir of her on p. 2.

is the match of any man's, but it is never drawn save in a good cause. She is frank and free-spoken ; when among friends the mood takes her, she can even sing a wanton song and accompany it on the viol ; but she is modest for all that, and woe to the man who attempts to take liberties ! She is acquainted with the shapes of iniquity, but she moves among them uncontaminated, and uses her knowledge not to practise but to defeat vice. She is a knight-errant who goes about succouring distressed lovers in the way of honesty, and she would like in her own person to avenge all the wrongs of women. She declares at the end that she will not marry until many wrongs are righted ;

> " Honesty and truth unslandered,
> Women manned but never pandered. "

"This sounds like doomsday," Lord Noland remarks. But Moll is content.

The Witch has been included in the present volume chiefly on account of its witch-scenes. They are interesting for their own sake, and also for comparison with the corresponding scenes in *Macbeth.* The old controversy as to Shakespeare's debt to Middleton, or Middleton's to Shakespeare, has died out. It seems now to be generally agreed that there was no debt on either side, but that subsequent adapters interpolated portions of Middleton's play into Shakespeare's. Putting aside the witch-scenes, this play is certainly not above Middleton's average level of excellence.

A Fair Quarrel, by Middleton and Rowley, has
of late years been chiefly associated with the name
of Middleton, and has, since the days of Charles
Lamb, deservedly ranked high on account of the
scenes of quarrel and reconciliation between Captain
Ager and the colonel. This play may be divided
into three fairly distinct parts, each with a manner
of its own : the story of Jane, Fitzallen, and the
physician ; the exploits of the roaring boys ; the
scenes between the captain and the colonel. The
first part is on the whole, I am inclined to think, by
Middleton.[1] The second part shows much of the
spirit of Middleton in realistic comedy, but it is
over-done, as Middleton's comedy rarely is, and we
are probably not mistaken in asserting that Rowley
had a considerable hand in this portion. The third
and most important part remains. This is marked
by impetuosity and vigour, combined with very
rough swift verse, and by an easy ascension to impossible heights of magnanimity, audacity, or resig-
nation. It has often been pointed out that Rowley
in his unaided work never achieved anything com-
parable to this. But there are two other points
which have not, so far as I know, been remarked
upon. The first is that neither does anything of
like kind occur in the unaided work of Middleton ;
the second, that precisely the same qualities are

[1] There are, however, distinct touches of Rowley also, as Mr
Bullen has pointed out. I note, for instance, that the action of
the well-bred Jane, in spitting at the physician who had insulted
her, is paralleled in Rowley's *All's Lost by Lust*, where th virtuous and high-born Jacinta spits at Lothario.

found in the other two great plays (*The Changeling*, and *The Spanish Gipsy*) in which Middleton and Rowley worked together. Middleton wrote a great many plays, and the qualities of his style in tragedy and serious romantic comedy are familiar to us. *The Witch*, though not a favourable example, is fairly typical. Spirited and swift as Middleton is in realistic comedy, he is always slow and deliberate in serious comedy, with many pauses for acute or noble reflection on life, sometimes of a Miltonic cast.[1] He had great knowledge of men, and his insight into human weaknesses was far too keen to permit of any enthusiasm for depicting unalloyed virtues or colossal vices. In his unaided work— rich and varied as it is—it is difficult to recall any heroic figure or any scene of high emotional intensity. Rowley, on the other hand, seems to have been a fitful and irregular artist, incapable of writing blank verse save in flashes of sudden inspiration, often incapable of constructing a sound plot, and maundering on piteously when he has to construct his own.[2] But his energy and spirit in taking up a subject already made for him were often of the most masculine order ; he had a rough but close grasp of the naked tragedy of events, well marked in the oft-treated subject of *All's Lost by Lust;* and he had an overmastering delight in all the manifesta-

[1] In his Introduction to the first volume of this edition of Middleton, Mr Swinburne has pointed out the attraction which the elder poet had for Milton.

[2] I agree with Mr Bullen that Rowley probably had very little to do with *A Match at Midnight.*

ions of strong passion, the magnanimous Julianus, the ferociously cruel Moor. It is Rowley's hand that we trace in the fiery impetuosity and saint-like submission of the ideal soldier-nature,—

> "his soul's wish to depart absolute man.
> In life a soldier, death a Christian."

Rowley was enamoured of the passions of the "absolute man," but of ordinary human weaknesses he knew nothing, and he could not build up a rational human creature. It is for this reason that the collaboration of Middleton and Rowley produced such happy results ; each supplied the other's deficiencies. That the work produced by this partnership is superior to anything produced by Rowley alone is undoubtedly true ; but it is of the same order, and differs in degree only.

The Mayor of Queenborough was published in 1661 as the work of Middleton. Of late years it has received such high praise that the reader will expect to find it in an edition of Middleton's best plays. I have, however, only included it after considerable hesitation. As a whole the play is obscure, roughly written and uninteresting ; the rare flashes of splendid or passionate poetry that redeem it might be gathered up into a very small space. The play is by no means characteristic of Middleton ; it has not been sufficiently pointed out how slender a thread of evidence connects it with him. It was not published with Middleton's name until the Restoration. After the great events that had

intervened and the complete interruption of theatri-
cal traditions, a play might easily be assigned
wrongly without any intention of fraud. It would
come with a very incomplete history into the pub-
lisher's hands ; some one would be found who
had witnessed its representation thirty years before
and who assigned it to this or that writer, and in
uncritical days the matter would be settled. In the
whole play it is difficult to find any passage that is
unmistakeably characteristic of Middleton ; the buf-
foonery of the comic interludes certainly cannot be
his,[1] and the serious portions of the play, inco-
herent, spasmodic, irregular, are at best as much in
the manner of his chief co-worker. It is interesting
to compare this play with Rowley's *Birth of Merlin*,
a related subject.

The Widow was published in Commonwealth
days by an actor who at that time helped to organ-
ise secret dramatic performances in noblemen's
houses, especially Holland House ; he "used to be
the jackal and give notice of time and place." It is
described on the title-page as the work of Jonson, .
Fletcher, and Middleton. Jonson assuredly had
nothing to do with it ; Fletcher may possibly have
had a finger in it ; the first two acts certainly recall
Fletcher's manner in plays of brilliant, rather licentious intrigue of the Spanish kind ; but this is soon
merged in what is unmistakably Middleton's more
wholesome style. And it is his most delightful

[1] I find that Mr Bullen is inclined to assign these scenes to
Rowley.

style of romantic comedy. *The Widow* has not hitherto attracted attention, but it deserves to be placed little below *The Spanish Gipsy;* it has not the energy which Rowley probably put into the early scenes of that play, but it is more evenly enjoyable, always bright and alert, with no jarring discord to spoil its joyous humanity. It is easy to understand how its unalloyed cheerfulness commended it in Commonwealth days and later. Morality here, so far as it exists at all, is a natural instinct, not a stern law ; the voice of the earnest Puritan's prayers, and the clash of his sword, are alike inaudible. We think of the little group of men and women, collected in secret by the "jackal" —like the devotees of a persecuted faith—to witness this glimpse of a large and sunny world that had vanished for ever.

H. E.

THE ROARING GIRL.

HE *Roaring Girl* was written by Middleton in conjunction with Dekker, acted at the Fortune Theatre, and published in 1611.

Mary Frith, commonly called Moll Cutpurse, on whose story the play is founded, was born in 1584, or rather later, in Aldersgate Street (according to the author of her "Life," published in 1662), her father being a shoemaker. She "delighted and sported," we are told, "only in boys' play and pastime, not minding or companying with the girls: she could not endure the sedentary life of sewing or stitching; a sampler was as grievous as a winding-sheet; her needle, bodkin, and thimble she could not think on quietly, wishing them changed into sword and dagger for a bout at cudgels." The experiment of sending this "lusty and sturdy wench" to domestic service was unsuccessfully attempted. She abandoned service, assumed male attire, and "to her dying day she would not leave it off." She is said to have been the first woman who vindicated for her sex the right of smoking.

In 1612 Mary Frith had to do penance at Paul's Cross, but for what offence is not known. We are told that she seemed very penitent, but it was discovered that she had "tippled off three quarts of sack before she came to her penance." It is related that she once robbed and wounded General Fairfax on Hounslow Heath. She lived to old age, although suffering latterly from dropsy, and died about the date of the Restoration of Charles II.

The portrait of Mary Frith, which forms the frontispiece to the present volume, has been copied from a woodcut printed on the title-page to the 1611 edition of *The Roaring Girl.*

TO THE COMIC PLAY-READERS, VENERY AND LAUGHTER.

HE fashion of play-making I can properly compare to nothing so naturally as the alteration in apparel ; for in the time of the great crop-doublet, your huge bombastic plays, quilted with mighty words to lean purpose, was only then in fashion : and as the doublet fell, neater inventions began to set up. Now, in the time of spruceness, our plays follow the niceness' of our garments, single plots, quaint conceits, lecherous jests, dressed up in hanging sleeves : and those are fit for the times and termers.[1] Such a kind of light-colour summer stuff, mingled with divers colours, you shall find this published comedy ; good to keep you in an afternoon from dice at home in your chambers : and for venery, you shall find enough for sixpence,[2] but well couched an you mark it ; for Venus, being a woman, passes through the play in doublet and breeches ; a brave disguise and a safe one, if the statute untie not her codpiece point. The book I make no question but is fit for many of your companies, as well as the person itself, and may be allowed both gallery-room at the playhouse, and chamber-room at your lodging. Worse things, I must needs confess, the world has taxed her for than has been written of her ; but 'tis the excellency of a writer to leave things better than he finds 'em ; though some obscene fellow, that cares not what he writes against others, yet keeps a mystical bawdyhouse himself, and entertains drunkards, to make use of their pockets and vent' his private bottle-ale at midnight,—though such a one would have ripped up the most nasty vice that ever hell belched forth, and presented it to a modest assembly, yet we rather wish in such discoveries, where reputation lies bleeding, a slackness of truth than fulness of slander.   THOMAS MIDDLETON.

[1] Frequenters of the law courts.   Many strangers came to London in term-time.   [2] The price of a play-book at the time.

PROLOGUE

A PLAY expected long makes the audience look
For wonders; that each scene should be a book,
Composed to all perfection : each one comes
And brings a play in's head with him ; up he sums
That he would of a Roaring Girl have writ;
If that he finds not here, he mews[1] at it.
Only we do entreat you think our scene
Cannot speak high, the subject being but mean ;
A Roaring Girl, whose notes till now ne'er were,
Shall fill with laughter our vast theatre.[2]
That's all which I dare promise : tragic passion,
And such grave stuff, is this day out of fashion.
I see Attention sets wide ope her gates
Of hearing, and with covetous listening waits,
To know what girl this Roaring Girl should be
For of that tribe are many.   One is she
That roars at midnight in deep tavern-bowls,
That beats the watch, and constables controls :
Another roars i' the daytime, swears, stabs, gives braves,
Yet sells her soul to the lust of fools and slaves :

---

[1] A common way of expressing disapproval at plays.

[2] The fortune in Golding Lane, built in 1600, and burnt down
in 1621. (See the frontispiece to *The Best Plays of Thomas
Dekker*, in this series).

Both these are sub-roarers. Then there's beside
A civil city Roaring Girl, whose pride,
Feasting, and riding, shakes her husband's state,
And leaves him roaring through an iron grate.[1]
None of these Roaring Girls is ours; she flies
With wings more lofty; thus her character lies—
Yet what need characters, when to give a guess
Is better than the person to express?
But would you know who 'tis? would you hear her name?
She's called Mad Moll; her life our acts proclaim.

[1] *i.e.* Of the debtors' prison.

DRAMATIS PERSONÆ.

Sir Alexander Wengrave.
Sebastian Wengrave, his son.
Sir Guy Fitzallard.
Sir Davy Dapper.
Jack Dapper, his son.
Sir Adam Appleton.
Sir Thomas Long.
Sir Beauteous Ganymede.
Lord Noland.
Goshawk.
Laxton.
Greenwit.
Gallipot, an apothecary.
Tiltyard, a feather-seller.
Openwork, a sempster.
Neatfoot, Sir A. Wengrave's man.
Gull, page to Jack Dapper.
Trapdoor.
Tearcat.
Coachman.
Porter.
Tailor.
Curtleax, a sergeant.
Hanger, his yeoman.
Gentlemen, Cutpurses, &c.

Moll, the Roaring Girl.
Mary Fitzallard, daughter of Sir Guy.
Mistress Gallipot.
Mistress Tiltyard.
Mistress Openwork.

SCENE—LONDON.

THE ROARING GIRL.

ACT THE FIRST.

SCENE I.

A Room in Sir Alexander Wengrave's *House.*

Enter Mary Fitzallard *disguised like a* Sempster, *with a case for bands, and* Neatfoot *with her, a napkin on his shoulder, and a trencher*[1] *in his hand, as from table.*

EAT. The young gentleman, our young master, Sir Alexander's son, is it into his ears, sweet damsel, emblem of fragility, you desire to have a message transported, or to be transcendent?

Mary. A private word or two, sir; nothing else.

Neat. You shall fructify in that which you come for; your pleasure shall be satisfied to your full contentment. I will, fairest tree of generation, watch when our young master is erected, that is to say, up, and deliver him to this your most white hand.

Mary. Thanks, sir.

[1] Wooden trenchers were still used at this date, even in the houses of the rich.

Neat. And withal certify him, that I have culled out for him, now his belly is replenished, a daintier bit or modicum than any lay upon his trencher at dinner. Hath he notion of your name, I beseech your chastity?

Mary. One, sir, of whom he bespake falling bands.[1]

Neat. Falling bands? It shall so be given him. If you please to venture your modesty in the hall amongst a curl-pated company of rude serving-men, and take such as they can set before you, you shall be most seriously and ingeniously[2] welcome.

Mary. I have dined indeed already, sir.

Neat. Or will you vouchsafe to kiss the lip of a cup of rich Orleans in the buttery amongst our waiting-women?

Mary. Not now, in truth, sir.

Neat. Our young master shall then have a feeling of your being here; presently it shall so be given him.

Mary. I humbly thank you, sir. But that my bosom
                                     [*Exit* NEATFOOT.
Is full of bitter sorrows, I could smile
To see this formal ape play antic tricks;
But in my breast a poisoned arrow sticks,
And smiles cannot become me. Love woven slightly,
Such as thy false heart makes, wears out as lightly;
But love being truly bred i' the soul, like mine,
Bleeds even to death at the least wound it takes,—
The more we quench this fire, the less it slakes:
O me!'

Enter SEBASTIAN WENGRAVE *with* NEATFOOT.

Seb. A sempster speak with me, sayest thou?

---

[1] They lay on the shoulders; "which new mode," said Evelyn, "succeeded the cumbersome ruff." Nares remarks that "the assumption of the band was, doubtless, originally a piece of coxcombry, as was the wearing of large wigs, though both are now thought to be connected with professional dignity."

[2] *i.e.* Sincerely.

Neat. Yes, sir; she's there, *viva voce* to deliver her auricular confession.

Seb. With me, sweetheart? what is't?

Mary. I have brought home your bands, sir.

Seb. Bands?—Neatfoot.

Neat. Sir?

Seb. Prithee, look in; for all the gentlemen are upon rising.

Neat. Yes, sir; a most methodical attendance shall be given.

Seb. And dost hear? if my father call for me, say I am busy with a sempster.

Neat. Yes, sir; he shall know it that you are busied with a needle-woman.

Seb. In's ear, good Neatfoot.

Neat. It shall be so given him.   [*Exit.*

Seb. Bands? you're mistaken, sweetheart, I bespake
          none:
When, where, I prithee? what bands? let me see them.

Mary. Yes, sir; a bond [1] fast sealed with solemn oaths,
Subscribed unto, as I thought, with your soul;
Delivered as your deed in sight of Heaven:
Is this bond cancelled? have you forgot me?

Seb. Ha! life of my life, Sir Guy Fitzallard's daughter?
What has transformed my love to this strange shape?
Stay; make all sure [*Shuts the door*]; so: now speak
          and be brief,
Because the wolf's at door that lies in wait
To prey upon us both.   Albeit mine eyes
Are blest by thine, yet this so strange disguise
Holds me with fear and wonder.

Mary. Mine's a loathed sight;
Why from it are you banished else so long?

Seb. I must cut short my speech: in broken language
Thus much, sweet Moll; I must thy company shun;
I court another Moll: my thoughts must run

          [1] "Bond" and "band" were synonymous.

As a horse runs that's blind round in a mill,
Out every step, yet keeping one path still.

   Mary. Umph! must you shun my company? in one
     knot
Have both our hands by the hands of Heaven been tied,
Now to be broke? I thought me once your bride;
Our fathers did agree on the time when:
And must another bedfellow fill my room?

   Seb. Sweet maid, let's lose no time; 'tis in Heaven's
     book
Set down, that I must have thee; an oath we took
To keep our vows: but when the knight your father
Was from mine parted, storms began to sit
Upon my covetous father's brows, which fell
From them on me. He reckoned up what gold
This marriage would draw from him; at which he swore,
To lose so much blood could not grieve him more:
He then dissuades me from thee, called thee not fair
And asked what is she but a beggar's heir?
He scorned thy dowry of five thousand marks.
If such a sum of money could be found,
And I would match with that, he'd not undo it,
Provided his bags might add nothing to it;
But vowed, if I took thee, nay, more, did swear it,
Save birth, from him I nothing should inherit.

   Mary. What follows then? my shipwreck?

   Seb. Dearest, no:
Though wildly in a labyrinth I go,
My end is to meet thee: with a side-wind
Must I now sail, else I no haven can find,
But both must sink for ever. There's a wench
Called Moll, mad Moll, or merry Moll; a creature
So strange in quality, a whole city takes
Note of her name and person: all that affection
I owe to thee, on her in counterfeit passion
I spend, to mad my father: he believes
I dote upon this Roaring Girl, and grieves

As it becomes a father for a son
That could be so bewitched : yet I'll go on
This crooked way, sigh still for her, feign dreams
In which I'll talk only of her : these streams
Shall, I hope, force my father to consent
That here I anchor, rather than be rent
Upon a rock so dangerous.   Art thou pleased,
Because thou seest we're waylaid, that I take
A path that's safe, though it be far about ?
   Mary. My prayers with Heaven guide thee !
   Seb. Then I will on :
My father is at hand ; kiss, and begone !
Hours shall be watched for meetings : I must now,
As men for fear, to a strange idol bow.
   Mary. Farewell !
   Seb. I'll guide thee forth : when next we meet,
A story of Moll shall make our mirth more sweet.
[Exeunt.

Enter Sir ALEXANDER WENGRAVE, Sir DAVY DAPPER,
   Sir ADAM APPLETON, GOSHAWK, LAXTON, *and*
   Gentlemen.

   All. Thanks, good Sir Alexander, for our bounteous
      cheer !
   Sir Alex. Fie, fie, in giving thanks you pay too dear.
   Sir Davy. When bounty spreads the table, faith, 'twere
      sin,
At going off if thanks should not step in.
   Sir Alex. No more of thanks, no more.   Ay, marry,
      sir.
The inner room was too close : how do you like
This parlour, gentlemen ?
   All. O, passing well !
   Sir Adam. What a sweet breath the air casts here, so
      cool !
   Gos. I like the prospect best.
   Lax. See how 'tis furnished !

Sir Davy. A very fair sweet room.

Sir Alex. Sir Davy Dapper,
The furniture that doth adorn this room
Cost many a fair gray groat ere it came here;
But good things are most cheap when they're most dear.
Nay, when you look into my galleries,
How bravely they're trimmed up, you all shall swear
You're highly pleased to see what's set down there:
Stories of men and women, mixed together,
Fair ones with foul, like sunshine in wet weather;
Within one square a thousand heads are laid,
So close that all of heads the room seems made;
As many faces there, filled with blithe looks,
Show like the promising titles of new books
Writ merrily, the readers being their own eyes,
Which seem to move and to give plaudites;
And here and there, whilst with obsequious ears
Thronged heaps do listen, a cut-purse thrusts and leers
With hawk's eyes for his prey; I need not show him;
By a hanging, villanous look yourselves may know him,
The face is drawn so rarely: then, sir, below
The very floor, as 'twere, waves to and fro,
And, like a floating island, seems to move
Upon a sea bound in with shores above.

All. These sights are excellent!

Sir Alex. I'll show you all:
Since we are met, make our parting comical.

Re-enter SEBASTIAN WENGRAVE *with* GREENWIT.

Seb. This gentleman, my friend, will take his leave, sir.

Sir Alex. Ha! take his leave, Sebastian, who?

Seb. This gentleman.

Sir Alex. Your love, sir, has already given me some
    time,
And if you please to trust my age with more,
It shall pay double interest: good sir, stay.

Green. I have been too bold.

Sir Alex. Not so, sir : a merry day
Mongst friends being spent, is better than gold saved.—
Some wine, some wine ! Where be these knaves I keep?

Re-enter NEATFOOT *with several* Servants.

Neat. At your worshipful elbow, sir.
Sir Alex. You're kissing my maids, drinking, or fast
    asleep.
Neat. Your worship has given it us right.
Sir Alex. You varlets, stir !
Chairs, stools, and cushions !—
                    [Servants *bring in wine, and place chairs, &c.*
                    Prithee, Sir Davy Dapper,
Make that chair thine.
Sir Davy. 'Tis but an easy gift;
And yet I thank you for it, sir : I'll take it.
Sir Alex. A chair for old Sir Adam Appleton !
Neat. A back friend to your worship.
Sir Adam. Marry, good Neatfoot,
I thank thee for't; back friends sometimes are good.
Sir Alex. Pray, make that stool your perch, good
    Master Goshawk.
Gos. I stoop to your lure, sir.
Sir Alex. Son Sebastian.
Take Master Greenwit to you.
Seb. Sit, dear friend.
Sir Alex. Nay, Master Laxton—furnish Master Laxton
With what he wants, a stone,—a stool, I would say,
A stool.
Lax. I had rather stand, sir.
Sir Alex. I know you had, good Master Laxton: so,
    so.   [*Exeunt* NEATFOOT *and* Servants.
Now here's a mess of friends ; and, gentlemen,
Because time's glass shall not be running long,
I'll quicken it with a pretty tale.
Sir Davy. Good tales do well
In these bad days, where vice does so excel.

Sir Adam. Begin, Sir Alexander.

Sir Alex. Last day I met

An agèd man, upon whose head was scored

A debt of just so many years as these

Which I owe to my grave: the man you all know.

All. His name, I pray you, sir.

Sir Alex. Nay, you shall pardon me:

But when he saw me, with a sigh that brake,

Or seemed to break, his heart-strings, thus he spake:

O my good knight, says he (and then his eyes

Were richer even by that which made them poor,

They'd spent so many tears they had no more),

O sir, says he, you know it! for you ha' seen

Blessings to rain upon mine house and me:

Fortune, who slaves men, was my slave; her wheel

Hath spun me golden threads; for, I thank Heaven,

I ne'er had but one cause to curse my stars.

I asked him then what that one cause might be.

All. So, sir.

Sir Alex. He paused: and as we often see

A sea so much becalmed, there can be found

No wrinkle on his brow, his waves being drowned

In their own rage; but when the imperious winds

Use strange invisible tyranny to shake

Both Heaven's and earth's foundation at their noise,

The seas, swelling with wrath to part that fray,

Rise up, and are more wild, more mad than they:

Even so this good old man was by my question

Stirred up to roughness; you might see his gall

Flow even in's eyes; then grew he fantastical.

Sir Davy. Fantastical? ha, ha!

Sir Alex. Yes; and talked oddly.

Sir Adam. Pray, sir, proceed:

How did this old man end?

Sir Alex. Marry, sir, thus:

He left his wild fit to read o'er his cards;

Yet then, though age cast snow on all his hairs.

He joyed, because, says he, the god of gold
Has been to me no niggard ; that disease,
Of which all old men sicken, avarice,
Never infected me——

  Lax. He means not himself, I'm sure.   [*Aside.*
  Sir Alex. For, like a lamp
Fed with continual oil, I spend and throw
My light to all that need it, yet have still
Enough to serve myself: O but, quoth he,
Though Heaven's dew fall thus on this aged tree,
I have a son that, like a wedge, doth cleave
My very heart-root !

  Sir Davy. Had he such a son?
  Seb. Now I do smell a fox strongly.   [*Aside.*
  Sir Alex. Let's see : no, Master Greenwit is not yet
So mellow in years as he ; but as like Sebastian,
Just like my son Sebastian, such another.

  Seb. How finely, like a fencer,
My father fetches his by-blows to hit me !
But if I beat you not at your own weapon
Of subtlety——   [*Aside.*

  Sir Alex. This son, saith he, that should be
The column and main arch unto my house,
The crutch unto my age, becomes a whirlwind
Shaking the firm foundation.

  Sir Adam. 'Tis some prodigal.
  Seb. Well shot, old Adam Bell ![1]   [*Aside.*
  Sir Alex. No city-monster neither, no prodigal,
But sparing, wary, civil, and, though wifeless,
An excellent husband ; and such a traveller,
He has more tongues in his head than some have
  teeth.

  Sir Davy. I have but two in mine.
  Gos. So sparing and so wary ?
What, then, could vex his father so ?

---

[1] A celebrated outlaw. The ballad of *Adam Bel, Clym of the
Cloughe and Wyllyam of Cloudesle* is well known.

Sir Alex. O, a woman !

Seb. A flesh-fly, that can vex any man.

Sir Alex. A scurvy woman,
On whom the passionate old man swore he doted :
A creature, saith he, nature hath brought forth
To mock the sex of woman.   It is a thing
One knows not how to name : her birth began
Ere she was all made : 'tis woman more than man,
Man more than woman ; and, which to none can hap,
The sun gives her two shadows to one shape ;
Nay, more, let this strange thing walk, stand, or sit,
No blazing star [1] draws more eyes after it.

Sir Davy. A monster ! 'tis some monster !

Sir Alex. She's a varlet.

Seb. Now is my cue to bristle. | *Aside.*

Sir Alex. A naughty pack.

Seb. 'Tis false !

Sir Alex. Ha, boy ?

Seb. 'Tis false !

Sir Alex. What's false ?   I say she's naught.

Seb. I say, that tongue
That dares speak so, but yours, sticks in the throat
Of a rank villain : set yourself aside——

Sir Alex. So, sir, what then ?

Seb. Any here else had lied.—
I think I shall fit you.   [*Aside.*

Sir Alex. Lie ?

Seb. Yes.

Sir Davy. Doth this concern him ?

Sir Alex. Ah, sirrah-boy,
Is your blood heated ? boils it ? are you stung ?
I'll pierce you deeper yet.—O my dear friends,
I am that wretched father ! this that son,
That sees his ruin, yet headlong on doth run.

Sir Adam. Will you love such a poison ?

Sir Davy. Fie, fie.

[1] Comet.

Seb. You're all mad.

Sir Alex. Thou'rt sick at heart, yet feel'st it not : **of**
all these,
What gentleman but thou, knowing his disease
Mortal, would shun the cure !—O Master Greenwit,
Would you to such an idol bow ?

Green. Not I, sir.

Sir Alex. Here's Master Laxton ; has he mind to a
woman
As thou hast ?

Lax. No, not I, sir.

Sir Alex. Sir, I know it.

Lax. Their good parts are so rare, their bad so
common,
I will have nought to do with any woman.

Sir Davy. 'Tis well done, Master Laxton. '

Sir Alex. O thou cruel boy,
Thou wouldst with lust an old man's life destroy !
Because thou seest I'm half-way in my grave,
Thou shovel'st dust upon me : would thou mightst have
Thy wish, most wicked, most unnatural !

Sir Davy. Why, sir, 'tis thought Sir Guy Fitzallard's
daughter
Shall wed your son Sebastian.

Sir Alex. Sir Davy Dapper,
I have upon my knees wooed this fond[1] boy
To take that virtuous maiden.

Seb. Hark you ; a word, sir.
You on your knees have cursed that virtuous maiden,
And me for loving her ; yet do you now
Thus baffle[2] me to my face ?   Wear not your knees
In such entreats ; give me Fitzallard's daughter.

Sir Alex. I'll give thee rats-bane rather.

---

[1] Foolish.

[2] Mock, baffle (**Fr.** *baffouer* or *baffoler*) was originally a **punish-**
ment of infamy, inflicted on recreant knights, one part of which
was hanging them up by the heels.—*Nares.*

Mid. II.   C

Seb. Well, then, you know
What dish I mean to feed upon.
  Sir Alex. Hark, gentlemen! he swears
To have this cut-purse drab, to spite my gall.
  All. Master Sebastian——
  Seb. I am deaf to you all.
I'm so bewitched, so bound to my desires,
Tears, prayers, threats, nothing can quench out ҭhose
    fires
That burn within me,   [*Exit.*
  Sir Alex. Her blood shall quench it, then.— [*Aside.*
Lose him not; O, dissuade him, gentlemen!
  Sir Davy. He shall be weaned, I warrant you.
  Sir Alex. Before his eyes
Lay down his shame, my grief, his miseries.
  All. No more, no more; away!
          [*Exeunt all but* Sir ALEXANDER WENGRAVE.
  Sir Alex. I wash a negro,
Losing both pains and cost: but take thy flight,
I'll be most near thee when I'm least in sight.
Wild buck, I'll hunt thee breathless: thou shalt run
    on,
But I will turn thee when I'm not thought upon

            Enter TRAPDOOR *with a letter.*

Now, sirrah, what are you? leave your ape's tricks, and
speak.
  Trap. A letter from my captain to your worship.
  Sir Alex. O, O, now I remember; 'tis to prefer thee
into my service.
  Trap. To be a shifter under your worship's nose of a
clean trencher, when there's a good bit upon't.
  Sir Alex. Troth, honest fellow—Hum—ha—let me
    see—
This knave shall be the axe to hew that down
At which I stumble; has a face that promiseth
Much of a villain: I will grind his wit,

And, if the edge prove fine, make use of it.— [*Aside.*
Come hither, sirrah : canst thou be secret, ha ?

Trap. As two crafty attorneys plotting the undoing of
their clients.

Sir Alex. Didst never, as thou'st walked about this town,
Hear of a wench called Moll,—mad, merry Moll ?

Trap. Moll Cut-purse, sir ?

Sir Alex. The same ; dost thou know her, then ?

Trap. As well as I know 'twill rain upon Simon and
Jude's day next : I will sift all the taverns i' the city, and
drink half-pots with all the watermen[1] a' the Bank-side,
but, if you will, sir, I'll find her out.

Sir Alex. That task is easy ; do't then : hold thy hand
up.
What's this ? is't burnt ?[2]

Trap. No, sir, no ; a little singed with making fire-
works.

Sir Alex. There's money, spend it ; that being spent,
fetch more. [*Gives money.*

Trap. O sir, that all the poor soldiers in England
had such a leader ! For fetching, no water spaniel is
like me.

Sir Alex. This wench we speak of strays so from her
kind,
Nature repents she made her : 'tis a mermaid
Has toled my son to shipwreck.

Trap. I'll cut her comb for you.

Sir Alex. I'll tell out gold for thee, then. Hunt her
forth,
Cast out a line hung full of silver hooks
To catch her to thy company : deep spendings
May draw her that's most chaste to a man's bosom.

Trap. The jingling of golden bells, and a good fool

---

[1] Taylor the water-poet asserts, that at this time, between
Windsor and Gravesend, there were not fewer than forty thousand
watermen.—*Reed.*

[2] Felons were frequently branded in the hand.

with a hobbyhorse, will draw all the whores i' the town
to dance in a morris.

Sir Alex. Or rather, for that's best (they say sometimes
She goes in breeches), follow her as her man.

Trap. And when her breeches are off, she shall follow
    me.

Sir Alex. Beat all thy brains to serve her.

Trap. Zounds, sir, as country wenches beat cream till
butter comes.

Sir Alex. Play thou the subtle spider; weave fine nets
To ensnare her very life.

Trap. Her life?

Sir Alex. Yes; suck
Her heart-blood, if thou canst: twist thou but cords
To catch her, I'll find law to hang her up.

Trap. Spoke like a worshipful bencher!

Sir Alex. Trace all her steps: at this she-fox's den
Watch what lambs enter; let me play the shepherd
To save their throats from bleeding, and cut hers.

Trap. This is the goll[1] shall do't.

Sir Alex. Be firm, and gain me
Ever thine own: this done, I entertain thee.
How is thy name?

Trap. My name, sir, is Ralph Trapdoor, honest Ralph.

Sir Alex. Trapdoor, be like thy name, a dangerous
    step
For her to venture on; but unto me——

Trap. As fast as your sole to your boot or shoe, sir.

Sir Alex. Hence, then; be little seen here as thou
    canst;
I'll still be at thine elbow.

Trap. The trapdoor's set.
Moll, if you budge, you're gone: this me shall crown;
A roaring boy the roaring girl puts down.

Sir Alex. God-a-mercy, lose no time.   [*Exeunt.*

    [1] Hand.

ACT THE SECOND

SCENE I.

*Three Shops open in a rank: the first an Apothecary's Shop,
the next a Feather-shop, the third a Sempster's Shop;
Mistress* GALLIPOT *in the first,* Mistress TILTYARD *in
the next,* OPENWORK *and* Mistress OPENWORK *in the
third.*

Enter LAXTON, GOSHAWK, *and* GREENWIT.

IS. OPEN. Gentlemen, what is't you
lack? what is't you buy? see fine
bands and ruffs, fine lawns, fine
cambrics: what is't you lack, gentle
men? what is't you buy?

 Lax. Yonder's the shop.

Gos. Is that she?

Lax. Peace.

Green. She that minces tobacco?[1]

Lax. Ay; she's a gentlewoman born, I can tell you,
though it be her hard fortune now to shred Indian pot
herbs.

Gos. O sir, 'tis many a good woman's fortune, when
her husband turns bankrout, to begin with pipes and set
up again.

Lax. And, indeed, the raising of the woman is the
lifting up of the man's head at all times; if one flourish,
t'other will bud as fast, I warrant ye.

---

[1] Tobacco was at this time sold by apothecaries.

Gos. Come, thou'rt familiarly acquainted there, I grope that.

Lax. An' you grope no better i' the dark, you may chance lie i' the ditch when you're drunk.

Gos. Go, thou'rt a mystical lecher !

Lax. I will not deny but my credit may take up an ounce of pure smoke.

Gos. May take up an ell of pure smock ! away, go !—'Tis the closest striker ![1] life, I think he commits venery forty foot deep ; no man's aware on't.   I, like a palpable smockster, go to work so openly with the tricks of art, that I'm as apparently seen as a naked boy in a phial ;[2] and were it not for a gift of treachery that I have in me, to betray my friend when he puts most trust in me—mass, yonder he is too !—and by his injury to make good my access to her, I should appear as defective in courting as a farmer's son the first day of his feather, that doth nothing at court but woo the hangings and glass windows for a month together, and some broken waiting-women for ever after.   I find those imperfections in my venery, that were't not for flattery and falsehood, I should want discourse and impudence ; and he that wants impudence among women is worthy to be kicked out at bed's feet. He shall not see me yet.   [*Aside.*

Green. Troth, this is finely shred.

Lax. O, women are the best mincers.

Mis. G. 'Thad been a good phrase for a cook's wife, sir.

Lax. But 'twill serve generally, like the front of a new almanac, as thus :—calculated for the meridian of cooks' wifes, but generally for all English women.

Mis. G. Nay, you shall ha't, sir ; I have filled it for you.   [*She puts the pipe to the fire.*

Lax. The pipe's in a good hand, and I wish mine always so.

[1] Wencher.

[2] Probably an abortion preserved in spirits.—*Steevens.*

Green. But not to be used a' that fashion.

Lax. O, pardon me, sir, I understand no French. I pray, be covered. Jack, a pipe of rich smoke!

Gos. Rich smoke? that's sixpence a pipe, is't?

Green. To me, sweet lady.

Mis. G. Be not forgetful; respect my credit; seem strange: art and wit makes a fool of suspicion; pray, be wary.

Lax. Pish! I warrant you.—Come, how is't, gallants?

Green. Pure and excellent.

Lax. I thought 'twas good, you were grown so silent: you are like those that love not to talk at victuals, though they make a worse noise i' the nose than a common fiddler's 'prentice, and discourse a whole supper with snuffling.—I must speak a word with you anon.

Mis. G. Make your way wisely, then.

Gos. O, what else, sir? he's perfection itself; full of manners,[1] but not an acre of ground belonging to 'em.

Green. Ay, and full of form; has ne'er a good stool in's chamber.

Gos. But above all, religious; he preyeth daily upon elder brothers.

Green. And valiant above measure; has run three streets from a sergeant.

Lax. Puh, puh.   [*He blows tobacco in their faces.*

Green. O, puh!

Gos. Ho, ho!

Lax. So, so.

Mis. G. What's the matter now, sir?

Lax. I protest I'm in extreme want of money; if you can supply me now with any means, you do me the greatest pleasure, next to the bounty of your love, as ever poor gentleman tasted.

Mis. G. What's the sum would pleasure ye, sir? though you deserve nothing less at my hands.

---

1 A quibble on " manners " and " manors."

Lax. Why, 'tis but for want of opportunity, thou knowest.—I put her off with opportunity still : by this light, I hate her, but for means to keep me in fashion with gallants ; for what I take from her, I spend upon other wenches ; bear her in hand [1] still : she has wit enough to rob her husband, and I ways enough to consume the money. [*Aside.*]—Why, how now ? what, the chin-cough ? [2]

Gos. Thou hast the cowardliest trick to come before a man's face, and strangle him ere he be aware ! I could find in my heart to make a quarrel in earnest.

Lax. Pox, an thou dost—thou knowest I never use to fight with my friends—thou'lt but lose thy labour in't. —Jack Dapper !

Enter JACK DAPPER *and* GULL.

Green. Monsieur Dapper, I dive down to your ankles.

J. Dap. Save ye, gentlemen all three, in a peculiar salute.

Gos. He were ill to make a lawyer ; he despatches three at once.

Lax. So, well said.—But is this [3] of the same tobacco, Mistress Gallipot ?

Mis. G. The same you had at first, sir.

Lax. I wish it no better : this will serve to drink [4] at my chamber.

Gos. Shall we taste a pipe on't ?

Lax. Not of this, by my troth, gentlemen, I have sworn before you.

Gos. What, not Jack Dapper ?

Lax. Pardon me, sweet Jack ; I'm sorry I made such

---

[1] *i.e.* Keep her in expectation.

[2] The whooping cough.

[3] She gives him money, and he pretends that he receives only tobacco from Mrs Gallipot.—*Collier.*

[4] To drink—meaning to smoke—tobacco was a common expression at the time.

a rash oath, but foolish oaths must stand: where art going, Jack?

J. Dap. Faith to buy one feather.

Lax. One feather? the fool's peculiar still.   [*Aside.*

J. Dap. Gull.

Gull. Master?

J. Dap. Here's three halfpence[1] for your ordinary, boy; meet me an hour hence in Paul's.

Gull. How? three single halfpence? life, this will scarce serve a man in sauce, a ha'p'orth of mustard, a ha'p'orth of oil, and a ha'p'orth of vinegar,—what's left then for the pickle herring? This shows like small beer i' the morning after a great surfeit of wine o'ernight: he could spend his three pound last night in a supper amongst girls and brave bawdyhouse boys: I thought his pockets cackled not for nothing: these are the eggs of three pound, I'll go sup 'em up presently.

[*Aside, and Exit.*

Lax. Eight, nine, ten angels:[2] good wench, i'faith, and one that loves darkness well; she puts out a candle with the best tricks of any drugster's wife in England: but that which mads her, I rail upon opportunity still, and take no notice on't. The other night she would needs lead me into a room with a candle in her hand to show me a naked picture, where no sooner entered, but the candle was sent of an errand: now, I not intending to understand her, but, like a puny[3] at the inns of venery, called for another light innocently; thus reward I all her cunning with simple mistaking. I know she cozens

---

[1] "And being almost upon dinner-time we hied us and took our repast at thrifty mother Walker's, where we found a whole nest of pinching batchelors, crowded together upon forms and benches in that most worshipful three-halfpenny ordinary."—Middleton's *Father Hubburd's Tales,* quoted by Bullen.

[2] Gold coins. He is reckoning the money he received from Mrs Callipot.

[3] An Oxford freshman. Marston has "a *puisné* of the lawyers' inn."

her husband to keep me, and I'll keep her honest as long
as I can, to make the poor man some part of amends.
An honest mind of a whoremaster! how think you
amongst you?   What, a fresh pipe? draw in a third
man?

  Gos. No, you're a hoarder, you engross by the
   ounces.
  J. Dap. [*At the feather-shop.*]—Pooh, I like it not.
  Mis. T. What feather is't you'd have, sir?
These are most worn and most in fashion :
Amongst the beaver gallants, the stone riders,
The private stage's audience, the twelvepenny-stool
   gentlemen,[1]
I can inform you 'tis the general feather.
  J. Dap. And therefore I mislike it: tell me of general!
Now, a continual Simon and Jude's rain
Beat all your feathers as flat down as pancakes!
Show me—a—spangled feather.
  Mis. T. O, to go a-feasting with;
You'd have it for a hench-boy,[2] you shall.
  Open. [*At the Sempster's shop.*]—Mass, I had quite
   forgot!
His honour's footman was here last night, wife;
Ha' you done with my lord's shirt?
  Mis. O. What's that to you, sir?
I was this morning at his honour's lodging,
Ere such a snake as you crept out of your shell.
  Open. O, 'twas well done, good wife!
  Mis. O. I hold it better, sir,
Than if you had done't yourself.
  Open. Nay, so say I :
But is the countess's smock almost done, mouse?[3]
  Mis. O. Here lies the cambric, sir; but wants, I fear
   me.

  [1] The usual charge for the use of a stool at the theatre was
sixpence.
  [2] Page.   [3] A term of endearment.

Open. I'll resolve you of that presently.

Mis. O. Heyday! O audacious groom!
Dare you presume to noble women's linen?
Keep you your yard to measure shepherd's holland:
I must confine you, I see that.

Gos. [*At the tobacco-shop.*]—What say you to this gear?

Lax. I dare the arrant'st critic in tobacco
To lay one fault upon't.

Enter MOLL, *in a frieze jerkin and a black safeguard.*[1]

Gos. Life, yonder's Moll!

Lax. Moll! which Moll?

Gos. Honest Moll.

Lax. Prithee, let's call her.—Moll!

Gos. Moll, Moll!

Green. Pist, Moll!

Moll. How now? what's the matter?

Gos. A pipe of good tobacco, Moll?

Moll. I cannot stay.

Gos. Nay, Moll, pooh, prithee, hark; but one word, i'faith.

Moll. Well, what is't?

Green. Prithee, come hither, sirrah.

Lax. Heart, I would give but too much money to be nibbling with that wench! life, sh'as the spirit of four great parishes, and a voice that will drown all the city! Methinks a brave captain might get all his soldiers upon her, and ne'er be beholding to a company of Mile End [2] milksops, if he could come on and come off quick enough: such a Moll were a marrow-bone before an Italian; he would cry *buona roba* till his ribs were nothing but bone.   I'll lay hard siege to her: money is that

---

[1] A sort of petticoat worn over the other clothes to protect them from the dirt, especially when travelling on horseback. It is still used in the West of England by farmers' wives and daughters, under the same name.

[2] Where the London trained bands were drilled and exercised.

aquafortis that eats into many a maidenhead; where the walls are flesh and blood, I'll ever pierce through with a golden auger. [*Aside.*

Gos. Now, thy judgment, Moll? is't not good?

Moll. Yes, faith, 'tis very good tobacco.—How do you sell an ounce? — Farewell. — God b'i' you, Mistress Gallipot.

Gos. Why, Moll, Moll!

Moll. I cannot stay now, i'faith: I am going .o buy a shag-ruff; the shop will be shut in presently.

Gos. 'Tis the maddest fantasticalest girl! I never knew so much flesh and so much nimbleness put together.

Lax. She slips from one company to another, like a fat eel between a Dutchman's fingers.—I'll watch my time for her. [*Aside.*

Mis. G. Some will not stick to say she is a man. And some, both man and woman.

Lax. That were excellent: she might first cuckold the husband, and then make him do as much for the wife.

Moll. [*At the feather-shop.*] Save you; how does Mistress Tiltyard?

J. Dap. Moll!

Moll. Jack Dapper!

J. Dap. How dost, Moll?

Moll. I'll tell thee by and by; I go but to the next shop.

J. Dap. Thou shalt find me here this hour about a feather.

Moll. Nay, an a feather hold you in play a whole hour, a goose will last you all the days of your life. —Let me see a good shag-ruff.

Open. [*At the Sempster's shop.*] Mistress Mary, that shalt thou, i'faith, and the best in the shop.

Mis. O. How now? greetings! love-terms, with a pox, between you! have I found out one of your haunts?

I send you for hollands, and you're i' the low countries
with a mischief.   I'm served with good ware by the shift;
that makes it lie dead so long upon my hands : I were
as good shut up shop, for when I open it I take nothing.

Open. Nay, an you fall a-ringing once, the devil cannot stop you.—I'll out of the belfry as fast as I can,
Moll.   [*Retires.*

Miss. O. Get you from my shop !

Moll. I come to buy. ·

Mis. O. I'll sell ye nothing ; I warn ye my house and
shop.

Moll. You, goody Openwork, you that prick out a
           poor living,
And sews many a bawdy skin-coat together ;
Thou private pandress between shirt and smock ;
I wish thee for a minute but a man,
Thou shouldst ne'er use more shapes ; but, as thou art,
I pity my revenge.   Now my spleen's up,
I would not mock it willingly.—

      Enter a Fellow, *with a long rapier by his side.*

                           . Ha ! be thankful ;
Now I forgive thee.

Mis. O. Marry, hang thee, I never asked forgiveness
in my life.

Moll. You, goodman swine's face !

Fel. What, will you murder me ?

Moll. You remember, slave, how you abused me t'other
night in a tavern.

Fel. Not I, by this light !

Moll. No, but by candle-light you did : you have tricks
to save your oaths ; reservations, have you ? and I have
reserved somewhat for you.   [*Strikes him.*]   As you like
that, call for more ; you know the sign again.

Fel. Pox on't, had I brought any company along with
me to have borne witness on't, 'twould ne'er have grieved
me ; but to be struck and nobody by, 'tis my ill fortune

still. Why, tread upon a worm, they say 'twill turn tail; but indeed a gentleman should have more manners.

[*Aside, and exit.*

Lax. Gallantly performed, i'faith, Moll, and manfully! I love thee for ever for't : base rogue, had he offered but the least counter-buff, by this hand, I was prepared for him !

Moll. You prepared for him ? **why** should you be prepared for him ? was he any more than a man ?

Lax. No, nor so much by a yard and a handful, London measure.

Moll. Why do you speak this then? do you think I cannot ride a stone-horse,[1] unless one lead him by the snaffle ?

Lax. Yes, and sit him bravely; I know thou canst, Moll : 'twas but an honest mistake through love, and I'll make amends for't anyway. Prithee, sweet, plump Moll, when shall thou and I go out a' town together?

Moll. Whither ? to Tyburn, prithee ?

Lax. Mass, that's out a' town indeed : thou hangest so many jests upon thy friends still ! I mean honestly to Brainford,[2] Staines, or Ware.

Moll. What to do there?

Lax. Nothing but be merry and lie together: I'll hire a coach with four horses.

Moll. I thought 'twould be a beastly journey. You may leave out one well; three horses will serve, if I play the jade myself.

Lax. Nay, pish, thou'rt such another kicking wench ? Prithee, be kind, and let's meet.

Moll. 'Tis hard but we shall meet, sir.

Lax. Nay, but appoint the place then; there's ten angels in fair gold, Moll : you see I do not trifle with you; do but say thou wilt meet me, and I'll have a coach ready for thee.

Moll. Why, here's my hand, I'll meet you, sir.

[1] **A stallion.**   [2] Brentford.

Lax. O good gold! [*Aside.*]—The place, sweet Moll?

Moll. It shall be your appointment.

Lax. Somewhat near Holborn, Moll.

Moll. In Gray's Inn Fields then.

Lax. A match.

Moll. I'll meet you there.

Lax. The hour?

Moll. Three.

Lax. That will be time enough to sup at Brainford.

Open. I am of such a nature, sir, I cannot endure the house when she scolds: sh'as a tongue will be heard further in a still morning than Saint Antling's bell.[1] She rails upon me for foreign wenching, that I being a free-man must needs keep a whore i' the suburbs, and seek to impoverish the liberties. When we fall out, I trouble you still to make all whole with my wife.

Gos. No trouble at all; 'tis a pleasure to me to join things together.

Open. Go thy ways, I do this but to try thy honesty, Goshawk.   [*Aside.*

J. Dap. [*At the feather-shop.*]—How likest thou this, Moll?

Moll. O, singularly; you're fitted now for a bunch.— He looks for all the world, with those spangled feathers, like a nobleman's bed-post. The purity of your wench would I fain try; she seems like Kent unconquered, and, I believe, as many wiles are in her. O, the gal-lants of these times are shallow lechers! they put not their courtship home enough to a wench: 'tis impossible to know what woman is throughly honest, because she's ne'er thoroughly tried; I am of that certain belief, there are more queans in this town of their own making than of any man's provoking: where lies the slackness then? many a poor soul would down, and there's no-body will push 'em:

---

[1] At St. Antholin's church there used to be a lecture early in the morning, which was much frequented by the Puritans.—*Reed.*

Women are courted, but ne'er soundly tried,
As many walk in spurs that never ride.   [*Aside.*

Mis. O. [*At the Sempster's shop.*]—O, abominable!

Gos. Nay, more, I tell you in private, he keeps a
whore i' the suburbs.

Mis. O. O spittle [1] dealing! I came to him a gentlewoman born: I'll show you mine arms when you please,
sir.

Gos. I had rather see your legs, and begin that way.
                              [*Aside.*

Mis. O. 'Tis well known he took me from a lady's
service, where I was well beloved of the steward: I had
my Latin tongue, and a spice of the French, before I
came to him; and now doth he keep a suburbian whore
under my nostrils?

Gos. There's ways enough to cry quit with him: hark
in thine ear.   [*Whispers her.*

Mis. O. There's a friend worth a million!

Moll. I'll try one spear against your chastity, Mistress
Tiltyard, though it prove too short by the burgh. [2]
                              [*Aside.*

Enter TRAPDOOR.

Trap. Mass, here she is: I'm bound already to serve
her, though it be but a sluttish trick. [*Aside.*]—Bless
my hopeful young mistress with long life and great
limbs; send her the upper hand of all bailiffs and their
hungry adherents!

Moll. How now? what art thou?

Trap. A poor ebbing gentleman, that would gladly
wait for the young flood of your service.

Moll. My service? what should move you to offer
your service to me, sir?

[1] Or "spital"—*i.e.*, hospital for diseased prostitutes.

[2] The burre is a broad ring of iron behind the handle [of a tilting
lance], and is brought into the sufflue or rest, when the tilter pre-
pareth to combat or encounter his adverse party.—Holme's *Acad.
of Armoury.*

Trap. The love I bear to your heroic spirit and masculine womanhood.

Moll. So, sir! put case we should retain you to us, what parts are there in you for a gentlewoman's service?

Trap. Of two kinds, right worshipful; moveable and immoveable—moveable to run of errands, and immoveable to stand when you have occasion to use me.

Moll. What strength have you?

Trap. Strength, Mistress Moll? I have gone up into a steeple, and stayed the great bell as't has been ringing; stopped a windmill going——

Moll. And never struck down yourself?

Trap. Stood as upright as I do at this present.

[MOLL *trips up his heels.*

Moll. Come, I pardon you for this; it shall be no disgrace to you: I have struck up the heels of the high German's[1] size ere now. What, not stand?

Trap. I am of that nature, where I love, I'll be at my mistress' foot to do her service.

Moll. Why, well said; but say your mistress should receive injury, have you the spirit of fighting in you? durst you second her?

Trap. Life, I have kept a bridge myself, and drove seven at a time before me!

Moll. Ay?

Trap. But they were all Lincolnshire bullocks, by my troth. [*Aside.*

Moll. Well, meet me in Gray's Inn Fields between three and four this afternoon, and, upon better consideration, we'll retain you.

Trap. I humbly thank your good mistresship.— I'll crack your neck for this kindness. [*Aside, and exit.*

Lax. Remember three. [MOLL *meets* LAXTON.

Moll. Nay, if I fail you, hang me.

Lax. Good wench, i'faith!

[1] The allusion is to a German fencer, who appears to have performed many notable exploits about this time.

Moll. [*Meeting* OPENWORK].   Who's this?

Open. 'Tis I, Moll.

Moll. Prithee, tend thy shop and prevent bastards.

Open. We'll have a pint of the same wine,[1] i'faith, Moll.

[Exit with MOLL.   A bell rings.

Gos. Hark, the bell rings! come, gentlemen.   Jack
Dapper, where shall's all munch?

J. Dap. I am for Parker's ordinary.

Lax. He's a good guest to'm. he deserves his board;
he draws all the gentlemen in a term-time thither.   We'll
be your followers, Jack; lead the way.—Look you, by
my faith, the fool has feathered his nest well.

[Exeunt JACK DAPPER, LAXTON, GOSHAWK,
and GREENWIT.

Enter GALLIPOT, TILTYARD, *and* Servants, *with water-*
spaniels and a duck.

Tilt. Come, shut up your shops.   Where's Master
Openwork?

Mis. G. Nay, ask not me, Master Tiltyard.

Tilt. Where's his water-dog? puh—pist—hur—hur—
pist!

Gal. Come, wenches, come; we're going all to Hogsdon.[2]

Mis. G. To Hogsdon, husband?

Gal. Ay, to Hogsdon, pigsnie.[3]

Mis. G. I'm not ready, husband.

Gal. Faith, that's well—hum—pist—pist.—

[Spits in the dog's mouth.[4]

Come, Mistress Openwork, you are so long!

---

[1] Meaning bastard wine, which was made from a bastard species
of the muscat grape, and came from the shores of the Mediter-
ranean.

[2] Hogsdon (Hoxton) was a favourite resort of holiday-makers;
the apprentices went there with their sweethearts to eat plum-cakes
and custards.—*Bullen.*

[3] Little pig.   A term of endearment.   [4] For good luck.

Mis. O. I have no joy of my life, Master Gallipot.

Gal. Pish, let your boy lead his water-spaniel along,
and we'll show you the bravest sport at Parlous Pond.[1] —
Hey, Trug, hey, Trug, hey, Trug ! here's the best duck
in England, except my wife ; hey, hey, hey ! fetch, fetch,
fetch !—

Come let's away :

Of all the year this is the sportful'st day.   [*Exeunt.*

SCENE II.

A Street.

Enter SEBASTIAN WENGRAVE.

Seb. If a man have a free will, where should the use
More perfect shine than in his will to love ?
All creatures have their liberty in that.

Enter behind Sir ALEXANDER WENGRAVE *listening.*

Though else kept under servile yoke and fear,
The very bond-slave has his freedom there.
Amongst a world of creatures voiced and silent,
Must my desires wear fetters ?—Yea, are you
So near ? then I must break with my heart's truth,
Meet grief at a back way.—Well : why, suppose
The two-leaved tongues of slander or of truth
Pronounce Moll loathsome ; if before my love
She appear fair, what injury have I ?

---

[1] This, I imagine, is the place now called " Peerless Pool." It
is situated near the Old-street Road, and was formerly a dangerous
pond, which, from the number of persons who lost their lives there,
obtained the name of Perilous Pool. In the year 1743 it was enclosed, and converted into a bathing-place. —*Reed.*

I have the thing I like : in all things else
Mine own eye guides me, and I find 'em prosper.
Life ! what should ail it now ?   I know that man
Ne'er truly loves,—if he gainsay't he lies,—
That winks and marries with his father's eyes :
I'll keep mine own wide open.

Enter MOLL *and a* Porter *with a viol on his back.*

Sir Alex. Here's brave wilfulness !
A made match ! here she comes ; they met a' purpose.
　　　　　　　　　　　　　　　　[*Aside.*

Por. Must I carry this great fiddle to your chamber,
Mistress Mary ?

Moll. Fiddle, goodman hog-rubber ?[1] Some of these
porters bear so much for others, they have no time to
carry wit for themselves.

Por. To your own chamber, Mistress Mary ?

Moll. Who'll hear an ass speak ? whither else, goodman pageant-bearer ? They're people of the worst
memories !　　　　　　　　　　　　　[*Exit* Porter.

Seb. Why, 'twere too great a burden, love, to have
　them
Carry things in their minds and a' their backs to-
　gether.

Moll. Pardon me, sir, I thought not you so near.

Sir Alex. So, so, so !　　　　　　　　[*Aside.*

Seb. I would be nearer to thee, and in that fashion
That makes the best part of all creatures honest :
No otherwise I wish it.

Moll. Sir, I am so poor to requite you, you must look
for nothing but thanks of me : I have no humour to
marry ; I love to lie a' both sides a' the bed myself : and
again, a' the other side, a wife, you know, ought to be
obedient, but I fear me I am too headstrong to obey ;
therefore I'll ne'er go about it. I love you so well, sir,

---

[1] A clownish person.

for your good will, I'd be loth you should repent your
bargain after; and therefore we'll ne'er come together
at first. I have the head now of myself, and am man
enough for a woman: marriage is but a chopping and
changing, where a maiden loses one head, and has a
worse i' the place.

Sir Alex. The most comfortablest answer from a roaring girl

That ever mine ears drunk in !   [*Aside.*

Seb. This were enough.

Now to afright a fool for ever from thee,
When 'tis the music that I love thee for.

Sir Alex. There's a boy spoils all again !   [*Aside.*

Moll. Believe it, sir, I am not of that disdainful temper
but I could love you faithfully.

Sir Alex. A pox on you for that word ! I like you
not now.

You're a cunning roarer, I see that already.   [*Aside.*

Moll. But sleep upon this once more, sir; you may
chance shift a mind to-morrow : be not too hasty to
wrong yourself; never while you live, sir, take a wife
running ; many have run out at heels that have done't.
You see, sir, I speak against myself ; and if every woman
would deal with their suitor so honestly, poor younger
brothers would not be so often gulled with old cozening
widows, that turn over all their wealth in trust to some
kinsman, and make the poor gentleman work hard for a
pension. Fare you well, sir.

Seb. Nay, prithee, one word more.

Sir Alex. How do I wrong this girl ! she puts him off
still.   [*Aside.*

Moll. Think upon this in cold blood, sir : you make
as much haste as if you were a-going upon a sturgeon
voyage. Take deliberation, sir ; never choose a wife as
if you were going to Virginia.[1]

---

[1] Attempts were being made about this time to settle Virginia.

Seb. And so we parted : my too-cursèd fate ! [1]

Sir Alex. She is but cunning, gives him longer time in't. [*Aside.*

Enter Tailor.

Tai. Mistress Moll, mistress Moll! so ho, ho, so ho !

Moll. There, boy, there, boy ! what dost thou go a-hawking after me with a red clout on thy finger?

Tai. I forgot to take measure on you for your new breeches.

Sir Alex. Hoyda, breeches? what, will he marry a monster with two trinkets? what age is this! if the wife go in breeches, the man must wear long coats [2] like a fool. [*Aside.*

Moll. What fiddling's here ! would not the old pattern have served your turn !

Tai. You change the fashion : you say you'll have the great Dutch slop,[3] Mistress Mary.

Moll. Why, sir, I say so still.

Tai. Your breeches, then, will take up a yard more.

Moll. Well, pray, look it be put in then.

Tai. It shall stand round and full, I warrant you.

Moll. Pray, make 'em easy enough.

Tai. I know my fault now, t'other was somewhat stiff between the legs; I'll make these open enough, I warrant you.

Sir Alex. Here's good gear towards ! I have brought up my son to marry a Dutch slop and a French doublet; a codpiece daughter ! [*Aside.*

Tai. So, I have gone as far as I can go.

Moll. Why, then, farewell.

Tai. If you go presently to your chamber, Mistress

---

[1] A quotation, probably.—*Dyce.*

i.e. Petticoats : in parts of Scotland they are worn by male idiots of the lowest class.—*Dyce.*

Wide loose breeches

Mary, pray, send me the measure of your thigh by some
honest body.

Moll. Well, sir, I'll send it by a porter presently. [*Exit.*

Tai. So you had need, it is a lusty one ; both of them
would make any porter's back ache in England. [*Exit.*

Seb. I have examined the best part of man,
Reason and judgment; and in love, they tell me,
They leave me uncontrolled : he that is swayed
By an unfeeling blood, past heat of love,
His spring-time must needs err; his watch ne'er goes
      right
That sets his dial by a rusty clock.

Sir Alex. [*Coming forward.*] So; and which is that
rusty clock, sir, you?

Seb. The clock at Ludgate, sir; it ne'er goes true.

Sir Alex. But thou go'st falser ; not thy father's cares
Can keep thee right: when that insensible work
Obeys the workman's art, lets off the hour,
And stops again when time is satisfied :
But thou runn'st on ; and judgment, thy main wheel,
Beats by all stops, as if the work would break,
Begun with long pains for a minute's ruin :
Much like a suffering man brought up with care,
At last bequeathed to shame and a short prayer.

Seb. I taste you bitterer than I can deserve, sir.

Sir Alex. What has betwitched thee, son? what devil
      or drug
Hath wrought upon the weakness of thy blood,
And betrayed all her hopes to ruinous folly?
O, wake from drowsy and enchanted shame,
Wherein thy soul sits, with a golden dream
Flattened and poisoned! I am old, my son ;
O, let me prevail quickly.
For I have weightier business of mine own
Than to chide thee : I must not to my grave
As a drunkard to his bed, whereon he lies
Only to sleep, and never cares to rise :

Let me despatch in time; come no more near her.

    Seb. Not honestly? not in the way of marriage?

    Sir Alex. What sayst thou? marriage? in what place?
        the Sessions-house?

And who shall give the bride, prithee? an indictment?

    Seb. Sir, now ye take part with the world to wrong
        her.

    Sir Alex. Why, wouldst thou   in marry to be pointed
        at?

Alas, the number's great! do not o'erburden't.
Why, as good marry a beacon on a hill,
Which all the country fix their eyes upon,
As her thy folly dotes on.   If thou long'st
To have the story of thy infamous fortunes
Serve for discourse in ordinaries and taverns,
Thou'rt in the way; or to confound thy name,
Keep on, thou canst not miss it; or to strike
Thy wretched father to untimely coldness,
Keep the left hand still, it will bring thee to't.
Yet, if no tears wrung from thy father's eyes,
Nor sighs that fly in sparkles from his sorrows,
Had power to alter what is wilful in thee,
Methinks her very name should fright thee from her,
And never trouble me.

    Seb. Why, is the name of Moll so fatal, sir?

    Sir Alex. Many one, sir, where suspect is entered ;
For, seek all London from one end to t'other,
More whores of that name than of any ten other.

    Seb. What's that to her? let those blush for them
        selves :

Can any gilt in others condemn her?
I've vowed to love her : let all storms oppose me
That ever beat against the breast of man,
Nothing but death's black tempest shall divide us.

    Sir Alex. O, folly that can dote on nought but shame !

    Seb. Put case, a wanton itch runs through one name
More than another; is that name the worse,

Where honesty sits possessed in't? it should rather
Appear more excellent, and deserve more praise,
When through foul mists a brightness it can raise.
Why, there are of the devils honest gentlemen
And well descended, keep an open house,
And some a' the good man's[1] that are arrant knaves.
He hates unworthily that by rote contemns,
For the name neither saves nor yet condemns;
And for her honesty, I've made such proof on't
In several forms, so nearly watched her ways,
I will maintain that strict against an army,
Excepting you, my father.   Here's her worst,
Sh'as a bold spirit that mingles with mankind,
But nothing else come's near it: and oftentimes
Through her apparel somewhat shames her birth;
But she is loose in nothing but in mirth;
Would all Molls were no worse!

   Sir Alex. This way I toil in vain, and give but aim [2]
To infamy and ruin: he will fall;
My blessing cannot stay him: all my joys
Stand at the brink of a devouring flood,
And will be wilfully swallowed, wilfully.
But why so vain let all these tears be lost?
I'll pursue her to shame, and so all's crossed.
                        [Aside, and exit.

   Seb. He's gone with some strange purpose, whose
      effect
Will hurt me little if he shoot so wide,
To think I love so blindly: I but feed
His heart to this match, to draw on the other,
Wherein my joy sits with a full wish crowned,
Only his mood excepted, which must change
By opposite policies, courses indirect;

----

[1] This seems to be an allusion to the proverbial saying, "God's
a good man."—*Dyce.*
[2] To give aim was to indicate when the arrow struck in archery.

Plain dealing in this world takes no effect.
This mad girl I'll acquaint with my intent,
    Get her assistance, make my fortunes known:
'Twixt lovers' hearts she's a fit instrument,
    And has the art to help them to their own.
By her advice, for in that craft she's wise,
My love and I may meet, spite of all spies.   [*Exit.*

ACT THE THIRD.

SCENE I.

Gray's Inn Fields.

Enter LAXTON *and* Coachman.

AX. Coachman.

    Coach. Here, sir.

    Lax. There's a tester[1] more; pri-
thee drive thy coach to the hither
end of Marybone-park, a fit place for
Moll to get in.

Coach. Marybone-park, sir?

Lax. Ay, it's in our way, thou knowest.

Coach. It shall be done, sir.

Lax. Coachman.

Coach. Anon, sir.

Lax. Are we fitted with good frampul[2] jades?

Coach. The best in Smithfield,[3] I warrant you, sir.

Lax. May we safely take the upper hand of any
coached velvet cap, or tuftaffety jacket? for they keep
a vile swaggering in coaches now-a-days; the highways
are stopped with them.

Coach. My life for yours, and baffle[4] 'em too, sir:
why, they are the same jades, believe it, sir, that have
drawn all your famous whores to Ware.

---

[1] Sixpence.   [2] Or frampold; restless, spirited.
[3] A noted market for worthless horses.   [4] See note *ante*, p. 17.

Lax. Nay, then they know their business ; they need no more instructions.

Coach. They're so used to such journeys, sir, I never use whip to 'em ; for if they catch but the scent of a wench once, they run like devils.

[*Exit* Coachman *with his whip.*

Lax. Fine Cerberus ! that rogue will have the start of a thousand ones ; for whilst others trot a' foot, he'll ride prancing to hell upon a coach - horse. Stay, 'tis now about the hour of her appointment, but yet I see her not. [*The clock strikes three.*] Hark ! what's this ? one, two, three : three by the clock at Savoy ; this is the hour, and Gray's Inn Fields the place, she swore she'd meet me. Ha ! yonder's two Inns-a'-court men with one wench, but that's not she ; they walk toward Islington out of my way. I see none yet dressed like her ; I must look for a shag-ruff, a frieze jerkin, a short sword, and a safe-guard,[1] or I get none. Why, Moll, prithee, make haste, or the coachman will curse us anon.

Enter MOLL, *dressed as a man.*

Moll. O, here's my gentleman ! If they would keep their days as well with their mercers as their hours with their harlots, no bankrout would give seven score pound for a sergeant's place ; for would you know a catchpoll rightly derived, the corruption of a citizen is the generation of a sergeant. How his eye hawks for venery ! [*Aside.*]—Come, are you ready, sir ?

Lax. Ready ? for what, sir ?

Moll. Do you ask that now, sir ?
Why was this meeting 'pointed ?

Lax. I thought you mistook me, sir : you seem to be
        some young barrister ;
I have no suit in law, all my land's sold ;
I praise Heaven for't, 't has rid me of much trouble.

---

[1] See note *ante*, p. 27.

Moll. Then I must wake you, sir; where stands the
Lax. Who's this? Moll, honest Moll? [coach?
Moll. So young, and purblind?
You're an old wanton in your eyes, I see that.

Lax. Thou'rt admirably suited for the Three Pigeons[1]
at Brainford. I'll swear I knew thee not.

Moll. I'll swear you did not; but you shall know me
now.

Lax. No, not here; we shall be spied, i'faith; the
coach is better: come.

Moll. Stay.   [*Puts off her cloak.*

Lax. What, wilt thou untruss a point,[2] Moll?

Moll. Yes; here's the point   [*Draws her sword.*
That I untruss; 't has but one tag, 'twill serve though
To tie up a rogue's tongue.

Lax. How!

Moll. There's the gold
With which you hired your hackney, here's her pace;
She racks hard, and perhaps your bones will feel it:
Ten angels of mine own I've put to thine;
Win 'em and wear 'em.

Lax. Hold, Moll! Mistress Mary——

Moll. Draw, or I'll serve an execution on thee,
Shall lay thee up till doomsday.

Lax. Draw upon a woman! why, what dost mean,
Moll?

Moll. To teach thy base thoughts manners: thou'rt
one of those
That thinks each woman thy fond flexible whore;
If she but cast a liberal eye upon thee,
Turn back her head, she's thine; or amongst company
By chance drink first to thee, then she's quite gone,
There is no means to help her: nay, for a need,
Wilt swear unto thy credulous fellow lechers,

---

[1] A much-frequented inn. At a later date it was kept by the
celebrated actor, Lowin.

[2] *i.e.* Untie the tags of her hose.

That thou art more in favour with a lady
At first sight than her monkey all her lifetime.
How many of our sex, by such as thou,
Have their good thoughts paid with a blasted name
That never deserved loosely, or did trip
In path of whoredom beyond cup and lip !
But for the stain of conscience and of soul,
Better had women fall into the hands
Of an act silent than a bragging nothing ;
There is no mercy in't. What durst move you, sir,
To think me whorish ? a name which I'd tear out
From the high German's[1] throat, if it lay leiger[2] there
To despatch privy slanders against me.
In thee I defy all men, their worst hates
And their best flatteries, all their golden witchcrafts,
With which they entangle the poor spirits of fools,
Distressèd needle-women and trade-fallen wives ;
Fish that must needs bite, or themselves be bitten ;
Such hungry things as these may soon be took
With a worm fastened on a golden hook :
Those are the lecher's food, his prey ; he watches
For quarrelling wedlocks[3] and poor shifting sisters ;
'Tis the best fish he takes. But why, good fisherman,
Am I thought meat for you, that never yet
Had angling rod cast towards me ? 'cause, you'll say,
I'm given to sport, I'm often merry, jest :
Had mirth no kindred in the world but lust,
O shame take all her friends then ! but, howe'er
Thou and the baser world censure my life,
I'll send 'em word by thee, and write so much
Upon thy breast, 'cause thou shalt bear't in mind,
Tell them 'twere base to yield where I have conquered ;
I scorn to prostitute myself to a man,
I that can prostitute a man to me ;
And so I greet thee.

[1] See note *ante*, p. 33.
[2] A resident ambassador at a foreign court.   [3] *i.e.* Wives.

Lax. Hear me——

Moll. Would the spirits
Of all my slanderers were clasped in thine,
That I might vex an army at one time !   [*They fight.*

Lax. I do repent me ; hold !

Moll. You'll die the better Christian then.

Lax. I do confess I have wronged thee, Moll.

Moll. Confession is but poor amends for wrong,
Unless a rope would follow.

Lax. I ask thee pardon.

Moll. I'm your hired whore, sir !

Lax. I yield both purse and body.

Moll. Both are mine,
And now at my disposing.

Lax. Spare my life !

Moll. I scorn to strike thee basely.

Lax. Spoke like a noble girl, i'faith !—Heart, I think
I fight with a familiar, or the ghost of a fencer. Sh'as
wounded me gallantly. Call you this a lecherous viage? [1]
here's blood would have served me this seven year in
broken heads and cut fingers ; and it now runs all out
together. Pox a' the Three Pigeons ! I would the coach
were here now to carry me to the surgeon's.

[*Aside, and exit.*

Moll. If I could meet my enemies one by one thus,
I might make pretty shift with 'em in time,
And make 'em know she that has wit and spirit,
May scorn
To live beholding to her body for meat ;
Or for apparel, like your common dame,
That makes shame get her clothes to cover shame.
Base is that mind that kneels unto her body,
As if a husband stood in awe on's wife !
My spirit shall be mistress of this house
As long as I have time in't.—O,

---

[1] Voyage.

Enter TRAPDOOR.

Here comes my man that would be : 'tis his hour.
Faith, a good well-set fellow, if his spirit
Be answerable to his umbles ;[1] he walks stiff,
But whether he'll stand to't stiffly, there's the point :
Has a good calf for't ; and ye shall have many a woman
Choose him she means to make her head by his calf :
I do not know their tricks in't.   Faith, he seems
A man without ; I'll try what he's within.

    Trap. She told me Gray's Inn Fields, 'twixt three and
        four ;
I'll fit her mistress-ship with a piece of service :
I'm hired to rid the town of one mad girl.
                          [MOLL *jostles him.*
What a pox ails you, sir ?

    Moll. He begins like a gentleman.

    Trap. Heart, is the field so narrow, or your eye-
        sight——
Life, he comes back again !

    Moll. Was this spoke to me, sir ?

    Trap. I cannot tell, sir.

    Moll. Go, you're a coxcomb !

    Trap. Coxcomb ?

    Moll. You're a slave !

    Trap. I hope there's law for you, sir.

    Moll. Yea, do you see, sir ?   [*Turns his hat.*

    Trap. Heart, this is no good dealing ! pray, let me
know what house you're of.

    Moll. One of the Temple, sir.   [*Fillips him.*

    Trap. Mass, so methinks.

    Moll. And yet sometime I lie about Chick Lane.

    Moll. A good shift ; but it shall not serve your turn.

    Trap. I like you the worse because you shift your lodg-
ing so often : I'll not meddle with you for that trick, sir.

---

[1] The entrails of a deer.

Trap. You'll give me leave to pass about my business, sir?

Moll. Your business? I'll make you wait on me
Before I ha' done, and glad to serve me too.

Trap. How, sir? serve you? not if there were no more men in England.

Moll. But if there were no more women in England, I hope you'd wait upon your mistress then?

Trap. Mistress?

Moll. O, you're a tried spirit at a push, sir?

Trap. What would your worship have me do?

Moll. You a fighter!

Trap. No, I praise Heaven, I had better grace and more manners.

Moll. As how, I pray, sir?

Trap. Life, 'thad been a beastly part of me to have drawn my weapons upon my mistress; all the world would a' cried shame of me for that.

Moll. Why, but you knew me not.

Trap. Do not say so, mistress; I knew you by your wide straddle, as well as if I had been in your belly.

Moll. Well, we shall try you further; i' the mean time We give you entertainment.

Trap. Thank your good mistress-ship.

Moll. How many suits have you?

Trap. No more suits than blacks,[1] mistress.

Moll. Well, if you deserve, I cast off this, next week, And you may creep into't.

Trap. Thank your good worship.

Moll. Come, follow me to St. Thomas Apostle's:
I'll put a livery cloak upon your back
The first thing I do.

Trap. I follow, my dear mistress.   [*Exeunt.*

---

[1] Mourning garments.

SCENE II.

GALLIPOT'S *Shop.*

Enter Mistress GALLIPOT *as from supper,* GALLIPOT
following her.

Gal. What, Pru! nay, sweet Prudence!

Mis. G. What a pruing keep you! I think the baby
would have a teat, it kyes[1] so. Pray, be not so fond of
me, leave your city humours; I'm vexed at you, to see
how like a calf you come bleating after me.

Gal. Nay, honey Pru, how does your rising up before
all the table show, and flinging from my friends so uncivilly! fie, Pru, fie! come.

Mis. G. Then up and ride, i'faith!

Gal. Up and ride? nay, my pretty Pru, that's far from
my thought, duck: why, mouse, thy mind is nibbling at
something; what is't? what lies upon thy stomach?

Mis. G. Such an ass as you: hoyda, you're best turn
midwife, or physician! you're a 'pothecary already, but
I'm none of your drugs.

Gal. Thou art a sweet drug, sweetest Pru, and the
more thou art pounded, the more precious.

Mis. G. Must you be prying into a woman's secrets,
say ye?

Gal. Woman's secrets?

Mis. G. What! I cannot have a qualm come upon
me, but your teeth waters till your nose hang over it!

Gal. It is my love, dear wife.

Mis. G. Your love? your love is all words; give me
deeds: I cannot abide a man that's too fond over me,—
so cookish! Thou dost not know how to handle a
woman in her kind.

Gal. No, Pru? why, I hope I have handled——

Mis. G. Handle a fool's head of your own,—fie, fie!

[1] Cries.

Gal. Ha, ha, 'tis such a wasp ! it does me good now to have her sting me, little rogue !

Mis. G. Now, fie, how you vex me ! I cannot abide these apron husbands; such cotqueans !¹ you overdo your things, they become you scurvily.

Gal. Upon my life she breeds : Heaven knows how I have strained myself to please her night and day. I wonder why we citizens should get children so fretful and untoward in the breeding, their fathers being for the most part as gentle as milch kine. [*Aside.*]—Shall I leave thee, my Pru.

Mis. G. Fie, fie, fie !

Gal. Thou shalt not be vexed no more, pretty, kind rogue ; take no cold, sweet Pru.   [*Exit.*

Mis. G. As your wit has done. Now, Master Laxton, show your head ; what news from you? would any husband suspect that a woman crying, " Buy any scurvy-grass," should bring love-letters amongst her herbs to his wife? pretty trick ! fine conveyance ! had jealousy a thousand eyes, a silly woman with scurvy grass blinds them all.

Laxton, with bays

Crown I thy wit for this, it deserves praise :

This makes me affect thee more, this proves thee wise :

'Lack, what poor shift is love forced to devise !—

To the point. [*Reads letter.*]—" O sweet creature "—a sweet beginning !—" pardon my long absence, for thou shalt shortly be possessed with my presence : though Demophoon was false to Phyllis, I will be to thee as Pan-da-rus was to Cres-sida ;² though Æneas made an ass of Dido, I will die to thee ere I do so. O sweetest creature, make much of me ! for no man beneath the silver moon shall make more of a woman than I do of thee : furnish me therefore with thirty pounds ; you must

¹ Men who meddle with women's affairs in the household.

² So in old ed., to mark the difficulty with which such hard names were read by Mistress Gallipot.—*Dyce.*

do it of necessity for me; I languish till I see some comfort come from thee.   Protesting not to die in thy debt,
but rather to live, so as hitherto I have and will,

" Thy true Laxton ever."

Alas, poor gentleman! troth, I pity him.
How shall I raise this money? thirty pound!
'Tis thirty sure, a 3 before an o;
I know his threes too well.   My childbed linen,
Shall I pawn that for him? then if my mark
Be known, I am undone; it may be thought
My husband's bankrout.   Which way shall I turn?
Laxton, what with my own fears and thy wants,
I'm like a needle 'twixt two adamants.

Re-enter GALLIPOT *hastily.*

Gal. Nay, nay, wife, the women are all up—Ha!
how? reading a' letters?   I smell a goose, a couple of
capons, and a gammon of bacon, from her mother out
of the country.   I hold my life—steal, steal——

[*Aside.*

Mis. G. O, beshrew your heart!
Gal. What letter's that?   I'll see't.

[Mistress GALLIPOT *tears the letter.*

Mis. G. O, would thou hadst no eyes to see the
        downfall
Of me and of thyself!   I am for ever,
For ever I'm undone!
Gal. What ails my Pru?
What paper's that thou tear'st?
Mis. G. Would I could tear
My very heart in pieces! for my soul
Lies on the rack of shame, that tortures me
Beyond a woman's suffering.
Gal. What means this?
Mis. G. Had you no other vengeance to throw down,
But even in height of all my joys——

Gal. Dear woman——

Mis. G. When the full sea of pleasure and content
Seemed to flow over me?

Gal. As thou desir'st
To keep me out of Bedlam, tell what troubles thee!
Is not thy child at nurse fallen sick, or dead?

Mis. G. O, no!

Gal. Heavens bless me! are my barns and houses
Yonder at Hockley-hole consumed with fire?
I can build more, sweet Pru.

Mis. G. 'Tis worse, 'tis worse!

Gal. My factor broke? or is the Jonas sunk?

Mis. G. Would all we had were swallowed in the
  waves,
Rather than both should be the scorn of slaves!

Gal. I'm at my wit's end.

Mis. G. O my dear husband!
Where once I thought myself a fixèd star,
Placed only in the Heaven of thine arms,
I fear now I shall prove a wanderer.
O Laxton, Laxton! is it then my fate
To be by thee o'erthrown?

Gal. Defend me, wisdom,
From falling into frenzy! On my knees,
Sweet Pru, speak; what's that Laxton, who so heavy
Lies on thy bosom?

Mis. G. I shall sure run mad!

Gal. I shall run mad for company then. Speak
  to me;
I'm Gallipot thy husband—Pru—why, Pru,
Art sick in conscience for some villanous deed
Thou wert about to act? didst mean to rob me?
Tush, I forgive thee: hast thou on my bed
Thrust my soft pillow under another's head?
I'll wink at all faults, Pru: 'las, that's no more
Than what some neighbours near thee have done before!
Sweet honey Pru, what's that Laxton?

Mis. G. O !

Gal. Out with him !

Mis. G. O, he's born to be my undoer !
This hand, which thou call'st thine, to him was given,
To him was I made sure[1] i' the sight of Heaven.

Gal. I never heard this thunder.

Mis. G. Yes, yes, before
I was to thee contracted, to him I swore :
Since last I saw him, twelve months three times told
The moon hath drawn through her light silver bow ;
For o'er the seas he went, and it was said,
But rumour lies, that he in France was dead :
But he's alive, O he's alive ! he sent
That letter to me, which in rage I rent ;
Swearing with oaths most damnably to have me,
Or tear me from this bosom : O Heavens, save me !

> *Gal.* My heart will break ; shamed and undone for
> ever !

> *Mis. G.* So black a day, poor wretch, went o'er thee
> never !

Gal. If thou should'st wrestle with him at the law,
Thou'rt sure to fall.   No odd sleight ? no prevention ?
I'll tell him thou'rt with child.

Mis. G. Umh !

Gal. Or give out
One of my men was ta'en a-bed with thee.

Mis. G. Umh, umh !

Gal. Before I lose thee, my dear Pru,
I'll drive it to that push.

Mis. G. Worse and worse still ;
You embrace a mischief, to prevent an ill.

Gal. I'll buy thee of him, stop his mouth with gold :
Think'st thou 'twill do ?

Mis. G. O me ! Heavens grant it would !
Yet now my senses are set more in tune.
He writ, as I remember, in his letter,

---

[1] Betrothed.

That he in riding up and down had spent,
Ere he could find me, thirty pounds: send that;
Stand not on thirty with him.

   Gal. Forty, Pru!
Say thou the word, 'tis done: we venture lives
For wealth, but must do more to keep our wives.
Thirty or forty, Pru?

   Mis. G. Thirty, good sweet;
Of an ill bargain let's save what we can :
I'll pay it him with my tears; he was a man,
When first I knew him, of a meek spirit,
All goodness is not yet dried up, I hope.

   Gal. He shall have thirty pound, let that stop all :
Love's sweets taste best when we have drunk down gall.

Enter TILTYARD, Mistress TILTYARD, GOSHAWK, *and*
Mistress OPENWORK.

God's-so, our friends! come, come, smooth your cheek :
After a storm the face of heaven looks sleek.

   Tilt. Did I not tell you these turtles were together?

   Mis. T. How dost thou, sirrah? why, sister Gallipot——

   Mis. O. Lord, how she's changed!

   Gos. Is your wife ill, sir?

   Gal. Yes, indeed, la, sir, very ill, very ill, never worse.

   Mis. T. How her head burns! feel how her pulses
work!

   Mis. O. Sister, lie down a little; that always does me
good.

   Mis. T. In good sadness,[1] I find best ease in that too.
Has she laid some hot thing to her stomach?

   Mis. G. No, but I will lay something anon.

   Tilt. Come, come, fools, you trouble her.—Shall's go,
Master Goshawk?

   Gos. Yes, sweet Master Tiltyard.—Sirrah Rosamond,
I hold my life Gallipot hath vexed his wife.

              [1] Seriousness.

Mis. O. She has a horrible high colour indeed.

Gos. We shall have your face painted with the same red soon at night, when your husband comes from his rubbers in a false alley: thou wilt not believe me that his bowls run with a wrong bias.

Mis. O. It cannot sink into me that he feeds upon stale mutton [1] abroad, having better and fresher at home.

Gos. What if I bring thee where thou shalt see him stand at rack and manger?

Mis. O. I'll saddle him in's kind, and spur him till he kick again.

Gos. Shall thou and I ride our journey then?

Mis. O. Here's my hand.

Gos. No more.—Come, Master Tiltyard, shall we leap into the stirrups with our women, and amble home?

Tilt. Yes, yes.—Come, wife.

Mis. T. In troth, sister, I hope you will do well for all this.

Mis. G. I hope I shall. Farewell, good sister. Sweet Master Goshawk.

Gal. Welcome, brother; most kindly welcome, sir.

All. Thanks, sir, for our good cheer.

[*Exeunt all but* GALLIPOT *and* Mistress GALLIPOT.

Gal. It shall be so: because a crafty knave
Shall not outreach me, nor walk by my door
With my wife arm in arm, as 'twere his whore.
I'll give him a golden coxcomb, thirty pound.
Tush, Pru, what's thirty pound? sweet duck, look
    cheerly.

Mis. G. Thou'rt worthy of my heart, thou buy'st it
    dearly.

Enter LAXTON *muffled.*

Lax. Uds light, the tide's against me; a pox of your 'pothecaryship! O for some glister to set him going! 'Tis one of Hercules' labours to tread one of these city

---

[1] A cant term for a prostitute.

hen's, because their cocks are still crowing over them.
There's no turning tail here, I must on.   [*Aside.*

Mis. G. O husband, see he comes !

Gal. Let me deal with him.

Lax. Bless you, sir.

Gal. Be you blest too, sir, if you come in peace.

Lax. Have you any good pudding tobacco,[1] sir?

Mis. G. O, pick no quarrels, gentle sir ! my husband
Is not a man of weapons, as you are ;
He knows all, I have opened all before him,
Concerning you.

Lax. Zounds, has she shown my letters ?   [*Aside.*

Mis. G. Suppose my case were yours, what would you
    do?
At such a pinch, such batteries, such assaults
Of father, mother, kindred, to dissolve
The knot you tied, and to be bound to him ;
How could you shift this storm off?

Lax. If I know, hang me !

Mis. G. Besides a story of your death was read
Each minute to me.

Lax. What a pox means this riddling ?   [*Aside.*

Gal. Be wise, sir ; let not you and I be tossed.
On lawyers' pens ; they have sharp nibs, and draw
Men's very heart-blood from them.   What need you, sir,
To beat the drum of my wife's infamy,
And call your friends together, sir, to prove
Your precontract, when sh'as confessed it?

Lax. Umh, sir,
Has she confessed it?

Gal. Sh'as, faith, to me, sir,
Upon your letter sending.

Mis G. I have, I have.

Lax. If I let this iron cool, call me slave.   [*Aside.*
Do you hear, you Dame Prudence? think'st thou, vile
    woman,

---

[1] Probably compressed tobacco.

I'll take these blows and wink?

   Mis. Gal. Upon my knees.   [*Kneeling.*

   Lax. Out, impudence!

   Gal. Good sir——

   Lax. You goatish slaves!

No wild fowl to cut up but mine?

   Gal. Alas, sir,

You make her flesh to tremble; fright her not:

She shall do reason, and what's fit.

   Lax. I'll have thee,

Wert thou more common than an hospital,

And more diseased.

   Gal. But one word, good sir!

   Lax. So, sir.

   Gal. I married her, have lien with her and got

Two children on her body: think but on that;

Have you so beggarly an appetite,

When I upon a dainty dish have fed

To dine upon my scraps, my leavings? ha, sir?

Do I come near you now, sir?

   Lax. Be-lady, [1] you touch me?

   Gal. Would not you scorn to wear my clothes, sir?

   Lax. Right, sir.

   Gal. Then, pray, sir, wear not her; for she's a garment

So fitting for my body, I am loth

Another should put it on: you'll undo both.

Your letter, as she said, complained you had spent,

In quest of her, some thirty pound; I'll pay it:

Shall that, sir, stop this gap up 'twixt you two?

   Lax. Well, if I swallow this wrong, let her thank you:

The money being paid, sir, I am gone:

Farewell.   O woman, happy's he trusts none!

   Mis. G. Despatch him hence, sweet husband.

   Gal. Yes, dear wife:

---

[1] A corruption of "By our lady," still used in some parts of the country.

Pray, sir, come in : ere Master Laxton part,
Thou shalt in wine drink to him.

 Mis. G. With all my heart.— [*Exit* GALLIPOT.
How dost thou like my wit?

 Lax. Rarely : that wile,
By which the serpent did the first woman beguile,
Did ever since all women's bosoms fill ;
You're apple-eaters all, deceivers still. [*Exeunt.*

SCENE III.

Holborn.

Enter Sir ALEXANDER WENGRAVE, Sir DAVY DAPPER,
 and Sir ADAM APPLETON *on one side, and* TRAPDOOR
 on the other.

 Sir Alex. Out with your tale, Sir Davy, to Sir Adam :
A knave is in mine eye deep in my debt.

 Sir Davy. Nay, if he be a knave, sir, hold him fast.
    [Sir DAVY *and* Sir ADAM *talk apart.*

 Sir Alex. Speak softly ; what egg is there hatching
now ?

 Trap. A duck's egg, sir, a duck that has eaten a
frog ; I have cracked the shell, and some villany or
other will peep out presently : the duck that sits is the
bouncing ramp,[1] that roaring girl my mistress ; the
drake that must tread is your son Sebastian.

 Sir Alex. Be quick.

 Trap. As the tongue of an oyster-wench.

 Sir Alex. And see thy news be true.

 Trap. As a barber's every Saturday night. Mad
Moll——

 Sir Alex. Ah——

    [1] *i.e.* Rampant creature.

Trap. Must be let in, without knocking, at your back gate.

Sir Alex. So.

Trap. Your chamber will be made bawdy.

Sir Alex. Good.

Trap. She comes in a shirt of mail.

Sir Alex. How? shirt of mail?

Trap. Yes, sir, or a male shirt; that's to say, in man's apparel.

Sir Alex. To my son?

Trap. Close to your son: your son and her moon will be in conjunction, if all almanacs lie not; her black safeguard is turned into a deep slop,[1] the holes of her upper body to button-holes, her waistcoat to a doublet, her placket[2] to the ancient seat of a cod-piece, and you shall take 'em both with standing collars.

Sir Alex. Art sure of this?

Trap. As every throng is sure of a pick-pocket; as sure as a whore is of the clients all Michaelmas term, and of the pox after the term.

Sir Alex. The time of their tilting?

Trap. Three.

Sir Alex. The day?

Trap. This.

Sir Alex. Away; ply it, watch her.

Trap. As the devil doth for the death of a bawd; I'll watch her, do you catch her.

Sir Alex. She's fast: here weave thou the nets. Hark.

Trap. They are made.

Sir Alex. I told them thou didst owe me money: hold it up; maintain't.

Trap. Stiffly, as a Puritan does contention.—Pox, I owe thee not the value of a halfpenny halter.

---

[1] See note *ante*, p. 38.
[2] The forepart of the shift; the word usually means an under-petticoat.

Sir Alex. Thou shalt be hanged in it ere thou 'scape
so :
Varlet, I'll make thee look through a grate ! [1]

Trap. I'll do't presently, through a tavern grate : [2]
drawer ! pish.   [*Exit.*

Sir Adam. Has the knave vexed you, sir ?

Sir Alex. Asked him my money,
He swears my son received it.   O, that boy
Will ne'er leave heaping sorrows on my heart,
Till he has broke it quite !

Sir Adam. Is he still wild ?

Sir Alex. As is a Russian bear.

Sir Adam. But he has left
His old haunt with that baggage ?

Sir Alex. Worse still and worse ;
He lays on me his shame, I on him my curse.

Sir Davy. My son, Jack Dapper, then shall run with
him
All in one pasture.

Sir Adam. Proves your son bad too, sir ?

Sir Davy. As villany can make him : your Sebastian
Dotes but on one drab, mine on a thousand ;
A noise [3] of fiddlers, tobacco, wine, and a whore,
A mercer that will let him take up more,
Dice, and a water-spaniel with a duck,—O
Bring him a-bed with these : when his purse jingles,
Roaring boys follow at's tail, fencers and ningles, [4]
Beasts Adam ne'er gave name to ; these horse-leeches
suck
My son ; he being drawn dry, they all live on smoke.

Sir Alex. Tobacco ?

Sir Davy. Right : but I have in my brain

[1] *i.e.* Of a prison.
[2] Meaning the red lattice which preceeded the use of glass
windows in places where drink was sold.
[3] A company of musicians.
[4] Or ingles ; familiar companions.

A windmill going that shall grind to dust
The follies of my son, and make him wise,
Or a stark fool.   Pray lend me your advice.
    Sir Alex., Sir Adam. 'That shall you, good Sir Davy.
    Sir Davy. Here's the springe
I ha' set to catch this woodcock[1] in : an action
In a false name, unknown to him, is entered
I' the Counter[2] to arrest Jack Dapper.
    Sir Alex., Sir Adam. Ha, ha, he !
    Sir Davy. Think you the Counter cannot break him?
    Sir Adam. Break him?
Yes, and break's heart too, if he lie there long.
    Sir Davy. I'll make him sing a counter-tenor sure.
    Sir Adam. No way to tame him like it; there he
        shall learn
What money is indeed, and how to spend it.
    Sir Davy. He's bridled there.
    Sir Alex. Ay, yet knows not how to mend it.
Bedlam cures not more madmen in a year
Than one of the Counters does; men pay more dear
There for their wit than anywhere : a Counter !
Why, 'tis an university, who not sees?
As scholars there, so here men take degrees,
And follow the same studies all alike.
Scholars learn first logic and rhetoric ;
So does a prisoner : with fine honeyed speech
At's first coming in he doth persuade, beseech
He may bê lodged with one that is not itchy,
To lie in a clean chamber, in sheets not lousy ;
But when he has no money, then does he try,
By subtle logic and quaint sophistry,
To make the keepers trust him.
    Sir Adam. Say they do.
    Sir Alex. Then he's a graduate.

   [1] A common saying, meaning a device to entrap a simpleton.
   [2] The Sheriff's prison : there were two Counters, one in Wood Street, Cheapside, and the other in the Poultry.

Sir Davy. Say they trust him not.

Sir Alex. Then is he held a freshman and a sot,
And never shall commence;[1] but being still barred,
Be expulsed from the Master's side[2] to the Twopenny
Or else i' the Hole beg place.   [ward,

Sir Adam. When then, I pray,
Proceeds a prisoner?

Sir Alex. When, money being the theme,
He can dispute with his hard creditors' hearts,
And get out clear, he's then a master of arts.
Sir Davy, send your son to Wood Street college,
A gentleman can no where get more knowledge.

Sir Davy. There gallants study hard.

Sir Alex. True, to get money.

Sir Davy. 'Lies by the heels, i'faith: thanks, thanks;
     I ha' sent
For a couple of bears shall paw him.

Sir Adam. Who comes yonder?

Sir Davy. They look like puttocks;[3] these should be
     they.

Enter CURTLEAX *and* HANGER.

Sir Alex. I know 'em,
They are officers; sir, we'll leave you.

Sir Davy. My good knights,
Leave me; you see I'm haunted now with sprites.

Sir Alex., Sir Adam. Fare you well, sir.   [*Exeunt.*

Cur. This old muzzle-chops should be he by the fellow's description.—Save you, sir.

Sir Davy. Come hither, you mad varlets; did not my
man tell you I watched here for you?

Cur. One in a blue-coat,[4] sir, told us that in this place

---

[1] *i.e.* Obtain his Master's degree.

[2] The governor of the prison was allowed to let certain rooms to
prisoners for his own profit. The poorest prisoners were placed in
the Hole.

[3] Kites.   [4] The usual dress of men-servants.

an old gentleman would watch for us; a thing contrary
to our oath, for we are to watch for every wicked
member in a city.

Sir Davy. You'll watch then for ten thousand: what's
thy name, honesty?

Cur. Sergeant Curtleax I, sir,

Sir Davy. An excellent name for a sergeant, Curtleax:

Sergeants indeed are weapons of the law;

When prodigal ruffians far in debt are grown,

Should not you cut them, citizens were o'erthrown.

Thou dwell'st hereby in Holborn, Curtleax?

Cur. That's my circuit, sir; I conjure most in that
circle.

Sir Davy. And what young toward whelp is this?

Han. Of the same litter; his yeoman, sir; my name's
Hanger.

Sir Davy. Yeoman Hanger:

One pair of shears[1] sure cut out both your coats;

You have two names most dangerous to men's throats;

You two are villanous loads on gentlemen's backs;

Dear ware this Hanger and this Curtleax!

Cur. We are as other men are, sir; I cannot see but
he who makes a show of honesty and religion, if his
claws can fasten to his liking, he draws blood: all that
live in the world are but great fish and little fish, and
feed upon one another; some eat up whole men, a
sergeant cares but for the shoulder of a man. They
call us knaves and curs; but many times he that sets
us on worries more lambs one year than we do in
seven.

Sir Davy. Spoke like a noble Cerberus! is the action
entered?

Han. His name is entered in the book of unbelievers.

Sir Davy. What book's that?

---

[1] "There went but a pair of shears between them," was a common proverbial expression.—*Nares.*

Cur. The book where all prisoners' names stand; and not one amongst forty, when he comes in, believes to come out in haste.

Sir Davy. Be as dogged to him as your office allows you to be.

Both. O sir!

Sir Davy. You know the unthrift, Jack Dapper?

Cur. Ay, ay, sir, that gull, as well as I know my yeoman.

Sir Davy. And you know his father too, Sir Davy Dapper?

Cur. As damned a usurer as ever was among Jews: if he were sure his father's skin would yield him any money, he would, when he dies, flay it off, and sell it to cover drums for children at Bartholomew fair.

Sir Davy. What toads are these to spit poison on a man to his face! [*Aside.*]—Do you see, my honest rascals? yonder Greyhound is the dog he hunts with; out of that tavern Jack Dapper will sally: sa, sa; give the counter; on, set upon him!

Both. We'll charge him upo' the back, sir.

Sir Davy. Take no bail; put mace[1] enough into his caudle; double your files, traverse your ground.

Both. Brave, sir.

Sir Davy. Cry arm, arm, arm!

Both. Thus, sir.

Sir Davy. There, boy, there, boy! away: look to your prey, my true English wolves; and so I vanish. [*Exit.*

Cur. Some warden of the sergeants begat this old fellow, upon my life: stand close.

Han. Shall the ambuscado lie in one place?

Cur. No; nook thou yonder. [*They retire.*

Enter MOLL *and* TRAPDOOR.

Moll. Ralph.

---

[1] A pun upon the sergeant's mace, which was the symbol of his authority.

Trap. What says my brave captain male and female?

Moll. This Holborn is such a wrangling street !

Trap. That's because lawyers walks to and fro in't.

Moll. Here's such jostling, as if every one we met were drunk and reeled.

Trap. Stand, mistress ! do you not smell carrion?

Moll. Carrion? no ; yet I spy ravens.

Trap. Some poor, wind-shaken gallant will anon fall into sore labour, and these men-midwives must bring him to bed i' the Counter : there all those that are great with child with debts lie in.

Moll. Stand up.

Trap. Like your new Maypole.

Han. Whist, whew !

Cur. Hump, no.

Moll. Peeping? it shall go hard, huntsmen, but I'll spoil your game. They look for all the world like two infected malt-mèn coming muffled up in their cloaks in a frosty morning to London.

Trap. A course, captain ; a bear comes to the stake.

Enter JACK DAPPER *and* GULL.

Moll. It should be so, for the dogs struggle to be let loose.

Han. Whew !

Cur. Hemp.

Moll. Hark, Trapdoor, follow your leader.

J. Dap. Gull.

Gull. Master?

J. Dap. Didst ever see such an ass as I am, boy?

Gull. No, by my troth, sir ; to lose all your money, yet have false dice of your own ; why, 'tis as I saw a great fellow used t'other day ; he had a fair sword and buckler, and yet a butcher dry-beat him with a cudgel.

Trap. Honest servant, fly !

Moll. Fly, Master Dapper ! you'll be arrested else.

J. Dap. Run, Gull, and draw.

Gull. Run, master; Gull follows you.

> [*Exeunt* DAPPER *and* GULL.

Cur. [MOLL *holding him.*] I know you well enough; you're but a whore to hang upon any man!

Moll. Whores, then, are like sergeants; so now hang you.—Draw, rogue, but strike not: for a broken pate they'll keep their beds, and recover twenty marks[1] damages.

Cur. You shall pay for this rescue.—Run down Shoe Lane and meet him.

Trap. Shu! is this a rescue, gentlemen, or no?

Moll. Rescue? a pox on 'em! Trapdoor, let's away;

> [*Exeunt* CURTLEAX *and* HANGER.

I'm glad I've done perfect one good work to-day.

If any gentleman be in scrivener's bands,

Send but for Moll, she'll bail him by these hands.

> [*Exeunt.*

---

[1] The mark was worth 13s. 4d.

ACT THE FOURTH.

SCENE I.

A Room in Sir Alexander Wengrave's *House.*

Enter Sir Alexander Wengrave.

IR ALEX. Unhappy in the follies of a
son,
Led against judgment, sense, obedience,
And all the powers of nobleness and
wit!

Enter Trapdoor.

O wretched father!—Now, Trapdoor, will she come?

Trap. In man's apparel, sir; I'm in her heart now,
And share in all her secrets.

Sir Alex. Peace, peace, peace!
Here, take my German watch, hang't up in sight,
That I may see her hang in English for't.

Trap. I warrant you for that now, next sessions rids
her, sir. This watch will bring her in better than a hundred constables. [*Hangs up the watch.*

Sir Alex. Good Trapdoor, sayst thou so? thou cheer'st
my heart
After a storm of sorrow. My gold chain too;
Here, take a hundred marks in yellow links.

Trap. That will do well to bring the watch to light,
sir;

And worth a thousand of your headborough's lanterns.

Sir Alex. Place that a' the court-cupboard;[1] let it lie
Full in the view of her thief-whorish eye.

Trap. She cannot miss it, sir; I see't so plain,
That I could steal't myself.   [*Places the chain.*

Sir Alex. Perhaps thou shalt too,
That or something as weighty : what she leaves
Thou shalt come closely in and filch away,
And all the weight upon her back I'll lay.

Trap. You cannot assure that, sir.

Sir Alex. No? what lets[2] it?

Trap. Being a stout girl, perhaps she'll desire pressing;
Then all the weight must lie upon her belly.

Sir Alex. Belly or back, I care not, so I've one.

Trap. You're of my mind for that, sir.

Sir Alex. Hang up my ruff-band with the diamond
        at it;
It may be she'll like that best.

Trap. [*Aside.*] It's well for her, that she must have
her choice; he thinks nothing too good for her.—If you
hold on this mind a little longer, it shall be the first work
I do to turn thief myself; 'twould do a man good to be
hanged when he is so well provided for.
                    [*Hangs up the ruff-band.*

Sir Alex. So, well said; all hangs well : would she
        hung so too !
The sight would please me more than all their glisterings.
O that my mysteries[3] to such straits should run,
That I must rob myself to bless my son !   [*Exeunt.*

Enter SEBASTIAN WENGRAVE, MARY FITZALLARD *dis-
    guised as a page, and* MOLL *in her male dress.*

Seb. Thou'st done me a kind office, without touch
Either of sin or shame; our loves are honest.

---

[1] A moveable side-board for displaying plate, etc.
[2] Hinders.   [3] Dyce suggested "miseries."

Moll. I'd scorn to make such shift to bring you
together else.

Seb. Now have I time and opportunity
Without all fear to bid thee welcome, love!

[*Kisses* MARY.

Mary. Never with more desire and harder venture!

Moll. How strange this shows, one man to kiss
another!

Seb. I'd kiss such men to choose, Moll;
Methinks a woman's lip tastes well in a doublet.

Moll. Many an old madam has the better fortune then,
Whose breaths grew stale before the fashion came:
If that will help 'em, as you think 'twill do,
They'll learn in time to pluck on the hose too.

Seb. The older they wax, Moll, troth I speak seriously,
As some have a conceit their drink tastes better
In an outlandish cup than in our own,
So methinks every kiss she gives me now
In this strange form is worth a pair of two.
Here we are safe, and furthest from the eye
Of all suspicion; this is my father's chamber,
Upon which floor he never steps till night:
Here he mistrusts me not, nor I his coming;
At mine own chamber he still pries unto me,
My freedom is not there at mine own finding,
Still checked and curbed; here he shall miss his purpose.

Moll. And what's your business, now you have your
mind, sir?
At your great suit I promised you to come:
I pitied her for name's sake, that a Moll
Should be so crossed in love, when there's so many
That owes nine lays[1] a-piece, and not so little.
My tailor fitted her; how like you his work?

Seb. So well, no art can mend it, for this purpose:
But to thy wit and help we're chief in debt,
And must live still beholding.

[1] Wagers.

Moll. Any honest pity
I'm willing to bestow upon poor ringdoves.

Seb. I'll offer no worse play.

Moll. Nay, an you should, sir,
I should draw first, and prove the quicker man.

Seb. Hold, there shall need no weapon at this meeting;
But 'cause thou shalt not loose thy fury idle,
Here take this viol, run upon the guts,
And end thy quarrel singing.

> [*Takes down and gives her a viol.*

Moll. Like a swan above bridge;[1]
For look you here's the bridge,[2] and here am I.

Seb. Hold on, sweet Moll!

Mary. I've heard her much commended, sir, for one
That was ne'er taught.

Moll. I'm much beholding to 'em.
Well, since you'll needs put us together, sir,
I'll play my part as well as I can : it shall ne'er
Be said I came into a gentleman's chamber,
And let his instrument hang by the walls.

Seb. Why, well said, Moll, i'faith ; it had been a shame
for that gentleman then that would have let it hung still,
and ne'er offered thee it.

Moll. There it should have been still then for Moll;
For though the world judge impudently of me,
I never came into that chamber yet
Where I took down the instrument myself.

Seb. Pish, let 'em prate abroad; thou'rt here where thou
art known and loved; there be a thousand close dames
that will call the viol an unmannerly instrument for a
woman, and therefore talk broadly of thee, when you
shall have them sit wider to a worse quality.

Moll. Pish,
I ever fall asleep and think not of 'em, sir ;
And thus I dream.

[1] When this play was written, the Thames abounded with swans.
[2] Of the viol-de-gambo.

Seb. Prithee, let's hear thy dream, Moll.
Moll [*Sings.*]

> I dream there is a mistress,
>   And she lays out the money;
> She goes unto her sisters,
>   She never comes at any.

Re-enter Sir ALEXANDER *behind.*

> She says she went to the Burse[1] for patterns;
> You shall find her at Saint Kathern's,
>   And comes home with never a penny.

Seb. That's a free mistress, faith!
Sir Alex. Ay, ay, ay,
Like her that sings it; one of thine own choosing.
                                        [*Aside.*

Moll. But shall I dream again?

[*Sings.*] Here comes a wench will brave ye:
>   Her courage was so great,
> She lay with one of the navy,
>   Her husband lying i' the Fleet.
> Yet oft with him she cavelled;
>   I wonder what she ails:
> Her husband's ship lay gravelled,
>   When hers could hoise up sails:
> Yet she began, like all my foes,
> To call whore first; for so do those—
>   A pox of all false tails!

Seb. Marry, amen, say I!
Sir Alex. So say I too.   [*Aside.*
Moll. Hang up the viol now, sir: all this while
I was in a dream; one shall lie rudely then;
But being awake, I keep my legs together.
A watch! what's a' clock here?
Sir Alex. Now, now she's trapped!   [*Aside.*

---

[1] The New Exchange in the Strand

Moll. Between one and two; nay, then I care not.
A watch and a musician are cousin-germans in one
thing, they must both keep time well, or there's no
goodness in 'em; the one else deserves to be dashed
against a wall, and t'other to have his brains knocked
out with a fiddle-case.
What! a loose chain and a dangling diamond?
Here were a brave booty for an evening thief now:
There's many a younger brother would be glad
To look twice in at a window for't,
And wriggle in and out, like an eel in a sand bag.
O, if men's secret youthful faults should judge 'em,
'Twould be the general'st execution
That e'er was seen in England!
There would be but few left to sing the ballads,
There would be so much work: mos of our brokers
Would be chosen for hangmen; a good day for them;
They might renew their wardrobes of free cost then.

Seb. This is the roaring wench must do us good.

Mary. No poison, sir, but serves us for some use;
Which is confirmed in her.

Seb. Peace, peace—
'Foot, I did hear him sure, where'er he be.

Moll. Who did you hear?

Seb. My father;
'Twas like a sigh of his: I must be wary.

Sir Alex. No? will't not be? am I alone so wretched
That nothing takes? I'll put him to his plunge[1] for't.
                                    [*Aside.*

Seb. Life! here he comes.—Sir, I beseech you take it;
Your way of teaching does so much content me,
I'll make it four pound; here's forty shillings, sir—
I think I name it right—help me, good Moll— [*Aside.*
Forty in hand.   [*Offering money.*

Moll. Sir, you shall pardon me:
I've more of the meanest scholar I can teach;

---

[1] Difficulty, straits.

This pays me more than you have offered yet.

Seb. At the next quarter,
When I receive the means my father 'lows me,
You shall have t'other forty.

Sir Alex. This were well now,
Were't to a man whose sorrows had blind eyes:
But mine behold his follies and untruths
With two clear glasses.—[*Aside, then coming forward.*]—
How now?

Seb. Sir?

Sir Alex. What's he there?

Seb. You're come in good time, sir; I've a suit to you;
I'd crave your present kindness.

Sir Alex. What's he there?

Seb. A gentleman, a musician, sir; one of excellent
fingering.

Sir Alex. Ay, I think so;—I wonder how they 'scaped
　　her.　　　　　　　　　　　　　　　　　　[*Aside.*

Seb. Has the most delicate stroke, sir.

Sir Alex. A stroke indeed!—I feel it at my heart.
　　　　　　　　　　　　　　　　　　　　　[*Aside.*

Seb. Puts down all your famous musicians.

Sir Alex. Ay, a whore may put down a hundred of
　　'em.　　　　　　　　　　　　　　　　　　[*Aside.*

Seb. Forty shillings is the agreement, sir, between us:
Now, sir, my present means mounts but to half on't.

Sir Alex. And he stands upon the whole?

Seb. Ay, indeed does he, sir.

Sir Alex. And will do still; he'll ne'er be in other
　　tale.

Seb. Therefore I'd stop his mouth, sir, an I could.

Sir Alex. Hum, true; there is no other way, indeed;—
His folly hardens; shame must needs succeed.—
　　　　　　　　　　　　　　　　　　　　　[*Aside.*

Now, sir, I understand you profess music.

Moll. I'm a poor servant to that liberal science, sir.

Sir Alex. Where is't you teach?

Moll. Right against Clifford's Inn.

Sir Alex. Hum, that's a fit place for't: you've many
scholars?

Moll. And some of worth, whom I may call my
masters.

Sir Alex. Ay, true, a company of whoremasters.—
[*Aside.*

You teach to sing, too?

Moll. Marry, do I, sir.

Sir Alex. I think you'll find an apt scholar of my
son,
Especially for prick-song.

Moll. I've much hope of him.

Sir Alex. I'm sorry for't, I have the less for that.—
[*Aside.*

You can play any lesson?

Moll. At first sight, sir.

Sir Alex. There's a thing called the Witch; can you
play that?

Moll. I would be sorry any one should mend me in't.

Sir Alex. Ay, I believe thee; thou'st so bewitched my
son,
No care will mend the work that thou hast done.
I have bethought myself, since my art fails,
I'll make her policy the art to trap her.
Here are four angels marked with holes in them
Fit for his cracked companions: gold he'll give her;
These will I make induction to her ruin,
And rid shame from my house, grief from my heart.—
[*Aside.*

Here, son, in what you take content and pleasure,
Want shall not curb you; pay the gentleman
His latter half in gold.   [*Gives money.*

Seb. I thank you, sir.

Sir Alex. O may the operation on't end three;
In her life, shame in him, and grief in me!
[*Aside and exit.*

Seb. Faith, thou shalt have 'em ; 'tis my father's gift :
Never was man beguiled with better shift.

Moll. He that can take me for a male musician,
I can't choose but make him my instrument,
And play upon him.   [*Exeunt.*

SCENE II.

Before GALLIPOT'S *Shop.*

Enter Mistress GALLIPOT *and* Mistress OPENWORK.

Mis. G. Is, then, that bird of yours, Master Goshawk,
so wild ?

Mis. O. A Goshawk ? a puttock ;[1] all for prey : he
angles for fish, but he loves flesh better.

Mis. G. Is't possible his smooth face should have
wrinkles in't, and we not see them ?

Mis. O. Possible ? why, have not many handsome
legs in silk stockings villanous splay feet, for all their
great roses ?[2]

Mis. G. Troth, sirrah, thou sayst true.

Mis. O. Didst never see an archer, as thou'st walked
by Bunhill,[3] look a-squint when he drew his bow ?

Mis. G. Yes, when his arrows have flien toward
Islington, his eyes have shot clean contrary towards
Pimlico.[4]

Mis. O. For all the world so does Master Goshawk
double with me.

---

[1] Kite.   [2] Rosettes.

[3] Where archery matches and artillery practice were held.   On
2nd September 1623, Middleton received twenty marks " for his
services at the shooting on Bunhill, and at the Conduit Head before
the Lord Mayor and Aldermen " (*Remembrancia*, p. 305).—*Bullen.*

[4] A part of Hoxton.

Mis. G. O, fie upon him: if he double once, he's not for me.

Mis. O. Because Goshawk goes in a shag-ruff band, with a face sticking up in't which shows like an agate set in a cramp ring,[1] he thinks I'm in love with him.

Mis. G. 'Las, I think he takes his mark amiss in thee!

Mis. O. He has, by often beating into me, made me believe my husband kept a whore.

Mis. G. Very good.

Mis. O. Swore to me that my husband this very morning went in a boat, with a tilt over it, to the Three Pigeons at Brainford, and his punk[2] with him under his tilt.

Mis. G. That were wholesome.

Mis. O. I believed it; fell a-swearing at him, cursing of harlots; made me ready to hoise up sail and be there as soon as he.

Mis. G. So, so.

Mis. O. And for that voyage Goshawk comes hither incontinently:[3] but, sirrah, this water-spaniel dives after no duck but me; his hope is having me at Brainford, to make me cry "quack."

Mis. G. Art sure of it?

Mis. O. Sure of it? my poor innocent Openwork came in as I was poking my ruff:[4] presently hit I him i' the teeth with the Three Pigeons; he forswore all; I up and opened all; and now stands he in a shop hard by, like a musket on a rest,[5] to hit Goshawk i' the eye, when he comes to fetch me to the boat.

Mis. G. Such another lame gelding offered to carry me through thick and thin,—Laxton, sirrah,—but I am rid of him now.

[1] Cramp rings were rings which had been consecrated on Good Friday and were supposed to preserve the wearer against cramp.

[2] Loose woman.   [3] Immediately.

[4] Setting the plaits with a steel rod.

[5] The ancient musket was supported on a strong pole provided with an iron spike at the end to fix it in the ground.

Mis. O Happy is the woman can be rid of 'em all!
'las, what are your whisking gallants to our husbands,
weigh 'em rightly, man for man?

Mis. G. Troth, mere shallow things.

Mis. O. Idle, simple things, running heads; and yet
let 'em run over us never so fast, we shopkeepers, when
all's done, are sure to have 'em in our purse-nets at
length; and when they are in, Lord, what simple animals
they are! then they hang the head——

Mis. G. Then they droop——

Mis. O. Then they write letters——

Mis. G. Then they cog ¹——

Mis. O. Then deal they underhand with us, and we
must ingle¹ with our husbands a-bed; and we must
swear they are our cousins, and able to do us a pleasure
at court.

Mis. G. And yet, when we have done our best, all's
but put into a riven dish; we are but frumped² at and
libelled upon.

Mis. O. O, if it were the good Lord's will there were
a law made, no citizen should trust any of 'em all!

Enter GOSHAWK.

Mis. G. Hush, sirrah! Goshawk flutters.

Gos. How now? are you ready?

Mis. O. Nay, are *you* ready? a little thing, you see
makes us ready.

Gos. Us? why, must she make one i' the voyage?

Mis. O. O, by any means! do I know how my husband will handle me?

Gos. 'Foot, how shall I find water to keep these two
mills going? [*Aside.*]—Well, since you'll needs be
clapped under hatches, if I sail not with you both till
all split,³ hang me up at the mainyard and duck me.—
It's but liquoring them both soundly, and then you shall

---

¹ Wheedle.   ² Mocked.   ³ A nautical phrase.

see their cork heels[1] fly up high, like two swans when
their tails are above water, and their long necks under
water diving to catch gudgeons. [*Aside.*]—Come, come,
oars stand ready; the tide's with us; on with those false
faces; blow winds and thou shalt take thy husband
casting out his net to catch fresh salmon at Brainford.

Mis. G. I believe you'll eat of a cod's head of your
own dressing before you reach half way thither.

      [*Aside ; she and* Mistress OPENWORK *then mask them-*
Gos. So, so, follow close; pin as you go.   [*selves.*

Enter LAXTON *muffled.*

Lax. Do you hear?

Mis. G. Yes, I thank my ears.

Lax. I must have a bout with your 'pothecaryship.

Mis. G. At what weapon?

Lax. I must speak with you.

Mis. G. No.

Lax. No? you shall.

Mis. G. Shall? away, soused sturgeon! half fish, half
flesh.

Lax. Faith, gib,[2] are you spitting? I'll cut your tail,
puss-cat, for this.

Mis. G. 'Las, poor Laxton, I think thy tail's cut
already! your worst.

Lax. If I do not——   [*Exit.*

Gos. Come, ha' you done?

Enter OPENWORK.

'Sfoot, Rosamond, your husband!

Open. How now? sweet Master Goshawk! none more
    welcome;

I've wanted your embracements : when friends meet,
The music of the spheres sounds not more sweet

---

  1 High cork heels were very fashionable at the time.
  2 Properly a male-cat : a common term of abuse.

Than does their conference.   Who's this?   Rosamond?
Wife? how now, sister?

   Gos. Silence, if you love me!

   Open. Why masked?

   Mis. O. Does a mask grieve you, sir?

   Open. It does.

   Mis. O. Then you're best get you a-mumming.[1]

   Gos. 'Sfoot, you'll spoil all!

   Mis. G. May not we cover our bare faces with masks,
As well as you cover your bald heads with hats?

   Open. No masks; why, they're thieves to beauty, that
      rob eyes
Of admiration in which true love lies.
Why are masks worn? why good? or why desired?
Unless by their gay covers wits are fired
To read the vilest looks: many bad faces,
Because rich gems are treasured up in cases,
Pass by their privilege current; but as caves
Damn misers' gold, so masks are beauties' graves.
Men ne'er meet women with such muffled eyes,
But they curse her that first did masks devise,
And swear it was some beldam.   Come, off with't.

   Mis. O. I will not.

   Open. Good faces masked are jewels kept by sprites;
Hide none but bad ones, for they poison men's sights;
Show, then, as shopkeepers do their broidered stuff,
By owl-light; fine wares can't be open enough.
Prithee, sweet Rose, come, strike this sail.

   Mis. O. Sail?

   Open. Ha!
Yes, wife, strike sail, for storms are in thine eyes.

   Mis. O. They're here, sir, in my brows, if any rise.

   Open. Ha, brows?—What says she, friend? pray, tell
      me why
Your two flags[2] were advanced; the comedy,

---

    [1] *i e.* Masquing.

    [2] Flags were placed at the tops of playhouses.

Come, what's the comedy?

Mis. G. *Westward ho.*[1]

Open. How?

Mis. O. 'Tis *Westward ho*, she says.

Gos. Are you both mad?

Mis. O. Is't market-day at Brainford, and your ware
Not sent up yet?

Open. What market-day? what ware?

Mis. O. A pie with three pigeons in't: 'tis drawn,
And stays your cutting up.

Gos. As you regard my credit——

Open. Art mad?

Mis. O. Yes, lecherous goat, baboon!

Open. Baboon? then toss me in a blanket.

Mis. O. Do I it well?

Mis. G. Rarely.

Gos. Belike, sir, she's not well; best leave her.

Open. No;
I'll stand the storm now, how fierce soe'er it blow.

Mis. O. Did I for this lose all my friends, refuse
Rich hopes and golden fortunes, to be made
A stale [2] to a common whore?

Open. This does amaze me.

Mis. O. O God, O God! feed at reversion now?
A strumpet's leaving?

Open. Rosamond!

Gos. I sweat; would I lay in Cold Harbour! [*Aside.*

Mis. O. Thou'st struck ten thousand daggers through
    my heart!

Open. Not I, by Heaven, sweet wife!

Mis. O. Go, devil, go; that which thou swear'st by
    damns thee!

---

[1] By Webster and Dekker, written before 1605. "Westward ho!"
was one of the Thames watermen's cries when seeking custom.

[2] Old writers use the term in the sense of a substitute for another
in wickedness, especially in adultery, or sometimes as a cover for
another's guilt. —*Halliwell.*

Gos. 'S heart, will you undo me?

Mis. O. Why stay you here? the star by which you sail
Shines yonder above Chelsea; you lose your shore;
If this moon light you, seek out your light whore.

Open. Ha!

Mis. G. Pish, your western pug!

Gos. Zounds, now hell roars!

Mis. O. With whom you tilted in a pair of oars
This very morning.

Open. Oars?

Mis. O. At Brainford, sir.

Open. Rack not my patience.—Master Goshawk,
Some slave has buzzed this into her, has he not?
I run a tilt in Brainford with a woman?
'Tis a lie!
What old bawd tells thee this? 'sdeath, 'tis a lie!

Mis. O. 'Tis one who to thy face shall justify
All that I speak.

Open. Ud'soul, do but name that rascal!

Mis. O. No, sir, I will not.

Gos. Keep thee there, girl, then!   [*Aside.*

Open. Sister, know you this varlet?

Mis. G. Yes.

Open. Swear true;
Is there a rogue so low damned? a second Judas?—
A common hangman, cutting a man's throat,
Does it to his face,—bite me behind my back?
A cur dog? swear if you know this hell-hound.

Mis. G. In truth, I do.

Open. His name?

Mis. G. Not for the world;
To have you to stab him.

Gos. O brave girls, worth gold![1]   [*Aside.*

Open. [*Drawing his sword.*]   A word, honest Master
      Goshawk.

Gos. What do you mean, sir?

---

[1] " A girl worth gold " was a proverbial expression.

Open. Keep off, and if the devil can give a name
To this new fury, holla it through my ear,
Or wrap it up in some hid character.
I'll ride to Oxford and watch out mine eyes,
But I will hear the Brazen Head speak,[1] or else
Show me but one hair of his head or beard,
That I may sample it.   If the fiend I meet
In mine own house, I'll kill him; in the street,
Or at the church-door,—there, 'cause he seeks t' untie
The knot God fastens, he deserves most to die.

Mis. O. My husband titles him!

Open. Master Goshawk, pray, sir,
Swear to me that you know him, or know him not,
Who makes me at Brainford to take up a petticoat
Besides my wife's.

Gos. By Heaven, that man I know not!

Mis. O. Come, come, you lie!

Gos. Will you not have all out!
By Heaven, I know no man beneath the moon
Should do you wrong, but if I had his name,
I'd print it in text letters.

Mis. O. Print thine own then:
Didst not thou swear to me he kept his whore?

Mis. G. And that in sinful Brainford they'd commit
That which our lips did water at, sir,—ha?

Mis. O. Thou spider that hast woven thy cunning web
In mine own house t' ensnare me! hast not thou
Sucked nourishment even underneath this roof,
And turned it all to poison, spitting it
On thy friend's face, my husband (he as 'twere sleeping),
Only to leave him ugly to mine eyes,
That they might glance on thee?

Mis. G. Speak, are these lies?

Gos. Mine own shame me confounds!

Open. No more; he's stung.
Who'd think that in one body there could dwell

---

[1] A fabulous achievement of Friar Bacon.

Deformity and beauty, Heaven and hell?
Goodness I see is but outside; we all set
In rings of gold stones that be counterfeit:
I thought you none.

 Gos. Pardon me!

 Open. Truth I do:
This blemish grows in nature, not in you;
For man's creation sticks even moles in scorn
On fairest cheeks.—Wife, nothing's perfect born.

 Mis. O. I thought you had been born perfect.

 Open. What's this whole world but a gilt rotten pill?
For at the heart lies the old core still.
I'll tell you, Master Goshawk, ay, in your eye
I have seen wanton fire; and then, to try
The soundness of my judgment, I told you
I kept a whore, made you believe 'twas true,
Only to feel how your pulse beat; but find
The world can hardly yield a perfect friend.
Come, come, a trick of youth, and 'tis forgiven;
This rub put by, our love shall run more even.

 Mis. O. You'll deal upon men's wives no more?

 Gos. No; you teach me
A trick for that.

 Mis. O. Troth, do not; they'll o'erreach thee.

 Open. Make my house yours, sir, still.

 Gos. No.

 Open. I say you shall:
Seeing thus besieged it holds out, 'twill never fall.

 Enter GALLIPOT, *followed by* GREENWIT *disguised as a
  Sumner;* [1] *and* LAXTON *muffled aloof off.*

 Open., Gos., &c. How now?

 Gal. With me, sir?

 Green. You, sir. I have gone snuffling up and down
by your door this hour, to watch for you.

---

[1] An apparitor who summoned delinquents to the Spiritual Court.

Mis. G. What's the matter, husband?

Green. I have caught a cold in my head, sir, by sitting up late in the Rose tavern; but I hope you understand my speech.

Gal. So, sir.

Green. I cite you by the name of Hippocrates Gallipot, and you by the name of Prudence Gallipot, to appear upon *Crastino,*—do you see?—*Crastino sancti Dunstani,* this Easter term, in Bow Church.

Gal. Where, sir? what says he?

Green. Bow, Bow Church, to answer to a libel of pre-contract on the part and behalf of the said Prudence and another: you're best, sir, take a copy of the citation, 'tis but twelvepence.

Open., Gos., &c. A citation!

Gal. You pocky-nosed rascal, what slave fees you to this!

Lax. [*Coming forward.*] Slave? I ha' nothing to do with you; do you hear, sir?

Gos. Laxton, is't not? What fagary[1] is this?

Gal. Trust me, I thought, sir, this storm long ago
Had been full laid, when, if you be remembered,
I paid you the last fifteen pound, besides
The thirty you had first; for then you swore——

Lax. Tush, tush, sir, oaths,—
Truth, yet I'm loth to vex you—tell you what,
Make up the money I had a hundred pound,
And take your bellyful of her.

Gal. An hundred pound?

Mis. G. What, a hundred pound? he gets none: what, a hundred pound?

Gal. Sweet Pru, be calm; the gentleman offers thus:
If I will make the moneys that are past
A hundred pound, he will discharge all courts,
And give his bond never to vex us more.

---

[1] Vagary.

Mis. G. A hundred pound? 'Las, take, sir, but threescore!
Do you seek my undoing?

Lax. I'll not bate one sixpence.—
I'll maul you, puss, for spitting.

Mis. G. Do thy worst.—
Will fourscore stop thy mouth?

Lax. No.

Mis. G. You're a slave;
Thou cheat, I'll now tear money from thy throat.—
Husband, lay hold on yonder tawny coat.[1]

Green. Nay, gentlemen, seeing your women are so
hot, I must lose my hair[2] in their company, I see.

　　　　　　　　　　　[Takes off his false hair.

Mis. O. His hair sheds off, and yet he speaks not so
much in the nose as he did before.

Gos. He has had the better surgeon.—Master Greenwit, is your wit so raw as to play no better a part than a
sumner's?

Gal. I pray, who plays *A Knack to know an Honest
Man,*[3] in this company?

Mis. G. Dear husband, pardon me, I did dissemble,
Told thee I was his precontracted wife,
When letters came from him for thirty pound:
I had no shift but that.

Gal. A very clean shift,
But able to make me lousy: on.

Mis. G. Husband, I plucked,
When he had tempted me to think well of him,
Gilt[4] feathers from thy wings, to make him fly
More lofty.

Gal. A' the top of you, wife: on.

Mis. G. He having wasted them, comes now for more,

---

[1] Sumners wore coats of this colour.
[2] One of the effects of syphilis.
[3] The title of an old comedy.
　" Get " in old ed.

Using me as a ruffian doth his whore,
Whose sin keeps him in breath. · By Heaven, I vow,
Thy bed he ne'er wronged more than he does now !
   Gal. My bed ? ha, ha ! like enough ; a shopboard
     will serve
To have a cuckold's coat cut out upon :
Of that we'll talk hereafter.—You're a villain.
   Lax. Hear me but speak, sir, you shall find me none.
   Open., Gos., &c. Pray, sir, be patient, and hear him.
   Gal. I'm muzzled for biting, sir ; use me how you will.
   Lax. The first hour that your wife was in my eye,
Myself with other gentlemen sitting by
In your shop tasting smoke, and speech being used,
That men who've fairest wives are most abused,
And hardly scape the horn, your wife maintained
That only such spots in city dames were stained
Justly but by men's slanders : for her own part,
She vowed that you had so much of her heart,
No man, by all his wit, by any wile
Never so fine-spun, should yourself beguile
Of what in her was yours.
   Gal. Yet, Pru, 'tis well.—
Play out your game at Irish,[1] sir : who wins ?
   Mis. O. The trial is when she comes to bearing.
   Lax. I scorned one woman thus should brave all men,
And, which more vexed me, a she-citizen ;
Therefore I laid siege to her ; out she held,
Gave many a brave repulse, and me compelled
With shame to sound retreat to my hot lust :
Then, seeing all base desires raked up in dust,
And that to tempt her modest ears, I swore
Ne'er to presume again : she said, her eye
Would ever give me welcome honestly ;
And, since I was a gentleman, if 't run low,
She would my state relieve, not to o'erthrow

   [1] A game resembling backgammon. " Bearing " is a term in
the game.

Your own and hers: did so; then seeing I wrought
Upon her meekness, me she set at nought;
And yet to try if I could turn that tide,
You see what stream I strove with; but, sir, I swear
By Heaven, and by those hopes men lay up there,
I neither have nor had a base intent
To wrong your bed! what's done, is merriment:
Your gold I pay back with this interest,
When I'd most power to do't, I wronged you least.

 Gal. If this no gullery be, sir——

 Open., Gos., &c. No, no, on my life!

 Gal. Then, sir, I am beholden—not to you, wife,—
But, Master Laxton, to your want of doing
Ill, which it seems you have not.—Gentlemen,
Tarry and dine here all.

 Open. Brother, we've a jest,
As good as yours, to furnish out a feast.

 Gal. We'll crown our table with't.—Wife, brag no
  more
Of holding out: who most brags is most whore.

         [Exeunt.

ACT THE FIFTH.

SCENE I.

A Street.

Enter JACK DAPPER, MOLL, Sir BEAUTEOUS GANYMEDE,
and Sir THOMAS LONG.

AP. But, prithee, Master Captain Jack, be plain and perspicuous with me; was it your Meg[1] of Westminster's courage that rescued me from the Poultry puttocks[2] indeed?

Moll. The valour of my wit, I ensure you, sir, fetched you off bravely, when you were i' the forlorn hope among those desperates. Sir Beauteous Ganymede here, and Sir Thomas Long, heard that cuckoo, my man Trapdoor, sing the note of your ransom from captivity.

Sir Beau. Uds so, Moll, where's that Trapdoor?

Moll. Hanged, I think, by this time: a justice in this town, that speaks nothing but "Make a mittimus, away with him to Newgate," used that rogue like a firework, to run upon a line betwixt him and me.

All. How, how?

Moll. Marry, to lay trains of villany to blow up my life: I smelt the powder, spied what linstock[3] gave fire

---

[1] *The Life and Pranks of Long Meg of Westminster* is the title of a pamphlet in which the career of this Amazon is set forth. She is often mentioned in old plays.

[2] Kites.

[3] The stick that held the gunner's match.

to shoot against the poor captain of the galley-foist,[1] and away slid I my man like a shovel-board shilling.[2] He struts up and down the suburbs, I think, and eats up whores, feeds upon a bawd's garbage.

Sir Tho. Sirrah, Jack Dapper——

J. Dap. What sayst, Tom Long?

Sir Tho. Thou hadst a sweet-faced boy, hail-fellow with thee, to your little gull: how is he spent?

J. Dap. Troth, I whistled the poor little buzzard off a' my fist, because, when he waited upon me at the ordinaries, the gallants hit me i' the teeth still, and said I looked like a painted alderman's tomb, and the boy at my elbow like a death's head.—Sirrah Jack, Moll——

Moll. What says my little Dapper?

Sir Beau. Come, come; walk and talk, walk and talk.

J. Dap. Moll and I'll be i' the midst.

Moll. These knights shall have squires' places belike then: well, Dapper, what say you?

J. Dap. Sirrah captain, mad Mary, the gull my own father, Dapper Sir Davy, laid these London boot-halers,[3] the catchpolls, in ambush to set upon me.

All. Your father? away, Jack!

J. Dap. By the tassels of this handkercher, 'tis true: and what was his warlike stratagem, think you? he thought, because a wicker cage tames a nightingale, a lousy prison could make an ass of me.

All. A nasty plot!

J. Dap. Ay, as though a Counter, which is a park in which all the wild beasts of the city run head by head, could tame me!

Moll. Yonder comes my Lord Noland.

Enter Lord NOLAND.

All. Save you, my lord.

---

[1] A long barge with oars; the Lord Mayor's was usually so called.
[2] A worn, smooth coin which slid easily.
[3] Freebooters, highwaymen.

Lord Nol. Well met, gentlemen all.—Good Sir Beauteous Ganymede, Sir Thomas Long,—and how does Master Dapper?

J. Dap. Thanks, my lord.

Moll. No tobacco, my lord?

Lord Nol. No, faith, Jack.

J. Dap. My Lord Noland, will you go to Pimlico with us? we are making a boon voyage to that nappy land of spice-cakes.

Lord Nol. Here's such a merry ging,[1] I could find in my heart to sail to the world's end with such company: come, gentlemen, let's on.

J. Dap. Here's most amorous weather, my lord.

All. Amorous weather!   [*They walk.*

J. Dap. Is not amorous a good word?

Enter TRAPDOOR *disguised as a poor Soldier with a patch over one eye, and* TEARCAT *all in tatters.*

Trap. Shall we set upon the infantry, these troops of foot? Zounds, yonder comes Moll, my whorish master and mistress! would I had her kidneys between my teeth!

Tear. I had rather have a cow-heel.

Trap. Zounds, I am so patched up, she cannot discover me: we'll on.

Tear. Alla corago,[2] then!

Trap. Good your honours and worships, enlarge the ears of commiseration, and let the sound of a hoarse military organ-pipe penetrate your pitiful bowels, to extract out of them so many small drops of silver as may give a hard straw-bed lodging to a couple of maimed soldiers.

J. Dap. Where are you maimed?

Tear. In both our nether limbs.

Moll. Come, come, Dapper, let's give 'em something 'las, poor men! what money have you? by my troth, I love a soldier with my soul.

---

[1] Gang.   [2] A corruption of *coraggio* (Ital.), courage.

Sir Beau. Stay, stay; where have you served?

Sir Tho. In any part of the Low Countries?

Trap. Not in the Low Countries, if it please your manhood, but in Hungary against the Turk at the siege of Belgrade.

Lord Nol. Who served there with you, sirrah?

Trap. Many Hungarians, Moldavians, Vallachians, and Transylvanians, with some Sclavonians; and retiring home, sir, the Venetian galleys took us prisoners, yet freed us, and suffered us to beg up and down the country.

J. Dap. You have ambled all over Italy, then?

Trap. O sir, from Venice to Roma, Vecchia, Bononia, Romagna, Bologna,[1] Modena, Piacenza, and Tuscana, with all her cities, as Pistoia, Valteria,[2] Mountepulchena,[3] Arezzo; with the Siennois, and divers others.

Moll. Mere rogues! put spurs to 'em once more.

J. Dap. Thou lookest like a strange creature, a fat butter-box, yet speakest English: what art thou?

Tear. Ick, mine here? ick bin den ruffling Tearcat, den brave soldado; ick bin dorick all Dutchlant gereisen; der schellum das meer ine beasa ine woert gaeb, ick slaag um stroakes on tom cop; dastick den hundred touzun divel halle, frollick, mine here.

Sir Beau. Here, here; let's be rid of their jabbering.

[*About to give money.*

Moll. Not a cross,[4] Sir Beauteous.—You base rogues, I have taken measure of you better than a tailor can; and I'll fit you, as you, monster with one eye, have fitted me.

Trap. Your worship will not abuse a soldier?

Moll. Soldier? thou deservest to be hanged up by that tongue which dishonours so noble a profession: soldier? you skeldering[5] varlet! hold, stand; there should be a trapdoor hereabouts.   [*Pulls off his patch.*

---

[1] Bononia and Bologna are the same place.

[2] Volterra.

[3] Montepulciano.

[4] Many coins bore a cross on one side.

[5] Cheating.

Trap. The balls of these glaziers[1] of mine, mine eyes, shall be shot up and down in any hot piece of service for my invincible mistress.

J. Dap. I did not think there had been such knavery in black patches[2] as now I see.

Moll. O sir, he hath been brought up in the Isle of Dogs,[3] and can both fawn like a spaniel, and bite like a mastiff, as he finds occasion.

Lord Nol. What are you, sirrah? a bird of this feather too?

Tear. A man beaten from the wars, sir.

Sir Tho. I think so, for you never stood to fight.

J. Dap. What's thy name, fellow soldier?

Tear. I am called by those that have seen my valour, Tearcat.

All. Tearcat?

Moll. A mere whip-jack,[4] and that is, in the commonwealth of rogues, a slave that can talk of sea-fight, name all your chief pirates, discover more countries to you than either the Dutch, Spanish, French, or English ever found out; yet indeed all his service is by land, and that is to rob a fair, or some such venturous exploit. Tearcat? 'foot, sirrah, I have your name, now I remember me, in my book of horners; horns for the thumb,[5] you know how.

Tear. No indeed, Captain Moll, for I know you by sight, I am no such nipping Christian, but a maunderer upon the pad,[6] I confess; and meeting with honest Trapdoor here, whom you had cashiered from bearing arms, out at elbows, under your colours, I instructed him in the

[1] A cant term for eyes.

[2] Black patches were worn by ladies and gallants of the time.

[3] Then a refuge for debtors and others who sought to evade the law.

[4] A pretended distressed sailor.

[5] A kind of horn thimble which thieves wore on the thumb to resist the edge of the knife when they were cutting purses.

[6] A beggar on the highway.

rudiments of roguery, and by my map made him sail over any country you can name, so that now he can maunder better than myself.

J. Dap. So, then, Trapdoor, thou art turned soldier now ?

Trap. Alas, sir, now there's no wars, 'tis the safest course of life I could take !

Moll. I hope, then, you can cant; for by your cudgels, you, sirrah, are an upright man.[1]

Trap. As any walks the highway, I assure you.

Moll. And, Tearcat, what are you ? a wild rogue,[2] an angler,[3] or a ruffler ?[4]

Tear. Brother to this upright man, flesh and blood ; ruffling Tearcat is my name, and a ruffler is my style, my title, my profession.

[1] " A sturdy big-bonde knaue, that neuer walkes but (like a Commander) with a short truncheon in his hand, which hee cals his Filchman. At Markets, Fayres, and other meetings his voice among Beggars is of the same sound that a Constables is of, it is not to be controld. He is free of all the shiers in England, but neuer stayes in any place long, &c. . . . These [upright men] cary the shapes of soldiers, and can talke of the Low Countries. though they neuer were beyond Dover."—Dekker's *Belman of London,* 1608. From this tract and from the same author's *Lanthorne and Candlelight* Dyce selected the quotations in the following notes.

[2] " These Wilde Rogues (like wilde geese) keepe in flocks, and all the day loyter in the fields, if the weather bee warme, and at Bricke-kils, or else disperse themselues in cold weather, to rich mens doores, and at night haue their meetings in Barnes or other out places."

[3] " In the day time, they beg from house to house, not so much for reliefe, as to spy what lyes fit for their nets, which in the night following they fish for. The Rod they angle with is a staffe of fiue or six foote in length, in which within one inch of the top is a little hole boared quite thorough, into which hole they put an yron hooke, and with the same doe they angle at windowes about midnight, the draught they pluck vp beeing apparell, sheetes, couerlets, or whatsoeuer their yron hookes can lay hold of."

[4] " The Ruffler and the Vpright-man are so like in conditions, that you would sweare them brothers."

Moll. Sirrah, where's your doxy? halt not with me.

All. Doxy, Moll? what's that?

Moll. His wench.

Trap. My doxy? I have, by the salomon,[1] a doxy that carries a kinchin mort[2] in her slate at her back, besides my dell and my dainty wild dell,[3] with all whom I'll tumble this next darkmans in the strommel, and drink ben bouse, and eat a fat gruntling cheat, a cackling cheat, and a quacking cheat.[4]

J. Dap. Here's old[5] cheating!

Trap. My doxy stays for me in a bousing ken, brave captain.

Moll. He says his wench stays for him in an ale-house. You are no pure rogues!

Tear. Pure rogues? no, we scorn to be pure rogues; but if you come to our lib ken or our stalling ken,[6] you shall find neither him nor me a queer cuffin.[7]

Moll. So, sir, no churl of you.

Tear. No, but a ben[8] cove, a brave cove, a gentry cuffin.

---

[1] By the mass.

[2] "Kinching-morts are girles of a yeare or two old, which the Morts (their mothers) cary at their backes in their Slates (which in the Canting-Tongue are Sheetes); if they haue no children of their owne, they will steale them from others, and by some meane disfigure them, that by their parents they shall neuer be knowne."—Dekker's *Bellman of London.*

[3] "A dell is a young wench, . . . but as yet not spoyled of her maidenhead. These Dells are reserued as dishes for the Vpright-men, for none but they must have the first taste of them. . . . Of these dells some are termed Wilde Dells, and those are such as are born and begotten under a hedge: the other are yong wenches that, either by death of parents, the Villainie of Executors, or the crueltie of maisters, and mistresses, fall into this infamous and damnable course of life."—*Ibid.*

[4] *i.e.* I'll tumble this next night in the straw, and drink good drink, and eat a fat pig, a capon, and a duck.

[5] Great.

[6] *i.e.* Our house to lie in, or place for receiving stolen goods.

[7] Fellow, the word is connected with "cove."   Good.

Lord Nol. Call you this canting?

J. Dap. Zounds, I'll give a schoolmaster half-a-crown a-week, and teach me this pedlar's French.[1]

Trap. Do but stroll, sir, half a harvest with us, sir, and you shall gabble your bellyful.

Moll. Come, you rogue, cant with me.

Sir Tho. Well said, Moll.—Cant with her, sirrah, and you shall have money, else not a penny.

Trap. I'll have a bout, if she please.

Moll. Come on, sirrah!

Trap. Ben mort, shall you and I heave a bough,[2] mill a ken, or nip a bung, and then we'll couch a hogshead under the ruffmans, and there you shall wap with me, and I'll niggle with you.

Moll. Out, you damned impudent rascal!

Trap. Cut benar whids, and hold your fambles and your stamps.[3]

Lord Nol. Nay, nay, Moll, why art thou angry? what was his gibberish?

Moll. Marry, this, my lord, says he: "Ben mort," good wench, "shall you and I heave a bough, mill a ken, or nip a bung?" shall you and I rob a house or cut a purse?

All. Very good.

Moll. "And then we'll couch a hogshead under the ruffmans;" and then we'll lie under a hedge.

Trap. That was my desire, captain, as 'tis fit a soldier should lie.

Moll. "And there you shall wap with me, and I'll niggle with you,"—and that's all.

Sir Beau. Nay, nay, Moll, what's that wap?

J. Dap. Nay, teach me what niggling is; I'd fain be niggling.

Moll. Wapping and niggling is all one, the rogue my man can tell you.

---

[1] The language of beggars.   [2] Rob a booth.
[3] *i.e.* Speak better words, and hold your hands and your legs.

Trap. 'Tis fadoodling, if it please you.

Sir Beau. This is excellent !   One fit more, good Moll.

Moll. Come, you rogue, sing with me.

SONG.

By MOLL *and* TEARCAT.

A gage of ben rom-bouse
In a bousing ken of Rom-vile,
Is benar than a caster,
Peck, pennam, lap,[1] or popler,
Which we mill in deuse a vile.
O I wud lib all the lightmans,
O I wud lib all the darkmans
By the salomon, under the ruffmans,
By the salomon, in the hartmans,
And scour the queer cramp ring,
And couch till a palliard docked my dell,
So my bousy nab might skew rom-bouse well.
Avast to the pad, let us bing ;
Avast to the pad, let us bing.[2]

All. Fine knaves, i'faith !

J. Dap. The grating of ten new cart-wheels, and the gruntling of five hundred hogs coming from Rumford market, cannot make a worse noise than this canting language does in my ears.   Pray, my Lord Noland, let's give these soldiers their pay.

Sir Beau. Agreed, and let them march.

Lord Nol. Here, Moll.   [*Gives money.*

Moll. Now I see that you are stalled[3] to the rogue,

---

[1] Old ed. "lay."

[2] *i.e.* "A quart pot of good wine in an alehouse of London is better than a cloak, meat, bread, butter-milk (or whey), or porridge, which we steal in the country.   O I would lie all the day, O I would lie all the night, by the mass, under the woods (or bushes), by the mass, in the stocks, and wear bolts (or fetters), and lie till a palliard lay with my wench, so my drunken head might quaff wine well. Avast to the highway, let us hence."— *Dyce.*

[3] Ordained.

and are not ashamed of your professions : look you, my
Lord Noland here and these gentlemen bestows upon
you two two boards and a half, that's two shillings
sixpence.

Trap. Thanks to your lordship.

Tear. Thanks, heroical captain.

Moll. Away !

Trap. We shall cut ben whids[1] of your masters and
mistress-ship wheresoever we come.

Moll. You'll maintain, sirrah, the old justice's plot to
his face?

Trap. Else trine me on the cheats,[2]—hang me.

Moll. Be sure you meet me there.

Trap. Without any more maundering,[3] I'll do't—
Follow, brave Tearcat.

Tear. *I præ, sequor :* let us go, mouse.

                    [*Exeunt* TRAPDOOR *and* TEARCAT.

Lord Nol. Moll, what was in that canting song?

Moll. Troth, my lord, only a praise of good drink, the
only milk which these wild beasts love to suck and thus
it was :

[*Sings.*]   A rich cup of wine,
                    O it is juice divine !
                    More wholesome for the head
                    Than meat, drink, or bread :
                    To fill my drunken pate
                    With that, I'd sit up late ;
                    By the heels would I lie,
                    Under a lowsy hedge die,
                    Let a slave have a pull
                    At my whore, so I be full
                    Of that precious liquor :

and a parcel of such stuff, my lord, not worth the opening.

---

[1] *i.e.* Speak good words.   [2] Hang me on the gallows.
[3] Muttering or mumbling like a beggar.

Enter a Cutpurse *very gallant,*[1] *with four or five others,
one having a wand.*

Lord Nol. What gallant comes yonder?

Sir Tho. Mass, I think I know him; 'tis one of Cumberland.

1st Cut. Shall we venture to shuffle in amongst yon heap of gallants, and strike?[2]

2nd Cut. 'Tis a question whether there be any silver shells[3] amongst them, for all their satin outsides.

The Others. Let's try.

Moll. Pox on him, a gallant? Shadow me, I know him; 'tis one that cumbers the land indeed; if he swim near to the shore of any of your pockets, look to your purses.

Lord Nol., Sir Beau., &c. Is't possible?

Moll. This brave[4] fellow is no better than a foist.

Lord Nol., Sir Beau., &c. Foist! what's that?

Moll. A diver with two fingers, a pickpocket; all his train study the figging-law, that's to say, cutting of purses and foisting.[5] One of them is a nip; I took him once i' the two-penny gallery[6] at the Fortune: then there's a cloyer[7] or snap, that dogs any new brother in that trade, and snaps will have half in any booty. He with the wand is both a stale, whose office is to face a man i' the streets, whilst shells are drawn by another, and then with his black conjuring rod in his hand, he, by the nimbleness of his eye and juggling stick, will, in cheaping a piece of plate at a goldsmith's stall, make four or five rings mount from the top of his *caduceus,* and, as if it were at leap-frog, they skip into his hand presently.

2nd Cut. Zounds, we are smoked!

[1] In fine clothes.   [2] Pick a purse.   [3] Money.
[4] Finely attired.   [5] Picking pockets.
[6] The cheapest part, but at some theatres there were penny seats.
[7] One who claimed a share in the plunder.

The Others. Ha !

2nd Cut. We are boiled,[1] pox on her ! see, Moll, the roaring drab !

1st Cut. All the diseases of sixteen hospitals boil her ! —Away !

Moll. Bless you, sir.

1st Cut. And you, good sir.

Moll. Dost not ken me, man ?

1st Cut. No, trust me, sir.

Moll. Heart, there's a knight, to whom I'm bound for many favours, lost his purse at the last new play i' the Swan,[2] seven angels in't: make it good, you're best; do you see ? no more.

1st Cut. A synagogue shall be called, Mistress Mary; disgrace me not; *pacus palabros*,[3] I will conjure for you : farewell.   [*Exit with his companions.*

Moll. Did not I tell you, my lord ?

Lord Nol. I wonder how thou camest to the knowledge of these nasty villains.

Sir Tho. And why do the foul mouths of the world call thee Moll Cutpurse ? a name, methinks, damned and odious.

Moll. Dare any step forth to my face and say,
I've ta'en thee doing so, Moll ? I must confess,
In younger days, when I was apt to stray,
I've sat among such adders ; seen their stings,
As any here might, and in full playhouses
Watched their quick-diving hands, to bring to shame
Such rogues, and in that stream met an ill name.
When next, my lord, you spy any one of those,
So he be in his art a scholar, question him ;
Tempt him with gold to open the large book
Of his close villanies ; and you yourself shall cant
Better than poor Moll can, and know more laws

---

[1] "Smoked" or "boiled" meant detected.

[2] One of the Bankside theatres.

[3] Properly *pocas palabras* (Span.) meaning, "few words."

Of cheaters, lifters, nips, foists, puggards, curbers,[1]
With all the devil's blackguard,[2] than it's fit
Should be discovered to a noble wit.
I know they have their orders, offices,
Circuits, and circles, unto which they're bound
To raise their own damnation in.

  J. Dap. How dost thou know it?

  Moll. As you do; I show't you, they to me show it.
Suppose, my lord, you were in Venice——

  Lord Nol. Well.

  Moll. If some Italian pander there would tell
All the close tricks of courtesans, would not you
Hearken to such a fellow?

  Lord Nol. Yes.

  Moll. And here,
Being come from Venice, to a friend most dear
That were to travel thither, you'd proclaim
Your knowledge in those villanies, to save
Your friend from their quick danger: must you have
A black ill name, because ill things you know?
Good troth, my lord, I'm made Moll Cutpurse so.
How many are whores in small ruffs and still looks!
How many chaste whose names fill slander's books!
Were all men cuckolds whom gallants in their scorns
Call so, we should not walk for goring horns.
Perhaps for my mad going some reprove me;
I please myself, and care not else who love me.

  Lord Nol., *Sir Beau.*, *&c.* A brave mind, Moll,
   i'faith!

  Sir Tho. Come, my lord, shall's to the ordinary?

  Lord Nol. Ay, 'tis noon, sure.

  Moll. Good my lord, let not my name condemn me

---

1 The cheator, or sharper, played with false dice; the lifter
lifted goods clean away; nips and foists were cut-purses; puggard
meant thief; and the curber hooked goods cut of a window.

2 The lowest class of menials employed in the court kitchens and
sculleries.

to you, or to the world : a fencer I hope may be called
a coward ; is he so for that ?   If all that have ill names
in London were to be whipped, and to pay but twelvepence a-piece to the beadle, I would rather have his
office than a constable's.

J. Dap. So would I, Captain Moll : 'twere a sweet
tickling office, i'faith.   [*Exeunt.*

SCENE II.

A Garden attached to Sir ALEXANDER WENGRAVE'S *House.*

Enter Sir ALEXANDER WENGRAVE, GOSHAWK,
GREENWIT, *and others.*

Sir Alex. My son marry a thief, that impudent girl,
Whom all the world stick their worst eyes upon !
    Green. How will your care prevent it ?
    Gos. 'Tis impossible :
They marry close, they're gone, but none knows whither.
    Sir Alex. O gentlemen, when has a father's heart-
        strings

Enter Servant.

Held out so long from breaking ?—Now what news, sir ?
    Seb. They were met upo' the water an hour since, sir,
Putting in towards the Sluice.
    Sir Alex. The Sluice ? come, gentlemen.
'Tis Lambeth works against us.   [*Exit* Servant.
    Green. And that Lambeth
Joins more mad matches than your six wet towns
'Twixt that and Windsor Bridge, where fares lie soaking.
    Sir Alex. **Delay** no time, sweet gentlemen : to Black-
        friars !
We'll take a pair of oars, and make after 'em.

Enter TRAPDOOR.

Trap. Your son and that bold masculine ramp[1] my
    mistress
Are landed now at Tower.

Sir Alex. Hoyda, at Tower?

Trap. I heard it now reported.

Sir Alex. Which way, gentlemen,
Shall I bestow my care? I'm drawn in pieces
Betwixt deceit and shame.

Enter Sir GUY FITZALLARD.

Sir Guy. Sir Alexander,
You are well met, and most rightly served;
My daughter was a scorn to you.

Sir Alex. Say not so, sir.

Sir Guy. A very abject she, poor gentlewoman!
Your house had been dishonoured. Give you joy, sir,
Of your son's gascoyne bride![2] you'll be a grandfather
    shortly
To a fine crew of roaring sons and daughters;
'Twill help to stock the suburbs passing well, sir.

Sir Alex. O, play not with the miseries of my heart!
Wounds should be dressed and healed, not vexed, or left
Wide open, to the anguish of the patient,
And scornful air let in; rather let pity
And advice charitably help to refresh 'em.

Sir Guy. Who'd place his charity so unworthily?
Like one that gives alms to a cursing beggar:
Had I but found one spark of goodness in you
Toward my deserving child, which then grew fond
Of your son's virtues, I had eased you now;
But I perceive both fire of youth and goodness
Are raked up in the ashes of your age,

---

[1] Rampant creature.
[2] Alluding to the gascoynes (or galligaskins), *i.e.* loose breeches,
worn by Moll.

Else no such shame should have come near your house,
Nor such ignoble sorrow touch your heart.

    Sir Alex. If not for worth, for pity's sake assist me !

    Green. You urge a thing past sense; how can he help
      you ?

All his assistance is as frail as ours:
Full as uncertain where's the place that holds 'em;
One brings us water-news; then comes another
With a full-charged mouth, like a culverin's[1] voice,
And he reports the Tower: whose sounds are truest ?

    Gos. In vain you flatter him.—Sir Alexander——

    Sir Guy. I flatter him ? gentlemen, you wrong me
      grossly.

    Green. He does it well, i'faith.

    Sir Guy. Both news are false,
Of Tower or water; they took no such way yet.

    Sir Alex. O strange ! hear you this, gentlemen ? yet
      more plunges.

    Sir Guy. They're nearer than you think for, yet more
Than if they were further off.   [close

    Sir Alex. How am I lost
In these distractions !

    Sir Guy. For your speeches, gentlemen,
In taxing me for rashness, 'fore you all
I will engage my state to half his wealth,
Nay, to his son's revenues, which are less,
And yet nothing at all till they come from him,
That I could, if my will stuck to my power,
Prevent this marriage yet, nay, banish her
For ever from his thoughts, much more his arms.

    Sir Alex. Slack not this goodness, though you heap
      upon me
Mountains of malice and revenge hereafter !
I'd willingly resign up half my state to him,
So he would marry the meanest drudge I hire.

    Green. He talks impossibilities, and you believe 'em.

                [1] A kind of cannon.

Sir Guy. I talk no more than I know how to finish,
My fortunes else are his that dares stake with me.
The poor young gentleman I love and pity;
And to keep shame from him (because the spring
Of his affection was my daughter's first,
Till his frown blasted all), do but estate him
In those possessions which your love and care
Once pointed out for him, that he may have room
To entertain fortunes of noble birth,
Where now his desperate wants casts him upon her;
And if I do not, for his own sake chiefly,
Rid him of this disease that now grows on him,
I'll forfeit my whole state before these gentlemen.

    Green. Troth, but you shall not undertake such
        matches;
We'll persuade so much with you.

    Sir Alex. Here's my ring;   [*Gives ring.*
He will believe this token. 'Fore these gentlemen
I will confirm it fully: all those lands
My first love 'lotted him, he shall straight possess
In that refusal.

    Sir Guy. If I change it not,
Change me into a beggar.

    Green. Are you mad, sir?

    Sir Guy. 'Tis done.

    Gos. Will you undo yourself by doing,
And show a prodigal trick in your old days?

    Sir Alex. 'Tis a match, gentlemen.

    Sir Guy. Ay, ay, sir, ay.
I ask no favour, trust to you for none;
My hope rests in the goodness of your son. .   [*Exit.*

    Green. He holds it up well yet.

    Gos. Of an old knight, i'faith.

    Sir Alex. Curst be the time I laid his first love barren,
Wilfully barren, that before this hour
Had sprung forth fruits of comfort and of honour!
He loved a virtuous gentlewoman.

Enter MOLL *in her male dress.*

Gos. Life, here's Moll !

Green. Jack ?

Gos. How dost thou, Jack ?

Moll. How dost thou, gallant?

Sir Alex. Impudence, where's my son ?

Moll. Weakness, go look him.

Sir Alex. Is this your wedding gown ?

Moll. The man talks monthly : [1]

Hot broth and a dark chamber for the knight !

I see he'll be stark mad at our next meeting.   [*Exit.*

Gos. Why, sir, take comfort now, there's no such

No priest will marry her, sir, for a woman   [matter,

Whiles that shape's on ; and it was never known

Two men were married and conjoined in one.

Your son hath made some shift to love another.

Sir Alex. Whate'er she be, she has my blessing with

May they be rich and fruitful, and receive   [her :

Like comfort to their issue as I take

In them ! has pleased me now ; marrying not this,

Through a whole world he could not choose amiss.

Green. Glad you're so penitent for your former sin, sir.

Gos. Say he should take a wench with her smock-

dowry,

No portion with her but her lips and arms ?

Sir Alex. Why, who thrive better, sir? they have most

blessing,

Though other have more wealth, and least repent :

Many that want most know the most content.

Green. Say he should marry a kind youthful sinner ?

Sir Alex. Age will quench that; any offence but theft

And drunkenness, nothing but death can wipe away ;

Their sins are green even when their heads are grey.

Nay, I despair not now; my heart's cheered, gentlemen;

No face can come unfortunately to me.—

[1] *i.e.* Madly ; as if under the influence of the moon.—*Steevens.*

Re-enter Servant.

Now, sir, your news?

Ser. Your son, with his fair bride,
Is near at hand.

    Sir Alex. Fair may their fortunes be!

    Green. Now you're resolved,[1] sir, it was never she.

    Sir Alex. I find it in the music of my heart.

Enter SEBASTIAN WENGRAVE *leading in* MOLL *in her female
dress and masked, and* Sir GUY FITZALLARD.

See where they come.

    Gos. A proper lusty presence, sir.

    Sir Alex. Now has he pleased me right: I always
       counselled him
To choose a goodly, personable creature:
Just of her pitch was my first wife his mother.

    Seb. Before I dare discover my offence,
I kneel for pardon.   [*Kneels.*

    Sir Alex. My heart gave it thee
Before thy tongue could ask it:
Rise; thou hast raised my joy to greater height
Than to that seat where grief dejected it.
Both welcome to my love and care for ever!
Hide not my happiness too long; all's pardoned;
Here are our friends.—Salute her, gentlemen.
                         [*They unmask her.*

    All. Heart, who's this? Moll!

    Sir Alex. O my reviving shame! is't I must live
To be struck blind? be it the work of sorrow,
Before age take't in hand!

    Sir Guy. Darkness and death!
Have you deceived me thus? did I engage
My whole estate for this?

    Sir Alex. You asked no favour,
And you shall find as little: since my comfort

               [1] Convinced.

Play false with me, I'll be as cruel to thee
As grief to fathers' hearts.

Moll. Why, what's the matter with you,
'Less too much joy should make your age forgetful?
Are you too well, too happy?

Sir Alex. With a vengeance!

Moll. Methinks you should be proud of such a
    daughter,
As good a man as your son.

Sir Alex. O monstrous impudence!

Moll. You had no note before, an unmarked knight;
Now all the town will take regard on you,
And all your enemies fear you for my sake:
You may pass where you list, through crowds most
    thick,
And come off bravely with your purse unpicked.
You do not know the benefits I bring with me;
No cheat dares work upon you with thumb[1] or knife,
While you've a roaring girl to your son's wife.

Sir Alex. A devil rampant!

Sir Guy. Have you so much charity
Yet to release me of my last rash bargain,
And I'll give in your pledge?

Sir Alex. No, sir, I stand to't;
I'll work upon advantage, as all mischiefs
Do upon me.

Sir Guy. Content.   Bear witness all, then,
His are the lands; and so contention ends:
Here comes your son's bride 'twixt two noble friends.

Enter Lord NOLAND *and* Sir BEAUTEOUS GANYMEDE
    with MARY FITZALLARD *between them;* GALLIPOT,
    TILTYARD, OPENWORK, *and their* Wives.

Moll. Now are you gulled as you would be; thank
    me for't,

---

[1] See note *ante,* p. 93.

I'd a forefinger in't.

Seb. Forgive me, father!
Though there before your eyes my sorrow feigned,
This still was she for whom true love complained.

Sir Alex. Blessings eternal, and the joys of angels,
Begin your peace here to be signed in Heaven!
How short my sleep of sorrow seems now to me,
To this eternity of boundless comforts,
That finds no want but utterance and expression!
My lord, your office here appears so honourably,
So full of ancient goodness, grace, and worthiness,
I never took more joy in sight of man
Than in your comfortable presence now.

Lord Nol. Nor I more delight in doing grace to virtue
Than in this worthy gentlewoman your son's bride,
Noble Fitzallard's daughter, to whose honour
And modest fame I am a servant vowed;
So is this knight.

Sir Alex. Your loves make my joys proud.
Bring forth those deeds of land my care laid ready,

[*Exit* Servant, *who presently returns with deeds.*

And which, old knight, thy nobleness may challenge,
Joined with thy daughter's virtues, whom I prize now
As dearly as that flesh I call mine own.
Forgive me, worthy gentlewoman; 'twas my blindness:
When I rejected thee, I saw thee not;
Sorrow and wilful rashness grew like films
Over the eyes of judgment; now so clear
I see the brightness of thy worth appear.

Mary. Duty and love may I deserve in those
And all my wishes have a perfect close.

Sir Alex. That tongue can never err, the sound's so
sweet.
Here, honest son, receive into thy hands
The keys of wealth, possession of those lands
Which my first care provided; they're thine own;
Heaven give thee a blessing with 'em! the best joys

That can in worldly shapes to man betide
Are fertile lands and a fair fruitful bride,
Of which I hope thou'rt sped.

 Seb. I hope so too, sir.

 Moll. Father and son, I ha' done you simple service
  here.

 Seb. For which thou shalt not part, Moll, unrequited.

 Sir Alex. Thou'rt a mad girl, and yet I cannot now
Condemn thee.

 Moll. Condemn me? troth, an you should, sir,
I'd make you seek out one to hang in my room:
– I'd give you the slip at gallows, and cozen the people.
Heard you this jest, my lord?

 Lord Nol. What is it, Jack?

 Moll. He was in fear his son would marry me,
But never dreamt that I would ne'er agree.

 Lord Nol. Why, thou hadst a suitor once, Jack: when
  wilt marry?

 Moll. Who, I, my lord? I'll tell you when, i'faith;
When you shall hear
Gallants void from sergeants' fear,
Honesty and truth unslandered,
Woman manned, but never pandered,
Cheats[1] booted, but not coached,
Vessels older ere they're broached;
If my mind be then not varied,
Next day following I'll be married.

 Lord Nol. This sounds like doomsday.

 Moll. Then were marriage best;
For if I should repent, I were soon at rest.

 Sir Alex. In troth, thou'rt a good wench: I'm sorry now
The opinion was so hard I conceived of thee:

Enter TRAPDOOR.

Some wrongs I've done thee.

 Trap. Is the wind there now?

---

[1] Dyce suggested "cheators."

'Tis time for me to kneel and confess first,
For fear it come too late, and my brains feel it.—[*Aside.*
Upon my paws I ask you pardon, mistress.

 Moll. Pardon! for what, sir? what has your rogueship
  done now?

 Trap. I've been from time to time hired to confound
  you
By this old gentleman.

 Moll. How!

 Trap. Pray, forgive him:
But may I counsel you, you should never do't.
Many a snare t' entrap your worship's life
Have I laid privily; chains, watches, jewels;
And when he saw nothing could mount you up,
Four hollow-hearted angels he then gave you,
By which he meant to trap you, I to save you.

 Sir Alex. To all which shame and grief in me cry
  guilty.
Forgive me: now I cast the world's eyes from me,
And look upon thee freely with mine own,
I see the most of many wrongs before me,
Cast from the jaws of Envy and her people,
And nothing foul but that.　I'll never more
Condemn by common voice, for that's the whore
That deceives man's opinion, mocks his trust,
Cozens his love, and makes his heart unjust.

 Moll.. Here be the angels, gentlemen; they were
  given me
As a musician: I pursue no pity;
Follow the law, an you can cuck[1] me, spare not;
Hang up my viol by me, and I care not.

 Sir Alex. So far I'm sorry, I'll thrice double 'em,
To make thy wrongs amends.
Come, worthy friends, my honourable lord,
Sir Beauteous Ganymede, and noble Fitzallard,
And you kind gentlewomen, whose sparkling presence

   [1] *i.e.* Put me in the cucking-stool.

Are glories set in marriage, beams of society,
For all your loves give lustre to my joys:
The happiness of this day shall be remembered
At the return of every smiling spring;
In my time now 'tis born; and may no sadness
Sit on the brows of men upon that day,
But as I am, so all go pleased away!   [*Exeunt.*

EPILOGUE.

A PAINTER having drawn with curious art
The picture of a woman, every part
Limned to the life, hung out the piece to sell.
People who passed along, viewing it well,
Gave several verdicts on it: some dispraised
The hair; some said the brows too high were raised;
Some hit her o'er the lips, misliked their colour;
Some wished her nose were shorter; some, the eyes
        fuller;
Others said roses on her cheeks should grow,
Swearing they looked too pale; others cried "no."
The workman still, as fault was found, did mend it,
In hope to please all: but this work being ended,
And hung open at stall, it was so vile,
So monstrous, and so ugly, all men did smile
At the poor painter's folly.   Such, we doubt,
Is this our comedy: some perhaps do flout
The plot, saying, 'tis too thin, too weak, too mean;
Some for the person will revile the scene,
And wonder that a creature of her being
Should be the subject of a poet, seeing
In the world's eye none weighs so light: others look

For all those base tricks, published in a book,
Foul as his brains they flowed from,[1] of cutpurses,
Of nips and foists, nasty, obscene discourses,
As full of lies as empty of worth or wit,
For any honest ear or eye unfit.
And thus,
If we to every brain that's humorous
Should fashion scenes, we, with the painter, shall,
In striving to please all, please none at all.
Yet for such faults as either the writer's wit
Or negligence of the actors do commit,
Both crave your pardons: if what both have done
Cannot full pay your expectation,
The Roaring Girl herself, some few days hence,
Shall on this stage give larger recompense.
Which mirth that you may share in, herself does woo you,
And craves this sign, your hands to beckon her to you.

[1] The book referred to cannot now be identified.

THE WITCH.

T is conjectured that the tragi-comedy of *The Witch* was a late production of Middleton's. The play was acted at the Blackfriars, but was not printed until 1778, from a unique MS. now in the Bodleian Library.

A portion of the plot was suggested (perhaps through the medium of the *Histoires Tragiques* of Belleforest) by the following story in Machiavelli's *Florentine History*:—"Their [the Lombards'] kingdom descending upon Alboinus, a bold and warlike man, they passed the Danube, and encountering Comundus King of the Lepides, then possessed of Pannonia, overthrew and slew him. Amongst the captives Alboinus finds Rosamund the daughter of Comundus, and taking her to wife becomes Lord of Pannonia ; but out of a brutish fierceness in his nature, he makes a drinking cup of Comundus's skull, and out of it used to carouse in memory of that victory. Invited now by Narsetes, with whom he had been in league during the Gothic war, he leaves Pannonia to the Huns, who, as we have said, were after the death of Attila returned into their own country, and comes into Italy, which finding so strangely divided, he in an instant possesses himself of Pavia, Milan, Verona, Vicenza, all Tuscany, and the greatest part of Flaminia, at this day called Romania. So that by these great and sudden victories judging himself already conqueror of Italy, he makes a solemn feast at Verona, and in the heat of wine growing merry, causes Comundus's skull to be filled full of wine, and would needs have it presented to Queen Rosamund, who sate at table over against him, telling her so loud that all might hear, that in such a time of mirth he would have her drink with her father; those words were as so many darts in the poor lady's bosom, and consulting with revenge, she bethought herself how Almachildis a noble Lombard, young and valiant,

courted one of the ladies of her bed-chamber; with her she con-
trives that she should promise Almachildis the kindness of admit-
ting him by night to her chamber ; and Almachildis according to
her assignation being received into a dark room, lies with the
Queen, whilst he thought he lay with the lady, who after the fact
discovers herself, offering to his choice either the killing of Alboinus
and enjoying her and the crown, or the being made his sacrifice for
defiling his bed. Almachildis consents to kill Alboinus ; but they
seeing afterwards their designs of seizing the kingdom prove un-
successful, nay rather fearing to be put to death by the Lombards
(such love bore they to Alboinus), they fled with all the royal
treasure to Longinus at Ravenna."

The main interest of this play centres around the witch-scenes
and their relation to *Macbeth.* This problem has given rise to a
multitude of theories. It seems most probable that *The Witch* was
the later play ; that Middleton was to some extent inspired by
Shakespeare, and that the players subsequently interpolated frag-
ments of *The Witch* into *Macbeth.*

TO THE TRULY WORTHY AND GENEROUSLY AFFECTED

THOMAS HOLMES, Esquire.

Noble Sir,

As a true testimony of my ready inclination to your
service, I have, merely upon a taste of your desire, recovered into
my hands, though not without much difficulty, this ignorantly ill-
fated labour of mine.

Witches are, *ipso facto,* by the law condemned, and that only, I
think, hath made her lie so long in an imprisoned obscurity.[1] For
your sake alone she hath thus far conjured herself abroad, and
bears no other charms about her but what may tend to your re-
creation, nor no other spell but to possess you with a belief, that
as she, so he that first taught her to enchant, will always be

Your devoted

Tho. Middleton.

---

[1] Probably amongst the manuscripts belonging to the King's Players.

Duke.

Lord Governor of Ravenna.

SEBASTIAN, formerly contracted to ISABELLA, now disguised as a servant.

FERNANDO, his friend.

ANTONIO, husband of ISABELLA.

ABERZANES, a gentleman.

ALMACHILDES, a gentleman.

GASPARO, }
HERMIO, } servants to ANTONIO.

FIRESTONE, the clown and HECATE'S son.

Servants, &c.

Duchess.

ISABELLA, wife of ANTONIO, and niece of the governor.

FRANCISCA, sister of ANTONIO.

AMORETTA, the duchess's woman.

FLORIDA, a courtesan.

HECATE, the chief witch.

STADLIN, }
HOPPO, } witches.

Other witches, &c.

SCENE—RAVENNA and its neighbourhood.

THE WITCH.

ACT THE FIRST.

SCENE I.

An Apartment in the House of the Lord Governor.
A Banquet set out.

Enter SEBASTIAN *and* FERNANDO.

EB. My three years spent in war has
 now undone
My peace for ever.
 Fer. Good, be patient, sir.
 Seb. She is my wife by contract
 before Heaven
And all the angels, sir.
 Fer. I do believe you;
But where's the remedy now? you see she's gone,
Another has possession.
 Seb. There's the torment!
 Fer. This day, being the first of your return, ·
Unluckily proves the first too of her fastening.
Her uncle, sir, the governor of Ravenna,
Holding a good opinion of the bridegroom,
As he's fair spoken, sir, and wondrous mild—
 Seb. There goes the devil in a sheep-skin!

Fer. With all speed
Clapped it up suddenly : I cannot think, sure,
That the maid over-loves him ; though being married,
Perhaps, for her own credit, now she intends
Performance of an honest, duteous wife.

Seb. Sir, I've a world of business : question nothing ;
You will but lose your labour ; 'tis not fit
For any, hardly mine own secrecy,
To know what I intend.   I take my leave, sir.
I find such strange employments in myself,
That unless death pity me and lay me down,
I shall not sleep these seven years ; that's the least, sir.
                                        [*Exit.*

Fer. That sorrow's dangerous can abide no counsel ;
'Tis like a wound past cure : wrongs done to love
Strike the heart deeply ; none can truly judge on't
But the poor sensible sufferer whom it racks
With unbelievèd pains, which men in health,
That enjoy love, not possibly can act,
Nay, not so much as think.   In troth, I pity him :
His sighs drink life-blood in this time of feasting.
A banquet towards too ! not yet hath riot
Played out her last scene? at such entertainments still
Forgetfulness obeys, and surfeit governs :
Here's marriage sweetly honoured in gorged stomachs
And overflowing cups !

Enter GASPARO *and* Servant.

Gas. Where is she, sirrah?
Ser. Not far off.
Gas. Prithee, where? go fetch her hither :
I'll rid him away straight.—   [*Exit* Servant.
                        The duke's now risen, sir.
Fer. I am a joyful man to hear it, sir,
It seems h'as drunk the less ; though I think he
That has the least has certainly enough.   [*Exit.*
Gas. I have observed this fellow : all the feast-time

He hath not pledged one cup, but looked most wickedly
Upon good Malaga; flies to the black-jack[1] still,
And sticks to small drink like a water-rat.
O, here she comes.

Enter FLORIDA.

Alas, the poor whore weeps!
'Tis not for grace now, all the world must judge;
It is for spleen and madness 'gainst this marriage:
I do but think how she could beat the vicar now,
Scratch the man horribly that gave the woman,
The woman worst of all if she durst do it.—   [*Aside.*
Why, how now, mistress? this weeping needs not; for
        though
My master marry for his reputation,
He means to keep you too.
    Flo. How, sir?
    Gas. He doth indeed;
He swore 't to me last night.   Are you so simple,
And have been five years traded, as to think
One woman would serve him? fie, not an empress!
Why, he'll be sick o' the wife within ten nights,
Or never trust my judgment.
    Flo. Will he, think'st thou?
    Gas. Will he!
    Flo. I find thee still so comfortable,
Beshrew my heart, if I know how to miss thee:
They talk of gentlemen, perfumers, and such things;
Give me the kindness of the master's man
In my distress, say I.
    Gas. 'Tis your great love, forsooth.
Please you withdraw yourself to yond private parlour;
I'll send you venison, custard, parsnip-pie;
For banqueting stuff, as suckets,[2] jellies, sirups,
I will bring in myself.

---

[1] A leathern beer-can. The Old Black Jack is still a tavern-sign,
[2] Sweetmeats.

Flo. I'll take 'em kindly, sir.   [*Exit.*

Gas. Sh'as your grand strumpet's complement to a
        tittle.
'Tis a fair building : it had need ; it has
Just at this time some one and twenty inmates ;
But half of 'em are young merchants, they'll depart
        shortly ;
They take but rooms for summer, and away they
When 't grows foul weather : marry, then come the
        termers,[1]
And commonly they're well-booted for all seasons
But peace, no word ; the guests are coming in.
                                        [*Retires.*

Enter ALMACHILDES *and* AMORETTA.

Alm. The fates have blessed me ; have I met you
        privately ?
Am. Why, sir, why, Almachildes !——
Alm. Not a kiss ?
Am. I'll call aloud, i'faith.
Alm. I'll stop your mouth.
Am. Upon my love to reputation,
I'll tell the duchess once more.
Alm. 'Tis the way
To make her laugh a little.
Am. She'll not think
That you dare use a maid of honour thus.
Alm. Amsterdam [2] swallow thee for a Puritan,
And Geneva cast thee up again ! like she that sunk
At Charing Cross, and rose again at Queenhithe ![3]
Am. Ay, these are the silly fruits of the sweet vine,
        sir.   [*Retires.*
Alm. Sweet venery be with thee, and I at the tail
Of my wish ! I am a little headstrong, and so

[1] See note *ante*, p. 3.
[2] The resort of persecuted Puritans.
[3] A legend concerning Elinor, wife of Edward I.

Are most of the company.   I will to the witches.
They say they have charms and tricks to make
A wench fall backwards, and lead a man herself
To a country-house, some mile out of the town,
Like a fire-drake.[1]   There be such whoreson kind girls
And such bawdy witches; and I'll try conclusions.[2]

Enter Duke, Duchess, Lord Governor, ANTONIO,
ISABELLA, *and* FRANCISCA.

Duke. A banquet yet! why surely, my lord governor,
Bacchus could ne'er boast of a day till now,
To spread his power, and make his glory known.

Duch. Sir, you've done nobly; though in modesty
You keep it from us, know, we understand so much,
All this day's cost 'tis your great love bestows,
In honour of the bride, your virtuous niece.

Gov. In love to goodness and your presence, madam;
So understood, 'tis rightly.

Duke. Now will I
Have a strange health after all these.

Gov. What's that, my lord?

Duke. A health in a strange cup; and 't shall go
    round.

Gov. Your grace need not doubt that, sir, having
    seen
So many pledged already: this fair company
Cannot shrink now for one, so it end there.

Duke. It shall, for all ends here: here's a full period.
                    [*Produces a skull set as a cup.*

Gov. A skull, my lord?

Duke. Call it a soldier's cup, man:
Fie, how you fright the women! I have sworn
It shall go round, excepting only you, sir,
For your late sickness, and the bride herself,
Whose health it is.

Isa. Marry, I thank Heaven for that!

---

[1] A meteor.   [2] Experiments.

Duke. Our duchess, I know, will pledge us, though
    the cup
Was once her father's head, which, as a trophy,
We'll keep till death in memory of that conquest.
He was the greatest foe our steel e'er struck at,
And he was bravely slain : then took we thee
Into our bosom's love : thou mad'st the peace
For all thy country, thou, that beauty, did.
We're dearer than a father, are we not?

Duch. Yes, sir, by much.

Duke. And we shall find that straight.

Ant. That's an ill bride-cup for a marriage-day,
I do not like the face on't.

Gov. Good my lord,
The duchess looks pale : let her not pledge you there.

Duke. Pale?

Duch. Sir, not I.

Duke. See how your lordship fails now ;
The rose not fresher, nor the sun at rising
More comfortably pleasing.

Duch. Sir, to you,
The lord of this day's honour.   [*Drinks.*

Ant. All first moving
From your grace, madam, and the duke's great favour,
Since it must.   [*Drinks.*

Fran. This the worst fright that could come
To a concealed great belly ! I'm with child ;
And this will bring it out, or make me come
Some seven weeks sooner than we maidens reckon,
                                [*Aside.*

Duch. Did ever cruel barbarous art match this?
Twice hath his surfeits brought my father's memory
Thus spitefully and scornfully to mine eyes ;
And I'll endure 't no more ; 'tis in my heart since :
I'll be revenged as far as death can lead me.   [*Aside.*

Alm. Am I the last man, then? I may deserve
To be first one day.   [*Drinks.*

Gov. Sir, it has gone round now.

Duke. The round?[1] an excellent way to train up
　soldiers!

Where's bride and bridegroom?

Ant. At your happy service.

Duke. A boy to-night at least; I charge you look to't,
Or I'll renounce you for industrious subjects.

Ant. Your grace speaks like a worthy and tried
　soldier.

Gas. And you'll do well for one that ne'er tossed pike,
　sir.　　　·　　　　　　　　　　　　　[*Exeunt.*

SCENE II.

The Abode of HECATE.

Enter HECATE.

Hec. Titty and Tiffin, Suckin and Pidgen, Liard and
Robin! white spirits, black spirits, grey spirits, red spirits!
devil-toad, devil-ram, devil-cat, and devil-dam! why,
Hoppo[2] and Stadlin, Hellwain and Puckle!

Stad. [*Within.*] Here, sweating at the vessel.

Hec. Boil it well.

Hop. [*Within.*] It gallops now.

---

[1] It was the duty of officers of inferior rank to go round and in-
spect the sentinels.

[2] These names are taken from Reginald Scot's *Witchcraft.* "On
9th June, 1604, a statute was passed, which enacted that ' if any
person shall practise or exercise any invocation or conjuration of
any evil or wicked spirit, or take up any man, woman, or child out
of his, her, or their grave, . . . or the skin, bone, or any other
part of any dead person to be employed or used in any manner of
witchcraft, . . . or shall . . . practise . . . any witchcraft
. . . whereby any person shall be killed, wasted, pined, or lamed
in his or her body or any part thereof, such offender shall suffer the
pains of death as felons without benefit of clergy or sanctuary.' " —
Bullen.

Hec. Are the flames blue enough?
Or shall I use a little seething more?
Stad. [*Within.*] The nips of fairies upon maids' white
    hips
Are not more perfect azure.
Hec. Tend it carefully.
Send Stadlin to me with a brazen dish,
That I may fall to work upon these serpents,
And squeeze 'em ready for the second hour:
Why, when?

Enter STADLIN *with a dish.*

Stad. Here's Stadlin and the dish.
Hec. There, take this unbaptizèd brat;[1]
    [*Giving the dead body of a child.*
Boil it well; preserve the fat:
You know 'tis precious to transfer
Our 'nointed flesh into the air,

---

[1] Here, and in the next three speeches of Hecate, Middleton
follows Reginald Scot, using sometimes the very words of that curious
writer. In the *Discouecie of Witchcraft*, Scot gives from "John Bapt.
Neap." *i.e.* Porta, the following receipts for the miraculous trans-
portation of witches: "℞. *The fat of yoong children, and seeth it
with water in a brasen vessell,* reseruing the thickest of that which
remaineth boiled in the bottome, which they laie vp and keepe,
vntill occasion serueth to vse it. *They put herevnto Eleoselinum,
Aconitum, frondes populeas, and soote.*" "℞. *Sium, acarum vulgare,
pentaphyllon, the bloud of a flitter-mouse, solanum somniferum et
oleum.* They stampe all these togither, and then they rubbe all
parts of their bodies exceedinglie, till they looke red and be verie
hot, so as the pores may be opened and their flesh soluble and loose.
They ioine herewithall either fat or oile in steed thereof, that the
force of the ointment maie the rather pearse inwardly, and so be
more effectual. By this means (saith he) *in a moone light night
they seeme to be carried in the aire, to feasting, singing, dansing,
kissing, culling, and other acts of venerie, with such youthes as they
loue and desire most,*" &c.—*Dyce.*

The *solanum somniferum* (or belladonna) is the chief active ingredient in the latter of these ancient receipts. It would certainly
produce hallucinations, with a considerable amount of general vas-
cular excitement.

In moonlight nights, on steeple-tops,
Mountains, and pine-trees, that like pricks or stops
Seem to our height; high towers and roofs óf princes
Like wrinkles in the earth; whole provinces
Appear to our sight then even leek [1]
A russet mole upon some lady's cheek.
When hundred leagues in air, we feast and sing,
Dance, kiss, and coll,[2] use everything :
What young man can we wish to pleasure us,
But we enjoy him in an incubus?
Thou know'st it, Stadlin?

   Stad. Usually that's done.

   Hec. Last night thou gott'st the mayor of Whelplie's
     son;
I knew him by his black cloak lined with yellow;
I think thou'st spoiled the youth, he's but seventeen :
I'll have him the next mounting.   Away, in :
Go, feed the vessel for the second hour.

   Stad. Where be the magical herbs?

   Hec. They're down his throat;
His mouth crammed full, his ears and nostrils stuffed.
I thrust in eleoselinum lately.
Aconitum, frondes populeas, and soot—
You may see that, he looks so black i' the mouth--
Then sium, acorum vulgare too,
Pentaphyllon, the blood of a flitter-mouse,[3]
Solanum somnificum et oleum.

   Stad. Then there's all, Hecate.

   Hec. Is the heart of wax
Stuck full of magic needles?

   Stad. 'Tis done, Hecate.

   Hec. And is the farmer's picture[4] and his wife's
Laid down to the fire yet?

---

[1] Like.   [2] Embrace.   [3] Bat.

[4] "He being further demanded to what end the spirits in the
likeness of toads and the pictures of man in wax or clay do serve,
he said that pictures made in wax will cause the party (for whom

Stad. They're a-roasting both too.

Hec. Good; [*Exit* STADLIN.] then their marrows are
    a-melting subtly,
And three months' sickness sucks up life in 'em.
They denied me often flour, barm, and milk,
Goose-grease and tar, when I ne'er hurt their churnings,
Their brew-locks, nor their batches, nor forespoke
Any of their breedings.   Now I'll be meet[1] with 'em:
Seven of their young pigs I've bewitched already,
Of the last litter;
Nine ducklings, thirteen goslings, and a hog,
Fell lame last Sunday after even-song too;
And mark how their sheep prosper, or what sup
Each milch-kine gives to the pail: I'll send these snakes
Shall milk 'em all
Beforehand; the dew-skirted dairy-wenches
Shall stroke dry dugs for this, and go home cursing;
I'll mar their sillabubs, and swathy[2] feastings
Under cows' bellies with the parish youths.
Where's Firestone, our son Firestone?

Enter FIRESTONE.

Fire.   Here am I, mother.

---

it is made) to continue sick two whole years, because it will be two
whole years ere the wax will be consumed.   And as for the pictures
of clay, their confection is after this manner.   They used to take
the earth of a new-made grave, the rib-bone of a man or woman
burned to ashes; if it be for a woman they take the bone of a
woman, if for a man the bone of a man; and a black spider with
an inner pith of an elder, tempered all in water, in the which water
the said toads must first be washed.   And after all ceremonies
ended, they put a prick, that is a pin or a thorn, in any member
where they would have the party grieved.   And if the said prick
be put to the heart, the party dieth within nine days, which image
they burn in the most moist place they can find."—*Examination of
John Walsh touching Witchcraft*, 1566, quoted by Bullen.

   [1] Even.

   [2] *i.e.* I suppose, feastings among the " swaths "—the mown rows
of grass.—*Dyce.*

Hec. Take in this brazen dish full of dear ware :

[*Gives dish.*

Thou shalt have all when I die ; and that will be
Even just at twelve a'clock at night come three year.

Fire. And may you not have one a'clock in to the
dozen, mother ?

Hec. No.

Fire. Your spirits are, then, more unconscionable than
bakers. You'll have lived then, mother, sixscore year
to the hundred ; and, methinks, after sixscore years, the
devil might give you a cast, for he's a fruiterer, too, and
has been from the beginning ; the first apple that e'er
was eaten came through his fingers : the costermonger's,[1]
then, I hold to be the ancientest trade, though some
would have the tailor pricked down before him.

Hec. Go, and take heed you shed not by the way ;
The hour must have her portion ! 'tis dear sirup ;
Each charmèd drop is able to confound
A family consisting of nineteen
Or one-and-twenty feeders.

Fire. Marry, here's stuff indeed !
Dear sirup call you it ? a little thing
Would make me give you a dram on't in a posset,
And cut you three years shorter.   [*Aside.*

Hec. Thou art now
About some villany.

Fire. Not I, forsooth.—
Truly the devil's in her, I think : how one villain smells
out another straight ! there's no knavery but is nosed
like a dog, and can smell out a dog's meaning. [*Aside.*]
—Mother, I pray, give me leave to ramble abroad to-
night with the Night-mare, for I have a great mind to
overlay a fat parson's daughter.

Hec. And who shall lie with me, then ?

---

[1] Apple-seller's. Costard is the name of a large kind of apple.

Mid. II.   K

Fire. The great cat
For one night, mother; 'tis but a night:
Make shift with him for once.

Hec. You're a kind son!
But 'tis the nature of you all; I see that
You had rather hunt after strange women still
Than lie with your own mothers.   Get thee gone;
Sweat thy six ounces out about the vessel,
And thou shalt play at midnight; the Night-mare
Shall call thee when it walks.

Fire. Thanks, most sweet mother.   [*Exit.*

Hec. Urchins, Elves, Hags, Satyrs, Pans, Fawns,
Sylvans, Kitt-with-the-candlestick, Tritons, Centaurs,
Dwarfs, Imps, the Spoorn, the Mare, the Man-i'-the-oak,
the Hellwain, the Fire-drake, the Puckle! A ab hur hus![1]

Enter SEBASTIAN.

Seb. Heaven knows with what unwillingness and hate
I enter this damned place: but such extremes
Of wrongs in love fight 'gainst religion's knowledge,
That were I led by this disease to deaths
As numberless as creatures that must die,
I could not shun the way.   I know what 'tis
To pity madmen now; they're wretched things
That ever were created, if they be
Of woman's making, and her faithless vows.
I fear they're now a-kissing: what's a'clock?

[1] Here again Middleton borrows from Reginald Scot: " And
they haue so fraied vs with bull beggers, spirits, witches, *vrchens,
elues, hags,* fairies, *satyrs, pans, faunes, sylens* [sylvans], *kit with
the cansticke, tritons, centaurs, dwarfes,* giants, *imps,* calcars,
coniurors, nymphes, changlings, Incubus, Robin good-fellowe, *the
spoorne, the mare, the man in the oke, the hell waine, the fierdrake,
the puckle,* Tom thombe, hob gobblin, Tom tumbler, boneles, and
such other bugs, that we are afraid of our owne shadowes."—
Discouerie of Witchcraft.   The words with which Hecate concludes
this speech, " A ab hur hus !" are also borrowed from R. Scot's
work, where they are mentioned as a charm against the toothache.—*Dyce.*

'Tis now but supper-time; but night will come,
And all new-married couples make short suppers.—
Whate'er thou art, I've no spare time to fear thee;
My horrors are so strong and great already,
That thou seemest nothing.   Up, and laze not.
Hadst thou my business, thou couldst ne'er sit so
'Twould firk thee into air a thousand mile,
Beyond thy ointments.   I would I were read
So much in thy black power as mine own griefs!
I'm in great need of help; wilt give me any?

Hec. Thy boldness takes me bravely; we're all sworn
To sweat for such a spirit: see, I regard thee;
I rise and bid thee welcome.   What's thy wish now?

Seb. O, my heart swells with't! I must take breath first.

Hec. Is't to confound some enemy on the seas?
It may be done to-night: Stadlin's[1] within;
She raises all your sudden ruinous storms,
That shipwreck barks, and tears up growing oaks,
Flies over houses, and takes *Anno Domini*[2]
Out of a rich man's chimney—a sweet place for't!
He'd be hanged ere he would set his own years there;
They must be chambered in a five-pound picture,
A green silk curtain drawn before the eyes on't;
His rotten, diseased years!—or dost thou envy
The fat prosperity of any neighbour?
I'll call forth Hoppo, and her incantation
Can straight destroy the young of all his cattle;
Blast vineyards, orchards, meadows; or in one night

---

[1] From R. Scot: "It is constantlie affirmed in M. Mal. that Stafus vsed alwaies to hide himselfe in a moushoall, and had a disciple called Hoppo, who made Stadlin a maister witch, and could all when they list inuisiblie transferre the third part of their neighbours doong, hay, corne, &c. into their own ground, make haile, tempests, and flouds, with thunder and lightning; and kill children, cattell, &c.: reueale things hidden, and many other tricks, when and where they list."—*Discouerie of Witchcraft.*   See also Sprenger's *Malleus Maleficarum.—Dyce.*
[2] The date at which the house was erected.

Transport his dung, hay, corn, by reeks,[1] whole stacks,
Into thine own ground.

   Seb. This would come most richly now
To many a country grazier; but my envy
Lies not so low as cattle, corn, or wines:
'Twill trouble your best powers to give me ease.

   Hec. Is it to starve up generation?
To strike a barrenness in man or woman?

   Seb. Hah!

   Hec. Hah, did you feel me there? I knew your grief.

   Seb. Can there be such things done?

   Hec. Are these the skins
Of serpents? these of snakes?

   Seb. I see they are.

   Hec. So sure into what house these are conveyed,

       [*Giving serpent-skins, &c., to* SEBASTIAN.
Knit with these charms and retentive knots,
Neither the man begets nor woman breeds,
No, nor performs the least desires of wedlock,
Being then a mutual duty. I could give thee
Chirocineta, adincantida,
Archimedon, marmaritin, calicia,[2]
Which I could sort to villanous barren ends;
But this leads the same way. More I could instance;
As, the same needles thrust into their pillows
That sews and socks up dead men in their sheets;
A privy gristle of a man that hangs
After sunset; good, excellent; yet all's there, sir.

   [1] Ricks.

   [2] "Pythagoras and Democritus giue vs the names of a great manie magicall hearbs and stones, whereof now both the vertue and the things themselues also are vnknowne; as *Marmaritin,* whereby spirits might be raised: *Archimedon,* which would make one bewraie in his sleepe all the secrets in his heart: *Adincantida, Calicia,* Meuais, *Chirocineta,* &c.: which had all their seuerall vertues, or rather poisons." Reginald Scot's *Discouerie of Witchcraft.*

Seb. You could not do a man that special kindness
To part 'em utterly now? could you do that?

Hec. No, time must do't: we cannot disjoin wedlock;
'Tis of Heaven's fastening. Well may we raise jars,
Jealousies, strifes, and heart-burning disagreements,
Like a thick scurf o'er life, as did our master
Upon that patient miracle;[1] but the work itself
Our power cannot disjoint.

Seb. I depart happy
In what I have then, being constrained to this.—
And grant, you greater powers that dispose men,
That I may never need this hag agen! [*Aside, and exit.*

Hec. I know he loves me not, nor there's no hope
  on't;
'Tis for the love of mischief I do this,
And that we're sworn to the first oath we take.

Re-enter FIRESTONE.

Fire. O mother, mother!

Hec. What's the news with thee now?

Fire. There's the bravest young gentleman within,
and the fineliest drunk! I thought he would have fallen
into the vessel; he stumbled at a pipkin of child's
grease; reeled against Stadlin, overthrew her, and in the
tumbling-cast struck up old Puckle's heels with her
clothes over her ears.

Hec. Hoyday!

Fire. I was fain to throw the cat upon her to save
her honesty, and all little enough; I cried out still, I
pray, be covered.[2] See where he comes now, mother.

Enter ALMACHILDES.

Alm. Call you these witches? they be tumblers
  methinks.
Very flat tumblers.

---

[1] *i.e.* Job.   [2] Which commonly meant " put on your hat."

Hec. 'Tis Almachildes—fresh blood stirs in me—
The man that I have lusted to enjoy :
I've had him thrice in incubus already. [*Aside.*
   Alm. Is your name Goody Hag?
   Hec. 'Tis anything :
Call me the horrid'st and unhallowed things
That life and nature trembles at, for thee
I'll be the same. Thou com'st for a love-charm now?
   Alm. Why, thou'rt a witch, I think.
   Hec. Thou shalt have choice of twenty, wet or dry.
   Alm. Nay, let's have dry ones.
   Hec. If thou wilt use't by way of cup and potion,
I'll give thee a remora[1] shall bewitch her straight.
   Alm. A remora? what's that?
   Hec. A little suck-stone ;
Some call it a sea-lamprey, a small fish.
   Alm. And must be buttered?
   Hec. The bones of a green frog too, wondrous precious,
The flesh consumed by pismires.
   Alm. Pismires? give me a chamber-pot!
   Fire. You shall see him go nigh to be so unmannerly,
he'll make water before my mother anon. [*Aside.*
   Alm. And now you talk of frogs, I've somewhat here ;
I come not empty-pocketed from a banquet,
I learned that of my haberdasher's wife ;
Look, goody witch, there's a toad in marchpane[2] for
      you. [*Gives marchpane.*
   Hec. O sir, you've fitted me?
   Alm. And here's a spawn or two
Of the same paddock-brood too, for your son.
        [*Gives other pieces of marchpan*

---

[1] Barnacle.
[2] Marchpane was composed of flour, pounded almonds and sugar, wrought into various figures, and then baked.

Fire. I thank your worship, sir : how comes your handkercher
So sweetly thus berayed ?[1] sure 'tis wet suckét,[2] sir.

Alm. 'Tis nothing but the sirup the toad spit ;
Take all, I prithee.

Hec. This was kindly done, sir ;
And you shall sup with me to-night for this.

Alm. How ? sup with thee ? dost think I'll eat fried rats
And pickled spiders ?

Hec. No ; I can command, sir,
The best meat i' the whole province for my friends,
And reverently served in to.

Alm. How ?

Hec. In good fashion.

Alm. Let me but see that, and I'll sup with you.

   [HECATE *conjures ; enter a Cat playing on a*
     fiddle, and Spirits with meat.

The Cat and Fiddle's an excellent ordinary :
You had a devil once in a fox-skin ? /

Hec. O, I have him still : come, walk with me, sir.

     [*Exeunt all except* FIRESTONE.

Fire. How apt and ready is a drunkard now to reel to the devil ! Well, I'll even in and see how he eats ; and I'll be hanged if I be not the fatter of the twain with laughing at him.   [*Exit.*

---

[1] Soiled.   [2] Sweetmeat.

ACT THE SECOND.

SCENE I.

A Hall in ANTONIO'S *House.*

Enter ANTONIO *and* GASPARO.

AS. Good sir, whence springs this sad-
    ness? trust me, sir,
    You look not like a man was married
       yesterday:
    There could come no ill tidings since
       last night
To cause that discontent. I was wont to know all,
Before you had a wife, sir: you ne'er found me
Without those parts of manhood, trust and secrecy.
  Ant. I will not tell thee this.
  Gas. Not your true servant, sir?
  Ant. True? you'll all flout according to your talent,
The best a man can keep of you: and a hell 'tis
For masters to pay wages to be laughed at.
Give order that two cocks be boiled to jelly.
  Gas. How? two cocks boiled to jelly?
  Ant. Fetch half an ounce of pearl.   [*Exit.*
  Gas. This is a cullis[1]
For a consumption; and I hope one night
Has not brought you to need the cook already,
And some part of the goldsmith: what, two trades

---

[1] Fr. *coulis.* A rich broth into the composition of which such
ingredients as powdered gold and gems occasionally entered.

In four-and-twenty hours, and less time?
Pray Heaven, the surgeon and the pothecary
Keep out! and then 'tis well.   You'd better fortune,
As far as I see, with your strumpet sojourner,
Your little four nobles[1] a-week : I ne'er knew you
Eat one panado[2] all the time you've kept her ;
And is't in one night now come up to two cock-broth?
I wonder at the alteration strangely.

Enter FRANCISCA.

Fran. Good morrow, Gaspar.
Gas. Your hearty wishes, mistress,
And your sweet dreams come upon you !
Fran. What's that, sir?
Gas. In a good husband ; that's my real meaning.
Fran. Saw you my brother lately?
Gas. Yes.
Fran. I met him now,
As sad, methought, as grief could make a man :
Know you the cause?
Gas. Not I : I know nothing,
But half an ounce of pearl, and kitchen business,
Which I will see performed with all fidelity :
I'll break my trust in nothing, not in porridge, I.   [*Exit.*
Fran. I have the hardest fortune, I think, of a hun-
dred gentlewomen :
Some can make merry with a friend seven year,
And nothing seen ; as perfect a maid still,
To the world's knowledge, as she came from rocking
But 'twas my luck, at the first hour, forsooth,
To prove too fruitful ; sure I'm near my time ;
I'm yet but a young scholar, I may fail
In my account ; but certainly I do not.

---

[1] The noble was worth 6s. 8d.
[2] Consisting of thin slices of bread, currants and spice, which
after being boiled in water was flavoured with rose-water and
sweetened.

These bastards come upon poor venturing gentlewomen
ten to one faster than your legitimate children : if I had
been married, I'll be hanged if I had been with child so
soon now.   When they are our husbands, they'll be
whipped ere they take such pains as a friend will do ; to
come by water to the back-door at midnight, there stay
perhaps an hour in all weathers, with a pair of reeking
watermen laden with bottles of wine, chewets,[1] and
currant-custards.   I may curse those egg-pies ; they are
meat that help forward too fast.

This hath been usual with me night by night,
Honesty forgive me ! when my brother has been
Dreaming of no such junkets ; yet he hath fared
The better for my sake, though he little think
For what, nor must he ever.   My friend promised me
To provide safely for me, and devise
A means to save my credit here i' the house.
My brother sure would kill me if he knew't,
And powder up my friend, and all his kindred,
For an East Indian voyage.

Enter ISABELLA.

Isa. Alone, sister?

Fran. No, there's another with me, though you see't
    not.--   [*Aside.*
Morrow, sweet sister : how have you slept to-night?

Isa. More than I thought I should ; I've had good
    rest.

Fran. I am glad to hear't.

Isa. Sister, methinks you are too long alone,
And lose much good time, sociable and honest :
I'm for the married life ; I must praise that now.

Fran. I cannot blame you, sister, to commend it ;
You've happened well, no doubt, on a kind husband,

---

[1] Minced or forced-meat pies.

And that's not every woman's fortune, sister :
You know if he were any but my brother,
My praises should not leave him yet so soon.

  Isa. I must acknowledge, sister, that my life
Is happily blest with him : he is no gamester,[1]
That ever I could find or hear of yet,
Nor midnight surfeiter ; he does intend
To leave tobacco too.

   Fran. Why, here's a husband !

  Isa. He saw it did offend me, and swore freely
He'd ne'er take pleasure in a toy[2] again
That should displease me : some knights' wives in town
Will have great hope, upon his reformation,
To bring their husbands' breaths into the old fashion,
And make 'em kiss like Christians, not like Pagans.

   Fran. I promise you, sister, 'twill be a worthy work
To put down all these pipers ; 'tis great pity
There should not be a statute against them,
As against fiddlers.

  Isa. These good offices,
If you had a husband, you might exercise,
To the good o' the commonwealth, and do much profit :
Beside, it is a comfort to a woman
T' have children, sister ; a great blessing certainly.

   Fran. They will come fast enough.

  Isa. Not so fast neither
As they're still welcome to an honest woman.

   Fran. How near she comes to me ! I protest she
     grates
My very skin.   *[Aside.*

  Isa. Were I conceived with child,
Beshrew my heart, I should be so proud on't !

   Fran. That's natural ; pride is a kind of swelling :—
But yet I've small cause to be proud of mine.   *[Aside.*

---

[1] Debauched fellow.   [2] Trifle.

Isa. You are no good companion for a wife :
Get you a husband ; prithee, sister, do,
That I may ask your counsel now and then :
'Twill mend your discourse much ; you maids know
        nothing.

   Fran. No, we are fools ; but commonly we prove
Quicker mothers than you that have husbands :—
I'm sure I shall else : I may speak for one.   [*Aside.*

Re-enter ANTONIO.

   Ant. I will not look upon her ; I'll pass by,
And make as though I see her not.   [*Aside.*
   Isa. Why, sir,—
Pray, your opinion, by the way, with leave, sir :
I'm counselling your sister here to marry.
   Ant. To marry ? soft ; the priest is not at leisure
        yet ;
Some five year hence.—Would you fain marry, sister ?
   Fra. I've no such hunger to't, sir,—for I think
I've a good bit that well may stay my stomach,
As well as any that broke fast, a sinner.   [*Aside.*
   Ant. Though she seem tall of growth, she's short in
        years
Of some that seem much lower.—How old, sister ?
Not seventeen, for a yard of lawn !
   Fran. Not yet, sir.
   Ant. I told you so.
   Fran. I would he'd laid a wager of old shirts rather,
I shall have more need of them shortly ; and yet,
A yard of lawn will serve for a christening-cloth ;
I've use for everything, as my case stands.   [*Aside.*
   Isa. I care not if I try my voice this morning ;
But I have got a cold, sir, by your means.
   Ant. I'll strive to mend that fault.
   Isa. I thank you, sir

[*Sings.*] In a maiden-time profest,
   Then we say that life is best ;
   Tasting once the married life,
   Then we only praise the wife :
   There's but one state more to try,
   Which makes women laugh or cry—
   Widow, widow : of these three
   The middle's best, and that give me.

 Ant. There's thy reward.   [*Kisses her.*

 Isa. I will not grumble, sir,
Like some musician ; if more come, 'tis welcome.

 Fran. Such tricks has made me do all that I have done :
Your kissing married folks spoil all the maids
That ever live i' the house with 'em.   O, here
He comes with his bags and bottles ; he was born
To lead poor watermen and I.   [*Aside.*

  Enter ABERZANES, *and* Servants *carrying baked meats
    and bottles.*

 Aber. Go, fellows, into the larder ; let the bake-meats
Be sorted by themselves.

 Ant. Why, sir—

 Aber. Look the canary bottles be well stopped ;
The three of claret shall be drunk at dinner.
        [*Exeunt* Servants.

 Ant. My   good   sir,   you're .too   plenteous   of   these
  courtesies,
Indeed you are ; forbear 'em, I beseech ye :
I know no merit in me, but poor love
And a true friend's well-wishing, that can cause
This kindness in excess.—I' the state that I am,
I shall go near to kick this fellow shortly,
And send him down stairs with his bag and baggage :
Why comes he now I'm married ? there's the point.—
         [*Aside.*

  ray, forbear these things.

Aber. Alas! you know, sir,
These idle toys, which you call courtesies,
They cost me nothing but my servants' travail!
One office must be kind, sir, to another:
You know the fashion. What! the gentlewoman
Your sister's sad, methinks.

Ant. I know no cause she has.

Fran. Nor shall you, by my good will.—[*Aside.*] What
do you mean, sir?
Shall I stay here, to shame myself and you?
The time may be to-night, for aught you know.

Aber. Peace; there's means wrought, I tell thee

Enter SEBASTIAN *and* Gentleman.

Fran. Ay, sir, when?

Ant. How now? what's he?

Isa. O, this is the man, sir,
I entertained this morning for my service;
Please you to give your liking.

Ant. Yes, he's welcome;
I like him not amiss.—Thou wouldst speak business,
Wouldst thou not?

Seb. Yes; may it please you, sir,
There is a gentleman from the northern parts
Hath brought a letter, as it seems, in haste.

Ant. From whom?

Gent. Your bonny lady mother, sir.
                              [*Giving letter to* ANTONIO.

Ant. You are kindly welcome, sir: how doth she:

Gent. I left her heal[1] varray well, sir.

Ant. [*Reads.*] " I pray send your sister down with all
speed to me: I hope it will prove much for her good in
the way of her preferment. Fail me not, I desire you,
son, nor let any excuse of hers withhold her: I have sent,
ready furnished, horse and man for her."

---

[1] Scotch : health.

Aber. Now, have I thought upon you?

Fran. Peace, good sir;
You're worthy of a kindness another time.

Ant. Her will shall be obeyed.—Sister, prepare yourself;
You must down with all speed.

Fran. I know, down I must;
And good speed send me!   [*Aside.*

Ant. 'Tis our mother's pleasure.

Fran. Good sir, write back again, and certify her
I'm at my heart's wish here; I'm with my friends,
And can be but well, say.

Ant. You shall pardon me, sister;
I hold it no wise part to contradict her,
Nor would I counsel you to't.

Fran. 'Tis so uncouth
Living i' the country, now I'm used to the city,
That I shall ne'er endure't.

Aber. Perhaps, forsooth,
'Tis not her meaning you shall live there long;
I do not think but after a month or so,
You'll be sent up again; that's my conceit.
However, let her have her will.

Ant. Ay, good sir,
Great reason 'tis she should.

Isa. I'm sorry, sister,
'Tis our hard fortune thus to part so soon.

Fran. The sorrow will be mine.

Ant. Please you walk in, sir;
We'll have one health unto those northern parts,
Though I be sick at heart.

        [*Exeunt* ANTONIO, ISABELLA, *and* Gentleman.

Aber. Ay, sir, a deep one—
Which you shall pledge too.

Fran. You shall pardon me;
I have pledged one too deep already, sir.

Aber. Peace ; all's provided for : thy wine's laid in,
Sugar and spice ; the place not ten mile hence.
What cause have maids now to complain of men,
When a farmhouse can make all whole agen ?

        [*Exeunt* ABERZANES *and* FRANCISCA.

Seb. It takes ; has no content : how well she bears
    it yet !
Hardly myself can find so much from her
That am acquainted with the cold disease :
O, honesty's a rare wealth in a woman !
It knows no want, at least will express none,
Not in a look.   Yet I'm not throughly happy :
His ill does me no good ; well may it keep me
From open rage and madness for a time,
But I feel heart's grief in the same place still.
What makes the greatest torment 'mongst lost souls ?
'Tis not so much the horror of their pains,
Though they be infinite, as the loss of joys ;
It is that deprivation is the mother
Of all the groans in hell, and here on earth
Of all the red sighs in the hearts of lovers.
Still she's not mine, that can be no man's else
Till I be nothing, if religion
Have the same strength for me as 't has for others :
Holy vows, witness that our souls were married !

    Re-enter GASPARO, *ushering in* Lord Governor
        attended by Gentlemen.

Gas. Where are you, sir ? come, pray, give your attend-
    ance ;
Here's my lord governor come.
    Gov. Where's our new kindred ?
Not stirring yet, I think.
    Gas. Yes, my good lord :
Please you, walk near.

Gov. Come, gentlemen, we'll enter.

Seb. I ha' done't upon a breach ; this is a less venture.

[*Exeunt.*

SCENE II.

A Gallery in the Duke's *House.*

Enter ALMACHILDES.

Alm. What a mad toy[1] took me to sup with witches !
Fie of all drunken humours ! by this hand,
I could beat myself when I think on't : and the rascals
Made me good cheer too ; and to my understanding then
Eat some of every dish, and spoiled the rest :
But coming to my lodging, I remember
I was as hungry as a tirèd foot-post.
What's this ?   [*Takes from his pocket a ribbon.*
             O, 'tis the charm her hagship gave me
For my duchess' obstinate woman ; round about
A threepenny silk ribbon of three colours,
Necte tribus nodis ternos Amoretta colores :
Amoretta ! why, there's her name indeed :
Necte Amoretta ; again, two boughts,[2]
Nodo et Veneris die vincula necte ;
Nay, if Veneris be one, I'm sure there's no dead flesh in't.
If I should undertake to construe this now,
I should make a fine piece of work of it,
For few young gallants are given to good construction
Of anything, hardly of their best friends' wives,
Sisters, or nieces.   Let me see what I can do now.
Necte tribus nodis,----Nick of the tribe of noddies :
Ternos colores,—that makes turned colours ;

---

          [1] Whim.   [2] Twists or knots.

Mid. II.   L

Nodo et Veneris,—goes to his venery like a noddy ;
Dic vincula,—with Dick the vintner's boy.
Here were a sweet charm now, if this were the meaning
on't, and very likely to overcome an honourable gentlewoman. The whorson old hellcat would have given me
the brain of a cat once in my handkercher ; I bade her
make sauce with't, with a vengeance ! and a little bone
in the hithermost part of a wolf's tail ; I bade her pick
her teeth with't, with a pestilence ! Nay, this is somewhat cleanly yet and handsome ; a coloured ribbon, a
fine, gentle charm ! a man may give't his sister, his
brother's wife, ordinarily. See, here she comes, luckily.

Enter AMORETTA.

Amo. Blest powers, what secret sin have I committed
That still you send this punishment upon me ?
Alm. 'Tis but a gentle punishment ; so take it.
Amo. Why, sir, what mean you ? will you ravish me ?
Alm. What, in the gallery, and the sun peep in ?
There's fitter time and place.—
                    [*As he embraces her, he thrusts the ribbon into her
                      bosom.*
                                'Tis in her bosom now. [*Aside.*
Amo. Go, you're the rudest thing e'er came at court ?
Alm. Well, well ; I hope you'll tell me another tale
Ere you be two hours older : a rude thing ?
I'll make you eat your word ; I'll make all split[1] else.
                                        [*Exit.*
Amo. Nay, now I think on't better, I'm to blame too ;
There's not a sweeter gentleman in court ;
Nobly descended too, and dances well.
Beshrew my heart, I'll take him when there's time ;
He will be catched up quickly. The duchess says
Sh'as some employment for him, and has sworn me

---

[1] A nautical phrase implying violence of action.

To use my best art in't ; life of my joys,
There were good stuff !   I will not trust her with him.
I'll call him back again ; he must not keep   ·
Out of my sight so long ; I shall grow mad then.

Enter Duchess.

Duch. He lives not now to see to-morrow spent,
If this means take effect, as there's no hardness in't.
Last night he played his horrid game again,
Came to my bedside at the full of midnight,
And in his hand that fatal, fearful cup ;
Waked me, and forced me pledge him, to my trembling
And my dead father's scorn : that wounds my sight,
That his remembrance should be raised in spite :
But either his confusion or mine ends it.—   [*Aside.*
O, Amoretta,—hast thou met him yet ?
Speak, wench, hast done that for me ?
    Amo. What, good madam ?
    Duch. Destruction of my hopes ! dost ask that now ?
Didst thou not swear to me, out of thy hate
To Almachildes, thou'dst dissemble him
A loving entertainment, and a meeting
Where I should work my will ?
    Amo. Good madam, pardon me :
A loving entertainment I do protest
Myself to give him, with all speed I can too ;
But, as I'm yet a maid, a perfect one
As the old time was wont to afford, when
There was few tricks and little cunning stirring,
I can dissemble none that will serve your turn ;
He must have even a right one and a plain one.
    Duch. Thou mak'st me doubt thy health ; speak, art
        thou well ?
    Amo. O, never better ! if he would make haste
And come back quickly ! he stays now too long.
            [*The ribbon falls out of her bosom.*

Duch. I'm quite lost in this woman : what's that fell
Out of her bosom now ? some love-token ?   [*Aside.*
  Amo. Nay, I'll say that for him, he's the uncivil'st
      gentleman,
And every way desertless.
  Duch. Who's that now
She discommends so fast ?   .   [*Aside.*
  Amo. I could not love him, madam,
Of any man in court.
  Duch. What's he now, prithee ?
  Amo. Who should it be but Almachildes, madam ?
I never hated man so deeply yet.
  Duch. As Almachildes ?
  Amo. I am sick, good madam,
When I but hear him named.
  Duch. How is this possible ?
But now thou saidst thou lov'dst him, and didst raise him
'Bove all the court in praises.
  Amo. How great people
May speak their pleasure, madam! but surely I
Should think the worse of my tongue while I lived then.
  Duch. No longer have I patience to forbear thee,
Thou that retain'st an envious soul to goodness !
He is a gentleman deserves as much
As ever fortune yet bestowed on man ;
The glory and prime lustre of our court ;
Nor can there any but ourself be worthy of him.
And take you notice of that now from me,
Say you have warning on't, if you did love him,
You must not now.
  Amo. Let your grace never fear it.
  Duch. Thy name is Amoretta, as ours is ;
'Thas made me love and trust thee.
  Amo. And my faithfulness
Has appeared well i' the proof still ; has't not, madam ?
  Duch. But if't fail now, 'tis nothing.

Amo. Then it shall not.
I know he will not be long from fluttering
'Bout this place, now has had a sight of me;
And I'll perform
In all that I vowed, madam, faithfully.

Duch. Then am I blest both in revenge and love,
And thou shalt taste the sweetness.   [*Exit.*

Amo. What your aims be
I list not to inquire; all I desire
Is to preserve a competent honesty,
Both for mine own and his use that shall have me,

Re-enter ALMACHILDES.

Whose luck soe'er it be.   O, he's returned already;
I knew he would not fail.

Alm. It works by this time,
Or the devil's in't, I think; I'll ne'er trust witch else,
Nor sup with 'em this twelvemonth.   [*Aside.*

Amo. I must soothe him now;
And 'tis great pain to do't against one's stomach. [*Aside.*

Alm. Now, Amoretta!

Amo. Now you're welcome, sir,
If you'd come always thus.

Alm. O, am I so?
Is the case altered[1] since?

Amo. If you'd be ruled,
And know your times, 'twere somewhat; a great comfort
'Las, I could be as loving and as venturous
As any woman—we're all flesh and blood, man—
If you could play the game out modestly,
And not betray your hand.   I must have care, sir;
You know I have a marriage-time to come,
And that's for life; your best folks will be merry,
But look to the main chance, that's reputation,
And then do what they list.

[1] "The case is altered" was a proverbial saying.

Alm. Wilt hear my oath ?
By the sweet health of youth, I will be careful,
And never prate on't, nor, like a cunning snarer,
Make thy clipped[1] name the bird to call in others.

Amo. Well, yielding then to such conditions
As my poor bashfulness shall require from you,
I shall yield shortly after.

Alm. I'll consent to 'em ;
And may thy sweet humility be a pattern
For all proud women living !

Amo. They're beholding to you.   [*Exeunt.*

SCENE III.

The Neighbourhood of Ravenna.

Enter ABERZANES, *and* Old Woman *carrying an infant.*

Aber. So, so, away with him !   I love to get 'em,
But not to keep 'em.   Dost thou know the house ?

Old Wom. No matter for the house, I know the porch.

Aber. There's sixpence more for that : away, keep
            close.—   [*Exit* Old Woman.
My tailor told me he sent away a maid-servant
Well ballast of all sides within these nine days ;
His wife ne'er dreamed on't ; gave the drab ten pounds,
And she ne'er troubles him : a common fashion
He told me 'twas to rid away a scape ;
And I have sent him this for't.   I remember
A friend of mine once served a prating tradesman
Just on this fashion, to a hair in troth.
'Tis a good ease to a man ; you can swell a maid up,

---

[1] Called.

And rid her for ten pound ; there's the purse back again,
Whate'er becomes of your money or your maid.
This comes of bragging, now.　It's well for the boy too ;
He'll get an excellent trade by't ; and on Sundays
Go like a gentleman that has pawned his rapier :
He need not care what countryman his father was,
Nor what his mother was when he was gotten :
The boy will do well certain : give him grace
To have a quick hand and convey things cleanly !

Enter FRANCISCA.

'Twill be his own another day.　O, well said !
Art almost furnished ? there's such a toil always
To set a woman to horse, a mighty trouble.
The letter came to your brother's hands, I know,
On Thursday last by noon : you were expected there
Yesterday night.
　Fran. It makes the better, sir.
　Aber. We must take heed we ride through all the
　　　　puddles
'Twixt this and that now, that your safeguard[1] there
May be most probably dabbled.
　Fran. Alas ! sir,
I never marked till now—I hate myself—
How monstrous thin I look !
　Aber. Not monstrous neither :
A little sharp i' the nose, like a country woodcock.
　Fran. Fie, fie, how pale I am ! I shall betray myself.
I would you'd box me well and handsomely,
To get me into colour.
　Aber. Not I, pardon me ;
That let a husband do when he has married you :
A friend at court will never offer that.

----

[1] See note *ante*, p. 27.

Come, how much spice and sugar have you left now.
At this poor one month's voyage ?

Fran. Sure, not much, sir ;
I think some quarter of a pound of sugar,
And half an ounce of spice.

Aber. Here's no sweet charge !
And there was thirty pound good weight and true,
Beside what my man stole when 'twas a-weighing,
And that was three pound more, I'll speak with least.
The Rhenish wine, is't all run out in caudles too ?

Fran. Do you ask that, sir ? 'tis of a week's departure.
You see what 'tis now to get children, sir.

Enter Boy.

Boy. Your mares are ready both, sir.

Aber. Come, we'll up, then.—
Youth, give my sister a straight wand : there's twopence.

Boy. I'll give her a fine whip, sir.

Aber. No, no, no ;
Though we have both deserved it.

Boy. Here's a new one.

Aber. Prithee, talk to us of no whips, good boy ;
My heart aches when I see 'em.—Let's away.   [*Exeunt.*

ACT THE THIRD.

SCENE I.

An Apartment in the Duke's *House.*

Enter Duchess, *leading* ALMACHILDES *blindfold.*

ALM. This you that was a maid? how are
        you born?
    To deceive men! I'd thought to have
        married you:
    I had been finely handled, had I not?
    I'll say that man is wise ever hereafter
That tries his wife beforehand. 'Tis no marvel
You should profess such bashfulness, to blind one,
As if you durst not look a man i' the face,
Your modesty would blush so. Why do you not run
And tell the duchess now? go; you should tell all:
Let her know this too.—Why, here's the plague now:
'Tis hard at first to win 'em; when they're gotten,
There's no way to be rid on 'em; they stick
To a man like bird-lime.—My oath is out:
Will you release me? I'll release myself else.
    Duch. Nay, sure, I'll bring you to your sight again.
            [*Taking off the bandage from his eyes.*
Say, thou must either die, or kill the duke;
For one of them thou must do.
    Alm. How, good madam?
    Duch. Thou hast thy choice, and to that purpose, sir,
I've given thee knowledge now of what thou hast,

And what thou must do, to be worthy on't.
You must not think to come by such a fortune
Without desert ; that were unreasonable.
He that's not born to honour must not look
To have it come with ease to him ; he must win't.
Take but unto thine actions wit and courage
That's all we ask of thee.   But if through weakness
Of a poor spirit thou deniest me this,
Think but how thou shalt die ! as I'll work means for't,
No murderer ever like thee ; for I purpose
To call this subtle, sinful snare of mine
An act of force from thee.   Thou'rt proud and youthful ;
I shall be believed : besides, thy wantonness
Is at this hour in question 'mongst our women
Which will make ill for thee.

   Alm. I had hard chance
To light upon this pleasure that's so costly ;
'Tis not content with what a man can do,
And give him breath, but seeks to have that too.

   Duch. Well, take thy choice.

   Alm. I see no choice in't, madam,
For 'tis all death, methinks.

   Duch. Thou'st an ill sight then
Of a young man.   'Tis death if thou refuse it ;
And say, my zeal has warned thee.   But consenting,
'Twill be new life, great honour, and my love,
Which in perpetual bands I'll fasten to thee.

   Alm. How, madam ?

   Duch. I'll do't religiously ;
Make thee my husband ; may I lose all sense
Of pleasure in life else, and be more miserable
Than ever creature was ! for nothing lives
But has a joy in somewhat.

   Alm. Then by all
The hopeful fortunes of a young man's rising,
I will perform it, madam.

Duch. There's a pledge then
Of a duchess' love for thee ; and now trust me
For thy most happy safety.   I will choose
That time shall never hurt thee : when a man
Shows resolution, and there's worth in him,
I'll have a care of him.   Part now for this time ;
But still be near about us, till thou canst
Be nearer, that's ourself.
 Alm. And that I'll venture hard for.
 Duch. Good speed to thee !   [*Exeunt.*

SCENE II.

An Apartment in ANTONIO'S *House.*

Enter GASPARO *and* FLORIDA.

 Flo. Prithee, be careful of me, very careful now
 Gas. I warrant you ; he that cannot be careful of a
quean, can be careful of nobody ; 'tis every man's
humour that : I should never look to a wife half so
handsomely.
 Flo. O softly, sweet sir ! should your mistress meet
   me now
In her own house, I were undone for ever.
 Gas. Never fear her : she's at her prick-song close ;
There's all the joy she has, or takes delight in.
Look, here's the garden key, my master gave't me,
And willed me to be careful : doubt not you on't.
 Flo. Your master is a noble complete gentleman
And does a woman all the right that may be.

Enter SEBASTIAN.

 Seb. How now ? what's she ?

Gas. A kind of doubtful creature :
I'll tell thee more anon.

                      [*Exeunt* GASPARO *and* FLORIDA.

  Seb. I know that face
To be a strumpet's, or mine eye is envious,
And would fain wish it so where I would have it.
I fail, if the condition[1] of this fellow
Wears not about it a strong scent of baseness.
I saw her once before here, five days since 'tis,
And the same wary panderous diligence
Was then bestowed on her : she came altered then,
And more inclining to the city-tuck.
Whom should this piece of transformation visit,
After the common courtesy of frailty,
In our house here ? surely not any servant ;
They are not kept so lusty, she so low.
I'm at a strange stand : love and luck assist me !

Re-enter GASPARO.

The truth I shall win from him by false play.
He's now returned.—Well, sir, as you were saying,—
Go forward with your tale.

  Gas. What ? I know nothing.

  Seb. The gentlewoman.

  Gas. She's gone out at the back-door now.

  Seb. Then farewell she, and you, if that be all.

  Gas. Come, come, thou shalt have more : I have no
      power
To lock myself up from thee.

  Seb. So methinks.

  Gas. You shall not think, trust me, sir, you shall not :
Your ear ; she's one o' the falling family,
A quean my master keeps ; she lies at Rutney's.

  Seb. Is't possible ? I thought I'd seen her somewhere,

---

[1] **Character.**

Gas. I tell you truth sincerely.   Sh'as been thrice here
By stealth within these ten days, and departed still
With pleasure and with thanks, sir; 'tis her luck.
Surely I think if ever there were man
Bewitched in this world, 'tis my master, sirrah.

 Seb. Thinks't thou so, Gaspar?

 Gas. O sir, too apparent.

 Seb. This may prove happy: 'tis the likeliest means
That fortune yet e'er showed me.   [*Aside.*

Enter ISABELLA with a letter.

 Isa. You're both here now,
And strangers newly lighted! where's your attendance?

 Seb. I know what makes you waspish: a pox on't!
She'll every day be angry now at nothing. [*Aside.*
      [*Exeunt* GASPARO *and* SEBASTIAN.

 Isa. I'll call her stranger in my heart:
Sh'as killed the name of sister through base lust,
And fled to shifts.   O how a brother's good thoughts
May be beguiled in woman! here's a letter,
Found in her absence, reports strangely of her,
And speaks her impudence: sh'as undone herself—
I could not hold from weeping when I read it—
Abused her brother's house and his good confidence.
'Twas done not like herself; I blame her much:
But if she can but keep it from his knowledge,
I will not grieve him first; it shall not come
By my means to his heart.—

Re-enter GASPARO.

      Now, sir, the news.

 Gas. You called 'em strangers; 'tis my master's sister,
  madam.

 Isa. O, is it so? she's welcome: who's come with
  her?

 Gas. I see none but Aberzanes.   [*Exit.*

Isa. He's enough
To bring a woman to confusion,   .
More than a wiser man or a far greater.
A letter came last week to her brother's hands,
To make way for her coming up again,   .
After her shame was lightened ; and she writ there,
The gentleman her mother wished her to,
Taking a violent surfeit at a wedding,
Died ere she came to see him : what strange cunning
Sin helps a woman to !   Here she comes now.—

Enter Francisca *and* Aberzanes.

Sister, you're welcome home again.
   Fran. Thanks, sweet sister.   -
   Isa. You've had good speed.
   Fran. What says she ? [*Aside.*]—I have made
All the best speed I could.
   Isa. I well believe you.—
Sir, we're all much beholding to your kindness.
   Aber. My service ever, madam, to a gentlewoman.
I took a bonny mare I keep, and met her
Some ten mile out of town,—eleven, I think.—
Twas at the stump I met you, I remember,
At bottom of the hill.
   Fran. 'Twas thereabout, sir.
   Aber. Full eleven then, by the rod, if they were
     measured.
   Isa. You look ill, methinks : have you been sick of
     late ?—
Troth, very bleak, doth she not ? how think you, sir ?
   Aber. No, no ; a little sharp with riding ; sh'as rid sore.
   Fran. I ever look lean after a journey, sister ;
One shall do that has travelled, travelled hard.
   Aber. Till evening I commend you to yourselves,
     ladies.   [*Exit.*
   Isa. And that's best trusting to, if you were hanged.—
                             [*Aside.*

You're well acquainted with his hand went out now ?
  Fran. His hand ?
    Isa. I speak of nothing else ; I think 'tis there
                              [*Giving letter.*
Please you to look upon't ; and when you've done,
If you did weep, it could not be amiss,
A sign you could say grace after a full meal.
You had not need look paler, yet you do.
'Twas ill done to abuse yourself and us,
To wrong so good a brother, and the thoughts
That we both held of you.   I did doubt you much
Before our marriage ; but then my strangeness[1]
And better hope still kept me off from speaking.
Yet may you find a kind and peaceful sister of me,
If you desist here, and shake hands with folly,
Which you ha' more cause to do than I to wish you.
As truly as I bear a love to goodness
Your brother knows not yet on't, nor shall ever
For my part, so you leave his company.
But if I find you impudent in sinning,
I will not keep't an hour, nay, prove your enemy,
And you know who will aid me.   As you've goodness,
You may make use of this ; I'll leave it with you. [*Exit.*
    Fran. Here's a sweet churching after a woman's
        labour,
And a fine Give you joy ! why, where the devil
Lay you to be found out ? the sudden hurry
Of hastening to prevent shame brought shame forth :
That's still the curse of all lascivious stuff ;
Misdeeds could never yet be wary enough.
Now must I stand in fear of every look,
Nay, tremble at a whisper.   She can keep it secret ?
That's very likely, and a woman too !
I'm sure I could not do't ; and I am made

---

[1] Shyness as a stranger.

As well as she can be for any purpose :
'Twould ne'er stay with me two days—I have cast[1] it—
The third would be a terrible sick day with me,
Not possible to bear it : should I then
Trust to her strength in't, that lies every night
Whispering the day's news in a husband's ear ?
No ; and I've thought upon the means : blest fortune !
I must be quit with her in the same fashion,
Or else 'tis nothing : there is no way like it,
To bring her honesty into question cunningly.
My brother will believe small likelihoods,
Coming from me too.   I lying now 'i the house
May work things to my will, beyond conceit too :
Disgrace her first, her tale will ne'er be heard ;
I learned that counsel first of a sound guard.
I do suspect Gaspar, my brother's squire there,
Had some hand in this mischief, for he's cunning
And I perhaps may fit him.

Enter ANTONIO.

Ant Your sister told me you were come ; thou'rt
   welcome.
Fran. Where is she ?
Ant. Who, my wife ?
Fran. ·Ay, sir.
Ant. Within.
Fran. Not within hearing, think you ?
Ant. Within hearing ?
What's thy conceit in that ? why shak'st thy head so,
And look'st so pale and poorly ?
Fran. I'm a fool indeed
To take such grief for others ; for your fortune, sir.
Ant. My fortune ? worse things yet ? farewell life then
Fran. I fear your're much deceived, sir, in this woman

----

[1] To cast meant both to plan and to vomit.

Ant. Who? in my wife? speak low; come hither;
    softly, sister.

Fran. I love her as a woman you made choice of;
But when she wrongs you, natural love is touched,
    brother,
And that will speak, you know.

Ant. I trust it will.

Fran. I held a shrewd suspicion of her lightness
At first, when I went down, which made me haste the
    sooner;
But more, to make amends, at my return now,
I found apparent signs.

Ant. Apparent, sayst thou?

Fran. Ay, and of base lust too : that makes the
    affliction.

Ant. There has been villany wrought upon me then :
'Tis too plain now.

Fran. Happy are they, I say still,
That have their sisters living i' the house with 'em,
Their mothers, or some kindred; a great comfort
To all poor married men; it is not possible
A young wife can abuse a husband then;
'Tis found straight.   But swear service to this, brother.

Ant. To this, and all thou wilt have.

Fran. Then this follows, sir.   [*Whispers him.*

Ant. I praise thy counsel well; I'll put't in use
    straight.
See where she comes herself.   [*Exit* FRANCISCA.

Re-enter ISABELLA.

                    Kind, honest lady,
I must now borrow a whole fortnight's leave of thee.

Isa. How, sir, a fortnight's?

Ant. It may be but ten days, I know not yet;
'Tis business for the state, and 't must be done.

Isa. I wish good speed to't then.

Mid. II.   M

Ant. Why, that was well spoke.
I'll take but a foot-boy ; I need no more ;
The rest I'll leave at home to do you service.

 Isa. Use your own pleasure, sir.

 Ant. Till my return
You'll be good company, my sister and you.

 Isa. We shall make shift, sir.

 Ant. I'm glad now she's come ;
And so the wishes of my love to both !

 Isa. And our good prayers with you, sir !
          [*Exit* ANTONIO.

    Re-enter SEBASTIAN.

 Seb. Now, my fortune !—   [*Aside.*
By your kind favour, madam.

 Isa. With me, sir ?

 Seb. The words shall not be many, but the faithfulness
And true respect that is included in 'em
Is worthy your attention, and may put upon me
The fair repute of a just, honest servant.

 Isa. What's here to do, sir,
There's such great preparation toward ?

 Seb. In brief, that goodness in you is abused, madam ;
You have the married life, but 'tis a strumpet
That has the joy on't and the fruitfulness ;
There goes away your comfort.

 Isa. How ? a strumpet ?

 Seb. Of five years' cost and upwards, a dear mischief,
As they are all of 'em ; his fortnight's journey
Is to that country : if it be not rudeness
To speak the truth, I've found it all out, madam.

 Isa. Thou'st found out thine own ruin ; for to my
   knowledge
Thou dost belie him basely : I dare swear
He's a gentleman as free from that folly
As ever took religious life upon him.

Seb. Be not too confident to your own abuse, madam.
Since I've begun the truth, neither your frowns—
The only curses that I have on earth,
Because my means depends upon your service—
Nor all the execration of man's fury,
Shall put me off: though I be poor, I'm honest,
And too just in this business. I perceive now
Too much respect and faithfulness to ladies
May be a wrong to servants.

Isa. Art thou yet
So impudent to stand in't?

Seb. Are you yet so cold, madam,
In the belief on't; there my wonder's fixed;
Having such blessèd health and youth about you,
Which makes the injury mighty.

Isa. Why, I tell thee,
It were too great a fortune for thy lowness
To find out such a thing; thou dost not look
As if thou'rt made for't.   By the sweets of love,
I would give half my wealth for such a bargain,
And think 'twere bought too cheap: thou canst not
      guess
Thy means and happiness, should I find this true
First, I'd prefer thee to the lord my uncle;
He's governor of Ravenna, all the advancements
I' the kingdom flows from him: what need I boast
      that
Which common fame can teach thee?

Seb. Then thus, madam :
Since I presume now on your height of spirit,
And your regard to your own youth and fruitfulness,
Which every woman naturally loves and covets,
Accept but of my labour in directions,
You shall both find your wrongs, which you may right
At your own pleasure, yet not missed to-night

Here in the house neither ; none shall take notice
Of any absence in you, as I've thought on't.
   Isa. Do this, and take my praise and thanks for ever.
   Seb. As I deserve, I wish 'em, and will serve you.
                                      [Exeunt.

SCENE III.

A Field.

Enter HECATE, STADLIN, HOPPO, *and other* Witches ;
FIRESTONE *in the background.*

   Hec. The moon's a gallant ; see how brisk she
      rides !
   Stad. Here's a rich evening, Hecate.
   Hec. Ay, is't not, wenches,
To take a journey of five thousand mile ?
   Hop. Ours will be more to-night.
   Hec. O 'twill be precious !
Heard you the owl yet ?
   Stad. Briefly in the copse,
As we came through now.
   Hec. 'Tis high time for us then.
   Stad. There was a bat hung at my lips three times
As we came through the woods, and drank her fill :
Old Puckle saw her.
   Hec. You are fortunate still ;
The very screech-owl lights upon your shoulder
And woos you, like a pigeon.   Are you furnished ?
Have you your ointments ?
   Stad. All.
   Hec. Prepare to flight then ;
I'll overtake you swiftly.

Stad. Hie thee, Hecate ;
We shall be up betimes.

Hec. I'll reach you quickly.

[*Exeunt all the* Witches *except* HECATE.

Fire. They are all going a-birding to-night : they
talk of fowls i' the air that fly by day ; I am sure they'll
be a company of foul sluts there to-night : if we have
not mortality after't, I'll be hanged, for they are able
to putrefy it, to infect a whole region. She spies me
now.

Hec. What, Firestone, our sweet son ?

Fire. A little sweeter than some of you, or a dunghill
were too good for me.   [*Aside.*

Hec. How much hast here ?

Fire. Nineteen, and all brave plump ones,
Besides six lizards and three serpentine eggs.

Hec. Dear and sweet boy ! what herbs hast thou ?

Fire. I have some marmartin and some mandragon.

Hec. Marmaritin and mandragora, thou wouldst say.

Fire. Here's panax too—I thank thee—my pan aches,
      I'm sure,
With kneeling down to cut 'em.

Hec. And selago,
Hedge-hyssop too : how near he goes my cuttings !
Were they all cropped by moonlight ?

Fire. Every blade of 'em,
Or I'm a moon-calf, mother.

Hec. Hie thee home with 'em :
Look well to the house to-night ; I'm for aloft.

Fire. Aloft, quoth you ? I would you would break
your neck once, that I might have all quickly ! [*Aside.*]
—Hark, hark, mother ! they are above the steeple already,
flying over your head with a noise[1] of musicians.

Hec. They're they indeed. Help, help me ; I'm too
      late else.

[1] Company.

SONG.

Voice. [*Above.*] Come away, come away,
    Hecate, Hecate, come away !
Hec. I come, I come, I come, I come,
    With all the speed I may,
    With all the speed I may.
    Where's Stadlin ?
Voice. [*Above.*] Here.
Hec. Where's Puckle ?
Voice. [*Above.*] Here ;
    And Hoppo too, and Hellwain too ;
    We lack but you, we lack but you ;
    Come away, make up the count.
Hec. I will but 'noint, and then I mount.
             [*A Spirit like a cat descends.*
Voice [*Above.*] There's one comes down to fetch his
    dues,
    A kiss, a coll,[1] a sip of blood ;
    And why thou stay'st so long
           I muse, I muse,
    Since the air's so sweet and good.
Hec. O, art thou come ?
           What news, what news ?
Spirit. All goes still to our delight :
    Either come, or else
           Refuse, refuse.
Hec. Now I'm furnished for the flight.
Fire. Hark, hark, the cat sings a brave treble in her
own language !
Hec. [*Going up.*] Now I go, now I fly,
    Malkin my sweet spirit and I.
    O what a dainty pleasure 'tis
    To ride in the air
    When the moon shines fair,
    And sing and dance, and toy and kiss

          [1] Embrace.

Over woods, high rocks, and mountains,
Over seas, our mistress' fountains,
Over steeples,[1] towers, and turrets,
We fly by night, 'mongst troops of spirits :
No ring of bells to our ear sounds,
No howls of wolves, no yelps of hounds ;
No, not the noise of water's breach,
Or cannon's throat our height can reach.

Voices. [*Above.*] No ring of bells, &c.

Fire. Well, mother, I thank your kindness : you must be gambolling i' the air, and leave me to walk here like a fool and a mortal.   [*Exit.*

[1] Previously printed "steep ; " witches were frequently associated with steeples ; and see *ante*, p. 127.

ACT THE FOURTH.

SCENE I.

An Apartment in the Duke's *House.*

Enter ALMACHILDES.

LM. Though the fates have endued me with a pretty kind of lightness, that I can laugh at the world in a corner on't, and can make myself merry on fasting nights to rub out a supper (which were a precious quality in a young formal student), yet let the world know there is some difference betwixt my jovial condition and the lunary state of madness. I am not quite out of my wits : I know a bawd from an aqua-vitæ shop, a strumpet from wildfire, and a beadle from brimstone. Now shall I try the honesty of a great woman soundly. She reckoning the duke's made away, I'll be hanged if I be not the next now. If I trust her, as she's a woman, let one of her long hairs wind about my heart, and be the end of me ; which were a piteous lamentable tragedy, and might be entituled "A fair warning for all hair-bracelets."
Already there's an insurrection
Among the people ; they are up in arms
Not out of any reason, but their wills,

Which are in them their saints, sweating and swearing,
Out of their zeal to rudeness, that no stranger,
As they term her, shall govern over them ;
They say they'll raise a duke among themselves first.

Enter Duchess.

Duch. O Almachildes, I perceive already
Our loves are born to curses ! we're beset
By multitudes ; and, which is worse, I fear me
Unfriended too of any : my chief care
Is for thy sweet youth's safety.
    Alm. He that believes you not
Goes the right way to Heaven, o' my conscience. [*Aside.*
    Duch. There is no trusting of 'em ; they're all as
        barren
In pity as in faith : he that puts confidence
In them, dies openly to the sight of all men,
Not with his friends and neighbours in peace private ;
But as his shame, so his cold farewell is,
Public and full of noise.   But keep you close, sir,
Not seen of any, till I see the way
Plain for your safety.   I expect the coming
Of the lord governor, whom I will flatter
With fair entreaties, to appease their wildness ;
And before him take a great grief upon me
For the duke's death, his strange and sudden loss
And when a quiet comes, expect thy joys.
    Alm. I do expect now to be made away
'Twixt this and Tuesday night : if I live Wednesday,
Say I have been careful, and shunned spoon-meat.[1]
                          [*Aside and exit.*
    Duch. This fellow lives too long after the deed ;
I'm weary of his sight, he must die quickly,
Or I've small hope of safety.   My great aim's

---

[1] Broth, in which poison could be easily administered.

At the lord governor's love ; he is a spirit
Can sway and countenance ; these obey and crouch.
My guiltiness had need of such a master,
That with a beck can suppress multitudes,
And dim misdeeds with radiance of his glory,
Not to be seen with dazzled popular eyes :
And here behold him come.

Enter Lord Governor, *attended by* Gentlemen.

   Gov. Return back to 'em,
Say we desire 'em to be friends of peace
Till they hear farther from us.   [*Exeunt* Gentlemen.
   Duch. O my lord,
I fly unto the pity of your nobleness,
That grieved'st lady that was e'er beset
With storms of sorrows, or wild rage of people !
Never was woman's grief for loss of lord
Dearer[1] than mine to me.
   Gov. There's no right done
To him now, madam, by wrong done to yourself ;
Your own good wisdom may instruct you so far :
And for the people's tumult, which oft grows
From liberty, or rankness of long peace,
I'll labour to restrain, as I've begun, madam.
   Duch. My thanks and praises shall ne'er forget you, sir,
And, in time to come, my love.
   Gov. Your love, sweet madam ?
You make my joys too happy ; I did covet
To be the fortunate man that blessing visits,
Which I'll esteem the crown and full reward
Of service present and deserts to come :
It is a happiness I'll be bold to sue for,
When I have set a calm upon these spirits
That now are up for ruin.

[1] *i.e.* Greater.

Duch. Sir, my wishes
Are so well met in yours, so fairly answered,
And nobly recompensed, it makes me suffer
In those extremes that few have ever felt ;
To hold two passions in one heart at once,
Of gladness and of sorrow.

   Gov. Then, as the olive
Is the meek ensign of fair fruitful peace,
So is this kiss of yours.

   Duch. Love's power be with you, sir !

   Gov. How sh'as betrayed her ! may I breathe no longer
Than to do virtue service, and bring forth
The fruits of noble thoughts, honest and loyal !
This will be worth the observing ; and I'll do't.

                            [Aside and exit.

   Duch. What a sure happiness confirms joy to me,
Now in the times of my most imminent dangers !
I looked for ruin, and increase of honour
Meets me auspiciously.   But my hopes are clogged now
With an unworthy weight ; there's the misfortune !
What course shall I take now with this young man ?
For he must be no hinderance : I have thought on't ;
I'll take some witch's counsel for his end,
That will be sur'st : mischief is mischief's friend. *[Exit.*

SCENE II.

An Apartment in FERNANDO'S *House.*

Enter SEBASTIAN *and* FERNANDO.

   Seb. If ever you knew force of love in life, sir,
Give to mine pity.

Fer. You do ill to doubt me.

Seb. I could make bold with no friend seemlier
Than with yourself, because you were in presence
At our vow-making.

Fer. I'm a witness to't.

Seb. Then you best understand, of all men living,
This is no wrong I offer, no abuse
Either to faith or friendship, for we're registered
Husband and wife in Heaven ; though there wants that
Which often keeps licentious men in awe
From starting from their wedlocks, the knot public,
'Tis in our souls knit fast ; and how more precious
The soul is than the body, so much judge
The sacred and celestial tie within us
More than the outward form, which calls but witness
Here upon earth to what is done in Heaven :
Though I must needs confess the least is honourable ;
As an ambassador sent from a king
Has honour by the employment, yet there's greater
Dwells in the king that sent him ; so in this.

Enter FLORIDA.

Fer. I approve all you speak, and will appear to you
A faithful, pitying friend.

Seb. Look, there is she, sir,
One good for nothing but to make use of ;
And I'm constrained t' employ her to make all things
Plain, easy, and probable : for when she comes
And finds one here that claims him, as I've taught
Both this to do't, and he to compound with her,
'Twill stir belief the more of such a business

Fer. I praise the carriage well.

Seb. Hark you, sweet mistress,
I shall do you a simple turn in this ;
For she disgraced thus, you are up in favour
For ever with her husband.

Flo. That's my hope, sir,
I would not take the pains else.   Have you the keys
Of the garden-side, that I may get betimes in
Closely, and take her lodging ?

Seb. Yes, I've thought upon you
Here be the keys.   [*Giving keys.*

Flo. Marry, and thanks, sweet sir :
Set me to work so still.

Seb. Your joys are false ones,
You're like to lie alone ; you'll be deceived
Of the bed-fellow you look for, else my purpose
Were in an ill case : he's on his fortnight's journey ;
You'll find cold comfort there ; a dream will be
Even the best market you can make to-night.   [*Aside.*
She'll not be long now : you may lose no time neither ;
If she but take you at the door, 'tis enough :
When a suspect doth catch once, it burns mainly.
There may you end your business, and as cunningly
As if you were i' the chamber, if you please
To use but the same art.

Flo. What need you urge that
Which comes so naturally I cannot miss on't ?
What makes the devil so greedy of a soul,
But 'cause h'as lost his own, to all joys lost ?
So 'tis our trade to set snares for other women,
'Cause we were once caught ourselves.   [*Exit.*

Seb. A sweet allusion !
Hell and a whore it seems are partners then
In one ambition : yet thou'rt here deceived now ;
Thou canst set none to hurt or wrong her honour,
It rather makes it perfect.   Best of friends
That ever love's extremities were blessed with,
I feel mine arms with thee, and call my peace
The offspring of thy friendship.   I will think
This night my wedding-night ; and with a joy
As reverend as religion can make man's,

I will embrace this blessing.   Honest actions
Are laws unto themselves, and that good fear
Which is on others forced, grows kindly there.

> [*Knocking within.*

 Fer. Hark, hark! one knocks : away, sir ; 'tis she
  certainly :   [*Exit* SEBASTIAN.
It sounds much like a woman's jealous 'larum.

Enter ISABELLA.

 Isa. By your leave, sir.
 Fer. You're welcome, gentlewoman.
 Isa. Our ladyship then stands us in no stead now.

> [*Aside.*

One word in private, sir.   [*Whispers him.*
 Fer. No, surely, forsooth,
There is no such here, you've mistook the house.
 Isa. O sir, that have I not ; excuse me there,
I come not with such ignorance ; think not so, sir.
'Twas told me at the entering of your house here
By one that knows him too well.
 Fer. Who should that be ?
 Isa. Nay, sir, betraying is not my profession :
But here I know he is ; and I presume
He would give me admittance, if he knew on't,
As one on's nearest friends.
 Fer. You're not his wife, forsooth ?
 Isa. Yes, by my faith, am I.
 Fer. Cry you mercy then, lady.
 Isa. She goes here by the name on's wife : good stuff!
But the bold strumpet never told me that. [*Aside.*
 Fer. We are so oft deceived that let out lodgings,
We know not whom to trust : 'tis such a world
There are so many odd tricks now-a-days
Put upon housekeepers.
 Isa. Why, do you think I'd wrong

You or the reputation of your house?
Pray, show me the way to him.
   Fer. He's asleep, lady,
The curtains drawn about him.
   Isa. Well, well, sir,
I'll have that care I'll not disease[1] him much,
Tread you but lightly.—O, of what gross falsehood
Is man's heart made of! had my first love lived
And returned safe, he would have been a light
To all men's actions, his faith shined so bright.
                    [*Aside, and exit with* FERNANDO.

Re-enter SEBASTIAN.

   Seb. I cannot so deceive her, 'twere too sinful,
There's more religion in my love than so.
It is not treacherous lust that gives content
T' an honest mind ; and this could prove no better.
Were it in me a part of manly justice,
That have sought strange hard means to keep her chaste
To her first vow, and I t' abuse her first?
Better I never knew what comfort were
In woman's love than wickedly to know it.
What could the falsehood of one night avail him
That must enjoy for ever, or he's lost?
'Tis the way rather to draw hate upon me ;
For, known, 'tis as impossible she should love me,
As youth in health to dote upon a grief,
Or one that's robbed and bound t' affect the thief :
No, he that would soul's sacred comfort win
Must burn in pure love, like a seraphin.

Re-enter ISABELLA.

Isa. Celio !
Seb. Sweet madam?

               [1] Disturb.

Isa. Thou hast deluded me ;
There's nobody.

Seb. How ? I wonder he would miss, madam,
Having appointed too ; 'twere a strange goodness
If Heaven should turn his heart now by the way.

Isa. O, never, Celio !

Seb. Yes, I ha' known the like :
Man is not at his own disposing, madam ;
The blessed powers have provided better for him,
Or he were miserable.   He may come yet ;
'Tis early, madam : if you would be pleased
T' embrace my counsel, you should see this night over,
Since you've bestowed this pains

Isa. I intend so.

Seb. That strumpet would be found, else she should go.
I curse the time now I did e'er make use
Of such a plague : sin knows not what it does.   [*Exeunt.*

SCENE III.

A Hall in ANTONIO'S *House.*

Enter FRANCISCA *above.*

Fran. 'Tis now my brother's time, even much about
      it;
For though he dissembled a whole fortnight's absence,
· He comes again to-night ; 'twas so agreed
Before he went.   I must bestir my wits now.
To catch this sister of mine, and bring her name
To some disgrace first, to preserve mine own :
There's profit in that cunning.   She cast off
My company betimes to-night by tricks and sleights,

And I was well contented.　I'm resolved[1]
There's no hate lost between us ; for I know
She does not love me now, but painfully,
Like one that's forced to smile upon a grief,
To bring some purpose forward ; and I'll pay her
In her own metal.　They're now all at rest,
And Gaspar there, and all : list ! fast asleep ;
He cries it hither :[2] I must disease[3] you straight, sir.
For the maid-servants and the girls o' the house,
I spiced them lately with a drowsy posset,
They will not hear in haste.　[*Noise within.*]　My
　　brother's come :
O, where's this key now for him ? here 'tis, happily :
But I must wake him first.—Why, Gaspar, Gaspar !
　　Gas. [*Within.*] What a pox gasp you for ?
　　Fran. Now I'll throw't down.
　　Gas. [*Within.*] Who's that called me now ? somebody
　　　　called Gaspar ?
　　Fran. O, up, as thou'rt an honest fellow, Gaspar !
　　Gas. [*Within.*] I shall not rise to-night then.　What's
　　　　the matter ?
Who's that ? young mistress ?
　　Fran. Ay ; up, up, sweet Gaspar !

Enter GASPARO.

My sister hath both knocked and called this hour,
And not a maid will stir.
　　Gas. They'll stir enough sometimes.
　　Fran. Hark, hark, again ! Gaspar, O, run, run, prithee!
　　Gas. Give me leave to clothe myself.
　　Fran. Stand'st upon clothing
In an extremity ?　Hark, hark again !
She may be dead ere thou com'st : O, in quickly !- -
　　　　　　　　　　　　　　　[*Exit* GASPARO.

---

[1] Convinced.　　[2] His snoring is audible.　　[3] Trouble.

He's gone : he cannot choose but be took now,
Or met in his return ; that will be enough.—

Enter ANTONIO.

Brother ? here, take this light.

    Ant. My careful sister !

    Fran. Look first in his own lodging ere you enter.

[Exit ANTONIO

    Ant. [*Within.*] O abused confidence ! there's nothing
But what betrays him more.   [of him

    Fran. Then 'tis too true, brother ?

    Ant. [*Within.*] I'll make base lust a terrible example ;
No villany e'er paid dearer.

    Flo. [*Within.*] Help ! hold, sir !

    Ant. [*Within.*] I'm deaf to all humanity.

    Fran. List, list !
A strange and sudden silence after all :
I trust h'as spoiled 'em both ; too dear a happiness !
O how I tremble between doubts and joys !

    Ant. [*Within.*] There perish both, down to the house
      of falsehood,
Where perjurous wedlock weeps !

Re-entering with his sword drawn.

O perjurous woman

Sh'ad took the innocence of sleep upon her
At my approach, and would not see me come ;
As if sh'ad lain there like a harmless soul,
And never dreamed of mischief. What's all this now ?
I feel no ease ; the burden's not yet off
So long as the abuse sticks in my knowledge.
O, 'tis a pain of hell to know one's shame !
Had it been hid and done, 't had been done happy,
For he that's ignorant lives long and merry.

    Fran. I shall know all now. [*Aside.*]—Brother !

    Ant. Come down quickly,
For I must kill thee too,

Fran. Me?

Ant. Stay not long :
If thou desir'st to die with little pain,
Make haste I'd wish thee, and come willingly ;
If I be forced to come, I shall be cruel
Above a man to thee.

Fran. Why, sir !—my brother ! — —

Ant. Talk to thy soul, if thou wilt talk at all ;
To me thou'rt lost for ever.

Fran. This is fearful in you :
Beyond all reason, brother, would you thus
Reward me for my care and truth shown to you ?

Ant. A curse upon 'em both, and thee for company !
'Tis that too diligent, thankless care of thine
Makes me a murderer, and that ruinous truth
That lights me to the knowledge of my shame.
Hadst thou been secret, then had I been happy,
And had a hope, like man, of joys to come :
Now here I stand a stain to my creation ;
And, which is heavier than all torments to me,
The understanding of this base adultery ;
And that thou toldst me first, which thou deserv'st
Death worthily for.

Fran. If that be the worst, hold, sir,
Hold, brother ; I can ease your knowledge straight,
By my soul's hopes, I can ! there's no such thing.

Ant. How ?

Fran. Bless me but with life, I'll tell you all :
Your bed was never wronged.

Ant. What ? never wronged ?

Fran. I ask but mercy as I deal with truth now :
'Twas only my deceit, my plot, and cunning,
To bring disgrace upon her ; by that means
To keep mine own hid, which none knew but she :
To speak troth, I had a child by Aberzanes, sir.

Ant. How ? Aberzanes ?

Fran. And my mother's letter
Was counterfeited, to get time and place
For my delivery.

Ant. O, my wrath's redoubled !

Fran. At my return she could speak all my folly,
And blamed me, with good counsel.   I, for fear
It should be made known, thus rewarded her ;
Wrought you into suspicion without cause,
And at your coming raised up Gaspar suddenly,
Sent him but in before you, by a falsehood,
Which to your kindled jealousy I knew
Would add enough : what's now confessed is true.

Ant. The more I hear, the worse it fares with me.
I ha' killed 'em now for nothing ; yet the shame
Follows my blood still.   Once more, come down :
Look you, my sword goes up.   [*Sheathing his sword.*
                      Call Hermio to me :
Let the new man alone ; he'll wake too soon
                      [*Exit* FRANCISCA *above.*
To find his mistress dead, and lose a service.
Already the day breaks upon my guilt ;

                   Enter HERMIO.

I must be brief and sudden.—Hermio.

Her. Sir ?

Ant. Run, knock up Aberzanes speedily ;
Say I desire his company this morning
To yonder horse-race, tell him ; that will fetch him :
O, hark you, by the way——   [*Whispers.*

Her. Yes, sir.

Ant. Use speed now,
Or I will ne'er use thee more ; and, perhaps,
I speak in a right hour.   My grief o'erflows ;
I must in private go and vent my woes.   [*Exeunt.*

ACT THE FIFTH.

SCENE I.

A Hall in ANTONIO'S *House.*

Enter ANTONIO *and* ABERZANES.

NT. You're welcome, sir.

    Aber. I think I'm worthy on't,
For, look you, sir, I come untrussed,[1] in
    troth.

    Ant. The more's the pity—honester
    men go to't—

That slaves should 'scape it. What blade have you got
    there?

    Aber. Nay, I know not that, sir : I am not acquainted greatly with the blade ; I am sure 'tis a good scabbard, and that satisfies me.

    Ant. 'Tis long enough indeed, if that be good.

    Aber. I love to wear a long weapon ; 'tis a thing commendable.

    Ant. I pray, draw it, sir.

    Aber. It is not to be drawn.

    Ant. Not to be drawn?

    Aber. I do not care to see't : to tell you troth, sir, 'tis only a holyday thing, to wear by a man's side.

    Ant. Draw it, or I'll rip thee down from neck to navel. Though there's small glory in't.

---

    [1] Partially dressed, the laces of his hose untied.

Aber. Are you in earnest, sir ?

Ant. I'll tell thee that anon.

Aber. Why, what's the matter, sir ?

Ant. What a base misery is this in life now
This slave had so much daring courage in him
To act a sin would shame whole generations,
But hath not so much honest strength about him
To draw a sword in way of satisfaction.
This shows thy great guilt, that thou dar'st not fight.

Aber. Yes, I dare fight, sir, in an honest cause.

Ant. Why, come then, slave ! thou'st made my sister
    whore.

Aber. Prove that an honest cause, and I'll be hanged

Ant. So many starting-holes ? can I light no way ?
Go to, you shall have your wish, all honest play.—
Come forth, thou fruitful wickedness, thou seed
Of shame and murder ! take to thee in wedlock
Baseness and cowardice, a fit match for thee !—
Come, sir, along with me.

Enter FRANCISCA.

Aber. 'Las, what to do ?
I am too young to take a wife, in troth.

Ant. But old enough to take a strumpet though :
You'd fain get all your children beforehand,
And marry when you've done ; that's a strange course
    sir.
This woman I bestow on thee : what dost thou say ?

Aber. I would I had such another to bestow on you
    sir.

Ant. Uncharitable slave ! dog, coward as thou art,
To wish a plague so great as thine to any !

Aber. To my friend, sir, where I think I may be
    bold.

Ant. Down, and do't solemnly ; contract yourselves
With truth and zeal, or ne'er rise up again.

I will not have her die i' the state of strumpet,
Though she took pride to live one.—Hermio, the wine !

Enter HERMIO *with wine.*

Her. 'Tis here, sir.—Troth, I wonder at some things ;
But I'll keep honest.   [*Aside.*
Ant. So, here's to you both now,   [*They drink.*
And to your joys, if't be your luck to find 'em :
I tell you, you must weep hard, if you do.
Divide it 'twixt you both ; you shall not need
A strong bill of divorcement after that,
If you mislike your bargain.   Go, get in now ;
Kneel and pray heartily to get forgiveness
Of those two souls whose bodies thou hast murdered. --
                    [*Exeunt* ABERZANES *and* FRANCISCA.
Spread, subtle poison !   Now my shame in her
Will die when I die ; there's some comfort yet.
I do but think how each man's punishment
Proves still a kind of justice to himself.
I was the man that told this innocent gentlewoman,
Whom I did falsely wed and falsely kill,
That he that was her husband first by contract
Was slain i' the field ; and he's known yet to live
So did I cruelly beguile his heart,   •
For which I'm well rewarded ; so is Gaspar,
Who, to befriend my love, swore fearful oaths
He saw the last breath fly from him.   I see now
'Tis a thing dreadful t' abuse holy vows,
And falls most weightily.
Her. Take comfort, sir ;
You're guilty of no death ; they're only hurt,
And that not mortally.

Enter GASPARO.

Ant. Thou breath'st untruths.
Her. Speak, Gaspar, for me then.

Gas. Your unjust rage, sir,
Has hurt me without cause.

Ant. 'Tis changed to grief for't.
How fares my wife?

Gas. No doubt, sir, she fares well,
For she ne'er felt your fury.   The poor sinner
That hath this seven year kept herself sound for you,
'Tis your luck to bring her into the surgeon's hands now.

Ant. Florida?

Gas. She : I know no other, sir ;
You were ne'er at charge yet but with one light-horse.

Ant. Why, where's your lady? where's my wife
    to-night then?

Gas. Nay, ask not me, sir ; your struck doe within
Tells a strange tale of her.

Ant. This is unsufferable !
Never had man such means to make him mad.
O that the poison would but spare my life
Till I had found her out !

Her. Your wish is granted, sir :
Upon the faithfulness of a pitying servant,
I gave you none at all ; my heart was kinder.
Let not conceit[1] abuse you ; you're as healthful,
For any drug, as life yet ever found you.

Ant. Why, here's a happiness wipes off mighty sorrows :
The benefit of ever-pleasing service
Bless thy profession !—

    Enter Lord Governor, *attended by* Gentlemen.

        O my worthy lord,
I've an ill bargain, never man had worse !
The woman that, unworthy, wears your blood
To countenance sin on her, your niece, she's false.

Gov. False?

Ant. Impudent, adulterous.

        [1] Apprehension.

Gov. You're too loud,
And grow too bold too with her virtuous meekness.

Enter FLORIDA.

Who dare accuse her ?
    Flo. Here's one dare and can.
She lies this night with Celio, her own servant :
The place, Fernando's house.
    Gov. Thou dost amaze us.
    Ant. Why, here's but lust translated from one baseness
Into another : here I thought t' have caught 'em,
But lighted wrong, by false intelligence,
And made me hurt the innocent.   But now
I'll make my revenge dreadfuller than a tempest ;
An army should not stop me, or a sea
Divide 'em from my revenge.   [*Exit.*
    Gov. I'll not speak
To have her spared, if she be base and guilty :
If otherwise, Heaven will not see her wronged,
I need not take care for her.   Let that woman
Be carefully looked to, both for health and sureness.—
It is not that mistaken wound thou wear'st
Shall be thy privilege.
    Flo. You cannot torture me
Worse than the surgeon does : so long I care not.
              [*Exit with* GASPARO *and a* Gentleman.
    Gov. If she be adulterous, I will never trust
Virtues in women ; they're but veils for lust.
                         [*Exit with* Gentlemen
    Her. To what a lasting ruin mischief runs !
I had thought I'd well and happily ended all,
In keeping back the poison ; and new rage now
Spreads a worse venom.   My poor lady grieves me :
'Tis strange to me that her sweet-seeming virtues
Should be so meanly overtook with Celio,
A servant : 'tis not possible.

Enter ISABELLA *and* SEBASTIAN

Isa. Good morrow, Hermio :
My sister stirring yet ?
   Her. How? stirring, forsooth !
Here has been simple stirring.   Are you not hurt, madam ?
Pray, speak ; we have a surgeon ready.
   Isa. How ? a surgeon !
   Her. Hath been at work these five hours.
   Isa. How he talks !
   Her. Did you not meet my master ?
   Isa. How, your master ?
Why, came he home to-night ?
   Her. Then know you nothing, madam ?
Please you but walk in, you shall hear strange business.
   Isa. I'm much beholding to your truth now, am I not ?
You've served me fair ; my credit's stained for ever !
                              [*Exit with* HERMIO.
   Seb. This is the wicked'st fortune that e'er blew :
We're both undone, for nothing : there's no way
Flatters recovery now, the thing's so gross :
Her disgrace grieves me more than a life's loss.   [*Exit.*

SCENE II.

The Abode of HECATE.   *A cauldron in the centre.*

Enter Duchess, HECATE, *and* FIRESTONE.

   Hec. What death is't you desire for Almachildes ?
   Duch. A sudden and a subtle
   Hec. Then I've fitted you.
   Here lie the gifts of both ; sudden and subtle :
His picture made in wax, and gently molten

By a blue fire kindled with dead men's eyes,
Will waste him by degrees.

Duch. In what time, prithee?

Hec. Perhaps in a moon's progress.

Duch. What, a month?
Out upon pictures, if they be so tedious!
Give me things with some life.

Hec. Then seek no farther.

Duch. This must be done with speed, dispatched this
If it may possible. [night,

Hec. I have it for you;
Here's that will do't : stay but perfection's time,
And that's not five hours hence.

Duch. Canst thou do this?

Hec. Can I!

Duch. I mean, so closely.

Hec. So closely
Do you mean too!

Duch. So artfully, so cunningly.

Hec. Worse and worse; doubts and incredulities!
They make me mad.   Let scrupulous creatures know
Cum[1] volui, ripis ipsis mirantibus, amnes
In fontes rediere suos ; concussaque sisto,
Stantia concutio cantu freta ; nubila pello,
Nubilaque induco ; ventos abigoque vocoque ;
Viperaes rumpo verbis et carmine fauces ;
Et silvas moveo ; jubeoque tremiscere montes,
Et mugire solum, manesque exire sepulchris.
Te quoque, luna, traho.   Can you doubt me then,
daughter,

---

[1] Ovid, *Met.* vii. 199, where the first line is
"Quorum ope, *cum volui, ripis mirantibus amnes :* "
but I find it quoted, as in our text, by Corn. Agrippa, *Occult.
Philos.*; by R. Scot, *Discouerie of Witchcraft*; and by Bodinus, *De
Magorum Dæmonomania.*   From the last mentioned work, indeed,
Middleton seems to have transcribed the passage, since he omits,
as Bodinus does, a line after " *Vitereas rumpo,*" &c. -- *Dyce.*

That can make mountains tremble, miles of woods walk,
Whole earth's foundations bellow, and the spirits
Of the entombed to burst out from their marbles,
Nay, draw yond moon to my involved designs ?

    Fire. I know as well as can be when my mother's mad,
and our great cat angry, for one spits French then, and
the other spits Latin.   [*Aside.*

    Duch. I did not doubt you, mother.

    Hec. No ! what did you ?
My power's so firm, it is not to be questioned.

    Duch. Forgive what's past : and now I know the
        offensiveness
That vexes art, I'll shun the occasion ever.

    Hec. Leave all to me and my five sisters, daughter :
It shall be conveyed in at howlet-time ;
Take you no care : my spirits know their moments ;
Raven or screech-owl never fly by the door
But they call in—I thank 'em—and they lose not by't
I give 'em barley soaked in infants' blood ;
They shall have *semina cum sanguine,*
Their gorge crammed full, if they come once to cur
    house ;
We are no niggard.   [*Exit* Duchess.

    Fire. They fare but too well when they come hither ;
they eat up as much t'other night as would have made
me a good conscionable pudding.

    Hec. Give me some lizard's-brain ; quickly, Firestone.

    [FIRESTONE *brings the different ingredients for the*
        charm, as HECATE *calls for them.*

Where's grannam Stadlin, and all the rest o' the sisters ?

    Fire. All at hand, forsooth.

    Enter STADLIN, HOPPO, *and other* Witches.

    Hec. Give me marmaritin, some bear-breech : when ?[1]

----

[1] An exclamation of impatience.

Fire. Here's bear-breech and lizard's-brain, forsooth.

Hec. Into the vessel;
And fetch three ounces of the red-haired girl
I killed last midnight.

Fire. Whereabouts, sweet mother?

Hec. Hip; hip or flank. Where is the acopus?[1]

Fire. You shall have acopus, forsooth.

Hec. Stir, stir about, whilst I begin the charm.

Black spirits and white, red spirits and gray,
Mingle, mingle, mingle, you that mingle may!
　　Titty, Tiffin,
　　Keep it stiff in;
　　Firedrake, Puckey,
　　Make it lucky;
　　Liard, Robin,
　　You must bob in.
Round, around, around, about, about!
All ill come running in, all good keep out!

1st Witch. Here's the blood of a bat.

Hec. Put in that, O, put in that!

2nd Witch. Here's libbard's-bane.

Hec. Put in again!

1st Witch. The juice of toad, the oil of adder.

2nd Witch. Those will make the younker madder.

Hec. Put in—there's all—and rid the stench.

Fire. Nay, here's three ounces of the red-haired
　　wench.

All the Witches. Round, around, around, &c.

Hec. So, so, enough: into the vessel with it.
There, 't hath the true perfection. I'm so light
At any mischief! there's no villany
But is a tune, methinks.

Fire. A tune? 'tis to the tune of damnation then I warrant you, and that song hath a villanous burthen. [*Aside.*

---

[1] A plant mentioned by Pliny.

Hec. Come, my sweet sisters; let the air strike our
   tune,
Whilst we show reverence to yond peeping moon.
          [*They dance the Witches' Dance, and exeunt.*[1]

SCENE III.

An Apartment in the House of the Lord Governor.

Enter Lord Governor, ISABELLA, FLORIDA, SEBASTIAN,
          GASPARO, *and* Servants.

Isa. My lord, I've given you nothing but the truth
Of a most plain and innocent intent.
My wrongs being so apparent in this woman—

[1] Though some resemblance may be traced between the charms
in *Macbeth* and the incantations in this play, which is supposed to
have preceded it, this coincidence will not detract much from the
originality of Shakespeare. His witches are distinguished from the
witches of Middleton by essential differences. These are creatures
to whom man or woman plotting some dire mischief might re. ort
for occasional consultation. Those originate deeds of blood and
begin bad impulses to men. From the moment that their eyes
first meet with Macbeth's, he is spell-bound. That meeting sways
his destiny. He can never break the fascination. These witches
can hurt the body; those have power over the soul. Hecate in
Middleton has a son, a low buffoon : the hags of Shakespeare have
neither child of their own, nor seem to be descended from any
p rent. They are foul anomalies, of whom we know not whence
they are sprung, nor whether they have beginning or ending. As
they are without human passions, so they seem to be without human
relations. They come with thunder and lightning, and vanish to
airy music. This is all we know of them. Except Hecate, they
have no names; which heightens their mysteriousness. The names
and some of the properties which Middleton has given to his hags
excite smiles. The Weird Sisters are serious things. Their
presence cannot coexist with mirth. But, in a lesser degree, the
witches of Middleton are fine creations. Their power too is, in
some measure, over the mind. They raise jars, jealousies, strifes,
like a thick scurf o'er life.—Charles Lamb.

A creature that robs wedlock of all comfort,
Where'er she fastens—I could do no less
But seek means privately to shame his folly.
No farther reached my malice ; and it glads me
That none but my base injurer is found
To be my false accuser.

  Gov. This is strange,
That he should give the wrongs, yet seek revenge.—
But, sirrah, you ; you are accused here doubly :
First, by your lady, for a false intelligence
That caused her absence, which much hurts her name,
Though her intents were blameless ; next, by this
    woman,
For an adulterous design and plot
Practised between you to entrap her honour,
Whilst she, for her hire, should enjoy her husband.
Your answer.

  Seb. Part of this is truth, my lord,
To which I'm guilty in a rash intent,
But clear in act ; and she most clear in both,
Not sanctity more spotless.

Enter HERMIO.

  Her. O, my lord !
  Gov. What news breaks there ?
  Her. Of strange destruction :
Here stands the lady that within this hour
Was made a widow.

  Gov. How ?
  Her. Your niece, my lord.
A fearful, unexpected accident
Brought death to meet his fury : for my lord
Entering Fernando's house, like a raised tempest,
Which nothing heeds but its own violent rage,
Blinded with wrath and jealousy, which scorn guides,
From a false trap-door fell into a depth

Exceeds a temple's height, which takes into it
Part of the dungeon that falls three-score fathom
Under the castle.

  Gov. O you seed of lust,
Wrongs and revenges wrongful, with what terrors
You do present yourselves to wretched man
When his soul least expects you !

  Isa. I forgive him
All his wrongs now, and sign it with my pity.

  Flo. O my sweet servant !   [*Swoons.*

  Gov. Look to yond light mistress.

  Gas. She's in a swoon, my lord.

  Gov. Convey her hence :
It is a sight would grieve the modest eye
To see a strumpet's soul sink into passion[1]
For him that was the husband of another.——

      [Servants *remove* FLORIDA.
Yet all this clears not you.

  Seb. Thanks to Heaven
That I am now of age to clear myself then.

      [*Discovers himself.*

  Gov. Sebastian !

  Seb. The same much wronged, sir.

  Isa. Am I certain
Of what mine eye takes joy to look upon ?

  Seb. Your service cannot alter me from knowledge ;
I am your servant ever.

  Gov. Welcome to life, sir.——
Gaspar, thou swor'st his death.

  Gas. I did indeed, my lord,
And have been since well paid for't : one forsworn mouth
Hath got me two or three more here.

  Seb. I was dead, sir,
Both to my joys and and all men's understanding,

     [1] **Violent grief.**

Till this my hour of life ; for 'twas my fortune
To make the first of my return to Urbin
A witness to that marriage ; since which time
I've walked beneath myself, and all my comforts
Like one on earth whose joys are laid above :
And though it had been offence small in me
T' enjoy mine own, I left her pure and free.
   Gov. The greater and more sacred is thy blessing ;
For where Heaven's bounty holy ground-work finds,
'Tis like a sea, encompassing chaste minds.
   Her. The duchess comes, my lord.

      Enter Duchess *and* AMORETTA.

   Gov. Be you then all witnesses
Of an intent most horrid.
   Duch. One poor night,
Ever[1] Almachildes now.
Better his meaner fortunes wept than ours,
That took the true height of a princess' spirit
To match unto their greatness.   Such lives as his
Were only made to break the force of fate
Ere it came at us, and receive the venom.
'Tis but a usual friendship for a mistress
To lose some forty years' life in hopeful time,
And hazard an eternal soul for ever :
As young as he has done't, and more desertful.   [*Aside.*
   Gov. Madam.
   Duch. My lord ?
   Gov. This is the hour that I've so long desired .
The tumult's full appeased : now may we both
Exchange embraces with a fortunate arm,
And practise to make love-knots, thus.
      [*A curtain is drawn, and the* Duke *discovered
        on a couch, as if dead.*

      [1] This passage is corrupt.
   Mid. II.   O

Duch. My lord !

Gov. Thus, lustful woman and bold murderess, thus.
Blessed powers,
To make my loyalty and truth so happy !
Look thee, thou shame of greatness, stain of honour,
Behold thy work, and weep before thy death !
If thou be'st blest with sorrow and a conscience,
Which is a gift from Heaven, and seldom knocks
At any murderer's breast with sounds of comfort,
See this thy worthy and unequalled piece ;
A fair encouragement for another husband !

Duch. Bestow me upon death, sir ; I am guilty,
And of a cruelty above my cause :
His injury was too low for my revenge.
Perform a justice that may light all others
To noble actions : life is hateful to me,
Beholding my dead lord.   Make us an one
In death, whom marriage made one of two living,
Till cursèd fury parted us : my lord,
I covet to be like him.

Gov. No, my sword
Shall never stain the virgin brightness on't
With blood of an adulteress.

Duch. There, my lord,
I dare my accusers, and defy the world,
Death, shame, and torment : blood I'm guilty of,
But not adultery, not the breach of honour.

Gov. No ?—Come forth, Almachildes !

Enter ALMACHILDES.

Duch. Almachildes ?
Hath time brought him about to save himself
By my destruction ?   I am justly doomed.

Gov. Do you know this woman ?

Alm. I've known her better, sir, than at this time.

Gov. But she defies you there.

Alm. That's the common trick of them all.

Duch. Nay, since I'm touched so near, before my
  death then,
In right of honour's innocence, I'm bold
To call Heaven and my woman here to witness.
My lord, let her speak truth, or may she perish !

Amo. Then, sir, by all the hopes of a maid's comfort
Either in faithful service or blest marriage,
The woman that his blinded folly knew
Was only a hired strumpet, a professor
Of lust and impudence, which here is ready
To approve what I have spoken.

Alm. A common strumpet ?
This comes of scarfs : I'll never more wear
An haberdasher's shop before mine eyes again.

Gov. My sword is proud thou'rt lightened of that sin :
Die then a murderess only !

Duke. [*Rising and embracing her.*] Live a duchess !
Better than never loved, embraced, and honoured.

Duch. My lord !

Duke. Nay, since in honour thou canst justly rise,
Vanish all wrongs, thy former practice dies !—
I thank thee, Almachildes, for my life,
This lord for truth, and Heaven for such a wife,
Who, though her intent sinned, yet she makes amends
With grief and honour, virtue's noblest ends.—
What grieved you then shall never more offend you ;
Your father's skull with honour we'll inter,
And give the peace due to the sepulchre :
And in all times may this day ever prove
A day of triumph, joy, and honest love !   [*Exeunt.*

A FAIR QUARREL

 *FAIR QUARREL*, written by Middleton
and Rowley, was published in 1617, "as
it was acted before the King and divers
times publikely by the Prince his High-
nes Servants." A second edition, "with
new additions of Mr Chough's and Trimtram's Roaring, and the Baud's Song,"
appeared in the same year. Another edition
followed in 1622.

TO THE NOBLY DISPOSED, VIRTUOUS, AND
FAITHFUL-BREASTED

ROBERT GREY, Esquire,

ONE OF THE GROOMS OF HIS HIGHNESS' BED-CHAMBER,

His poor well-willer wisheth his best wishes, hic et supra.

Worthy Sir,

IS but a play, and a play is but a butt, against which many shoot many arrows of envy; 'tis the weaker part, and how much more noble shall it be in you to defend it: yet if it be (as some philosophers have left behind 'em), that this megacosm, this great world, is no more than a stage, where every one must act his part, you shall of necessity have many partakers, some long, some short, some indifferent, all some; whilst indeed the players themselves have the least part of it, for I know few that have lands (which are a part of the world), and therefore no grounded men; but howsoever they serve for mutes, happily they must wear good clothes for attendance, yet all have exits, and must all be stripped in the tiring-house (viz. the grave), for none must carry any thing out of the stock. You see, sir, I write as I speak, and I speak as I am, and that's excuse enough for me. I did not mean to write an epistle of praise to you; it looks so like a thing I know you love not, flattery, which you exceedingly hate actively, and unpleasingly accept passively: indeed, I meant to tell you your own, that is, that this child of the Muses is yours: whoever begat it, 'tis laid to your charge, and, for aught I know, you must father and keep it too: if it please you, I hope you shall not be ashamed of it neither, for it has been seen, though I say it, in good companies, and many have said it is a handsome, pretty-spoken infant. Now be your own judge; at your leisure look on it, at your pleasure laugh at it; and if you be sorry it is no better, you may be glad it is no bigger.

Yours ever,

WILLIAM ROWLEY.

DRAMATIS PERSONÆ.

RUSSELL, brother of Lady AGER and father of JANE.
The Colonel.
Captain AGER, son of Lady AGER.
Friends of the Colonel.
Friends of Captain AGER.
FITZALLEN, privately married to JANE.
CHOUGH, a Cornish gentleman.
TRIMTRAM, his servant.
Physician.
Surgeon.
Usher of the Roaring School.
Captain ALBO, a pander.
VAPOUR, a tobacco-seller.
Sergeants, Roarers, Servants.

Lady AGER, mother of the Captain, and sister of RUSSELL.
JANE, daughter of RUSSELL, and privately married to
      FITZALLEN.
The Colonel's sister.
ANNE, sister of the physician.
Dutch Nurse.
MEG, a bawd.
PRISS, a harlot.

SCENE—LONDON and its Neighbourhood.

A FAIR QUARREL.

ACT THE FIRST.

SCENE I.

A Court before RUSSELL'S *House.*

Enter RUSSELL

RUS. It must be all my care ; there's all
    my love,
    And that pulls on the t'other. Had
      I been left
    In a son behind me, while I had been
      here
    He should have shifted as I did before
Lived on the freeborn portion of his wit ;   [him,
But a daughter, and that an only one,—O,
We cannot be too careful o' her, too tender :
'Tis such
A brittle niceness, a mere cupboard of glasses,
The least shake breaks or cracks 'em. All my aim is
To cast her upon riches ; that's the thing
We rich men call perfection ; for the world
Can perfect nought without it : 'tis not neatness,
Either in handsome wit or handsome outside,

With which one gentleman, far in debt, has courted
    her ;
Which boldness he shall rue.   He thinks me blind
And ignorant : I've let him play a long time,
Seemed to believe his worth, which I know nothing :
He may perhaps laugh at my easy confidence,
Which closely I requite upon his fondness
For this hour snaps him ; and before his mistress,
His saint, forsooth, which he inscribes my girl,
He shall be rudely taken and disgraced.
The trick will prove an everlasting scarecrow
To fright poor gallants from our rich men's daughters.

Enter Lady AGER *and two* Servants.

Sister ! I've such a joy to make you a welome of,
Better you never tasted.
    Lady Ager. Good, sir, spare it not.
    Rus. Colonel's come, and your son Captain Ager.
    Lady Ager. My son ?   [*Weeps.*
    Rus. I know your eye would be first served ;
That's the soul's taster still for grief or joy.
    Lady Ager. O, if a mother's dear suit may prevail witn
    him,
From England he shall never part again !
    Rus. No question he'll be ruled, and grant you that.
    Lady Ager. I'll bring all my desires to that request.
                        [*Exit with* Servants.
    Rus. Affectionate sister ! she has no daughter now ;
It follows all the love must come to him,
And he has a worth deserves it, were it dearer.

Enter Friend *of the* Colonel *and* Friend *of*
Captain AGER.

    Col.'s Fr. I must give way to't.
    Rus. What's here to question ?   [*Aside.*

Col.'s Fr. Compare young Captain Ager with the
    colonel !

Cap.'s Fr. Young ? why, do you
Make youth stand for an imputation ?
That which you now produce for his disgrace
Infers his nobleness, that, being young,
Should have an anger more inclined to courage
And moderation than the colonel ;
A virtue as rarè as chastity in youth ;
And let the cause be good—conscience in him,
Which ever crowns his acts, and is indeed
Valour's prosperity—he dares then as much
As ever made him famous that you plead for.

    Col.'s Fr. Then I forbear too long.

    Cap.'s Fr. His worth for me !   [*They fight.*

    Rus. Here's noble youths ! belike some wench has
    crossed 'em,
And now they know not what to do with their blood.
                              [*Aside.*

     Enter the Colonel *and* Captain AGER.

    Col. How now ?

    Cap. Ager. Hold, hold ! what's the incitement ?

    Col. So serious at your game ! come, come, the
    quarrel ?

    Col.'s Fr. Nothing, good faith, sir.

    Col. Nothing ? and you bleed ?

    Col.'s Fr. Bleed ! where ? pish, a little scratch by
    chance, sir.

    Col. What need this niceness,[1] when you know so
    well
That I must know these things, and truly know 'em ?
Your daintiness makes me but more impatient ;
This strange concealment frets me.

    Col.'s Fr. Words did pass

               [1] Scrupulousness.

Which I was bound to answer, as my opinion
And love instructed me ;
And should I take in general fame into 'em,
I think I should commit no error in't.

 Col. What words, sir, and of whom ?

 Col.'s Fr. This gentleman
Paralleled Captain Ager's worth with yours.

 Col. With mine ?

 Col.'s Fr. It was a thing I could not listen to
With any patience.

 Cap. Ager. What should ail you, sir ?
There was little wrong done to your friend i' that.

 Col. How ? little wrong to me ?

 Cap. Ager. I said so, friend,
And I suppose that you'll esteem it so.

 Col. Comparisons !

 Cap. Ager. Why, sir, 'twixt friend and friend
There is so even and level a degree,
I will admit of no superlative.

 Col. Not in terms of manhood ?

 Rus. [*Coming forward.*] Nay, gentlemen——

 Col. Good sir, give me leave—in terms of manhood,
What can you dispute more questionable ?
You're a captain, sir ; I give you all your due.

 Cap. Ager. And you are a colonel, a title
Which may include within it many captains :
Yet, sir, but throwing by those titular shadows,
Which add no substance to the men themselves,
And take them uncompounded, man and man,
They may be so with fair equality.

 Col. You're a boy, sir !

 Cap. Ager. And you have a beard, sir :
Virginity and marriage are both worthy ;
And the positive purity there are some
Have made the nobler.

 Col. How now ?

Rus. Nay, good sir——

Cap. Ager. I shrink not ; he that goes the foremost may

Be overtaken.

Col. Death, how am I weighed !

Cap. Ager. In an even balance, sir ; a beard put in
Gives but a small advantage : man and man,
And lift the scales.

Col. Patience shall be my curse,
If it ride me further !   [*They draw their swords.*

Rus. How now, gallants ?
Believe me then, I must give aim[1] no longer :
Can words beget swords, and bring 'em forth, ha ?
Come, they're abortive propagations ;
Hide 'em, for shame !   I had thought soldiers
Had been musical, would not strike out of time,
But to the consort[2] of drum, trumps, and fife :
Tis madman-like to dance without music,
And most unpleasing shows to the beholders,
A Lydian ditty to a Doric note.
Friends embrace with steel hands ! fie, it meets too hard !
I must have those encounters here debarred.

Col. Shall I lose here what I have safe brought home
Through many dangers ?

Cap. Ager. What's that, sir ?

Col. My fame,
Life of the life, my reputation.
Death ! I am squared and measured out ;
My heights, depths, breadth, all my dimensions taken !
Sure I have yet beyond your astrolabe
A spirit unbounded.

Cap. Ager. Sir, you might weigh——

Rus. Tush !

----

[1] See note *ante*, p. 41.   [2] Concert.

All this is weighing fire, vain and fruitless :
The further it runs into argument,
The further plunged ; beseech you, no more on't.
I have a little claim, sir, in your blood,
As near as the brother to your mother,
If that may serve for power to move your quiet :
The rest I shall make up with courtesy
And an uncle's love.

    Cap. Ager. I have done, sir, but— —
    Rus. But ? I'll have no more shooting at these butts.
    Col. We'll to pricks[1] when he please.
    Rus. You rove all still.
Sir, I have no motive proof to disgest[2]
Your raisèd choler back into temperate blood ;
But if you'll make mine age a counsellor,—
As all ages have hitherto allowed it,
Wisdom in men grows up as years increase,—
You shall make me blessèd in making peace,
And do your judgment right.

    Col. In peace at home
Grey hairs are senators, but to determine
Soldiers and their actions——

            Enter FITZALLEN *and* JANE.

    Rus. 'Tis peace here, sir :
And see, here comes a happy interim ;
Here enters now a scene of loving arms ;
This couple will not quarrel so.

    Col.'s Fr. Be advised, sir ;
This gentleman, Fitzallen, is your kinsman ;
You may o'erthrow his long-laboured fortunes
With one angry minute, 'tis a rich churl,

---

  [1] The " prick " was the point or mark in the centre of the butts.
To " rove " was to shoot an arrow in an upward direction,
not point-blank.
  [2] Digest.

And this his sole inheritrix ; blast not
His hopes with this tempest.
    Col. It shall calm me :
All the town's conjurers and their demons could not
Have laid my spirit so.
    Fitz. Worthy coz,
I gratulate your fair return to peace !
Your swift fame was at home long before you.
    Col. It meets, I hope, your happy fortunes here,
And I am glad in't.   I must salute your joys, coz.
With a soldier's encounter   [*Kisses* JANE.
    Fitz. Worthy Captain Ager !
I hope, my kinsman shortly.
    Rus. You must come short indeed,
Or the length of my device will be ill-shrunk.—   [*Aside.*
Why, now it shows finely !   I'll tell you, sir,—
Sir ?—nay, son, I know, i' the end 'twill be so—
    Fitz. I hope so, sir.
    Rus. Hope ? nay, 'tis past all hope, son :
Here has been such a stormy encounter 'twixt
My cousin[1] captain and this brave colonel,
About I know not what—nothing indeed—
Competitions, degrees, and comparatives
Of soldiership ; but this smooth passage of love
Has calmed it all.—Come, I will have it sound ;
Let me see your hearts combined in your hands,
And then I will believe the league is good :
It shall be the grape's, if we drink any blood.
    Col. I have no anger, sir.
    Cap. Ager. I have had none,
My blood has not yet rose to a quarrel ;
Nor have you had cause——
    Col. No cause of quarrel ?
Death ! if my father should tell me so——

---

[1] Cousin was used familiarly to express various degrees of relationship.

Rus. Again ?

Fitz. Good sir, for my sake——

Col. Faith, I have done, coz ;

You do too hastily believe mine anger :
And yet, to say diminiting[1] valour
In a soldier is no cause of quarrel——

    Rus. Nay, then, I'll remove the cause, to kill the effect.

Kinsman, I'll press you to't, if either love
Or consanguinity may move you to't.
I must disarm you ; though ye are a soldier,
Pray, grant me your weapon ; it shall be safe

                [Takes Captain AGER'S *sword.*

At your regress from my house.   Now I know
No words can move this noble soldier's sword
To a man undefenced so : we shall parley,
And safely make all perfect friends again.

    Col. To show my will, sir, accept mine to you ;

                [Gives his sword to RUSSELL.

As good not wear it as not dare to use it.

    Col.'s Fr. Nay, then, sir, we will be all exampled ;
We'll have no arms here now but lovers' arms.

                [Gives his sword to RUSSELL.

    Cap.'s Fr. No seconds must begin a quarrel : take
        mine, sir.   *[Gives his sword to* RUSSELL.

    Rus. Why, la, what a fine sunshine's here !   these clouds

My breath has blown into another climate.
I'll be your armourer ; they are not pawned.—
These were the fish that I did angle for ;
I have caught 'em finely.   Now for my trick ;
My project's lusty, and will hit the nick.

                [Exit with weapon.

    Col. What, is't a match, beauty ?   I would now have
Alliance with my worthy Captain Ager,

            [1] Diminishing.

To knit our loves the faster : here is witness
Enough, if you confirm it now.

   Jane. Sir, my voice
Was long since given, since that I gave my hand.

   Col. Would you had sealed too !

   Jane. That wish comes too late,   [*Aside.*
For I too soon fear my delivery.——
My father's hand sticks yet, sir ; you may now
Challenge a lawful interest in his :
He took your hand from your enragèd blood,
And gave it freely to your opposite,
My cousin Ager : methinks you should claim from
       him,
In the less quality of calmer blood,
To join the hands of two divided friends,
Even these two that would offer willingly
Their own embrace.

   Col.'s Fr. Troth, she instructs you well,
Colonel, and you shall do a lover's part
Worth one brave act of valour.

   Col. Why, I did
Misdoubt no scruple ; is there doubt in it ?

   Fitz. Faith, sir, delays, which at the least are doubts ;
But here's a constant resolution fixed,
Which we wish willingly he would accord to.

   Col. Tush, he shall do't, I will not be denied ;
He owes me so much in the recompense
Of my reconcilement.—Captain Ager,
You will take our parts against your uncle
In this quarrel ?

   Cap. Ager. I shall do my best, sir ;
Two denials shall not repulse me : I love
Your worthy kinsman, and wish him mine ; I know
He doubts it not.

   Col. See, he's returned.

     Mid. II.   P

Re-enter RUSSELL *with* Servant.

Rus. Your cue,
Be sure you keep it ; 'twill be spoken quickly,
Therefore watch it.   [*Exit* Servant.

   Col. Let's set on him all at once.

   All. Sir, we have a suit to you.

   Rus. What, all at once ?

   All. All, all, i'faith, sir.

   Rus. One speaker may yet deliver : say, say ;
I shall not dare to stand out 'gainst so many.

   Col. Faith, sir, here's a brabbling[1] matter hangs on
     demur ;
I make the motion for all without a fee ;
Pray you, let it be ended this term.

   Rus. Ha, ha, ha !—
That is the rascal's cue, and he has missed it.—   [*Aside.*
What is't, what is't, sir ?

   Col. Why, sir, here's a man
And here's a woman—you're scholar good enough—
Put 'em together, and tell me what it spells ?

   Rus. Ha, ha, ha !—
There's his cue once again :

Re-enter Servant.

             O, he's come—humph !   [*Aside.*

   Ser. My master laughs ; that is his cue to mischief.
                             [*Aside.*

   Col. What say you, sir ?

   Ser. Sir——

   Rus. Ha ! what say you, sir ?

   Ser. Sir, there's a couple desire speedily to speak
     with you.

   Rus. A couple, sir, of what ? hounds or horses ?

   Ser. Men, sir ; gentlemen or yeomen, I know not
     which,

              [1] Brawling.

But the one, sure, they are.

Rus. Hast thou no other description of them ?

Ser. They come with commission, they say, sir, to
taste of your earth ; if they like it, they'll turn it into
gunpowder.

Rus. O, they are saltpetre-men—before me, [1]
And they bring commission, the king's power indeed ! [2]
They must have entrance : but the knaves will be bribed ;
There's all the hope we have in officers ;
They were too dangerous in a commonwealth,
But that they will be very well corrupted ;
Necessary varlets.

Ser. Shall I enter in, [3] sir ?

Rus. By all fair means, sir,
And with all speed, sir : give 'em very good words,
To save my ground unravished, unbroke up :
Mine's yet   [*Exit* Servant.
A virgin earth ; the worm hath not been seen
To wriggle in her chaste bowels, and I'd be loth
A gunpowder fellow should deflower her now.

Col. Our suit is yet delayed by this means, sir.

Rus. Alas ! I cannot help it ! these fellows gone
As I hope I shall despatch 'em quickly,
A few articles shall conclude your suit :
Who ? Master Fitzallen ? the only man
That my adoption aims at.

Col. There's good hope then.

---

[1] A form of asseveration.

[2] In October, 1595, the Lord Mayor wrote to the Lords in Council
to protest against the high-handed way in which the saltpetre
men executed their commission. . . . . " Before the discovery and importation of Indian nitre, saltpetre was manufactured
from earth impregnated with animal matter, and, being the chief
ingredient of gunpowder, was claimed by the Government.
. . . . and the saltpetre-man was empowered to break open
all premises, and to dig up the floors of stables, and even dwelling
houses."—*Remembrancia—Bullen.*

[3] *i.e.* Show them in.

Enter two Sergeants *in disguise*

1st Serg. Save you, sir.

Rus. You are welcome, sir, for aught I know yet.

2nd Serg. We come to take a view and taste of your
  ground, sir.

Rus. I'd rather feed you with better meat, gentlemen ;
But do your pleasures, pray.

1st Serg. This is our pleasures :—We arrest you, sir,
In the king's name.   [*They arrest* FITZALLEN.

Fitz. Ha ! at whose suit ?

Rus. How's that ?

Col. Our weapons, good sir, furnish us !

Jane. Ay me !

Rus. Stay, stay, gentlemen, let's inquire the cause :
It may be but a trifle ; a small debt
Shall need no rescue here.

2nd Serg. Sir, betwixt three creditors, Master Leach,
Master Swallow, and Master Bonesuck, the debts are a
thousand pounds.

Rus. A thousand pounds ! beshrew me, a good man's
  substance !

Col. Good sir, our weapons ! we'll teach these varlets
  to walk.
In their own parti-coloured coats, that they
May be distinguishèd from honest men.

1st Serg. Sir, attempt no rescue ; he's our prisoner :
You'll make the danger worse by violence.

Col. A plague upon your gunpowder-treason,
Ye quick-damned varlets ! is this your saltpetre-proving,
Your tasting earth ? would you might ne'er feed better,
Nor none of your catchpoll tribe !—Our weapons, good
We'll yet deliver him.   [sir !

Rus. Pardon me, sir ;
I dare not suffer rescue here,

At least not by so great an accessary
As to furnish you : had you had your weapons—
But to see the ill fate on't !—My fine trick, i'faith !
Let beggars beware to love rich men's daughters :
I'll teach 'em the new morrice ; I learnt it myself
Of another careful father.

    Fitz. May I not be bailed ?

    2nd Serg. Yes, but not with swords.

    Col. Slaves, here are sufficient men !

    1st Serg. Ay, i' the field,
But not in the city.—Sir, if this gentleman
Will be one, we'll easily admit the second.

    Rus. Who, I ? sir, pray, pardon me : I am wronged,
Very much wronged in this ; I must needs speak it.—
Sir, you have not dealt like an honest lover
With me nor my child : here you boast to me
Of a great revenue, a large substance,
Wherein you would endow and state my daughter :
Had I missed this, my opinion yet
Thought you a frugal man, to understand
The sure wards against all necessities ;
Boldly to defend your wife and family,
To walk unmuffled, dreadless of these flesh-hooks,
Even in the daring'st streets through all the city ;
But now I find you a loose prodigal,
A large unthrift : a whole thousand pound !
Come from him, girl, his inside is not sound.

    Fitz. Sir, I am wronged ; these are malicious plots
Of some obscure enemies that I have ;
These debts are none of mine.

    Rus. Ay, all say so :
Perhaps you stand engaged for other men ;
If so you do, you must then call't your own :
The like arrearage do I run into
Should I bail you ; but I have vowed against it,
And I will keep my vows ; that is religious.

Fitz. All this is nothing so, sir.

Rus. Nothing so?
By my faith, 'tis, sir; my vows are firm.

Fitz. I neither
Owe these debts, nor am I engaged for others.

Rus. The easier is your liberty regained:
These appear proofs to me.

Col. Liberty, sir?
I hope you will not see him go to prison.

Rus. I do not mean to bear him company
So far, but I will see him out of my doors:
O, sir, let him go to prison! 'tis a school
To tame wild bloods, he'll be much better for't.

Col. Better for lying in prison?

Rus. In prison; believe it,
Many an honest man lies in prison, else all
The keepers are knaves; they told me so themselves.

Col. Sir, I do now suspect you have betrayed him
And us, to cause us to be weaponless:
If it be so, you're a blood-sucking churl,
One that was born in a great frost, when charity
Could not stir a finger; and you shall die
In heat of a burning fever i' the dog-days,
To begin your hell to you: I've said your grace for you;
Now get you to supper as soon as you can;
Pluto, the master of the house, is set already.

Cap. Ager. Sir, you do wrong mine uncle.

Col. Pox on your uncle
And all his kin! if my kinsman mingle
No blood with him.

Cap. Ager. You are a foul-mouthed fellow!

Col. Foul-mouthed I will be—thou'rt the son of a
whore!

Cap. Ager. Ha! whore? plagues and furies! I'll
thrust that back,
Or pluck thy heart out after!—son of a whore?

Col. On thy life I'll prove it.

Cap. Ager. Death, I am naked!—
Uncle, I'll give you my left hand for my sword
To arm my right with—O, this fire will flame me
Into present ashes!

Col. Sir, give us weapons;
We ask our own; you will not rob us of them?

Rus. No, sir, but still restrain your furies here:
At my door I'll give you them, nor at this time
My nephew's; a time will better suit you:
And I must tell you, sir, you have spoke swords,
And 'gainst the law of arms, poisoned the blades,
And with them wounded the reputation
Of an unblemished woman: would you were out of my
        doors!

Col. Pox on your doors, and let it run all your house
Give me my sword!   [o'er!

Cap. Ager. We shall meet, colonel?

Col. Yes, better provided: to spur thee more,
I do repeat my words—son of a whore!
                              [*Exit with his* Friend.

Cap.'s Fr. Come, sir; 'tis no worse than it was; you can
Do nothing now.   [*Exit with* Captain AGER.

Rus. No, I'll bar him now.—Away with that beggar!
                                             [*Exit.*

Jane. Good sir,
Let this persuade you for two minutes' stay:
At this price, I know, you can wait all day.
                              [*Giving money.*

1st Serg. You know the remora[1] that stays our ship
    always.

Jane. Your ship sinks many when this hold let's go.—
O my Fitzallen! what is to be done?

Fitz. To be still thine is all my part to be,
Whether in freedom or captivity.

                    [1] Barnacle.

Jane. But art thou so engaged as this pretends?

Fitz. By Heaven, sweet Jane, 'tis all a hellish plot
Your cruel-smiling father all this while
Has candied o'er a bitter pill for me;
Thinking by my remove to plant some other,
And then let go his fangs.

Jane. Plant some other?
Thou hast too firmly stamped me for thine own,
Ever to be rased out : I am not current
In any other's hand ; I fear too soon
I shall discover it.

Fitz. Let come the worst ;
Bind but this knot with an unloosèd line,
I will be still thine own.

Jane. And I'll be thine.

1st Serg. My watch has gone two minutes, master.

Fitz. It shall not be renewed ; I go, sir—Farewell !

Jane. Farewell ! we both are prisoned, though not
        together ;
But here's the difference in our luckless chance,
I fear mine own, wish thy deliverance.

Fitz. Our hearts shall hourly visit : I'll send to thee ;
Then 'tis no prison where the mind is free.

[Exit with Sergeants.

Re-enter RUSSELL.

Rus. So, let him go !—Now, wench, I bring thee joys,
A fair sunshine after this angry storm.
It was my policy to remove this beggar :
What ? shall rich men wed their only daughters
To two fair suits of clothes, and perhaps yet
The poor tailor is unpaid ? no, no, my girl,
I have a lad of thousands coming in :
Suppose he have more wealth than wit to guide it,
Why, there's thy gains ; thou keep'st the keys of all,
Disposest all ; and for generation,

Man does most seldom stamp 'em from the brain ;
Wise men begets fools, and fools are the fathers
To many wise children ; *hysteron proteron,*
A great scholar may beget an idiot,
And from the plough-tail may come a great scholar ;
Nay, they are frequent propagations.

 Jane. I am not well, sir.

 Rus. Ha ! not well, my girl ?
Thou shalt have a physician then,
The best that gold can fetch upon his footcloth,[1]
Thou know'st my tender pity to thee ever ;
Want nothing that thy wishes can instruct thee
To call for,—'fore me, and thou look'st half-ill indeed !
But I'll bring one within a day to thee
Shall rouse thee up, for he's come up already ;
One Master Chough, a Cornish gentleman ;
Has as much land of his own fee-simple
As a crow can fly over in half a day :
And now I think on't, at the Crow at Aldgate
His lodging is :—he shall so stir thee up !—
Come, come, be cheered ! think of thy preferment :
Honour and attendance, these will bring thee health :
And the way to 'em is to climb by wealth.   [*Exeunt.*

[1] Long cloth housings (of a horse or mule) were formerly considered indispensable articles for a physician of standing.

ACT THE SECOND.

SCENE I.

A Room in Lady AGER'S *House.*

Enter Captain AGER.

CAP. AGER. The son of a whore !
There is not such another murdering-
piece[1]
In all the stock of calumny ; it kills
At one report two reputations,
A mother's and a son's. If it were
possible
That souls could fight after the bodies fell,
This was a quarrel for 'em ; he should be one, indeed,
That never heard of Heaven's joys or hell's torments,
To fight this out : I am too full of conscience,
Knowledge, and patience, to give justice to't ;
So careful of my eternity, which consists
Of upright actions, that unless I knew
It were a truth I stood for, any coward
Might make my breast his foot-pace : and who lives
That can assure the truth of his conception,
More than a mother's carriage makes it hopeful ?
And is't not miserable valour then,

[1] A small piece of artillery.

That man should hazard all upon things doubtful?
O, there's the cruelty of my foe's advantage!
Could but my soul resolve my cause were just,
Earth's mountain nor sea's surge should hide him from
    me!
E'en to hell's threshold would I follow him,
And see the slanderer in before I left him!
But as it is, it fears me; and I never
Appeared too conscionably just till now.
My good opinion of her life and virtues
Bids me go on, and fain would I be ruled by't;
But when my judgement tells me she's but woman,
Whose frailty let in death to all mankind,
My valour shrinks at that.   Certain, she's good;
There only wants but my assurance in't,
And all things then were perfect: how I thirst for't!
Here comes the only she that could resolve—
But 'tis too vile a question to demand indeed.

Enter Lady AGER.

Laay Ager. Son, I've a suit to you.
    Cap. Ager. That may do well.—   [*Aside.*
To me, good madam? you're most sure to speed in't,
Be't i' my power to grant it.
    Lady Ager. 'Tis my love
Makes the request, that you would never part
From England more.
    Cap. Ager. With all my heart 'tis granted!
I'm sure I'm i' the way never to part from't.   [*Aside.*
    Lady Ager. Where left you your dear friend the
        colonel?
    Cap. Ager. O, the dear colonel,—I should meet him
        soon.
    Lady Ager. O, fail him not then! he's a gentleman
The fame and reputation of your time
Is much engaged to.

Cap. Ager. Yes, an you knew all, mother.

Lady Ager. I thought I'd known so much of his fair
goodness,
More could not have been looked for.

Cap. Ager. O, yes, yes, madam,
And this his last exceeded all the rest.

Lady Ager. For gratitude's sake, let me know this, I
prithee !

Cap. Ager. Then thus ; and I aesire your censure[1]
freely,
Whether it appeared not a strange noble kindness in him.

Lady Ager. Trust me, I long to hear't.

Cap. Ager. You know he's hasty,—
That by the way.

Lady Ager. So are the best conditions ;[2]
Your father was the like.

Cap. Ager. I begin now
To doubt me more : why am not I so too then
Blood follows blood through forty generations,
And I've a slow-paced wrath—a shrewd dilemma

                                               [Aside.

Lady Ager. Well, as you were saying, sir——

Cap. Ager. Marry, thus, good madam :
There was in company a foul-mouthed villain—
Stay, stay,
Who should I liken him to that you have seen ?
He comes so near one that I would not match him with ;
Faith, just a' the colonel's pitch,[3] he's ne'er the worse
man ;
Usurers have been compared to magistrates,
Extortioners to lawyers, and the like ;
But they all prove ne'er the worse men for that.

Lady Ager. That's bad enough ; they need not.

Cap. Ager. This rude fellow,

---

[1] Judgment.   [2] Dispositions.   [3] Heigh

A shame to all humanity or manners,
Breathes from the rottenness of his gall and malice
The foulest stain that ever man's fame blemished ;
Part of which fell upon your honour, madam,
Which heightened my affliction.

    Lady Ager. Mine ? my honour, sir ?

    Cap. Ager. The colonel, soon enraged, as he's all
        touchwood,
Takes fire before me, makes the quarrel his,
Appoints the field : my wrath could not be heard,
His was so high-pitched, so gloriously mounted
Now, what's the friendly fear that fights within me,
Should his brave noble fury undertake
A cause that were unjust in our defence,
And so to lose him everlastingly
In that dark depth where all bad quarrels sink
Never to rise again, what pity 'twere
First to die here, and never to die there !

    Lady Ager. Why, what's the quarrel—speak, sir—that
        should raise
Such fearful doubt, my honour bearing part on't ?—
The words, whate'er they were.

    Cap. Ager. Son of a whore !

    Lady Ager. Thou liest   [*Strikes him.*
And were my love ten thousand times more to thee,
Which is as much now as e'er mother's was,
So thou should'st feel my anger.   Dost thou call
That quarrel doubtful ? where are all my merits ?
Not one stand up to tell this man his error ?
Thou might'st as well bring the sun's truth in question
As thy birth or my honour !

    Cap. Ager. Now blessings crown you for't !
It is the joyfull'st blow that e'er flesh felt.

    Lady Ager. Nay, stay, stay, sir ; thou art not left so
        soon :
This is no question to be slighted off,

And at your pleasure closed up fair again,
As though you'd never touched it : no, honour doubted
Is honour deeply wounded ; and it rages
More than a common smart, being of thy making ;
For thee to fear my truth, it kills my comfort :
Where should fame seek for her reward, when he
That is her own by the great tie of blood
Is farthest off in bounty ?   O poor goodness !
That only pay'st thyself with thy own works,
For nothing else look towards thee.   Tell me, pray,
Which of my loving cares dost thou requite
With this vile thought, which of my prayers or wishes ?
Many thou ow'st me for : this seven year hast thou
   known me
A widow, only married to my vow ;
That's no small witness of my faith and love
To him that in life was thy honoured father ;
And live I now to know that good mistrusted ?
 Cap. Ager. No ; 't shall appear that my belief is
  cheerful,
For never was a mother's reputation
Noblier defended : 'tis my joy and pride
I have a firm faith to bestow upon it.
 Lady Ager. What's that you said, sir ?
 Cap. Ager. 'Twere too bold and soon yet
To crave forgiveness of you : I'll earn it first :
Dead or alive I know I shall enjoy it.
 Lady Ager. What's all this, sir ?
 Cap. Ager. My joy's beyond expression !
I do but think how wretched I had been
Were this another's quarrel, and not mine.
 Lady Ager. Why, is it yours ?
 Cap. Ager. Mine ? think me not so miserable
Not to be mine ; then were I worse than abject,
More to be loathed than vileness or sin's dunghill :
Nor did I fear your goodness, faithful madam,

But come with greedy joy to be confirmed in't,
To give the nobler onset.   Then shines valour,
And admiration from her fixed sphere draws,
When it comes burnished with a righteous cause ;
Without which I'm ten fathoms under coward,
That now am ten degress above a man,
Which is but one of virtue's easiest wonders.

   Lady Ager. But, pray, stay ; all this while I understand you
The colonel was the man.

   Cap. Ager. Yes, he's the man,
The man of injury, reproach, and slander,
Which I must turn into his soul again.

   Lady Ager. The colonel do't ? that's strange !

   Cap. Ager. The villain did it ;
That's not so strange :—your blessing and your leave.

   Lady Ager. Come, come, you shall not go !

   Cap. Ager. Not go !   Were Death
Sent now to summons me to my eternity,
I'd put him off an hour ; why, the whole world
Has not chains strong enough to bind me from't :
The strongest is my reverence to you,
Which if you force upon me in this case,
I must be forced to break it.

   Lady Ager. Stay, I say !

   Cap. Ager. In anything command me but in this,
madam.

   Lady Ager. 'Las, I shall lose him ! [*Aside.*] You
will hear me first ?

   Cap. Ager. At my return I will.

   Lady Ager. You'll never hear me more, then.

   Cap. Ager. How ?

   Lady Ager. Come back, I say !
You may well think there's cause I call so often.

   Cap. Ager. Ha, cause ! what cause ?

   Lady Ager. So much, you must not go.

Cap. Ager. How?

Lady Ager. You must not go.

Cap. Ager. Must not! why?

Lady Ager. I know a reason for't,
Which I could wish you'd yield to, and not know;
If not, it must come forth: faith, do not know,
And yet obey my will.

Cap. Ager. Why, I desire
To know no other than the cause I have,
Nor should you wish it, if you take your injury,
For one more great I know the world includes not.

Lady Ager. Yes, one that makes this nothing: yet be
    ruled,
And if you understand not, seek no further.

Cap. Ager. I must; for this is nothing.

Lady Ager. Then take all;
And if amongst it you receive that secret
That will offend you, though you condemn me,
Yet blame yourself a little; for, perhaps,
I would have made my reputation sound
Upon another's hazard with less pity;
But upon yours I dare not.

Cap. Ager. How?

Lady Ager. I dare not:
'Twas your own seeking this.

Cap. Ager. If you mean evilly,
I cannot understand you; nor for all the riches
This life has, would I.

Lady Ager. Would you never might!

Cap. Ager. Why, 'tis your goodness that I joy to fight for.

Lady Ager. In that you neither right your joy nor me.

Cap. Ager. What an ill orator has virtue got here!
Why, shall I dare to think it a thing possible
That you were ever false?

Lady Ager. O, fearfully!
As much as you come to.

Cap. Ager. O silence, cover me!
I've felt a deadlier wound than man can give me.
False!
    Lady Ager. I was betrayed to a most sinful hour
By a corrupted soul I put in trust once,
A kinswoman.
    Cap. Ager. Where is she? let me pay her!
    Lady Ager. O, dead long since!
    Cap. Ager. Nay, then, sh'as all her wages.
False! do not say't, for honour's goodness, do not
You never could be so.   He I called father
Deserved you at your best, when youth and merit
Could boast at highest in you; y'had no grace
Or virtue that he matched not, no delight
That you invented but he sent it crowned
To your full-wishing soul.
    Lady Ager. That heaps my guiltiness.
    Cap. Ager. O, were you so unhappy to be false
Both to yourself and me? but to me chiefly.
What a day's hope is here lost! and with it
The joys of a just cause!   Had you but thought
On such a noble quarrel, you'd ha' died
Ere you'd ha' yielded; for the sin's hate first,
Next for the shame of this hour's cowardice.
Curst be the heat that lost me such a cause,
A work that I was made for!   Quench, my spirit,
And out with honour's flaming lights within thee!
Be dark and dead to all respects of manhood!
I never shall have use of valour more.
Put off your vow for shame! why should you hoard up
Such justice for a barren widowhood,
That was so injurious to the faith of wedlock?
                                   [*Exit* Lady AGER.
I should be dead, for all my life's work's ended;
I dare not fight a stroke now, nor engage
The noble resolution of my friends:
        Mid. II.   Q

Enter two Friends *of* Captain AGER.

That were more vile.—They're here : kill me, my shame!

　　　　　　　　　　　　　　　　　　　[*Aside.*

I am not for the fellowship of honour.

　　1st Fr. Captain! fie, come, sir! we've been seeking
　　　　for you

Very late to-day ; this was not wont to be :

Your enemy's i' the field.

　　Cap. Ager. Truth enters cheerfully.

　　2nd Fr. Good faith, sir, you've a royal quarrel on't.

　　Cap. Ager. Yes, in some other country, Spain or
　　　　Italy,

It would be held so.

　　1st Fr. How? and is't not here so?

　　Cap. Ager. 'Tis not so contumeliously received

In these parts, an you mark it.

　　1st Fr. Not in these?

Why, prithee, what is more, or can be?

　　Cap. Ager. Yes ;

That ordinary commotioner, the lie,

Is father of most quarrels in this climate,

And held here capital, an you go to that.

　　2nd Fr. But, sir, I hope you will not go to that,

Or change your own for it : son of a whore!

Why, there's the lie down to posterity,

The lie to birth, the lie to honesty.

Why would you cozen yourself so, and beguile

So brave a cause, manhood's best masterpiece?

Do you e'er hope for one so brave again?

　　Cap. Ager. Consider then the man, the colonel,

Exactly worthy, absolutely noble,

However spleen and rage abuses him ;

And 'tis not well or manly to pursue

A man's infirmity.

1st Fr. O miracle!
So hopeful, valiant, and complete a captain
Possessed with a tame devil! Come out! thou spoilest
The most improved young soldier of seven kingdoms;
Made captain at nineteen; which was deserved
The year before, but honour comes behind still:
Come out, I say! This was not wont to be;
That spirit ne'er stood in need of provocation,
Nor shall it now: away, sir!

   Cap. Ager. Urge me not.

   1st Fr. By manhood's reverend honour, but we
     must!

   Cap. Ager. I will not fight a stroke.

   1st Fr. O blasphemy
To sacred valour!

   Cap. Ager. Lead me where you list.

   1st Fr. Pardon this traitorous slumber, clogged with
     evils:

Give captains rather wives than such tame devils!

                        [Exeunt.

SCENE II.

A Room in RUSSELL'S *House.*

Enter Physician *and* JANE.

   Phy. Nay, mistress, you must not be covered to me;
The patient must ope to the physician
All her dearest sorrows: art is blinded else,
And cannot show her mystical effects.

   Jane. Can art be so dim-sighted, learnèd sir?
I did not think her so incapacious.

You train me, as I guess, like a conjuror,
One of our fine oraculous wizards,
Who, from the help of his examinant,
By the near guess of his suspicion,
Points out the thief by the marks he tells him.
Have you no skill in physiognomy?
What colour, says your coat, is my disease?
I am unmarried, and it cannot be yellow;[1]
If it be maiden-green, you cannot miss it.

  Phy. I cannot see that vacuum in your blood:
But, gentlewoman, if you love yourself,
Love my advice; be free and plain with me:
Where lies your grief?

    Jane. Where lies my grief indeed?
I cannot tell the truth, where my grief lies,
But my joy is imprisoned.

    Phy. This is mystical!

    Jane. Lord, what plain questions you make problems
      of!
Your art is such a regular highway,
That put you out of it, and you are lost:
My heart's imprisoned in my body, sir;
There is all my joy; and my sorrow too
Lies very near it.

  Phy. They are bad adjuncts;
Your joy and grief, lying so near together,
Can propagate no happy issue: remove
The one, and let it be the worst—your grief—
If you'll propose the best unto your joy.

    Jane. Why, now comes your skill: what physic for it?

    Phy. Now I have found you out; you are in love.

    Jane. I think I am: what's your appliance now?
Can all your Paracelsian mixtures cure it?
'T must be a surgeon of the civil law,
I fear, that must cure me.

              [1] The hue of jealousy.

Phy. Gentlewoman,
If you knew well my heart, you would not be
So circular;[1] the very common name
Of physician might reprove your niceness;[2]
We are as secret as your confessors,
And as firm obliged; 'tis a fine like death
For us to blab.
　　Jane. I will trust you; yet, sir,
I'd rather do it by attorney to you;
I else have blushes that will stop my tongue:
Have you no friend so friendly as yourself,
Of mine own sex, to whom I might impart
My sorrows to you at the second hand?
　　Phy. Why, la, there I hit you! and be confirmed
I'll give you such a bosom-counsellor,
That your own tongue shall be sooner false to you.
Make yourself unready,[3] and be naked to her;
I'll fetch her presently.　　　　　　　　　　[*Exit.*
　　Jane. I must reveal;
My shame will else take tongue, and speak before me;
'Tis a necessity impulsive drives me.
O my hard fate, but my more hard father,
That father of my fate!—a father, said I?
What a strange paradox I run into!
I must accuse two fathers of my fate
And fault, a reciprocal generation:
The father of my fault would have repaired
His faulty issue, but my fate's father hinders it:
Then fate and fault, wherever I begin,
I must blame both, and yet 'twas love did sin.

　　　　　Re-enter Physician *with* ANNE.

　　Phy. Look you, mistress, here's your closet; put in
What you please, you ever keep the key of it.

---

[1] Roundabout.　　[2] Scrupulousness.　　[3] Undress yourself.

Jane. Let me speak private, sir.

Phy. With all my heart;
I will be more than mine ears' length from you.

                                       [*Retires.*

Jane. You hold some endeared place with this gentleman?

Anne. He is my brother, forsooth, I his creature;
He does command me any lawful office,
Either in act or counsel.

Jane. I must not doubt you;
Your brother has protested secrecy,
And strengthened me in you: I must lay ope
A guilty sorrow to you; I'm with child.
'Tis no black swan I show you; these spots stick
Upon the face of many go for maids:
I that had face enough to do the deed,
Cannot want tongue to speak it; but 'tis to you,
Whom I accept my helper.

Anne. Mistress, 'tis locked
Within a castle that's invincible:
It is too late to wish it were undone.

Jane. I've scarce a wish within myself so strong,
For, understand me, 'tis not all so ill
As you may yet conceit [1] it: this deed was done
When Heaven had witness to the jugal [2] knot;
Only the barren ceremony wants,
Which by an adverse father is abridged.

Anne. Would my pity could help you!

Jane. Your counsel may.
My father yet shoots widest from my sorrow,
And, with a care indulgent, seeing me changed
From what I was, sends for your good brother
To find my grief, and practise remedy:
You know it, give it him; but if a fourth
Be added to this counsel, I will say

           [1] Suspect.   [2] Conjugal.

Ye're worse than you can call me at the worst,
At this advantage of my reputation.
    Anne. I will revive a reputation
That women long has lost; I will keep counsel:
I'll only now oblige my teeth to you,
And they shall bite the blabber, if it offer
To breathe on an offending syllable.
    Jane. I trust you; go, whisper.[1] Here comes my
        father.

Enter RUSSELL, CHOUGH, *and* TRIMTRAM.

    Rus. Sir, you are welcome, more, and most wel-
        come,
All the degrees of welcome; thrice welcome, sir.
    Chough. Is this your daughter, sir?
    Rus. Mine only joy, sir.
    Chough. I'll show her the Cornish hug, sir. [*Embraces
her.*] I have kissed you now, sweetheart, and I never
do any kindness to my friends but I use to hit 'em in
the teeth with it presently.
    Trim. My name is Trimtram, forsooth; look, what
my master does, I use to do the like.
                    [*Attempts to kiss* ANNE.
    Anne. You are deceived, sir; I am not this gentle-
woman's servant, to make your courtesy equal.
    Chough. You do not know me, mistress?
    Jane. No, indeed.—I doubt I shall learn too soon.
                                        [*Aside.*
    Chough. My name is Chough,[2] a Cornish gentleman;
my man's mine own countryman too, i'faith: I warrant
you took us for some of the small islanders.

---

[1] *i.e.* To your brother.
[2] Chough or chuff is a sea-bird, generally thought a stupid one,
common in Cornwall: and a *Cornish chough* appears to have been a
name for a silly fellow from the country.—*Dyce.*

Jane. I did indeed, between the Scotch and Irish.

Chough. Red-shanks?[1] I thought so, by my truth:
    no, truly,
We are right Cornish diamonds.

Trim. Yes, we cut
Out quarrels[2] and break glasses where we go.

Phy. [*Conversing apart with* ANNE.] If it be hidden
    from her father, yet
His ignorance understands well his knowledge,
For this I guess to be some rich coxcomb
He'd put upon his daughter.

Anne. That's plainly so.

Phy. Then only she's beholding to our help
For the close delivery of her burden,
Else all's overthrown.

Anne. And, pray, be faithful in that, sir.

Phy. Tush, we physicians are the truest
Alchemists, that from the ore and dross of sin
Can new distil a maidenhead again.

Rus. How do you like her, sir?

Chough. Troth, I do like her, sir, in the way of comparison, to anything that a man would desire; I am as high as the Mount[3] in love with her already, and that's as far as I can go by land; but I hope to go farther by water with her one day.

Rus. I tell you, sir, she has lost some colour
By wrestling with a peevish sickness now of late.

Chough. Wrestle? nay, an she love wrestling, I'll teach her a trick to overthrow any peevish sickness in London, whate'er it be.

Rus. Well, she had a rich beauty, though I say't;
Nor is it lost; a little thing repairs it.

---

[1] A contemptuous term applied to the Scottish Highlanders and native Irish, from their going barelegged.

[2] Square-shaped panes of glass.

[3] St. Michael's Mount in Cornwall.

Chough. She shall command the best thing that I
    have.
In Middlesex, i'faith.

Rus. Well, sir, talk with her;
Give her a relish of your good liking to her;
You shall have time and free
Access to finish what you now begin.

Jane. What means my father? my love's unjust
    restraint,
My shame, were it published, both together
Could not afflict me like this odious fool:
Now I see why he hated my Fitzallen.   [*Aside.*

Chough. Sweet lady, your father says you are a
wrestler: if you love that sport, I love you the better:
i'faith, I love it as well as I love my meat after supper;
'tis indeed meat, drink, and cloth to me.

Jane. Methinks it should tear your clothes, sir.

Chough. Not a rag, i'faith.—Trimtram, hold my cloak.
[*Gives his cloak to* TRIMTRAM.]—I'll wrestle a fall with
you now; I'll show you a trick that you never saw in
your life.

Jane. O, good sir, forbear! I am no wrestler.

Phy. Good sir, take heed, you'll hurt the gentle-
    woman.

Chough. I will not catch beneath the waist, believe
    it;
I know fair play.

Jane. 'Tis no woman's exercise in London, sir.

Chough. I'll ne'er believe that: the hug and the lock
between man and woman, with a fair fall, is as sweet
an exercise for the body as you'll desire in a summer's
evening.

Phy. Sir, the gentlewoman is not well.

Chough. It may be you are a physician, sir?

Phy. 'Tis so, sir.

Chough. I say, then, and I'll stand to't, three ounces

of wrestling with two hips, a yard of a green gown[1] put
together in the inturn, is as good a medicine for the
green sickness as ever breathed.

    Trim. Come, sir, take your cloak again; I see here
will be ne'er a match.   [*Returns the cloak.*

    Jane. A match?
I had rather be matched from a musket's mouth,
And shot unto my death.   [*Aside.*

    Chough. I'll wrestle with any man for a good supper.

    Trim. Ay, marry, sir, I'll take your part there, catch
that catch may.

    Phy. [*To* Russell.] Sir, she is willing to't: there at
      my house
She shall be private, and near to my attendance:
I know you'll not mistrust my faithful care;
I shall return her soon and perfectly.

    Rus. Take your charge, sir.—Go with this gentleman,
      Jane;
But, prithee, look well this way ere thou go'st;
'Tis a rich simplicity of great estate,
A thing that will be ruled, and thou shalt rule;
Consider of your sex's general aim,
That domination is a woman's Heaven.

    Jane. I'll think on't, sir.

    Rus. My daughter is retiring, sir.

    Chough. I will part at Dartmouth with her, sir.
[*Kisses her.*]—O that thou didst but love wrestling! I
would give any man three foils on that condition!

    Trim. There's three sorts of men that would thank
you for 'em, either cutlers, fencers, or players.

---

    [1] There is usually a spice of naughtiness intended when "green
gowns" are mentioned. Cf. Ben Jonson's *Bartholomew Fair*, iv.
3 :—"Ursula, take them in and fit them to their calling. Green
gowns, crimson petticoats, green women, my lord mayor's green
women! guests o' the game, true bred." See the charming ballad
of *Green Gown* in Mr. Ebsworth's edition of the *Westminster
Drollery.—Bullen.*

Rus. Sir, as I began I end,—wondrous welcome !

[*Exeunt all except* CHOUGH *and* TRIMTRAM.

Trim. What, will you go to school to-day ? you are entered, you know, and your quarterage runs on.

Chough. What, to the roaring school ?[1] pox on't, 'tis such a damnable noise, I shall never attain it neither. I do wonder they have never a wrestling school ; that were worth twenty of your fencing or dancing schools.

Trim. Well, you must learn to roar here in London ; you'll never proceed in the reputation of gallantry else.

Chough. How long has roaring been an exercise, thinkest thou, Trimtram ?

Trim. Ever since guns came up ; the first was your roaring Meg.[2]

Chough. Meg ? then 'twas a woman was the first roarer ?

Trim. Ay, a fire of her touch-hole, that cost many a proper man's life since that time ; and then the lions, they learnt it from the guns, living so near 'em ;[3] then it was heard to the Bankside, and the bears[4] they began to roar ; then the boys got it, and so ever since there have been a company of roaring boys.

Chough. And how long will it last, thinkest thou ?

Trim. As long as the water runs under London Bridge, or watermen ply at Westminster stairs.

Chough. Well, I will begin to roar too, since it is in fashion. O, Corineus,[5] this was not in thy time ! I should have heard on't by the tradition of mine ancestors—for I'm sure there were Choughs in thy days—if it had been so : when Hercules and thou wert on

The roaring boys were the hectoring bullies of the time.

[2] A name for a cannon, after Long Meg of Westminster, a noted virago of Henry VIII.'s time.

In the Tower.   [4] In Paris Garden.

A fabulous Cornish hero, who wrestled with the giant Gogmagog.

the Olympic Mount together, then was wrestling in request.

Trim. Ay, and that Mount is now the Mount in Cornwall: Corineus brought it thither under one of his arms, they say.

Chough. O Corineus, my predecessor, that I had but lived in those days to see thee wrestle! on that condition I had died seven year ago.

Trim. Nay, it should have been a dozen at least, i'faith, on that condition.   [*Exeunt.*

ACT THE THIRD.

SCENE I.

A Field.

Enter Captain AGER *and two* Friends.

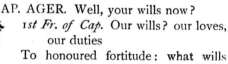AP. AGER. Well, your wills now?
     1st Fr. of Cap. Our wills? our loves,
       our duties
     To honoured fortitude: what wills
       have we
     But our desires to nobleness and
       merit,
Valour's advancement, and the sacred rectitude
Due to a valorous cause?
   Cap. Ager. O, that's not mine!
   2nd Fr. of Cap. War has his court of justice, that's
     the field,
Where all cases of manhood are determined,
And your case is no mean one.
   Cap. Ager. True; then 'twere virtuous;
But mine is in extremes, foul and unjust.
Well, now you've got me hither, you're as far
To seek in your desire as at first minute;
For, by the strength and honour of a vow,
I will not lift a finger in this quarrel.

1st Fr. of Cap. How? not in this? be not so rash
    a sinner:
Why, sir, do you ever hope to fight again then?
Take heed on't; you must never look for that:
Why, the universal stock of the world's injury
Will be too poor to find a quarrel for you.
Give up your right and title to desert, sir:
If you fail Virtue here, she needs you not
All your time after; let her take this wrong,
And never presume then to serve her more:
Bid farewell to the integrity of arms,
And let that honourable name of soldier
Fall from you like a shivered wreath of laurel
By thunder struck from a desertless forehead,
That wears another's right by usurpation.
Good captain, do not wilfully cast away
At one hour all the fame your life has won:
This is your native seat; here you should seek
Most to preserve it; or if you will dote
So much on life,—poor life, which in respect
Of life in honour is but death and darkness,—
That you will prove neglectful of yourself,
Which is to me too fearful too imagine,
Yet for that virtuous lady's cause, your mother,
Her reputation dear to nobleness
As grace to penitence, whose fair memory
E'en crowns fame in your issue, for that blessedness
Give not this ill place, but in spite of hell,
And all her base fears, be exactly valiant.
    Cap. Ager. O, O!
    2nd Fr. of Cap. Why, well said, there's fair hope in that;
Another such a one!
    Cap. Ager. Came they in thousands,
'Tis all against you.
    1st Fr. of Cap. Then, poor friendless merit,
Heaven be good to thee! thy professor leaves thee.

Enter the Colonel *and two* Friends.

He's come; do but you draw, we'll fight it for you.

    Cap. Ager. I know too much to grant that.

    1st Fr. of Cap. O dead manhood!

Had ever such a cause so faint a servant?

Shame brand me, if I do not suffer for him!

    Col. I've heard, sir, you've been guilty of much
        boasting

For your brave earliness at such a meeting:

You've lost the glory of that way this morning;

I was the first to-day.

    Cap. Ager. So were you ever

In my respect, sir.

    1st Fr. of Cap. O most base præludium!

    Cap. Ager. I never thought on Victory, our mistress,

With greater reverence than I have your worth,

Nor ever loved her better.

    1st Fr. of Cap. 'Slight, I could knock

His brains 'bout his heels, methinks!

    2nd Fr. of Cap. Peace, prithee, peace.

    Cap. Ager. Success in you has been my absolute joy;

And when I've wished content, I've wished your friend-
        ship.

    1st Fr. of Cap. Stay, let me but run him through
        the tongue a little;

There's lawyer's blood in't, you shall see foul gear
        straight.

    2nd Fr. of Cap. Come, you're as mad now as he's
        cowardous.

    Col. I came not hither, sir, for an encomium.

    1st Fr. of Cap. No, the more coxcomb he that claws
        the head

Of your vainglory with't!   *[Aside.*

    Col. I came provided

For storms and tempests, and the foulest season

That ever rage let forth, or blew in wildness
From the incensèd prison of man's blood.

    Cap. Ager. 'Tis otherwise with me; I come with
        mildness,
Peace, constant amity, and calm forgiveness,
The weather of a Christian and a friend.

    1st Fr. of Cap. Give me a valiant Turk, though not
        worth tenpence,[1] rather.

    Cap. Ager. Yet, sir, the world will judge the injury
        mine,
Insufferably mine, mine beyond injury:
Thousands have made a less wrong reach to hell,
Ay, and rejoiced in his most endless vengeance,
A miserable triumph, though a just one!
But when I call to memory our long friendship,
Methinks it cannot be too great a wrong
That then I should not pardon.   Why should man,
For a poor hasty syllable or two,
And vented only in forgetful fury,
Chain all the hopes and riches of his soul
To the revenge of that, die lost for ever?
For he that makes his last peace with his Maker
In anger, anger is his peace eternally:
He must expect the same return again
Whose venture is deceitful; must he not, sir?

    Col. I see what I must do, fairly put up again;
For here'll be nothing done, I perceive that.

    Cap. Ager. What shall be done in such a worthless
        business
But to be sorry, and to be forgiven;
You, sir, to bring repentance, and I pardon?

    Col. I bring repentance, sir?

    Cap. Ager. If't be too much

---

[1] This seems to have been the amount at which the Elizabethans
usually rated a Turk. Marlowe uses "Turk of tenpence" as a
term of abuse.

To say repentance, call it what you please, sir;
Choose your own word : I know you're sorry for't,
And that's as good.

    Col. I sorry? by fame's honour, I am wronged!
Do you seek for peace, and draw the quarrel larger?

    Cap. Ager. Then 'tis I am sorry that I thought you
      so.

    1st Fr. of Cap. A captain! I could gnaw his title off.

    Cap. Ager. Nor is it any misbecoming virtue, sir,
In the best manliness to repent a wrong,
Which made me bold with you.

    1st Fr. of Cap. I could cuff his head off.

    2nd Fr. of Cap. Nay, pish!

    1st Fr. of Cap. Pox on him, I could eat his buttock
    baked, methinks!

    Col. So, once again take thou thy peaceful rest, then ;
                    [*Sheathing his sword.*
But, as I put thee up, I must proclaim
This captain here, both to his friends and mine,
That only came to see fair valour righted,
A base submissive coward ; so I leave him.
                    [*Offers to go away.*

    Cap. Ager. O, Heaven has pitied my excessive patience,
And sent me a cause! now I have a cause ;
A coward I was never.—Come you back, sir!

    Col. How?

    Cap. Ager. You left a coward here.

    Col. Yes, sir, with you.

    Cap. Ager. 'Tis such base metal, sir, 'twill not be
    taken ;
It must home again with you.

    2nd Fr. of Cap. Should this be true now!

    1st Fr. of Cap. Impossible! coward do more than
    bastard?

    Col. I prithee mock me not, take heed you do not ;
For if I draw once more, I shall grow terrible,
    Mid. II.   R

And rage will force me do what will grieve honour.
    Cap. Ager. Ha, ha, ha!
    Col. He smiles; dare it be he?—What think you,
        gentlemen?
Your judgments, shall I not be cozened in him?
This cannot be the man: why, he was bookish,
Made an invective lately against fighting,
A thing, in troth, that moved a little with me,
Put up a fouler contumely far
Than thousand cowards came to, and grew thankful.
    Cap. Ager. Blessèd remembrance in time of need!
I'd lost my honour else.
    2nd Fr. of Cap. Do you note his joy?
    Cap. Ager. I never felt a more severe necessity;
Then came thy excellent pity. Not yet ready?
Have you such confidence in my just manhood
That you dare so long trust me, and yet tempt me
Beyond the toleration of man's virtue?
Why, would you be more cruel than your injury?
Do you first take pride to wrong me, and then think
    me
Not worth your fury? do not use me so;
I shall deceive you then. Sir, either draw,
And that not slightingly, but with the care
Of your best preservation, with that watchfulness
As you'd defend yourself from circular fire,
Your sin's rage, or her lord—this will require it—
Or you'll be too soon lost, for I've an anger
Has gathered mighty strength against you, mighty:
Yet you shall find it honest to the last,
Noble and fair.
    Col. I'll venture't once again;
And if't be but as true as it is wondrous,
I shall have that I come for: your leave, gentlemen.
    1st Fr. of Cap. If he should do't indeed, and de-
    ceive's all now!

Stay, by this hand he offers—fights, i'faith !

> [*The* Colonel *and* Captain AGER *fight.*

Fights, by this light he fights, sir !

    2nd Fr. of Cap. So methinks, sir.

    1st Fr. of Cap. An absolute punto, hey ?

    2nd Fr. of Cap. 'Twas a passado, sir.

    1st Fr. of. Cap. Why, let it pass, an 'twas ; I'm sure
      'twas somewhat.

What's that now ?

    2nd Fr. of Cap. That's a punto.

    1st Fr. of Cap. O, go to, then ;

I knew 'twas not far off.   What a world's this !

Is coward a more stirring meat than bastard, my
    masters ?

Put in more eggs, for shame, when you get children,

And make it true court-custard.—Ho, I honour thee !

'Tis right and fair ; and he that breathes against it,

He breathes against the justice of a man,

And man to cut him off 'tis no injustice.

> [*The* Colonel *falls.*

Thanks, thanks for this most unexpected nobleness !

    Cap. Ager. Truth never fails her servant, sir, nor leaves
      him

With the day's shame upon him.

    1st Fr. of Cap. Thou'st redeemed

Thy worth to the same height 'twas first esteemed.

> [*Exit* Captain AGER *with his* Friends.

    1st Fr. of Col. Alas, how is it, sir? give us some hope

Of your stay with us : let your spirit be seen

Above your fortune ; the best fortitude

Has been of fate ill-friended : now force your empire,

And reign above your blood, spite of dejection ;

Reduce [1] the monarchy of your abler mind,

Let not flesh straiten it.

    Col. O, just Heaven has found me,

---

[1] Bring back.

And turned the stings of my too hasty injuries
Into my own blood! I pursued my ruin,
And urged him past the patience of an angel :
Could man's revenge extend beyond man's life,
This would ha' waked it. If this flame will light me
But till I see my sister, 'tis a kind one ;
More I expect not from't. Noble deserver ! .
Farewell, most valiant and most wronged of men ;
Do but forgive me, and I'm victor then.[1]

> [*Exit, led off by his* Friends.

[1] The insipid levelling morality to which the modern stage is tied down would not admit of such admirable passions as these scenes are filled with. A puritanical obtuseness of sentiment, a stupid infantile goodness, is creeping among us, instead of the vigorous passions, and virtues clad in flesh and blood, with which the old dramatists present us. Those noble and liberal casuists could discern in the differences, the quarrels, the animosities of man, a beauty and truth of moral feeling, no less than in the iterately inculcated duties of forgiveness and atonement. With us all is hypocritical meekness. A reconciliation scene (let the occasion be never so absurd or unnatural), is always sure of applause. Our audiences come to the theatre to be complimented on their goodness. They compare notes with the amiable characters in the play, and find a wonderful similarity of disposition between them. We have a common stock of dramatic morality, out of which a writer may be supplied, without the trouble of copying it from originals within his own breast. To know the boundaries of honour, to be judiciously valiant, to have a temperance which shall beget a smoothness in the angry swellings of youth, to esteem life as nothing when the sacred reputation of a parent is to be defended, yet to shake and tremble under a pious cowardice when that ark of an honest confidence is found to be frail and tottering, to feel the true blows of a real disgrace blunting that sword which the imaginary strokes of a supposed false imputation had put so keen an edge upon but lately ; to do, or to imagine this done in a feigned story, asks something more of a moral sense, somewhat a greater delicacy of perception in questions of right and wrong, than goes to the writing of two or three hackneyed sentences about the laws of honour as opposed to the laws of the land, or a commonplace against duelling. Yet such things would stand a writer now-a-days in far better stead than Captain Ager and his conscientious honour ; and he would be

SCENE II.

A Room in the Physician's *House.*

Enter Physician, JANE, ANNE, *and* Dutch Nurse *with a* Child.

Phy. Sweet fro,[1] to your most indulgent care
Take this my heart's joy; I must not tell you
The value of this jewel in my bosom.

Nurse. Dat you may vell, sir; der can niet forstoore you.

Phy. Indeed I cannot tell you; you know, nurse,
These are above the quantity of price:
Where is the glory of the goodliest trees
But in the fruit and branches? the old stock
Must decay; and sprigs, scions such as these,
Must become new stocks, for us to glory
In their fruitful issue; so we are made
Immortal one by other.

Nurse. You spreek a most lieben fader, and ich sall
do de best of tender nurses to dis infant, my pretty
frokin.

Phy. I know you will be loving: here, sweet friend;
[*Gives money.*
Here's earnest of a large sum of love and coin
To quit[2] your tender care.

Jane. I have some reason too
To purchase your dear care unto this infant.
[*Gives money.*

Nurse. You be de witness of de baptim, dat is, as
you spreken, de godmother, ich vell forstoore it so.

Jane. Yes, I'm the bad mother,—if it be offence.
[*Aside.*

considered as a far better teacher of morality than old Rowley or
Middleton if they were living.—*Charles Lamb.*

[1] Dutch : *frow,* woman.   [2] Requite.

Anne. I must be a little kind too.   [*Gives money.*

Nurse. Much tanks to you all! dis child is much
beloved; and ich sall see much care over it.

Phy. Farewell.—Good sister, show her the way forth.—
I shall often visit you, kind nurse.

Nurse. You sall be velcome.

[*Exeunt* ANNE *and* Nurse.

Jane. O sir, what a friend have I found in you!
Where my poor power shall stay in the requital,
Yourself must from your fair condition [1]
Make up in mere acceptance of my will.

Phy. O, pray you, urge it not! we are not born
For ourselves only; self-love is a sin;
But in our loving donatives to others
Man's virtue best consists: love all begets;
Without, all are adulterate and counterfeit.

Jane. Your boundless love I cannot satisfy
But with a mental memory of your virtues:
Yet let me not engage your cost withal;
Beseech you then take restitution
Of pains and bounty which you have disbursed
For your poor debtor.

Phy. You will not offer it?
Do not esteem my love so mercenary
To be the hire of coin: sure, I shall think
You do not hold so worthily of me
As I wish to deserve.

Jane. Not recompense?
Then you will beggar me with too much credit:
Is't not sufficient you preserve my name,
Which I had forfeited to shame and scorn,
Cover my vices with a veil of love,
Defend and keep me from a father's rage,
Whose love yet infinite, not knowing this,

[1] Disposition.

Might, knowing, turn a hate as infinite;
Sure he would throw me ever from his blessings,
And cast his curses on me!   Yes, further,   ·
Your secrecy keeps me in the state of woman;
For else what husband would choose me his wife,
Knowing the honour of a bride were lost?
I cannot number half the good you do me
In the concealed retention of my sin;
Then make me not worse than I was before,
In my ingratitude, good sir.
    Phy. Again?
I shall repent my love, if you'll so call't,
To be made such a hackney: give me coin?
I had as lief you gave me poison, lady,
For I have art and antidotes 'gainst that;
I might take that, but this I will refuse.
    Jane. Will you then teach me how I may requite you
In some small quantity?
    Phy. 'Twas that I looked for.—   [*Aside.*
Yes, I will tell you, lady, a full quittance,
And how you may become my creditress.
    Jane. I beseech you, do, sir!
    Phy. Indeed I will, lady:
Not in coin, mistress; for silver, though white,
Yet it draws black lines; it shall not rule my palm,
There to mark forth his base corruption:
Pay me again in the same quality
That I to you tendered,—that is, love for love.
Can you love me, lady? you have confessed
My love to you.   .
    Jane. Most amply.
    Phy. Why, faith, then,
Pay me back that way.
    Jane. How do you mean, sir?
    Phy. Tush, our meanings are better understood
Than shifted to the tongue; it brings along

A little blabbing blood into our cheeks,
That shames us when we speak.

    Jane. I understand you not.

    Phy. Fie, you do; make not yourself ignorant
In what you know; you have ta'en forth the lesson
That I would read to you.

    Jane. Sure then I need not
Read it again, sir.

    Phy. Yes, it makes perfect:
You know the way unto Achilles' spear;[1]
If that hurt you, I have the cure, you see.

    Jane. Come, you're a good man; I do perceive you,
You put a trial to me; I thank you;
You are my just confessor, and, believe me,
I'll have no further penance for this sin.
Convert a year unto a lasting ever,
And call't Apollo's smile: 'twas once, then never.

    Phy. Pray you, mistake not; indeed I love you.

    Jane. Indeed? what deed?

    Phy. The deed that you have done.

    Jane. I cannot believe you.

    Phy. Believe the deed then!

    Jane. Away, you are a blackamoor! you love me?
I hate you for your love!   Are you the man
That in your painted outside seemed so white?
O, you're a foul dissembling hypocrite!
You saved me from a thief, that yourself might rob me;
Skinned over a green wound to breed an ulcer:
Is this the practice of your physic-college?

    Phy. Have you yet uttered all your niceness forth?
If you have more, vent it; certes,[1] I think
Your first grant was not yielded with less pain;
If 'twere, you have your price, yield it again.

---

[1] Telephus, wounded by Achilles' spear, could only be cured by rust scraped from the weapon.

Jane. Pray you, tell me, sir,—I asked it before,—
Is it a practice amongst you physicians?

Phy. Tush, that's a secret; we cast all waters:
Should I reveal, you would mistrust my counsel:
The lawyer and physician here agrees,
To women-clients they give back their fees;
And is not that kindness?

Jane. This for thy love!   [*Spits at him.*
Out, outside of a man: thou cinnamon-tree,
That but thy bark hast nothing good about thee!
The unicorn is hunted for his horn,
The rest is left for carrion: thou false man,
Thou'st fished with silver hooks and golden baits;
But I'll avoid all thy deceiving sleights.

Phy. Do what you list, I will do something too;
Remember yet what I have done for you:
You have a good face now, but 'twill grow rugged;
Ere you grow old, old men will despise you:
Think on your grandame Helen, the fairest queen;
When in a new glass she spied her old face,
She, smiling, wept to think upon the change:
Take your time; you're crazed, you're an apple fallen
From the tree; if you be kept long, you'll rot.
Study your answer well: yet I love you;
If you refuse, I have a hand above you.   [*Exit.*

Jane. Poison thyself, thou foul empoisoner!
Of thine own practique drink the theory!
What a white devil[2] have I met withal!
What shall I do?—what do? is it a question?
Nor shame, nor hate, nor fear, nor lust, nor force,
Now being too bad, shall ever make me worse.

---

[1] Certainly.
[2] "Lately we were troubled with White Devils, who, under pretence
of extraordinary sanctity, published open heresy and blasphemy
against God, His word, His works, and ordinances."—Hall's *Down-
fall of Maygames,* 1661.

Re-enter ANNE.

What have we here? a second spirit?
   Anne. Mistress,
I am sent to you.
   Jane. Is your message good?
   Anne. As you receive it:
My brother sent me, and you know he loves you.
   Jane. I heard say so; but 'twas a false report.
   Anne. Pray, pardon me, I must do my message;
Who lives commanded must obey his keeper:
I must persuade you to this act of woman.
   Jane. Woman? of strumpet!
   Anne. Indeed, of strumpet;
He takes you at advantage of your fall,
Seeing you down before.
   Jane. Curse on his feigned smiles!
   Anne. He's my brother, mistress; and a curse on you,
If e'er you bless him with that cursèd deed!
Hang him, poison him! he held out a rose,
To draw the yielding sense, which, come to hand,
He shifts, and gives a canker.[1]
   Jane. You speak well yet.
   Anne. Ay, but, mistress, now I consider it,
Your reputation lies at his mercy,
Your fault dwells in his breast; say he throw't out,
It will be known; how are you then undone!
Think on't, your good name; and they're not to be sold
In every market: a good name is dear,
And indeed more esteemèd than our actions,
By which we should deserve it.
   Jane. Ay me, most wretched!
   Anne. What? do you shrink at that?
Would you not wear one spot upon your face,

---

[1] Dog-rose.

To keep your whole body from a leprosy,
Though it were undiscovered ever?   Hang him!
Fear him not: horse leeches suck out his corrupt blood!
Draw you none from him, 'less it be pure and good.

    Jane. Do you speak your soul?

    Anne. By my soul do I!

    Jane. Then yet I have a friend: but thus exhort me,
And I have still a column to support me.

    Anne. One fault
Heaven soon forgives, and 'tis on earth forgot;
The moon herself is not without one spot.   [*Exeunt.*

SCENE III.

A Room in Lady AGER'S *House.*

Enter Lady AGER, *meeting a* Servant.

    Lady Ager. Now, sir, where is he? speak, why comes
        he not?
I sent you for him.—Bless this fellow's senses!
What has he seen? a soul nine hours entranced,
Hovering 'twixt hell and Heaven, could not wake ghast-
        lier.
Nor yet return an answer?—

Enter a 2nd Servant.

                What say you, sir?

Where is he?

    2nd Serv. Gone.

    Lady Ager. What say'st thou!

    2nd Serv. He is gone, madam;

But, as we heard, unwillingly he went
As ever blood enforced.

    Lady Ager. Went? whither went he?

    2nd Serv. Madam, I fear I ha' said too much already.

    Lady Ager. These men are both agreed.—Speak,
        whither went he?

    2nd Serv. Why, to—I would you'd think the rest
        yourself, madam.

    Lady Ager. Meek patience bless me!

    2nd Serv. To the field.

    1st Serv. To fight, madam.

    Lady Ager. To fight?

    1st Serv. There came two urging gentlemen,
That called themselves his seconds; both so powerful,
As 'tis reported, they prevailed with him
With little labour.

    Lady Ager. O, he's lost, he's gone!
For all my pains, he's gone! two meeting torrents
Are not so merciless as their two rages:
He never comes again.   Wretched affection!
Have I belied my faith, injured my goodness,
Slandered my honour for his preservation,
Having but only him, and yet no happier?
'Tis then a judgment plain; truth's angry with me,
In that I would abuse her sacred whiteness
For any worldly temporal respect:
Forgive me then. thou glorious woman's virtue,
Admired where'er thy habitation is,
Especially in us weak ones!   O, forgive me,
For 'tis thy vengeance this!   To belie truth,
Which is so hardly ours, with such pain purchased,
Fastings and prayers, continence and care,
Misery must needs ensue.   Let him not die
In that unchaste belief of his false birth,
And my disgrace! whatever angel guides him,
May this request be with my tears obtained,

Let his soul know my honour is unstained !—   [*Aside.*
Run, seek away ! if there be any hope,
Let me not lose him yet.   [*Exeunt* Servants.]   When I
      think on him,
His dearness and his worth, it earns [1] me more :
They that know riches tremble to be poor.
My passion is not every woman's sorrow :
She must be truly honest feels my grief,
And only known to one ; if such there be,
They know the sorrow that oppresseth me.   [*Exit.*

            [1] Yearns.

ACT THE FOURTH.

SCENE I.

The Roaring-School.

Enter the Colonel's Friend, CHOUGH, TRIMTRAM, Usher, *and several* Roarers.

OL'S FR. Truth, sir, I must needs blame you for a truant, having but one lesson read to you, and neglect so soon; fie, I must see you once a day at least.

Chough. Would I were whipped, tutor, if it were not 'long of my man Trimtram here!

Trim.. Who, of me?

Chough. Take't upon thee, Trim; I'll give thee five shillings, as I am a gentleman.

Trim. I'll see you whipped first:—well, I will too.— Faith, sir, I saw he was not perfect, and I was loth he should come before to shame himself.

Col.'s Fr. How? shame, sir? is it a shame for scholars to learn? Sir, there are great scholars that are but slenderly read in our profession: sir, first it must be economical, then ecumenical: shame not to practise in the house how to perform in the field: the nail that is driven takes a little hold at the first stroke, but more at

the second, and more at the third, but when 'tis home
to the head, then 'tis firm.

Chough. Faith, I have been driving it home to the
head this two days.

Trim. I helped to hammer it in as well as I could
too, sir.

Col.'s Fr. Well, sir, I will hear you rehearse anon:
meantime peruse the exemplary of my bills, and tell me
in what language I shall roar a lecture to you; or I'll
read to you the mathematical science of roaring.

Chough. Is it mathematical?

Col.'s Fr. O, sir, does not the wind roar, the sea
roar, the welkin roar?—indeed most things do roar by
nature—and is not the knowledge of these things mathematical?

Chough. Pray, proceed, sir.

Col.'s Fr. [*Reads.*] "The names of the languages,
the Sclavonian, Parthamenian, Barmeothian, Tyburnian,
Wappinganian, or the modern Londonian: any man or
woman that is desirous to roar in any of these languages,
in a week they shall be perfect if they will take pains; so
let 'em repair into Holborn to the sign of the Cheat-loaf."

Chough. Now your bill speaks of that I was wonder-
ing a good while at, your sign; the loaf looks very like
bread, i'faith, but why is it called the Cheat-loaf?

Col.'s Fr. This house was sometimes a baker's, sir,
that served the court, where the bread is called
cheat.[1]

Trim. Ay, ay, 'twas a baker that cheated the court
with bread.

Col.'s Fr. Well, sir, choose your languages; and your
lectures shall be read, between my usher and myself, for

---

[1] Cheat was wheaten bread of the second quality, ranking next
to manchet. There were two sorts, the fine and the coarse, the
latter, according to Harrison, being "used in the halles of the
nobilitie and gentrie onelie."

your better instruction, provided your conditions be performed in the premises beforesaid.

Chough. Look you, sir, there's twenty pound in hand, and twenty more I am to pay when I am allowed a sufficient roarer.   [*Gives money.*

Col.'s Fr. You speak in good earnest, sir?

Chough. Yes, faith do I: Trimtram shall be my witness.

Trim. Yes, indeed, sir, twenty pound is very good earnest.

Ush. Sir, one thing I must tell you belongs to my place: you are the youngest scholar; and till another comes under you, there is a certain garnish belongs to the school; for in our practice we grow to a quarrel; then there must be wine ready to make all friends, for that's the end of roaring, 'tis valiant, but harmless; and this charge is yours.

Chough. With all my heart, i'faith, and I like it the better because no blood comes on it: who shall fetch?

1st Roar. I'll be your spaniel, sir.

Col.'s Fr. Bid Vapour bring some tobacco too.

Chough. Do, and here's money for't.

Ush. No, you shall not; let me see the money: so [*Takes the money*], I'll keep it, and discharge him after the combat. [*Exit* 1st Roarer.] For your practice' sake, you and your man shall roar him out on't—for indeed you must pay your debts so, for that's one of the main ends of roaring—and when you have left him in a chafe, then I'll qualify the rascal.

Chough. Content.—I'faith, Trim, we'll roar the rusty rascal out of his tobacco.

Trim. Ay, an he had the best craccus [1] in London.

Col.'s Fr. Observe, sir, we could now roar in the Sclavonian language, but this practice hath been a little sublime, some hair's-breadth or so above your caput; I

---

[1] A species of tobacco.

take it, for your use and understanding both, it were
fitter for you to taste the modern assault, only the
Londonian roar.

Chough. I'faith, sir, that's for my purpose, for I shall
use all my roaring here in London : in Cornwall we are
all for wrestling, and I do not mean to travel over sea
to roar there.

Col.'s Fr. Observe then, sir ;—but it were necessary
you took forth your tables [1] to note the most difficult
points for the better assistance of your memory.

Chough. Nay, sir, my man and I keep two tables.

Trim. Ay, sir, and as many trenchers, cats' meat and
dogs' meat enough.

Col.'s Fr. Note, sir.—Dost thou confront my cyclops ?

Ush. With a Briarean brousted.

Chough. Cyclops.   [*Writes.*

Trim. Briarean.   [*Writes.*

Col.'s Fr. I know thee and thy lineal pedigree.

Ush. It is collateral, as Brutus and Posthumus.

Trim. Brutus.   [*Writes.*

Chough. Posthumus.   [*Writes.*

Col.'s Fr. False as the face of Hecate ! thy sister
is a——

Ush. What is my sister, centaur?

Col.'s Fr. I say thy sister is a bronstrops. [2]

Ush. A bronstrops?

Chough. Tutor, tutor, ere you go any further, tell
me the English of that ; what is a bronstrops, pray ?

Col.'s Fr. A bronstrops is in English a hippocrene.

Chough. A hippocrene ; note it, Trim : I love to
understand the English as I go.   [*Writes.*

Trim. What's the English of hippocrene?

Chough. Why, bronstrops.

Ush. Thou dost obtrect [3] my flesh and blood.

Col.'s Fr. Again I denounce, thy sister is a fructifer.

[1] Memorandum book.   [2] Prostitute.—*Halliwell.*   [3] Slander.
Mid. II.   s

Chough. What's that, tutor?

Col's Fr. That is in English a fucus or a minotaur.

Chough. A minotaur. [*Writes.*

Trim. A fucus. [*Writes.*

Ush. I say thy mother is a callicut, a panagron, a duplar, and a sindicus.

Col.'s Fr. Dislocate thy bladud![1]

Ush. Bladud shall conjure, if his demons once appear.

Re-enter 1st Roarer *with wine, followed by* VAPOUR *with tobacco.*

Col.'s Fr. Advance thy respondency.

Chough. Nay, good gentlemen, do not fall out.—A cup of wine quickly, Trintram!

Ush. See, my steel hath a glister!

Chough. Pray wipe him, and put him up again, good usher.

Ush. Sir, at your request I pull down the flag **of** defiance.

Col.'s Fr. Give me a bowl of wine, my fury shall be quenched: here, usher! [*Drinks.*

Ush. I pledge thee in good friendship. [*Drinks.*

Chough. I like the conclusion of roaring very well, i'faith.

Trim. It has an excellent conclusion indeed,—if **the** wine be good, always provided.

Col.'s Fr. O, the wine must be always provided, **be** sure of that.

Ush. Else you spoil the conclusion, and that **you** know crowns all.

Chough. 'Tis much like wrestling, i'faith, for we **shake** hands ere we begin; now that's to avoid the law, **for** then if he throw him a furlong into the ground, he **can-**

[1] *i.e.* I suppose, "draw thy sword."— *Dyce.* King Bladud was **a** famous magician.

not recover himself upon him, because 'twas done in cold friendship.

Col.'s Fr. I believe you, sir.

Chough. And then we drink afterwards, just in this fashion : wrestling and roaring are as like as can be, i'faith, even like long sword and half pike.

Col.'s Fr. Nay, they are reciprocal, if you mark it, for as there is a great roaring at wrestling, so there is a kind of wrestling and contention at roaring.

Chough. True, i'faith, for I have heard 'em roar from the six windmills [1] to Islington : those have been great falls then.

Col.'s Fr. Come, now, a brief rehearsal of your other day's lesson, betwixt your man and you, and then for to-day we break up school.

Chough. Come, Trimtram.—If I be out, tutor, I'll be bold to look in my tables, because I doubt I am scarce perfect

Col.'s Fr. Well, well, I will not see small faults.

Chough. The wall !

Trim. The wall of me? to thy kennel, spaniel !

Chough. Wilt thou not yield precedency?

Trim. To thee? I know thee and thy brood.

Chough. Knowest thou my brood?   I know thy brood too, thou art a rook.

Trim. The nearer akin to the choughs.

Chough. The rooks akin to the choughs?

Col.'s Fr. Very well maintained !

Chough. Dungcoer, thou liest !

Trim. Lie? enucleate the kernel of thy scabbard.

Chough. Now if I durst draw my sword, 'twere valiant, 'faith.

[1] In Finsbury fields near Moorgate. They were erected on a deposit of more than a thousand cartloads of bones that had been removed from the charnel of old St Paul's, when the charnel house was destroyed in 1549.

Col.'s Fr. Draw, draw, howsoever!

Chough. Have some wine ready to make us friends, I pray you.

Trim. Chough, I will make thee fly and roar.

Chough. I will roar if thou strikest me.

Col.'s Fr. So, 'tis enough; now conclude in wine: I see you will prove an excellent practitioner: wondrous well performed on both sides!

Chough. Here, Trimtram, I drink to thee. [*Drinks.*

Trim. I'll pledge you in good friendship. [*Drinks.*

Enter Servant.

Serv. Is there not one Master Chough here?

Ush. This is the gentleman, sir.

Serv. My master, sir, your elected father-in-law, desires speedily to speak with you.

Chough. Friend, I will follow thee: I would thou hadst come a little sooner! thou shouldst have seen roaring sport, i'faith.

Serv. Sir, I'll return that you are following.

Chough. Do so. [*Exit* Servant.]—I'll tell thee, tutor, I am to marry shortly; but I will defer it a while till I can roar perfectly, that I may get the upper hand of my wife on the wedding-day; 't must be done at first or never.

Col.'s Fr. 'Twill serve you to good use in that, sir.

Chough. How likest thou this, whiffler?[1]

Vap. Very valiantly, i'faith, sir.

Chough. Tush, thou shalt see more by and by.

Vap. I can stay no longer indeed, sir: who pays me for my tobacco?

Chough. How? pay for tobacco? away, ye sooty-mouthed piper! you rusty piece of Martlemas bacon, away!

---

[1] Puffer of tobacco.

Trim. Let me give him a mark[1] for't.

Chough. No, Trimtram, do not strike him; we'll only roar out a curse upon him.

Trim. Well, do you begin then.

Chough. May thy roll rot, and thy pudding[2] drop in pieces, being sophisticated with filthy urine!

Trim. May sergeants dwell on either side of thee, to fright away the twopenny customers!

Chough. And for thy penny ones, let them suck thee dry!

Trim. When thou art dead, mayst thou have no other sheets to be buried in but mouldy tobacco-leaves!

Chough. And no strawings to stick thy carcase but the bitter stalks!

Trim. Thy mourners all greasy tapsters!

Chough. With foul tobacco-pipes in their hats, instead of rotten rosemary;[3] and last of all, may my man and I live to see all this performed, and to piss reeking even upon thy grave!

Trim. And last of all for me, let this epitaph be re-membered over thee:

> Here coldly now within is laid to rot
> A man that yesterday was piping hot:
> Some say he died by pudding, some by prick,[4]
> Others by roll and ball, some leaf;[5] all stick
> Fast in censure,[6] yet think it strange and rare,
> He lived by smoke, yet died for want of air:
> But then the surgeon said, when he beheld him,
> It was the burning of his pipe that killed him.

Chough. So, are you paid now, whiffler?

---

[1] A coin worth 13s. 4d.　Trimtram is of course punning on the word.

[2] Roll and pudding were tobacco made up in particular forms.

[3] Rosemary was worn at funerals.

[4] Pudding-prick was the skewer which fastened the pudding-bag.

[5] Another kind of tobacco.　　　　　　[6] Opinion.

Vap. All this is but smoke out of a stinking pipe.

Chough. So, so, pay him now, usher.

　　　　　　[VAPOUR *is paid by the* Usher, *and exit.*

Col.'s Fr. Do not henceforth neglect your schooling, Master Chough.

Chough. Call me rook, if I do, tutor.

Trim. And me raven, though my name be Trimtram.

Chough. Farewell, tutor.

Trim. Farewell, usher.

　　　　　　[*Exeunt* CHOUGH *and* TRIMTRAM.

Col.'s Fr. Thus when the drum's unbraced, and trumpets cease,

Soldiers must get pay for to live in peace.　　　[*Exeunt.*

SCENE II.

A Chamber in the Colonel's *House.*

The Colonel *discovered lying on a couch, several of his* Friends *watching him: as the* Surgeon *is going out, the* Colonel's Sister *enters.*

Col.'s Sist. O my most worthy brother, thy hard fate 'twas!—

Come hither, honest surgeon, and deal faithfully

With a distressèd virgin: what hope is there?

Surg. Hope? chilis[1] was 'scaped miraculously, lady.

Col.'s Sist. What's that, sir?

Surg. Cava vena: I care but little for his wound i' the œsophag, not thus much, trust me; but when they come to diaphragma once, the small intestines, or the

　　　[1] *i.e.* The *vena cava,* the largest vein in the body.

spinal medul, or i' the roots of the emunctories of the
noble parts, then straight I fear a syncope; the flanks
retiring towards the back, the urine bloody, the excre-
ments purulent, and the dolour pricking or pungent.

Col's Sist. Alas, I'm ne'er the better for this answer!

Surg. Now I must tell you his principal dolour lies i'
the region of the liver, and there's both inflammation
and tumefaction feared; marry, I made him a quadran-
gular plumation, where I used sanguis draconis, by my
faith, with powders incarnative, which I tempered with
oil of hypericon, and other liquors mundificative.

Col.'s Sist. Pox a' your mundies figatives! I would
they were all fired!

Surg. But I purpose, lady, to make another experiment at next dressing with a sarcotic medicament made
of iris of Florence; thus, mastic, calaphena, opoponax,
sacrocolla [1]——

Col.'s Sist. Sacro-halter! what comfort is i' this to
a poor gentlewoman? pray tell me in plain terms what
you think of him.

Surg. Marry, in plain terms I know not what to say
to him: the wound, I can assure you, inclines to para-
lism, and I find his body cacochymic: being then in
fear of fever and inflammation, I nourish him altogether
with viands refrigerative, and give for potion the juice
of savicola dissolved with water cerefolium: I could
do no more, lady, if his best ginglymus [2] were dissevered.

                                                    [*Exit.*

Col.'s Sist. What thankless pains does the tongue
          often take
To make the whole man most ridiculous!
I come to him for comfort, and he tires me
Worse than my sorrow: what a precious good
May be delivered sweetly in few words!
And what a mount of nothing has he cast forth :

          [1] A Persian gum.   [2] Joint.

Alas, his strength decays!   [*Aside*].—How cheer you, sir,
My honoured brother?

   Col. In soul never better;
I feel an excellent health there, such a stoutness
My invisible enemies fly me : seeing me armed
With penitence and forgiveness, they fall backward,
Whether through admiration, not imagining
There were such armoury in a soldier's soul
As pardon and repentance, or through power
Of ghostly valour.   But I have been lord
Of a more happy conquest in nine hours now
Than in nine years before.—O kind lieutenants,
This is the only war we should provide for !
Where he that forgives largest, and sighs strongest,
Is a tried soldier, a true man indeed,
And wins the best field, makes his own heart bleed.
Read the last part of that will, sir.

   1st Fr. of Col. [*Reads.*] " I also require at the hands of
my most beloved sister, whom I make full executrix, the
disposure of my body in burial at Saint Martin's i' the
Field; and to cause to be distributed to the poor of the same
parish forty mark, and to the hospital of maimed soldiers
a hundred: lastly, I give and bequeath to my kind, dear,
and virtuous sister the full possession of my present estate
in riches, whether it be in lands, leases, money, goods,
plate, jewels, or what kind soever, upon this condition
following that she forthwith tender both herself and all
these infeoffments to that noble captain, my late enemy,
Captain Ager."

   Col.'s Sist. How, sir?

   Col. Read it again, sir; let her hear it plain.

   Col.'s Sist. Pray, spare your pains, sir; 'tis too plain
       already.—

Good sir, how do you? is your memory perfect?
This will makes question of you : I bestowed
So much grief and compassion a' your wound,

I never looked into your senses' epilepsy :
The sickness and infirmity of your judgment
Is to be doubted now more than your body's.
Why, is your love no dearer to me, sir,
Than to dispose me so upon the man
Whose fury is your body's present torment,
The author of your danger? one I hate
Beyond the bounds of malice.   Do you not feel
His wrath upon you?   I beseech you, sir,
Alter that cruel article !
   Col. Cruel, sister?—
Forgive me, natural love, I must offend thee,
Speaking to this woman.—Am I content,
Having much kindred, yet to give thee all,
Because in thee I'd raise my means to goodness,
And canst thou prove so thankless to my bounty,
To grudge my soul her peace? is my intent
To leave her rich, whose only desire is
To send me poorer into the next world
Than ever usurer went, or politic statist?
Is it so burdensome for thee to love
Where I forgive?   O, wretched is the man
That builds the last hopes of his saving comforts
Upon a woman's charity ! he's most miserable :
If it were possible, her obstinate will
Will pull him down in his midway to Heaven.
I've wronged that worthy man past recompense,
And in my anger robbed him of fair fame ;
And thou the fairest restitution art
My life could yield him : if I knew a fairer,
I'd set thee by and thy unwilling goodness,
And never make my sacred peace of thee :
But there's the cruelty of a fate debarred
Thou art the last, and all, and thou art hard !
   Col.'s Sist. Let your grieved heart hold better thoughts
     of me ;

I will not prove so, sir; but since you enforce it
With such a strength of passion, I'll perform
What by your will you have enjoined me to,
Though the world never show me joy again.

   Col. O, this may be fair cunning for the time,
To put me off, knowing I hold not long;
And when I look to have my joys accomplished,
I shall find no such things: that were vile cozenage,
And not to be repented.

   Col.'s Sist. By all the blessedness
Truth and a good life looks for, I will do't, sir!

   Col. Comforts reward you for't whene'er you grieve!
I know if you dare swear, I may believe.

           [*Exit the* Colonel's Sister. *Scene closes.*

SCENE III.

A Room in Lady AGER'S *House.*

Enter Captain AGER.

   Cap. Ager. No sooner have I entrance i' this house
       now
But all my joy falls from me, which was wont
To be the sanctuary of my comforts:
Methought I loved it with a reverent gladness,
As holy men do consecrated temples
For the saint's sake, which I believed my mother;
But proved a false faith since, a fearful heresy.
O, who'd erect the assurance of his joys
Upon a woman's goodness! whose best virtue
Is to commit unseen, and highest secrecy
To hide but her own sin: there's their perfection:

And if she be so good, which many fail of too,
When these are bad, how wondrous ill are they!
What comfort is't to fight, win this day's fame,
When all my after-days are lamps of shame?

Enter Lady AGER.

Lady Ager. Blessings be firm to me! he's come, 'tis
    he!—   [*Aside.*
A surgeon speedily!

Cap. Ager. A surgeon? why, madam?

Lady Ager. Perhaps you'll say 'tis but a little wound;
Good to prevent a danger:—quick, a surgeon!

Cap. Ager. Why, madam?

Lady Ager. Ay, ay, that's all the fault of valiant
    men,
They'll not be known a' their hurts till they're past help,
And then too late they wish for't.

Cap. Ager. Will you hear me?

Lady Ager. 'Tis no disparagement to confess a wound;
I'm glad, sir, 'tis no worse:—a surgeon quickly!

Cap. Ager. Madam——

Lady Ager. Come, come, sir, a wound's honourable,
And never shames the wearer.

Cap. Ager. By the justice
I owe to honour, I came off untouched!

Lady Ager. I'd rather believe that.

Cap. Ager. You believe truth so.

Lady Ager. My tears prevail then. Welcome, welcome,
    sir,
As peace and mercy to one new departed!
Why would you go though, and deceive me so,
When my abundant love took all the course
That might be to prevent it?   I did that
For my affection's sake—goodness forgive me for't!—
That were my own life's safety put upon't,
I'd rather die than do't.   Think how you used me then

And yet would you go and hazard yourself too!
'Twas but unkindly done.

    Cap. Ager. What's all this, madam?

    Lady Ager. See, then, how rash you were and short in
        wisdom!

Why, wrong my faith I did, slandered my constancy,
Belied my truth; that which few mothers will,
Or fewer can, I did, out of true fear
And loving care, only to keep thee here.

    Cap. Ager. I doubt I'm too quick of apprehension
        now,

And that's a general fault when we hear joyfully,
With the desire of longing for't: I ask it,
Why, were you never false?

    Lady Ager. May death come to me
Before repentance then!

    Cap. Ager. I heard it plain sure—
Not false at all?

    Lady Ager. By the reward of truth,
I never knew that deed that claims the name on't!

    Cap. Ager. May, then, that glorious reward you swore
        by

Be never-failing to you! all the blessings
That you have given me, since obedient custom
Taught me to kneel and ask 'em, are not valuable
With this immaculate blessing of your truth:
This is the palm to victory,
The crown for all deserts past and to come:
Let 'em be numberless; they are rewarded,
Already they're rewarded. Bless this frame,
I feel it much too weak to bear the joy on't.   [*Kneels.*

    Lady Ager. Rise, sir.

    Cap. Ager. O, pardon me!
I cannot honour you too much, too long.
I kneel not only to a mother now,
But to a woman that was never false:

Ye're dear, and ye're good too; I think a' that:
What reverence does she merit! 'tis fit such
Should be distinguished from the prostrate sex;
And what distinction properer can be shown,
Than honour done to her that keeps her own?

   Lady Ager. Come, sir, I'll have you rise.

   Cap. Ager. To do a deed, then,   [*Rises.*
That shall for ever raise me.   O my glory,
Why, this, this is the quarrel that I looked for!
The t'other but a shift to hold time play.
You sacred ministers of preservation,
For Heaven's sake send him life,
And with it mighty health, and such a strength
May equal but the cause!   I wish no foul things:
If life but glow in him, he shall know instantly
That I'm resolved to call him to account for't.

   Lady Ager. Why, hark you, sir——

   Cap. Ager. I bind you by your honour, madam,
You speak no hindrance to's; take heed, you ought
    not.

   Lady Ager. What an unhappiness have I in good-
    ness!
'Tis ever my desire to intend well,
But have no fortunate way in't.   For all this
Deserve I yet no better of you
But to be grieved again?   Are you not well
With honest gain of fame, with safety purchased?
Will you needs tempt a ruin that avoids you?   [*Exit.*

   Cap. Ager. No, you've prevailed; things of this nature
    sprung,
When they use action must use little tongue.—

Enter Servant.

Now, sir, the news?

   Ser. Sir, there's a gentlewoman
Desires some conference with you.

   Cap. Ager. How, with me?
A gentlewoman? what is she?
   Ser. Her attendant
Delivered her to be the colonel's sister.
   Cap. Ager. O, for a storm then! [*Exit* Servant.] 'las,
      poor, virtuous gentlewoman,
I will endure her violence with much pity!
She comes to ease her heart, good, noble soul;
'Tis e'en a charity to release the burden;
Were not that remedy ordained for women,
Their hearts would never hold three years together:
And here she comes; I never marked so much of her;

        Enter the Colonel's Sister.

That face can be the mistress of no anger
But I might very well endure a month, methinks.—
I am the man; speak, lady; I'll stand fair.
   Col's Sist. And I'm enjoined by vow to fall thus low,
                          [*Kneels.*
And, from the dying hand of a repentant,
Offer, for expiation of wrongs done you,
Myself, and with myself all that was his,
Which upon that condition was made mine,
Being his soul's wish to depart absolute man,
In life a soldier, death a Christian.
   Cap. Ager. O, Heaven has touched him nobly! how it
      shames
My virtue's slow perfection! Rise, dear brightness—
I forget manners too—up, matchless sweetness!
   Col's. Sist. I must not, sir; there is not in my vow
That liberty; I must be received first,
Or all denied; if either, I am free.
   Cap. Ager. He must be without soul should deny
      thee;
And with that reverence I receive the gift

As it was sent me. [*Raises her.*]   Worthy colonel,
Has such a conquering way i' the blest things !
Whoever overcomes, he only wins.   [*Exeunt.*

SCENE IV.[1]

A Street.   A noise of "hem"[2] within.

Enter Captain ALBO, MEG, *and* PRISS.

Meg. Hark of these hard-hearted bloodhounds ! these
butchers are e'en as merciless as their dogs ; they knock
down a women's fame e'en as it walks the streets by 'em.

Priss. And the captain here that should defend us
walks by like John of the apple-loft.[3]

Cap. Albo. What for interjections, Priss, *hem, evax,
vah ?* let the carnifexes[4] scour their throats ! thou
knowest there is a curse hangs over their bloody heads ;
this year there shall be more butchers' pricks burnt than
of all trades besides.

Meg. I do wonder how thou camest to be a captain.

Cap. Albo. As thou camest to be a bawd, Meg, and
Priss to be a whore ; every one by their deserts.

Meg. Bawd and whore? out, you unprofitable rascal !
hast not thou been at the new play yet, to teach thee

---

[1] This scene is not in the original impression. It was added
when the unsold copies were re-issued with a fresh title-page. --
Bullen.

[2] Compare *The Honest Whore*, Part ii. iv. 1, where Bellafront says
that during her days of vice, when she appeared in the street,
"though with face masked," she "could not scape the *hem.*" --*Dyce.*

[3] "John of the apple-loft" seems to be synonymous with "apple-
squire," a cant term for a pimp.

[4] Scoundrels (literally, hangmen).

better manners? truly they say they are the finest players, and good speakers of gentlewomen of our quality ; bawd and whore is not mentioned amongst 'em, but the handsomest narrow-mouthed names they have for us, that some of them may serve as well for a lady as for one of our occupation.

Priss. Prithee, patroness, let's go see a piece of that play ; if we shall have good words for our money, 'tis as much as we can deserve, i'faith.

Meg. I doubt 'tis too late now ; but another time, servant.

Cap. Albo. Let's go now, sweet face ; I am acquainted with one of the pantomimics ; the bulchins [1] will use the Irish captain with respect, and you two shall be boxed amongst the better sort.

Priss. Sirrah Captain Albo, I doubt you are but white-livered ; look that you defend us valiantly, you know your penance else.—Patroness, you remember how you used him once?

Meg. Ay, servant, and I shall never forget it till I use him so again.—Do you remember, captain?

Cap. Albo. Mum, Meg ; I will not hear on't now.

Meg. How I and my amazons stript you as naked as an Indian——

Cap. Albo. Why, Meg——

Meg. And then how I bound you to the good behaviour in the open fields——

Priss. And then you strowed oats upon his hoppers——

Cap. Albo. Prithee, sweet face——

Priss. And then brought your ducks to nibble upon him.—You remember?

Cap. Albo. O, the remembrance tortures me again ! no more, good sweet face.

Meg. Well, lead on, sir ; but hark a little.

---

[1] Bulkins, bull-calves.

Enter CHOUGH *and* TRIMTRAM.

Chough. Didst thou bargain for the bladders with the butcher, Trim?

Trim. Ay, sir, I have 'em here; I'll practise to swim too, sir, and then I may roar with the water at London Bridge: he that roars by land and by water both is the perfect roarer.

Chough. Well, I'll venture to swim too: if my father-in-law gives me a good dowry with his daughter, I shall hold up my head well enough.

Trim. Peace, sir; here's practice for our roaring, here's a centaur and two hippocrenes.

Chough. Offer the jostle, Trim.

                [TRIMTRAM *jostles* Captain ALBO.

Cap. Albo. Ha! what meanest thou by that?

Trim. I mean to confront thee, cyclops.

Chough. I'll tell thee what 'a means—is this thy sister?

Cap. Albo. How then, sir?

Chough. Why, then, I say she is a bronstrops;[1] and this is a fucus.

Priss. No, indeed, sir; we are both fucusses.

Cap. Albo. Art thou military? art thou a soldier?

Chough. A soldier? no, I scorn to be so poor; I am a roarer.

Cap. Albo. A roarer?

Trim. Ay, sir, two roarers.

Cap. Albo. Know, then, my fresh-water friends, that I am a captain.

Chough. What, and have but two to serve under you?

Cap. Albo. I am now retiring the field.

Trim. You may see that by his bag and baggage.

Chough. Deliver up thy panagron to me.

[1] Prostitute.

Trim. And give me thy sindicus.

Cap. Albo. Deliver?

Meg. I pray you, captain, be contented; the gentlemen seem to give us very good words.

Chough. Good words? ay, if you could understand 'em; the words cost twenty pound.

Meg. What is your pleasure, gentlemen?

Chough. I would enucleate my fructifier.

Priss. What says he, patroness?

Meg. He would enoculate: I understand the gentleman very pithily.

Cap. Albo. Speak, are you gentle or plebeian? can you give arms?[1]

Chough. Arms? ay, sir; you shall feel our arms presently.

Trim. 'Sault you the women; I'll pepper him till he stinks again: I perceive what countrymen he is; let me alone with him.

Cap. Albo. Darest thou charge a captain?

Trim. Yes, and discharge upon him too.

Cap. Albo. Foh, 'tis poison to my country, the slave has eaten pippins! O, shoot no more! turn both thy broadsides rather than thy poop; 'tis foul play; my country breeds no poison.[2] I yield; the great O Toole[3] shall yield on these conditions.

Chough. I have given one of 'em a fair fall, Trim.

Trim. Then thus far we bring home conquest.— Follow me, captain; the cyclops doth command.

Chough. Follow me, tweaks,[4] the centaur doth command.

[1] "Give arms" is to bear arms in an heraldic sense.

[2] According to the legend, St Patrick purged Ireland from all venomous creatures.

[3] Notorious for his romantic bravery, vanity, and eccentricity. His own country was not the only one in which he figured; for he served as a volunteer, and displayed his courage and absurdities in various parts of Europe.   [4] Prostitutes.

Meg. Anything, sweet gentlemen: will't please you
to lead to the tavern, where we'll make all friends?

Trim. Why, now you come to the conclusion.

Chough. Stay, Trim; I have heard your tweaks are
like your mermaids, they have sweet voices to entice the
passengers: let's have a song, and then we'll set 'em at
liberty.

Trim. In the commendation of roaring, not else, sir.

Chough. Ay, in the commendation of roaring.

Meg. The best we can, gentlemen.

[*Sings,* PRISS *joining in chorus.*

> Then here thou shalt resign
>   Both captain and commander;
> That name was never thine,
>   But apple-squire[1] and pander;
> And henceforth will we grant,
>   In pillage or in monies,
> In clothing or provant,[2]
>   Whate'er we get by conies:
> With a hone, a hone, a hone,
>   No cheaters nor decoys
> Shall have a share, but alone
>   The bravest roaring boys.
>
> Whate'er we get by gulls
>   Of country or of city,
> Old flat-caps[3] or young heirs,
>   Or lawyers' clerks so witty;
> By sailors newly landed,
>   To put in for fresh waters;
> By wandering gander-mooners,[4]
>   Or muffled late night-walkers.
>   With a hone, &c.

[1] Pimp.   [2] Provisions.

[3] A nick-name for citizens.

[4] Gander-mooner is one who practised gallantry during the time
his wife was lying in a period that was known as the gand r-month.

Whate'er we get by strangers,
  The Scotch, the Dutch, or Irish,
Or, to come nearer home,
  By masters of the parish;
It is concluded thus,
  By all and every wench,
To take of all their coins,
  And pay 'em back in French.
    With a hone, &c.

Chough. Melodious minotaur!

Trim. Harmonious hippocrene!

Chough. Sweet-breasted [1] bronstrops!

Trim. Most tunable tweak!

Chough. Delicious duplar!

Trim. Putrefactious panagron!

Chough. Calumnious callicut!

Trim. And most singular sindicus!

Meg. We shall never be able to deserve these good words at your hands, gentlemen.

Cap. Albo. Shake golls [2] with the captain; he shall be thy valiant friend.

Chough. Not yet, captain; we must make an end of our roaring first.

Trim. We'll serve 'em as we did the tobacco-man, lay a curse upon 'em; marry, we'll lay it on gently, because they have used us so kindly, and then we'll shake golls together.

Priss. As gently as you can, sweet gentlemen.

Chough. For thee, O pander, mayst thou trudge till the damned soles of thy boots fleet into dirt, but never rise into air!

Trim. Next, mayst thou fleet so long from place to place, till thou be'st kicked out of Fleet Street!

---

[1] Sweet-voiced   [2] Cant term for hands.

Chough. As thou hast lived by bad flesh, so rotten mutton be thy bane!

Trim. When thou art dead, may twenty whores follow thee, that thou mayst go a squire [1] to thy grave!

Cap. Albo. Enough for me, sweet faces; let me sleep in my grave.

Chough. For thee, old sindicus, may I see thee ride in a caroch with two wheels, and drawn with one horse.[2]

Trim. Ten beadles running by, instead of footmen!

Chough. With every one a whip, 'stead of an Irish dart![3]

Trim. Forty barbers' basins [4] sounding before, instead of trumpets!

Meg. This will be comely indeed, sweet gentlemen roarers.

Trim. Thy ruff starched yellow with rotten eggs!

Chough. And mayst thou then be drawn from Holborn to Hounslow Heath!

Trim. And then be burnt to Colebrook, for destroying of Maidenhead!

Meg. I will study to deserve this kindness at your hands, gentlemen.

Chough. Now, for thee, little fucus; mayst thou first serve out thy time as a tweak, and then become a bronstrops, as she is!

Trim. Mayst thou have a reasonable good spring, for thou art likely to have many dangerous foul falls!

Chough. Mayst thou have two ruffs torn in one week!

Trim. May spiders only weave thy cobweb-lawn!

Chough. Mayst thou set up in Rogue-lane——

[1] Pimp.   [2] Meaning may you be carted as a bawd.

[3] An allusion to the darts carried by Irish running-footmen.—*Dyce.*

[4] When bawds were carted, a mob preceded them, beating metal basins. The hiring of their basins for this purpose was a source of profit to the barbers.—*Nares.*

Trim. Live till thou stinkest in Garden-alleys——

Chough. And die sweetly in Tower-ditch!

Priss. I thank you for that, good sir roarer.

Chough. Come, shall we go now, Trim? my father-in-law stays for me all this while.

Trim. Nay, I'll serve 'em as we did the tobacco-man; I'll bury 'em altogether, and give 'em an epitaph.

Chough. All together, Trim? why, then, the epitaph will be accessary to the sin.

Trim. Alas, he has kept the door[1] all his life-time! for pity, let 'em lie together in their graves.

Cap. Albo. E'en as thou wilt, Trim, and I thank you too, sir.

Trim. He that the reason would know, let him hark,
Why these three were buried near Marybone Park:
These three were a pander, a bawd, and a whore,
That sucked many dry to the bones before.
Will you know how they lived? here't may be read:
The Low Countries did ever find 'em bread;
They lived by Flushing, by Sluys, and the Groyne,
Sickened in France, and died under the Line.
Three letters at last commended 'em hither,
But the hangman broke one in putting together:
P was the first, who cries out for a pardon,
O craves his book, yet could not read such a hard one,
An X was the last, which in conjunction
Was broke by Brandon;[2] and here's the conclusion:
By three trees, three letters, these three, pander, bawd,
        whore,
Now stink below ground, stunk long above before.

Chough. So, now we have done with you; remember roaring boys.

Trim. Farewell, centaur!

---

[1] *i.e.* Been a pander.

[2] Gregory Brandon, the common hangman, and father of Richard, who is supposed to have beheaded Charles I.

Chough. Farewell, bronstrops!

Trim. Farewell, fucus!

              [*Exeunt* CHOUGH *and* TRIMTRAM.

Cap. Albo. Well, Meg, I will learn to roar, and still maintain the name of captain over these lance-presadoes.[1]

Meg. If thou dost not, mayst thou be buried under the roaring curse!   [*Exeunt.*

       [1] Lance-corporals, "leaders of half a file."

ACT THE FIFTH.

SCENE I.

A Room in RUSSELL'S *House.*

Enter Physician, *and* JANE *dressed as a bride.*

HY. Will you be obstinate?
 Jane. Torment me not,
Thou lingering executioner to death,
Greatest disease to nature, that striv'st by art
To make men long a-dying! your practice is
Upon men's bodies; as men pull roses
For their own relish, but to kill the flower,
So you maintain your lives by others' deaths:
What eat you then but carrion?
 Phy. Fie, bitterness!
Ye'd need to candy o'er your tongue a little,
Your words will hardly be digested else.
 Jane. You can give yourself a vomit to return 'em,
If they offend your stomach.
 Phy. Hear my vow;
You are to be married to-day——
 Jane. A second torment,
Worse than the first, 'cause unavoidable!

I would I could as soon annihilate
My father's will in that as forbid thy lust!

 Phy. If you then tender an unwilling hand,
Meet it with revenge, marry a cuckold.

 Jane. If thou wilt marry me, I'll make that vow,
And give my body for satisfaction
To him that should enjoy me for his wife.

 Phy. Go to; I'll mar your marriage.

 Jane. Do; plague me so:
I'll rather bear the brand of all that's past,
In capital characters upon my brow,
Than think to be thy whore or marry him.

 Phy. I will defame thee ever——

 Jane. Spare me not.

 Phy. I will produce thy bastard,
Bring thee to public penance——

 Jane. No matter, I care not;
I shall then have a clean sheet; I'll wear twenty,
Rather than one defiled with thee.

 Phy. Look for revenge!

 Jane. Pursue it fully then.—Out of his hate
I shall escape, I hope, a loathed fate.   [*Aside and exit.*

 Phy. Am I rejected, all my baits nibbled off,
And not the fish caught? I'll trouble the whole stream,
And choke it in the mud: since hooks not take,
I'll throw in nets that shall or kill or break.

Enter TRIMTRAM *with rosemary.*[1]

This is the bridegroom's man.—Hark, sir, a word.

 Trim. 'Tis a busy day, sir, nor I need no physic;
You see I scour about my business.

 Phy. Pray you, a word, sir: your master is to be
married to-day?

 Trim. Else all this rosemary's lost.

 . Rosemary was used both at weddings and funerals.

Phy. I would speak with your master, sir.

Trim. My master, sir, is to be married this morning,
and cannot be within while [1] soon at night.

Phy. If you will do your master the best service
That e'er you did him; if he shall not curse
Your negligence hereafter slacking it;
If he shall bless me for the dearest friend
That ever his acquaintance met withal;
Let me speak with him ere he go to church.

Trim. A right physician! you would have none go to
the church nor churchyard till you send them thither:
well, if Death do not spare you yourselves, he deals hardly
with you, for you are better benefactors and send more
to him than all diseases besides.

Chough. [*Within.*] What, Trimtram, Trimtram!

Trim. I come, sir.—Hark you, you may hear him!
he's upon the spur, and would fain mount the saddle of
matrimony; but, if I can, I'll persuade him to come to
you.

Phy. Pray you, do, sir. [*Exit* TRIMTRAM.]—I'll teach
　　all peevish niceness
To beware the strong advantage of revenge.

Enter CHOUGH.

Chough. Who's that would speak with me?

Phy. None but a friend, sir; I would speak with you.

Chough. Why, sir, and I dare speak with any man
under the universe. Can you roar, sir?

Phy. No, in faith, sir;
I come to tell you mildly for your good,
If you please to hear me: you are upon marriage?

Chough. No, sir; I am towards it, but not upon it
yet.

Phy. Do you know what you do?

　　　　　　　[1] Until.

Chough. Yes, sir, I have practised what to do before now ; I would be ashamed to be married else : I have seen a bronstrops in my time, and a hippocrene, and a tweak too.

Phy. Take fair heed, sir; the wife that you would
          marry
Is not fit for you.

Chough. Why, sir, have you tried her?

Phy. Not I, believe it, sir ; but believe withal
She has been tried.

Chough. Why, sir, is she a fructifer or a fucus?

Phy. All that I speak, sir, is in love to you :
Your bride, that may be, has not that portion
That a bride should have.

Chough. Why, sir, she has a thousand and a better
penny.

Phy. I do not speak of rubbish, dross, and ore,
But the refinèd metal, honour, sir.

Chough. What she wants in honour shall be made up
in worship, sir ; money will purchase both.

Phy. To be plain with you, she's naught.

Chough. If thou canst not roar, thou'rt a dead man !
my bride naught?   [*Drawing his sword.*

Phy. Sir, I do not fear you that way ; what I speak
                               [*Drawing his sword.*
My life shall maintain ; I say she is naught.

Chough. Dost thou not fear me?

Phy. Indeed I do not, sir.

Chough. I'll never draw upon thee while I live for
that trick ; put up and speak freely.

Phy. Your intended bride is a whore ; that's freely,
          sir.

Chough. Yes, faith, a whore's free enough, an she
hath a conscience : is she a whore? foot, I warrant she
has the pox then.

Phy. Worse, the plague ; 'tis more incurable.

Chough. A plaguy whore? a pox on her, I'll none of her!

Phy. Mine accusation shall have firm evidence;
I will produce an unavoided[1] witness,
A bastard of her bearing.

Chough. A bastard? 'snails,[2] there's great suspicion she's a whore then! I'll wrestle a fall with her father for putting this trick upon me, as I am a gentleman.

Phy. Good sir, mistake me not; I do not speak
To break the contract of united hearts;
I will not pull that curse upon my head,
To separate the husband and the wife;
But this, in love, I thought fit to reveal,
As the due office betwixt man and man,
That you might not be ignorant of your ills.
Consider now of my premonishment
As yourself shall please.

Chough. I'll burn all the rosemary to sweeten the house, for, in my conscience, 'tis infected: has she drunk bastard?[3] if she would piss me wine-vinegar now nine times a day, I'd never have her, and I thank you too.

Re-enter TRIMTRAM.

Trim. Come, will you come away, sir? they have all rosemary, and stay for you to lead the way.

Chough. I'll not be married to-day, Trimtram: hast e'er an almanac about thee? this is the nineteenth of August, look what day of the month 'tis.

Trim. 'Tis tenty-nine[4] indeed, sir.

[*Looks in an almanac.*

Chough. What's the word?[5] what says Bretnor?[6]

---

[1] Irrefutable.　　　　[2] A corruption of God's nails.

[3] A common wine of the period.

[4] *i.e.* Ten and nine.　　　　[5] Motto.

[6] A celebrated almanac-maker and soothsayer.

Trim. The word is, sir, " There's a hole in her coat."

Chough. I thought so; the physician agrees with him; I'll not marry to-day.

Trim. I pray you, sir; there will be charges for new rosemary else; this will be withered by to-morrow.

Chough. Make a bonfire on't, to sweeten Rosemary-lane: prithee, Trim, entreat my father-in-law that might have been, to come and speak with me.

Trim. The bride cries already and looks t'other way; an you be so backward too, we shall have a fine arse-ward wedding on't.   [*Exit.*

Chough. You'll stand to your words, sir?

Phy. I'll not fly the house, sir;
When you have need, call me to evidence.

Chough. If you'll prove she has borne a bastard, I'll stand to't she's a whore.   [*Exit* Physician.

Enter RUSSELL *and* TRIMTRAM.

Rus. Why, how now, son? what causeth these delays?
All stay for your leading.

Chough. Came I from the Mount to be confronted?

Rus. How's that, sir?

Chough. Canst thou roar, old man?

Rus. Roar? how mean you, sir?

Chough. Why, then, I'll tell thee plainly, thy daughter is a bronstrops.

Rus. A bronstrops? what's that, sir?

Trim. Sir, if she be so, she is a hippocrene.

Chough. Nay, worse, she is a fructifer.

Trim. Nay, then, she is a fucus, a minotaur, and a tweak.

Rus. Pray you, speak to my understanding, sir.

Chough. If thou wilt have it in plain terms, she is a callicut and a panagron.

Trim. Nay, then, she is a duplar and a sindicus.

Rus. Good, sir, speak English to me.

Chough. All this is Cornish to thee; I say thy daughter has drunk bastard in her time.

Rus. Bastard? you do not mean to make her a whore?

Chough. Yes, but I do, if she make a fool of me; I'll ne'er make her my wife till she have her maidenhead again.

Rus. A whore? I do defy this calumny.

Chough. Dost thou? I defy thee then.

Trim. Do you, sir? then I defy thee too: fight with us both at once in this quarrel, if thou darest!

Chough. I could have had a whore at Plymouth.

Trim. Ay, or at Pe'ryn.[1]

Chough. Ay, or under the Mount.

Trim. Or as you came at Ivel.[2]

Chough. Or at Wookey-Hole in Somersetshire.

Trim. Or at the Hanging-stones in Wiltshire.

Chough. Or at Maidenhead in Berkshire: and did I come in by Maidenhead to go out by Staines? O, that man, woman, or child would wrestle with me for a pound of patience!

Rus. Some thief has put in poison at your ears,
To steal the good name of my child from me;
Or if it be a malice of your own,
Be sure I will enforce a proof from you.

Chough. He's a goose and a woodcock that says
I will not prove any word that I speak.

Trim. Ay, either goose or woodcock; he shall, sir, with any man.

Chough. Phy-si-ci-an! mauz avez[3] physician!

Rus. Is he the author?

---

[1] Penryn.   [2] Yeovil.
[3] Is this Cornish?—*Dyce.*

Re-enter Physician.

Phy. Sir, with much sorrow for your sorrow's sake,
I must deliver this most certain truth ;
Your daughter is an honour-stainèd bride,
Indeed she is the mother to a child   ·
Before the lawful wife unto a husband.

Chough. La, that's worse than I told thee ; I said she
had borne a bastard, and he says she was the mother
on't too.

Rus. I'm yet an infidel against all this,
And will believe the sun is made of brass,
The stars of amber——

Chough. And the moon of a Holland cheese.

Rus. Rather than this impossibility.
O, here she comes.

Re-enter JANE *with* ANNE.

Nay, come, daughter, stand at the bar of shame ;
Either now quit thyself, or kill me ever :
Your marriage-day is spoiled, if all be true.

Jane. A happy misery ! who's my accuser?

Phy. I am, that knows it true I speak.

Chough. Yes, and I'm his witness.

Trim. And I.

Chough. And I again.

Trim. And I again too ; there's four, that's enough, I
hope.

Rus. How can you witness, sir, that nothing know
But what you have received from his report?

Chough. Must we not believe our physicians? pray
you, think I know as much as every fool does.

Trim. Let me be Trimtram, I pray you too, sir.

Jane. Sir, if this bad man have laid a blemish

On my white name, he is a most false one,
Defaming me for the just denial
Of his foul lust.—Nay, now you shall be known,
    sir.

Anne. Sir, I'm his sister, and do better know him
Than all of you : give not too much belief
To his wild words; he's oftentimes mad, sir.

Phy. I thank you, good sister!

Anne. Are you not mad
To do this office? fie upon your malice!

Phy. I'll presently produce both nurse and child,
Whose very eyes shall call her mother before it speaks.

                                   [*Exit.*

Chough. Ha, ha, ha, ha! by my troth, I'd spend a
shilling on that condition to hear that : I think in my
conscience I shall take the physician in a lie; if the child
call her mother before it can speak, I'll never wrestle
while I live again.

Trim. It must be a she child, if it do, sir; and
those speak the soonest of any living creatures, they
say.

Chough. Baw, waw! a dog will bark a month sooner;
he's a very puppy else.

Rus. Come, tell truth 'twixt ourselves; here's none
    but friends:
One spot a father's love will soon wipe off;
The truth, and thereby try my love abundant;
I'll cover it with all the care I have,
And yet, perhaps, make up a marriage-day.

Jane. Then it's true, sir, I have a child.

Rus. Hast thou?
Well, wipe thine eyes; I'm a grandfather then.
If all bastards were banished, the city would be thin
In the thickest term-time.   Well, now let me alone,
I'll try my wits for thee.—Richard, Francis, Andrew!
None of my knaves within?

Enter Servant.

Ser. Here's one of 'em, sir: the guests come in apace.

Rus. Do they, Dick? let 'em have wine and sugar;
we'll be for 'em presently; but hark, Dick.

[*Whispers* Servant.

Chough. I long to hear this child speak, i'faith, Trim;
I would this foolish physician would come once.

Trim. If it calls her mother, I hope it shall never call
you father.

Chough. No; an it do, I'll whip it, i'faith, and give
thee leave to whip me.

Rus. Run on thy best legs, Dick.

Ser. I'll be here in a twinkling, sir.　　　[*Exit.*

Re-enter Physician *with* Dutch Nurse *and* Child.

Phy. Now, gentlemen, believe your eyes, if not
My tongue.—Do not you call this your child?

Chough. Phew, that's not the point! you promised us
the child should call her mother; if it does this month,
I'll ne'er go to the roaring school again.

Rus. Whose child is this, nurse?

Nurse. Dis gentleman's, so he to me readen.

[*Points to the* Physician.

Chough. 'Snails, she's the physician's bronstrops,
Trim!

Trim. His fucus, his very tweak, i'faith.

Chough. A glister in his teeth! let him take her, with
a purgation to him!

Rus. 'Tis as your sister said, you are stark mad,
　　　sir,
This much confirms it; you have defamed
Mine honest daughter; I'll have you punished for't,
Besides the civil penance of your sin,
And keeping of your bastard.

　　Mid. II.　　　　　　　　　　　　　U

Phy. This is fine!
All your wit and wealth must not thus carry it.

Rus. Sir Chough, a word with you.

Cough. I'll not have her, i'faith, sir; if Trimtram
will have her, an he will, let him.

Trim. Who, I, sir? I scorn it: if you'll have her,
I'll have her too; I'll do as you do, and no otherwise.

Rus. I do not mean't to either; this only, sir,
That whatsoe'er you've seen, you would be silent;
Hinder not my child of another husband,
Though you forsake her.

Chough. I'll not speak a word, i'faith.

Rus. As you are a gentleman?

Chough. By these basket-hilts, as I am a youth, a
gentleman, a roarer.

Rus. Charm your man,[1] I beseech you, too.

Chough. I warrant you, sir, he shall do nothing but
what I do before him.

Rus. I shall most dearly thank you.—

Re-enter Servant *with* FITZALLEN.

O, are you come?
Welcome, son-in-law! this was beyond your hope:
We old men have pretty conceits sometimes;
Your wedding-day's prepared, and this is it;
How think you of it?

Fitz. As of the joyfullest
That ever welcomed me! you show yourself now
A pattern to all kind fathers.—My sweetest Jane!

Rus. Your captivity I meant but as sauce
Unto your wedding-dinner; now I'm sure
'Tis far more welcome in this short restraint
Than had it freely come.

Fitz. A thousandfold.

[1] Cause him to keep silent.

Jane. I like this well. [*Aside.*

Chough. I have not the heart to see this gentleman gulled so; I will reveal; I make it mine own case; 'tis a foul case.

Trim. Remember you have sworn by your hilts.

Chough. I'll break my hilts rather than conceal: I have a trick; do thou follow me; I will reveal it, and yet not speak it neither.

Trim. 'Tis my duty to follow you, sir.

Chough. [*Sings.*] "Take heed in time, O man, unto thy head!"

Trim. [*Sings.*] "All is not gold that glistereth in bed."

Rus. Why, sir,—why, sir!

Chough. [*Sings.*] "Look to't, I say, thy bride is a bronstrops."

Trim. [*Sings.*] "And knows the thing that men wear in their slops."

Fitz. How's this, sir?

Chough. [*Sings.*] "A hippocrene, a tweak, for and[1] a fucus."

Trim. [*Sings.*] "Let not fond love with foretops so rebuke us."

Rus. Good sir——

Chough. [*Sings.*] "Behold a baby of this maid's begetting."

Trim. [*Sings.*] "A deed of darkness after the sunsetting."

Rus. Your oath, sir!

Chough. [*Sings.*] "I swear and sing thy bride has taken physic."

Trim. [*Sings.*] "This was the doctor cured her of that phthisic."

Chough. [*Sings.*] "If you'll believe me, I will say no more."

Trim. [*Sings.*] "Thy bride's a tweak, as we do say that roar."

And also.

Chough. Bear witness, gentlemen, I have not spoke a
word ; my hilts are whole still.

Fitz. This is a sweet epithalamium
Unto the marriage-bed, a musical,
Harmonious Iö ! Sir, you have wronged me,
And basely wronged me ! was this your cunning fetch,
To fetch me out of prison, for ever to marry me
Unto a strumpet?

Rus. None of those words, good sir ;
'Tis but a fault, and 'tis a sweet one too.
Come, sir, your means is short; lengthen your fortunes
With a fair proffer : I'll put a thousand pieces
Into the scale, to help her to weigh it up,
Above the first dowry.

Fitz. Ha ? you say well ;
Shame may be bought out at a dear rate ;
A thousand pieces added to her dowry !

Rus. There's five hundred of 'em to make the bar-
gain ;   [*Gives money.*
I've worthy guests coming, and would not delude 'em ;
Say, speak like a son to me.

Fitz. Your blessing, sir ;
We are both yours :—witness, gentlemen,
These must be made up a thousand pieces,
Added to a first thousand for her dowry,
To father that child.

Phy. O, is it out now ?

Chough. For t'other thousand, I'll do't myself yet.

Trim. Or I, if my master will.

Fitz. The bargain's made, sir ; I have the tender
And possession both, and will keep my purchase.

Chough. Take her e'en to you with all her moveables;
I'll wear my bachelor's buttons still.

Trim. So will I, i'faith ; they are the best flowers in
any man's garden, next to heart's-ease.

Fitz. This is as welcome as the other, sir.

And both as the best bliss that e'er on earth
I shall enjoy.   Sir, this is mine own child;
You could not have found out a fitter father;
Nor is it basely bred, as you imagine,
For we were wedded by the hand of Heaven
Ere this work was begun.

 Chough. At Pancridge,[1] I'll lay my life on't.

 Trim. I'll lay my life on't too, 'twas there.

 Fitz. Somewhere it was, sir.

 Rus. Was't so, i'faith, son?

 Jane. And that I must have revealed to you, sir,
Ere I had gone to church with this fair groom;
But, thank this gentleman, he prevented[2] me.—
I am much bound unto your malice, sir.

 Phy. I am ashamed.

 Jane. Shame to amendment then.

 Rus. Now get you together for a couple of cunning
  ones!
But, son, a word; the latter thousand pieces
Is now more than the bargain.

 Fitz. No, by my faith, sir,
Here's witness enough on it; it must serve
To pay my fees, imprisonment is costly.

 Chough. By my troth, the old man has gulled himself
finely! Well, sir, I'll bid myself a guest, though not a
groom; I'll dine, and dance, and roar at the wedding
for all this.

 Trim. So will I, sir, if my master does.

 Rus. Well, sir, you're welcome: but now no more
  words on't
Till we be set at dinner, for there will mirth
Be the most useful for digestion:
See, my best guests are coming.

---

 [1] Pancras.   A "Pancridge parson" was the convenient clergyman
of that day.—*Bullen.*

 [2] Anticipated.

Enter Lady AGER, *the* Colonel's Sister, Captain AGER,
his two Friends, *and* Surgeon.

Cap. Ager. Recovered, sayst thou?

Surg. May I be excluded quite out of Surgeons' Hall
else! marry, I must tell you the wound was fain to be
twice corroded; 'twas a plain gastroraphe, and a deep
one; but I closed the lips on't with bandages and
sutures, which is a kind conjunction of the parts
separated against the course of nature.

Cap. Ager. Well, sir, he is well.

Surg. I feared him, I assure you, captain; before the
suture in the belly, it grew almost to a convulsion, and
there was like to be a bloody issue from the hollow
vessels of the kidneys.

Cap. Ager. There's that, to thank thy news and thy
      art together.   [*Gives him money.*

Surg. And if your worship at any time stand in need
of incision, if it be your fortune to light into my hands,
I'll give you the best.

Cap. Ager. Uncle, the noble colonel's recovered.

Rus. Recovered?
Then honour is not dead in all parts, coz.

Enter the Colonel *and two* Friends.

1st Fr. of Cap. Behold him yonder, sir.

Cap. Ager. My much unworthiness
Is now found out; thou'st not a face to fit it.

1st Fr. of Col. Sir, yonder's Captain Ager.

Col. O lieutenant,
The wrong I've done his fame puts me to silence;
Shame so confounds me, that I dare not see him.

Cap. Ager. I never knew how poor my deserts were
Till he appeared; no way to give requital!
Here shame me lastingly, do't with his own:

Return this to him; tell him I have riches
In that abundance in his sister's love,
These come but to oppress me, and confound
All my deservings everlastingly;
I never shall requite my wealth in her, say.
> [*Giving the will to his* Friend, *who delivers it to
> the* Colonel.

How soon from virtue and an honoured spirit
May man receive what he may never merit!

　Col. This comes most happily, to express me better;
For since this will was made, there fell to me
The manor of Fitzdale; give him that too;
> [*Returning the will with other papers.*

He's like to have charge,
There's fair hope of my sister's fruitfulness:
For me, I never mean to change my mistress,
And war is able to maintain her servant.

　1*st Fr. of Cap.* Read there; a fair increase, sir, oy
　　my faith;
He has sent it back, sir, with new additions.

　Cap. Ager. How miserable he makes me! this en-
　　forces me
To break through all the passages oi shame,
And headlong fall——

　Col. Into my arms, dear worthy!

　Cap. Ager. You have a goodness
Has put me past my answers; you may speak
What you please now,-I must be silent ever.

　Col. This day has shown me joy's unvalued treasure;
I would not change this brotherhood with a monarch;
Into which blest alliance sacred Heaven
Has placed my kinsman, and given him his ends:
Fair be that quarrel makes such happy friends!
> [*Exeunt.*

THE MAYOR
OF QUEENBOROUGH.

 HE MAYOR OF QUEENBOROUGH was not printed until 1661, when it appeared as "a Comedy, as it hath been often Acted with much Applause at Black-Fryars, By his Majesties Servants. Written by Tho. Middleton." Mr. Dyce considered it a very early work of Middleton's; Mr. Bullen thinks that "it underwent considerable revision at a later date, and has descended in its revised form." Until recent years it attracted little attention.

Prefixed to the First Edition of the Play.

Gentlemen,

OU have the first flight of him, I assure you. This *Mayor of Queenborough*, whom you have all heard of, and some of you beheld upon the stage, now begins to walk abroad in print : he has been known sufficiently by the reputation of his wit, which is enough, by the way, to distinguish him from ordinary mayors ; but wit, you know, has skulked in corners for many years past,[1] and he was thought to have most of it that could best hide himself. Now, whether this magistrate feared the decimating times, or kept up the state of other mayors, that are bound not to go out of their liberties during the time of their mayoralty, I know not : 'tis enough for me to put him into your hands, under the title of an honest man, which will appear plainly to you, because you shall find him all along to have a great pique to the rebel Oliver. I am told his drollery yields to none the English drama did ever produce ; and, though I would not put his modesty to the blush, by speaking too much in his commendation, yet I know you will agree with me, upon your better acquaintance with him, that there is some difference in point of wit betwixt the *Mayor of Queenborough* and the *Mayor of Huntingdon.*[2]

1 In allusion to the play-houses having been closed by the Puritans.
2 Huntingdon was the birth-place of Cromwell, after whom the rebel Oliver of the play was probably named or re-named.

DRAMATIS PERSONÆ.

CONSTANTIUS,
AURELIUS AMBROSIUS, } sons of CONSTANTINE.
UTHER PENDRAGON,
VORTIGER.
VORTIMER, his son.
DEVONSHIRE, } British lords.
STAFFORD,
GERMANUS, } monks.
LUPUS,
HENGIST.
HORSUS.
SIMON, a tanner, Mayor of Queenborough.
AMINADAB, his clerk.
OLIVER, a fustian-weaver.
Glover.
Barber,
Tailor.
Feltmonger.
Button-maker.
Graziers.
Players.
Gentlemen.
Murderers.
Soldiers, Footmen, &c.

CASTIZA, daughter of DEVONSHIRE.
ROXENA daughter of HENGIST.
Ladies.

RAYNULPH HIGDEN, Monk of Chester, as Chorus.

SCENE—KENT, and other parts of England, with the exception of the final scene, which is in Wales.

THE MAYOR
OF QUEENBOROUGH.

ACT THE FIRST.

Enter RAYNULPH, *as* Chorus.[1]

AY. What Raynulph, monk of Chester, can
Raise from his Polychronicon,
That raiseth him, as works do men,
To see long-parted light agen,
That best may please this round fair ring,
With sparkling diamonds circled in,
I shall produce. If all my powers
Can win the grace of two poor hours,
Well apaid I go to rest.
Ancient stories have been best ;
Fashions, that are now called new,
Have been worn by more than you ;
Elder times have used the same,
Though these new ones get the name :

---

[1] Raynulph Higden of St. Werberg's monastery, in Chester, was
the compiler of the *Polychronicon*, up to the year 1357.

So in story what now told
That takes not part with days of old ?
Then to approve time's mutual glory,
Join new time's love to old time's story.   [*Exit.*

SCENE I.

Before a Monastery.

Shouts within ; then enter VORTIGER, *carrying the crown.*

Vort. Will that wide-throated beast, the multitude,
Never leave bellowing ?   Courtiers are ill
Advisèd when they first make such monsters.
How near was I to a sceptre and a crown !
Fair power was even upon me ; my desires
Were casting glory, till this forkèd rabble,
With their infectious acclamations,
Poisoned my fortunes for Constantine's sons.
Well, though I rise not king, I'll seek the means
To grow as near to one as policy can,
And choke their expectations.

Enter DEVONSHIRE *and* STAFFORD.

Now, good lords,
In whose kind loves and wishes I am built
As high as human dignity can aspire,
Are yet those trunks, that have no other souls
But noise and ignorance, something more quiet ?
Devon. Nor are they like to be, for aught we gather
There wills are up still ; nothing can appease them ;
Good speeches are but cast away upon them.
Vort. Then, since necessity and fate withstand me,

I'll strive to enter at a straiter passage.
Your sudden aid and counsels, good my lords.
   Staff. They're ours no longer than they do you
     service.

Enter CONSTANTIUS *in the habit of a monk, attended by*
    GERMANUS *and* LUPUS : *as they are going into the*
    monastery, VORTIGER *stays them.*

   Vort. Vessels of sanctity, be pleased a while
To give attention to the general peace,
Wherein Heaven is served too, though not so purely.
Constantius, eldest son of Constantine,
We here seize on thee for the general good,
And in thy right of birth.
   Const. On me ! for what, lords ?
   Vort. The kingdom's government.
   Const. O powers of blessedness,,
Keep me from growing downwards into earth again !
I hope I'm further on my way than so.
Set forwards !
   Vort. You must not.
   Const. How !
   Vort. I know your wisdom
Will light upon a way to pardon us,
When you shall read in every Briton's brow
The urged necessity of the times.
   Const. What necessity can there be in the world,
But prayer and repentance ? and that is business
I am about now.
   Vort. Hark, afar off still !
We lose and hazard much.—Holy Germanus
And reverend Lupus, with all expedition
Set the crown on him.
   Const. No such mark of fortune
Comes near my head.

Vort. My lord, we're forced to rule you.

Const. Dare you receive Heaven's light in at your eye-
      lids,
And offer violence to religion ?
Take heed ;
The very beam let in to comfort you
May be the fire to burn you.   On these knees,

                                    [*Kneeling.*

Hardened with zealous prayers, I entreat you
Bring not my cares into the world again !
Think with how much unwillingness and anguish
A glorified soul parted from the body
Would to that loathsome jail again return ;
With such great pain a well-subdued affection
Re-enters worldly business.

      Vort. Good my lord,
I know you cannot lodge so many virtues,
But patience must be one.   As low as earth

            [*Kneeling with* DEVONSHIRE *and* STAFFORD.

We beg the freeness of your own consent,
Which else must be constrained ; and time it were
Either agreed or forced.   Speak, good my lord,
For you bind up more sins in this delay
Than thousand prayers can absolve again.

      Const. Were't but my death, you should not kneel so
            long for't.

      Vort. 'Twill be the death of millions if you rise not
And that betimes too.—Lend your help, my lords,
For fear all come too late.

                  [*They rise and raise* CONSTANTIUS.

      Const. This is a cruelty
That peaceful man did never suffer yet,
To make me die again, that once was dead,
And begin all that ended long before.
Hold, Lupus and Germanus : you are lights
Of holiness and religion : can you offer

The thing that is not lawful ? stand not I
Clear from all temporal charge by my profession ?
   Ger. Not when a time so violent calls upon you
Who's born a prince, is born for general peace,
Not his own only : Heaven will look for him
In others' acts, and will require him there.
What is in you religious, must be shown
In saving many more souls than your own.
   Const. Did not great Constantine, our noble father,
Deem me unfit for government and rule,
And therefore pressed me into this profession ?
Which I've held strict, and love it above glory.
Nor is there want of me : yourselves can witness,
Heaven hath provided largely for your peace,
And blessed you with the lives of my two brothers :
Fix your obedience there, leave me a servant.
   [*They put the Crown on the head of* CONSTANTIUS.
   All. Long live Constantius, son of Constantine,
King of Great Britain !
   Const. I do feel a want
And extreme poverty of joy within ;
The peace I had is parted 'mongst rude men ;
To keep them quiet, I have lost it all.
What can the kingdom gain by my undoing ?
That riches is not best, though it be mighty,
That's purchased by the ruin of another ;
Nor can the peace, so filched, e'er thrive with them :
And if't be worthily held sacrilege
To rob a temple, 'tis no less offence
To ravish meditations from the soul,
The consecrated altar in a man :
And all their hopes will be beguiled in me ;
I know no more the way to temporal rule,
Than he that's born and has his years come to him
In a rough desert. Well may the weight kill me :
And that's the fairest good I look for from it.

   Mid II.   X

Vort. Not so, great king: here stoops a faithful
    servant
Would sooner perish under it with cheerfulness,
Than your meek soul should feel oppression
Of ruder cares : such common coarse employments
Cast upon me your servant, upon Vortiger.
I see you are not made for noise and pains,
Clamours of suitors, injuries, and redresses,
Millions of actions, rising with the sun,
Like laws still ending, and yet never done,
Of power to turn a great man to the state
Of his marble monument with over-watching.
To be oppressed is not required of you, my lord,
But only to be king.   The broken sleeps
Let me take from you, sir ; the toils and troubles,
All that is burthenous in authority,
Please you lay it on me, and what is glorious
Receive't to your own brightness.
    Const. Worthy Vortiger,
If 'twere not sin to grieve another's patience
With what we cannot tolerate ourself,
How happy were I in thee and thy love !
There's nothing makes man feel his miseries
But knowledge only : reason, that is placed
For man's director, is his chief afflictor ;
For, though I cannot bear the weight myself,
I cannot have that barrenness of remorse, [1]
To see another groan under my burthen.
    Vort. I'm quite blown up a conscionable way :
There's even a trick of murdering in some pity.
The death of all my hopes I see already :
There was no other likelihood, for religion
Was never friend of mine yet.   [*Aside.*
    Const. Holy partners in strictest abstinence,
Cruel necessity hath forced me from you :

----

[1] *i.e.* Pity.

We part, I fear, for ever ; but in mind
I will be always here ; here let me stay.

   Devon. My lord, you know the times.

   Const. Farewell, blest souls ; I fear I shall offend
He that draws tears from you takes your best friend.

      [*Exeunt* CONSTANTIUS, DEVONSHIRE, *and* STAF-
        FORD ; *while* LUPUS *and* GERMANUS *enter the*
        monastery.

   Vort. Can the great motion of ambition stand,
Like wheels false wrought by an unskilful hand ?
Then, Time, stand thou too : let no hopes arrive
At their sweet wishfulness, till mine set forwards.
Would I could stay thy existence, as I can
Thy glassy counterfeit in hours of sand !
I'd keep thee turned down, till my wishes rose ;
Then we'd both rise together.
What several inclinations are in nature !
How much is he disquieted, and wears royalty
Disdainfully upon him, like a curse !
Calls a fair crown the weight of his afflictions !
When here's a soul would sink under the burthen,
Yet well recover't. I will use all means
To vex authority from him, and in all
Study what most may discontent his blood,
Making my mask my zeal to the public good :
Not possible a richer policy
Can have conception in the thought of man.

        Enter two Graziers.

   1st Graz. An honourable life enclose your lordship !

   Vort. Now, what are you ?

   2nd Graz. Graziers, if't like your lordship.

   Vort. So it should seem by your enclosures.
What's your affair with me ?

   1st Graz. We are your
Petitioners, my lord.

Vort. For what ? depart :
Petitioners to me ! you've well deserved
My grace and favour.   Have you not a ruler
After your own election ? hie you to court ;
Get near and close, be loud and bold enough,
You cannot choose but speed.   [*Exit.*

   2nd Graz. If that will do't,
We have throats wide enough ; well put them to't.
                                    [*Exeunt.*

DUMB SHOW.

FORTUNE *discovered, in her hand a round ball full of
lots ; then enters* HENGIST *and* HORSUS, *with
others ; they draw lots, and having opened them,
all depart save* HENGIST *and* HORSUS, *who kneel
and embrace : then enter* ROXENA, *seeming to take
leave of* HENGIST *in great passion,*[1] *but more
especially and warily of* HORSUS, *her lover : she
departs one way,* HENGIST *and* HORSUS *another.*

Enter RAYNULPH.

Ray. When Germany was overgrown
With sons of peace too thickly sown,
Several guides were chosen then
By destined lots, to lead out men ;
And they whom Fortune here withstands
Must prove their fates in other lands.
On these two captains fell the lot ;
But that which must not be forgot
Was Roxena's cunning grief ;
Who from her father, like a thief,

      [1] *i.e.* Sorrow.

Hid her best and truest tears,
Which her lustful lover wears
In many a stolen and wary kiss,
Unseen of father.   Maids do this,
Yet highly scorn to be called strumpets too :
But what they lack of't, I'll be judged by you.   [*Exit.*

SCENE II.

A Hall in the Palace.

Enter VORTIGER, Feltmonger, Button-maker, Glaziers,
and other Petitioners.

Vort. This way his majesty comes.
All. Thank your good lordship.
Vort. When you hear yon door open—
All. Very good, my lord.
Vort. Be ready with your several suits ; put forward.
Graz. That's a thing every man does naturally, sir,
That is a suitor, and doth mean to speed.
Vort. 'Tis well you're so deep learned.   Take no
    denials.
All. No, my good lord.
Vort. Not any, if you love
The prosperity of your suits : you mar all utterly,
And overthrow your fruitful hopes for ever,
If either fifth or sixth, nay, tenth repulse
Fasten upon your bashfulness.
All. Say you so, my lord ?
We can be troublesome if we list.
Vort. I know it :
I felt it but too late in the general sum
Of your rank brotherhood, which now I thank you for —

While this vexation is in play, I'll study
For a second ; then a third to that ; one still
To vex another, that he shall be glad
To yield up power ; if not, it shall be had.

[*Aside and exit.*

Butt. Hark ! I protest, my heart was coming upwards :
I thought the door had opened.

Graz. Marry, would it had, sir !

Butt. I have such a treacherous heart of my own, 'twill
throb at the very fall of a farthingale.

Graz. Not if it fall on the rushes.[1]

Butt. Yes, truly ; if there be no light in the room, I
shall throb presently.[2] The first time it took me, my
wife was in the company : I remember the room was not
half so light as this ; but I'll be sworn I was a whole
hour in finding her.

Graz. By'r lady, y'had a long time of throbbing of it
then.

Butt. Still I felt men, but I could feel no women ; I
thought they had been all sunk. I have made a vow
for't, I'll never have meeting, while I live, by candle-
light again.

Graz. Yes, sir, in lanterns.

Butt. Yes, sir, in lanterns ; but I'll never trust candle
naked again.

Graz. Hark, hark ! stand close : it opens now indeed !

Butt. O majesty, what art thou ! I'd give any man
half my suit to deliver my petition : it is in the behalf of
button-makers, and so it seems by my flesh.

Enter CONSTANTIUS *in regal attire, and two* Gentlemen.

Const. Pray do not follow me, unless you do it
To wonder at my garments ; there's no cause
I give you why you should : 'tis shame enough,

---

[1] With which floors were commonly strewn.   [2] Immediately.

Methinks, to look upon myself ;
It grieves me that more should.   The other weeds
Became me better, but the lords are pleased
To force me to wear these ; I would not else :
I pray be satisfied ; I called you not.
Wonder of madness ! can you stand so idle,
And know that you must die ?

  1st Gent. We're all commanded, sir ;
Besides, it is our duties to your grace,
To give attendance.

  Const. What a wild thing is this !
No marvel though you tremble at death's name,
When you'll not see the cause why you are fools.
For charity's sake, desist here, I pray you !
Make not my presence guilty of your sloth :
Withdraw, young men, and find you honest business.

    2nd Gent. What hopes have we to rise by following
        him ?
I'll give him over shortly.

    1st Gent. He's too nice,
Too holy for young gentlemen to follow
That have good faces and sweet running fortunes.

                    [*Exeunt* Gentlemen.

  Const. Eight hours a-day in serious contemplation
Is but a bare allowance ; no higher food
To the soul than bread and water to the body ;
And that's but needful ; then more would do better.

  Butt. Let us all kneel together ; 'twill move pity :
. I've been at the begging of a hundred suits.

                    [*All the* Petitioners *kneel.*

  Const. How happy am I in the sight of you !
Here are religious souls, that lose not time :
With what devotion do they point at Heaven,
And seem to check me that am too remiss !
I bring my zeal among you, holy men :
If I see any kneel, and I sit out,   [*Kneels.*

That hour is not well spent.   Methinks, strict souls,
You have been of some order in your times.

Graz. Graziers and braziers some, and this a felt-maker.

Butt. Here's his petition and mine, if it like your
grace.   [*Giving petitions.*

Graz. Look upon mine, I am the longest suitor ; I was
undone seven years ago.

Const. [*Rising with the others.*] You've mocked my
        good hopes. Call you these petitions ?
Why, there's no form of prayer among them all.

Butt. Yes, in the bottom there is half a line
Prays for your majesty, if you look on mine.

Const. Make your requests to Heaven, not to me.

Butt. 'Las! mine's a supplication for brass buttons, sir.

Felt. There's a great enormity in wool ; I beseech your
grace consider it.

Graz. Pastures rise two-pence an acre ; what will this
world come to !

Butt. I do beseech your grace——— -

Graz. Good your grace——— -

Const. O, this is one of my afflictions
That with the crown enclosed me ! I must bear it.

Graz. Your grace's answer to my supplication.

Butt. Mine, my lord.

Const. No violent storm lasts ever ;
This is the comfort of't.

Felt. Your highness's answer.

Graz. We are almost all undone, the country beggared.

Butt. See, see, he points at Heaven, as who should say
There's enough there : but 'tis a great way thither.
There's no good to be done, I see that already ; we may
all spend our mouths like a company of hounds in chase
of a royal deer, and then go home and fall to cold mutton-
bones, when we have done.

Graz. My wife will hang me, that's my currish destiny.
                        [*Exeunt all except* CONSTANTIUS.

Const. Thanks, Heaven ! 'tis o'er now : we should ne'er
    know rightly
The sweetness of a calm, but for a storm.
Here's a wished hour for contemplation now ;
All's still and silent ; here is a true kingdom.

Re-enter VORTIGER.

Vort. My lord.
Const. Again ?
Vort. Alas, this is but early
And gentle to the troops of businesses
That flock about authority ! you must forthwith
Settle your mind to marry.
    Const. How ! to marry ?
    Vort. And suddenly, there's no pause to be given ;
The people's wills are violent, and covetous
Of a succession from your loins.
    Const. From me
There can come none : a professed abstinence
Hath set a virgin seal upon my blood,
And altered all the course ; the heat I have
Is all enclosed within a zeal to virtue,
And that's not fit for earthly propagation.
Alas, I shall but forfeit all their hopes !
I'm a man made without desires, tell them.
    Vort. I proved them with such words, but all were
    fruitless.
A virgin of the highest subject's blood
They have picked out for your embrace, and send her
Blessed with their general wishes, into fruitfulness.
Lo ! where she comes, my lord.

Enter CASTIZA.

Const. I never felt
The unhappy hand of misery till this touch :
A patience I could find for all but this.

Cast. My lord, your vowed love ventures me but dan-
　　gerously.

Vort. 'Tis but to strengthen a vexation politic.

Cast. That's an uncharitable practice, trust me, sir.

Vort. No more of that.

Cast. But say he should affect me, sir,
How should I 'scape him then ?　I have but one
Faith, my lord, and that you have already ;
Our late contràct is a divine witness to't.

Vort. I am not void of shifting-rooms and helps
For all projècts that I commit with you.　　　　*[Exit.*

Cast. This is an ungodly way to come to honour ;
I do not like it : I love Lord Vortiger,
But not these practices ; they're too uncharitable. *[Aside.*

Const. Are you a virgin ?

Cast. Never yet, my lord,
Known to the will of man.

Const. O blessèd creature !
And does too much felicity make you surfeit ?
Are you in soul assured there is a state
Prepared for you, for you, a glorious one,
In midst of Heaven, now in the state you stand in,
And had you rather, after much known misery,
Cares and hard labours, mingled with a curse,
Throng but to the door, and hardly get a place there ?
Think, hath the world a folly like this madness ?
Keep still that holy and immaculate fire,
You chaste lamp of eternity ! 'tis a treasure
Too precious for death's moment to partake,
This twinkling of short life.　Disdain as much
To let mortality know you, as stars
To kiss the pavements ; you've a substance as
Excellent as theirs, holding your pureness :
They look upon corruption, as you do,
But are stars still ; be you a virgin too.

Cast. I'll never marry.　What though my truth be
　　engaged

To Vortiger? forsaking all the world
I save it well, and do my faith no wrong.——   [*Aside.*
You've mightily prevailed, great virtuous sir ;
I'm bound eternally to praise your goodness :
My thoughts henceforth shall be as pure from man,
As ever made a virgin's name immortal.

   Const. I will do that for joy, I never did,
Nor ever will again.

     As he kisses her, re-enter VORTIGER *and* Gentlemen.

   1st Gent. My lord, he's taken.
   Vort. I'm sorry for't, I like not that so well ;
They're something too familiar for their time, methinks.
This way of kissing is no way to vex him :
Why I, that have a weaker faith and patience,
Could endure more than that, coming from a woman.
Despatch, and bring his answer speedily.   [*Exit*
   1st Gent. My lord, my gracious lord !
   Const. Beshrew thy heart !
   2nd Gent. They all attend your grace.
   Const. I would not have them :
'Twould please me better, if they'd all depart,
And leave me to myself ; or put me out,
And take it to themselves.
   1st Gent. The noon is past ;
Meat's on the table.
   Const. Meat ! away, get from me ;
Thy memory is diseased ; what saint's eve's this ?
   1st Gent. Saint Agatha's, I take it
   Const. Is it so ?
I am not worthy to be served before her ;
And so return, I pray.
   2nd Gent. He'll starve the guard, if this be suffered ; if
we set court bellies by a monastery clock, he that breaks
a fellow's pate now, will not be able to crack a louse
within this twelvemonth. [*Aside and exeunt* Gentlemen.

Const. 'Tis sure forgetfulness, and not man's will,
That leads him forth into licentious ways ;
We cannot certainly commit such errors,
And think upon them truly as they're acting.
Why's abstinence ordained, but for such seasons ?

Re-enter VORTIGER.

Vort. My lord, you've pleased to put us to much pains,
But we confess 'tis portion of our duty.
Will your grace please to walk ? dinner stays for you.
   Const. I've answered that already.
   Vort. But, my lord,
We must not so yield to you : pardon me,
'Tis for the general good : you must be ruled, sir ;
Your health and life is dearer to us now :
Think where you are, at court : this is no monastery.
   Const. But, sir, my conscience keeps still where it was :
I may not eat this day.
   Vort. We've sworn you shall,
And plentifully too : we must preserve you, sir,
Though you be wilful ; 'tis no slight condition
To be a king.
   Const. Would I were less than man !
   Vort. You will make the people rise, my lord,
In great despair of your continuance,
If you neglect the means that must sustain you.
   Const. I never eat on eves.
   Vort. But now you must ;
It concerns others' healths that you take food :
I've changed your life, you well may change your mood.
   Const. This is beyond all cruelty.
   Vort. 'Tis our care, my lord.   [*Exeunt.*

ACT THE SECOND.

SCENE I.

A Room in the Palace.

Enter VORTIGER *and* CASTIZA.

CAST. My lord, I am resolved ; tempt
    me no farther ;
'Tis all to fruitless purpose.
  Vort. Are you well ?
  Cast. Never so perfect in the **truth**
    of health
As at this instant.
  Vort. Then I doubt my **own**,
Or that I am not waking.
  Cast. Would you were then !
You'd praise my resolution.
  Vort. This is wondrous !
Are you not mine by contract ?
  Cast. 'Tis most true, my lord,
And I am better blessed in't than I looked for,
In that I am confined in faith so strictly :
I'm bound, my lord, to marry none but you, --
You'll grant me that,—and you I'll never marry.
  Vort. It draws me **into violence** and hazard :
I saw you kiss the king.
  Cast. I grant you so, sir ;

Where could I take my leave of the world better?
I wronged not you in that; you will acknowledge
A king is the best part of't.

    Vort. O, my passion!

    Cast. I see you something yielding to infirmity, sir;
I take my leave.

    Vort. Why, 'tis not possible!

    Cast. The fault is in your faith; time I were gone
To give it better strengthening.

    Vort. Hark you, lady——

    Cast. Send your intent to the next monastery;
There you shall find my answer ever after;
And so with my last duty to your lordship,
For whose prosperity I will pray as heartily
As for my own.   [*Exit.*

    Vort. How am I served in this?
I offer a vexation to the king;
He sends it home into my blood with vantage.
I'll put off time no longer: I have brought him
Into most men's neglects, calling his zeal
A deep pride hallowed over, love of ease
More than devotion or the public benefit;
Which catcheth many men's beliefs. I'm strong too
In people's wishes; their affections point at me.
I lose much time and glory; that redeemed,
She that now flies returns with joy and wonder:
Greatness and woman's wish ne'er keep asunder.   [*Exit.*

DUMB SHOW.

Enter two Villains; *to them* VORTIGER, *who seems
to solicit them with gold, then swears them, and
exit.* Enter CONSTANTIUS *meditating; they
rudely strike down his book, and draw their*

swords ; he kneels and spreads his arms ; they kill him, and hurry off the body. Enter VOR-TIGER, DEVONSHIRE, *and* STAFFORD, *in conference ; to them the two* Villains *presenting the head of* CONSTANTIUS ; VORTIGER *seems sorrowful, and in rage stabs them both. Then the lords crown* VORTIGER, *and fetch in* CASTIZA, *who comes unwillingly ;* VORTIGER *hales her, and they crown her :* AURELIUS *and* UTHER, *brothers of* CONSTANTIUS, *seeing him crowned, draw and fly.*

Enter RAYNULPH.

Ray. When nothing could prevail to tire
The good king's patience, they did hire
Two wicked rogues to take his life ;
In whom a while there fell a strife
Of pity and fury ; but the gold
Made pity faint, and fury bold.
Then to Vortiger they bring
The head of that religious king ;
Who feigning grief, to clear his guilt,
Makes the slaughterers' blood be spilt.
Then crown they him, and force the maid,
That vowed a virgin-life, to wed ;
Such a strength great power extends,
It conquers fathers, kindred, friends,
And since fate's pleased to change her life,
She proves as holy in a wife.
More to tell, were to betray
What deeds in their own tongues must say :
Only this, the good king dead,
The brothers poor in safety fled.   [*Exit*

SCENE II.

A Hall in the Palace

Enter VORTIGER *crowned, a* Gentleman *meeting him.*

Gent. My lord !

Vort. I fear thy news will fetch a curse, it comes
With such a violence.

Gent. The people are up
In arms against you.

Vort. O this dream of glory !
Sweet power, before I can have time to taste thee,
Must I for ever lose thee?—What's the imposthume
That swells them now ?

Gent. The murder of Constantius.

Vort. Ulcers of realms ! they hated him alive,
Grew weary of the minute of his reign,
Called him an evil of their own electing.
And is their ignorant zeal so fiery now,
When all their thanks are cold ? the mutable hearts
That move in their false breasts !—Provide me safety :

[*Noise within.*

Hark ! I hear ruin threaten me with a voice
That imitates thunder.

Enter 2nd Gentleman.

2nd Gent. Where's the king ?

Vort. Who takes him ?

2nd Gent. Send peace to all your royal thoughts,
my lord :
A fleet of valiant Saxons newly landed
Offer the truth of all their service to you.

Vort. Saxons ! my wishes : let them have free entrance.
And plenteous welcomes from all hearts that love us ;

[*Exit* 2nd Gentleman.

They never could come happier.

*Re-enter-*2nd Gentleman *with* HENGIST, HORSUS, *and*
Soldiers.

Heng. Health, power, and victory to Vortiger !

Vort. There can be no more pleasure to a king,
If all the languages earth spake were ransacked.
Your names I know not ; but so much good fortune
And warranted worth lightens your fair aspècts,
I cannot but in arms of love enfold you.

Heng. The mistress of our birth's hope, fruitful Ger-
Calls me Hengistus, and this captain Horsus ;   [many,
A man low-built, but yet in deeds of arms
Flame is not swifter.   We are all, my lord,
The sons of Fortune ; she has sent us forth
To thrive by the red sweat of our own merits ;
And since, after the rage of many a tempest,
Our fates have cast us upon Britain's bounds,
We offer you the first-fruits of our wounds.

Vort. Which we shall dearly prize : the mean'st blood
spent
Shall at wealth's fountain make its own content.

Heng. You double vigour in us then, my lord :
Pay is the soul of such as thrive by the sword. [*Exeunt.*

SCENE III.

Near the Palace.

Enter VORTIGER *and* Gentlemen.   *Alarm and noise of*
skirmishes within.

1st Gent. My lord, these Saxons bring a fortune
with them
Stays[1] any Roman success.

¹ Qy. Stains?—*Dyce.*

Vort. On, speak, forwards !
I will not take one minute from thy tidings.

1st Gent. The main supporters of this insurrection
They've taken prisoners, and the rest so tamed,
They stoop to the least grace that flows from mercy.

Vort. Never came power guided by better stars
Than these men's fortitudes : yet they're misbelievers,
Which to my reason is wondrous.

Enter HENGIST, HORSUS, *and* Soldiers, *with* Prisoners.

You've given me such a first taste of your worth,
'Twill never from my love ; when life is gone,
The memory sure will follow, my soul still
Participating immortality with it.
But here's the misery of earth's limited glory,
There's not a way revealed to any honour
Above the fame which your own merits give you.

Heng. Indeed, my lord, we hold, when all's summed
        up
That can be made for worth to be expressed,
The fame that a man wins himself is best ;
That he may call his own.   Honours put to him
Make him no more a man than his clothes do,
And are as soon ta'en off ; for in the warmth
The heat comes from the body, not the weeds :
So man's true fame must strike from his own deeds.
And since by this event which fortune speaks us,
The land appears the fair predestined soil
Ordained for our good hap, we crave, my lord,
A little earth to thrive on, what you please,
Where we'll but keep a nursery of good spirits
To fight for you and yours.

Vort. Sir, for our treasure,
'Tis open to your merits, as our love ;

But for ye're strangers in religion chiefly—
Which is the greatest alienation can be,
And breeds most factions in the bloods of men—
I must not yield to that.

Enter SIMON *with a hide.*

 Heng. 'Sprecious, my lord,
I see a pattern ; be it but so little
As yon poor hide will compass.
 Vort. How, the hide !
 Heng. Rather than nothing, sir.
 Vort. Since you're so reasonable,
Take so much in the best part of our kingdom.
 Heng. We thank your grace.
      [*Exit* VORTIGER *with* Gentlemen.
      Rivers from bubbling springs
Have rise at first, and great from abject things.
Stay yonder fellow : he came luckily,
And he shall fare well for't, whate'er he be ;
We'll thank our fortune in rewarding him.
 Hor. Stay, fellow !
 Sim. How, fellow ? 'tis more than you know, whether
I be your fellow or no ; I am sure you see me not.
 Heng. Come, what's the price of your hide ?
 Sim. O unreasonable villain ! he would buy the house
over a man's head. I'll be sure now to make my
bargain wisely ; they may buy me out of my skin else.
[*Aside.*]—Whose hide would you buy, mine or the
beast's ? There is little difference in their complexions :
I think mine is the blacker of the two : you shall see for
your love, and buy for your money.—A pestilence on
you all, how have you deceived me ; you buy an ox-hide '
you buy a calf's gather ! They are all hungry soldiers, and
I took them for honest shoemakers.   [*Aside.*

Heng. Hold, fellow ; prithee, hold ;—right a fool
      worldling
That kicks at all good fortune ; whose man art thou ?

Sim. I am a servant, yet a masterless man, sir.

Heng. Prithee, how can that be ?

Sim. Very nimbly, sir ; my master is dead, and now
I serve my mistress ; ergo, I am a masterless man : she
is now a widow, and I am the foreman of her tan-pit.

Heng. Hold you, and thank your fortune, not your
      wit.   [*Gives him money.*

Sim. Faith, and I thank your bounty, and not your
wisdom : you are not troubled with wit neither greatly, it
seems.   Now, by this light, a nest of yellow-hammers ;
what will become of me ? if I can keep all these without
hanging myself, I am happier than a hundred of my
neighbours.   You shall have my skin into the bargain ;
then if I chance to die like a dog, the labour will be
saved of flaying me : I'll undertake, sir, you shall have
all the skins in our parish at this price, men's and
women's.

Heng. Sirrah, give good ear to me : now take the
      hide
And cut it all into the slenderest thongs
That can bear strength to hold.

Sim. That were a jest, i'faith : spoil all the leather ?
sin and pity ! why, 'twould shoe half your army.

Heng. Do it, I bid you.

Sim. What, cut it all in thongs ? Hum, this is like the
vanity of your Roman gallants, that cannot wear good
suits, but they must have them cut and slashed in
giggets,[1] that the very crimson taffaties sit blushing at
their follies.   I would I might persuade you from this
humour of cutting ; 'tis but a swaggering condition,[2] and

---

[1] Giggets seems to refer to the stripes or "panes" in the hose.
[2] "Cutter," a bully or sharper.

nothing profitable: what if it were but well pinked?
'twould last longer for a summer suit.

Heng. What a cross lump of ignorance have I lighted
on !
I must be forced to beat my drift into him.—   [*Aside.*
Look you, to make you wiser than your parents,
I have so much ground given me as this hide
Will compass, which, as it is, is nothing.

Sim. Nothing, quotha ?
Why, 'twill not keep a hog.

Heng. Now with the vantage
Cut into several pieces, 'twill stretch far,
And make a liberal circuit.

Sim. A shame on your crafty hide ! is this your
cunning? I have learnt more knavery now than ever I
shall claw off while I live. I'll go purchase land by
cow-tails, and undo the parish ; three good bulls' pizzles
would set up a man for ever: this is like a pin a-day to
set up a haberdasher of small wares.

Heng. Thus men that mean to thrive, as we, must
learn
Set in a foot at first.

Sim. A foot do you call it? The devil is in that foot
that takes up all this leather.

Heng. Despatch, and cut it carefully with all
The advantage, sirrah.

Sim. You could never have lighted upon such a fellow
to serve your turn, captain. I have such a trick of
stretching, too ! I learned it of a tanner's man that was
hanged last sessions at Maidstone : I'll warrant you, I'll
get you a mile and a half more than you're aware of.

Heng. Pray, serve me so as oft as you will, sir.

Sim. I am casting about for nine acres to make a
garden-plot out of one of the buttocks.

Heng. 'Twill be a good soil for nosegays.

Sim. 'Twill be a good soil for cabbages, to stuff out the guts of your followers there.

Heng. Go, see it carefully performed :

                    [*Exit* SIMON *with* Soldiers.

It is the first foundation of our fortunes
On Britain's earth, and ought to be embraced
With a respect near linked to adoration.
Methinks it sounds to me a fair assurance
Of large honours and hopes ; does it not, captain ?

Hor. How many have begun with less at first,
That have had emperors from their bodies sprung,
And left their carcasses as much in monument
As would erect a college !

Heng. There's the fruits
Of their religious show too ; to lie rotting
Under a million spent in gold and marble.

Hor. But where shall we make choice of our ground, captain ?

Heng. About the fruitful flanks of uberous[1] Kent,
A fat and olive soil ; there we came in.
O captain, he has given he knows not what !

Hor. Long may he give so !

Heng. I tell thee, sirrah, he that begged a field
Of fourscore acres for a garden-plot,
'Twas pretty well ; but he came short of this.

Hor. Send over for more Saxons.

Heng. With all speed, captain.

Hor. Especially for Roxena.

Heng. Who, my daughter ?

Hor. That star of Germany, forget not her, sir :
She is a fair fortunate maid.—
Fair she is, and fortunate may she be ;
But in maid lost for ever.   My desire
Has been the close confusion of that name.

             [1] Fruitful.

A treasure 'tis, able to make more thieves
Than cabinets set open to entice ;
Which learn them theft that never knew the vice. [*Aside.*
    Heng. Come, I'll despatch with speed.
    Hor. Do, forget none.
    Heng. Marry, pray help my memory.
    Hor. Roxena, you remember ?
    Heng. What more, dear sir ?
    Hor. I see your memory's clear, sir.   [*Shouts within.*
    Heng. Those shouts leaped from our army.
    Hor. They were too cheerful
To voice a bad event.

Enter a Gentleman.

    Heng. Now, sir, your news ?
    Gent. Roxena the fair—
    Heng. True, she shall be sent for.
    Gent. She's here, sir.
    Heng. What say'st ?
    Gent. She's come, sir.
    Hor. A new youth
Begins me o'er again.   [*Aside.*
    Gent. Followed you close, sir,
With such a zeal as daughter never equalled ;
Exposed herself to all the merciless dangers
Set in mankind or fortune ; not regarding
Aught but your sight.
    Heng. Her love is infinite to me.
    Hor. Most charitably censured ; 'tis her cunning,
The love of her own lust, which makes a woman
Gallop down hill as fearless as a drunkard.
There's no true loadstone in the world but that ;
It draws them through all storms by sea or shame :
Life's loss is thought too small to pay that game. [*Aside.*

Gent. What follows more of her will take you strongly.

Heng. How!

Gent. Nay, 'tis worth your wonder.
Her heart, joy-ravished with your late success,
Being the early morning of your fortunes,
So prosperously new opening at her coming,
She takes a cup of gold, and, midst the army,
Teaching her knee a reverend cheerfulness,
Which well became her, drank a liberal health
To the king's joys and yours, the king in presence;
Who with her sight, but her behaviour chiefly,
Or chief but one or both, I know not which,—
But he's so far 'bove my expression caught,
'Twere art enough for one man's time and portion
To speak him and miss nothing.

Heng. This is astonishing!

Hor. O, this ends bitter now! our close-hid flame
Will break out of my heart; I cannot keep it.   [*Aside.*

Heng. Gave you attention, captain? how now, man?

Hor. A kind of grief 'bout these times of the moon
    still:
I feel a pain like a convulsion,
A cramp at heart; I know not what name fits it.

Heng. Nor never seek one for it, let it go
Without a name; would all griefs were served so!

Flourish.   Re-enter VORTIGER, *with* ROXENA *and*
Attendants.

Hor. A love-knot already? arm in arm!   [*Aside.*

Vort. What's he
Lays claim to her?

Heng. In right of fatherhood
I challenge an obedient part.

Vort. Take it,
And send me back the rest.

    Heng, What means your grace ?

    Vort. You'll keep no more than what belongs to
      you ?

    Heng. That's all, my lord ; it all belongs to me ;
I keep the husband's interest till he come :
Yet out of duty and respect to majesty,
I send her back your servant.

    Vort. My mistress, sir, or nothing.

    Heng. Come again ;
I never thought to hear so ill of thee.

    Vort. How, sir, so ill ?

    Heng. So beyond detestable.
To be an honest vassal is some calling,
Poor is the worst of that, shame comes not to't ;
But mistress, that's the only common bait
Fortune sets at all hours, catching whore with it,
And plucks them up by clusters.   There's my sword, my
      lord ;   [*Offering his sword to* VORTIGER.
And if your strong desires aim at my blood,
Which runs too purely there, a nobler way
Quench it in mine.

    Vort. I ne'er took sword in vain :
Hengist, we here create thee Earl of Kent.

    Hor. O, that will do't !   [*Aside, and falls.*

    Vort. What ails our friend ? look to him.

    Rox. O, 'tis his epilepsy ; I know it well :
I helped him once in Germany ; comes it again ?
A virgin's right hand stroked upon his heart
Gives him ease straight ; but it must be a pure virgin,
Or else it brings no comfort.

    Vort. What a task
She puts upon herself, unurgèd purity !
The truth of this will bring love's rage into me.

Rox. O, this would mad a woman ! there's no proof
In love to indiscretion.[1]

Hor. Pish ! this cures not.

Rox. Dost think I'll ever wrong thee ?

Hor. O, most feelingly !
But I'll prevent it now, and break thy neck
With thy own cunning.   Thou has undertaken
To give me help, to bring in royal credit
Thy cracked virginity, but I'll spoil all :
I will not stand on purpose, though I could,
But fall still to disgrace thee.

Rox. What, you will not?

Hor. I have no other way to help myself ;
For when thou'rt known to be a whore imposterous,[2]
I shall be sure to keep thee.

Rox. O sir, shame me not !
You've had what is most precious ; try my faith :
Undo me not at first in chaste opinion.

Hor. All this art shall not make me feel my legs.

Rox. I prithee, do not wilfully confound me.

Hor. Well, I'm content for this time to recover,
To save thy credit, and bite in my pain ;
But if thou ever fail'st me, I will fall,
And thou shalt never get me up again.   [*Rises.*

Rox. Agreed 'twixt you and I, sir.—See, my lord,
A poor maid's work ! the man may pass for health now
Among the clearest bloods, and those are nicest.

Vort. I've heard of women brought men on their
            knees,
But few that e'er restored them.—How now, captain .

Hor. My lord, methinks I could do things past man
I'm so renewed in vigour ; I long most

---

[1] *i.e.* No trial compared to that which is occasioned by the
indiscretion of the object beloved.—*Dyce.*

[2] Deceitful.

For violent exercise to take me down :
My joy's so high in blood, I'm above frailty.

    Vort. My lord of Kent.

    Heng. Your love's unworthy creature.

    Vort. See'st thou this fair chain? think upon the
        means
To keep it linked for ever.

    Heng. O my lord,
'Tis many degrees sundered from my hope !
Besides, your grace has a young virtuous queen.

    Vort. I say, think on it.

    Hor. If this wind hold, I fall to my old disease.

                                [*Aside.*

    Vort. There's no fault in thee but to come so late ;
All else is excellent : I chide none but fate.   [*Exeunt.*

ACT THE THIRD.

SCENE I.

A Room in the Palace.

Enter HORSUS *and* ROXENA.

ROX. I've no conceit now that you ever
    loved me,
    But as lust led you for the time.
      Hor. See, see !
      Rox. Do you pine at my advance-
ment, sir?
  Hor. O barrenness
Of understanding ! what a right love's this !
'Tis you that fall, I that am reprehended :
What height of honours, eminence of fortune,
Should ravish me from you ?
    Rox. Who can tell that, sir?
What's he can judge of a man's appetite
Before he sees him eat ?
Who knows the strength of any's constancy
That never yet was tempted ?   We can call
Nothing our own, if they be deeds to come ;
They're only ours when they are passed and done.
How blest are you above your apprehension,
If your desire would lend you so much patience,
To examine the adventurous condition
Of our affections, which are full of hazard,
And draw in the time's goodness to defend us !

First, this bold course of ours cannot last long,
Nor ever does in any without shame,
And that, you know, brings danger ; and the greater
My father is in blood, as he's well risen,
The greater will the storm of his rage be ‾
'Gainst his blood's wronging : I have cast[1] for this.
'Tis not advancement that I love alone ;
'Tis love of shelter, to keep shame unknown.

   Hor. O, were I sure of thee, as 'tis impossible
There to be ever sure where there's no hold,
Your pregnant hopes should not be long in rising !

   Rox. By what assurance have you held me thus far,
Which you found firm, despair you not in that.

   Hor. True, that was good security for the time ;
But in a change of state, when you're advanced,
You women have a French toy in your pride,
You make your friend come crouching : or perhaps,
To bow in the hams the better, he is put
To compliment three hours with your chief woman,
Then perhaps not admitted ; no, nor ever,
That's the more noble fashion.   Forgetfulness
Is the most pleasing virtue they can have,
That do spring up from nothing ; for by the same
Forgetting all, they forget whence they came,
An excellent property of oblivion.

   Rox. I pity all the fortunes of poor women
In my own unhappiness.   When we have given
All that we have to men, what's our requital ?
An ill-faced jealousy, that resembles much
The mistrustfulness of an insatiate thief,
That scarce believes he has all, though he has stripped
The true[2] man naked, and left nothing on him
But the hard cord that binds him : so are we
First robbed, and then left bound by jealousy.

       [1] Contrived.   [2] *i.e.* Honest.

Take reason's advice, and you'll find it impossible
For you to lose me in this king's advancement,
Who's an usurper here ; and as the kingdom,
So shall he have my love by usurpation ;
The right shall be in thee still.   My ascension
To dignity is but to waft thee higher ;
And all usurpers have the falling-sickness,
They cannot keep up long.
   Hor. May credulous man
Put all his confidence in so weak a bottom,
And make a saving voyage?
   Rox. Nay, as gainful
As ever man yet made.
   Hor. Go, take thy fortunes,
Aspire with my consent,
So thy ambition will be sure to prosper ;
Speak the fair certainties of Britain's queen
Home to thy wishes.
   Rox. Speak in hope I may,
But not in certainty.
   Hor. I say in both :
Hope, and be sure I'll soon remove the let[1]
That stands between thee and glory.
   Rox. Life of love !
If lost virginity can win such a day,
I'll have no daughter but shall learn my way.   [*Exit.*
   Hor. 'Twill be good work for him that first instructs
      them :
May be some sons of mine, got by this woman too,
May match with their own sisters.   Peace, 'tis he.

Enter VORTIGER.

Invention, fail me not : 'tis a gallant credit
To marry one's whore bravely.   [*Aside.*

---

[1] **Hindrance.**

Vort. Have I power
Of life and death, and cannot command ease
In my own blood? After I was a king,
I thought I never should have felt pain more ;
That there had been a ceasing of all passions
And common stings, which subjects use to feel,
That were created with a patience fit
For all extremities. But such as we
Know not the way to suffer ; then to do it
How most preposterous 'tis ! Tush, riddles, riddles !
I'll break through custom. Why should not the mind,
The nobler part that's of us, be allowed
Change of affections, as our bodies are
Change of food and raiment ? I'll have it so.
All fashions appear strange at first production ;
But this would be well followed.—O, captain !

Hor. My lord, I grieve for you ; I scarce fetch breath,
But a sigh hangs at the end of it : but this
Is not the way, if you'd give way to counsel.

Vort. Set me right, then, or I shall heavily curse thee
For lifting up my understanding to me,
To show that I was wrong. Ignorance is safe ;
I then slept happily : if knowledge mend me not,
Thou hast committed a most cruel sin,
To wake me into judgment, and then leave me.

Hor. I will not leave you, sir; that were rudely
      done.
First, you've a flame too open and too violent,
Which, like blood-guiltiness in an offender,
Betrays him when nought else can. Out with't, sir ;
Or let some cunning coverture be made
Before your practice[1] enters : 'twill spoil all else.

 . *Vort.* Why, look you, sir ; I can be as calm as silence
All the while music plays. Strike on, sweet friend,

---

[1] Artifice, insidious design.

As mild and merry as the heart of innocence ;
I prithee, take my temper.   Has a virgin
A heat more modest ?

    Hor. He does well to ask me ;
I could have told him once.   [*Aside.*]—Why, here's a
        government !
There's not a sweeter amity in friendship
Than in this league 'twixt you and health.

    Vort. Then since
Thou find'st me capable of happiness,
Instruct me with the practice.

    Hor. What will you say, my lord,
If I ensnare her in an act of lust ?

    Vort. O, there were art to the life ! but 'tis impossible ;
I prithee, flatter me no further with it.
Fie ! so much sin as goes to make up that
Will ne'er prevail with her.   Why, I'll tell you, sir,
She's so sin-killing modest, that if only
To move the question were enough adultery
To cause a separation, there's no gallant
So brassy-impudent durst undertake
The words that shall belong to't.

    Hor. Say you so, sir ?
There's nothing made in the world but has a way to't ;
Though some be harder than the rest to find,
Yet one there is, that's certain ; and I think
I've took the course to light on't.

    Vort. O, I pray for't !

    Hor. I heard you lately say (from whence, my lord,
My practice received life first), that your queen
Still consecrates her time to contemplation,
Takes solitary walks.

    Vort. Nay, late and early
Commands her weak guard from her, which are but
Women at strongest.

Hor. I like all this, my lord :
And now, sir, you shall know what net is used
In many places to catch modest women,
Such as will never yield by prayers or gifts.
Now there be some will catch up men as fast ;
But those she-fowlers nothing concern us ;
Their birding is at windows ; ours abroad,
Where ring-doves should be caught, that's married wives,
Or chaste maids ; what the appetite has a mind to.

Vort. Make no pause then.

Hor. The honest gentlewoman,
When nothing will prevail—I pity her now—
Poor soul, she's enticed forth by her own sex
To be betrayed to man ; who in some garden-house[1]
Or remote walk, taking his lustful time,
Binds darkness on her eye-lids, surprises her ;
And having a coach ready, turns her in,
Hurrying her where he list for the sin's safety,
Making a rape of honour without words ;
And at the low ebb of his lust, perhaps
Some three days after, sends her coached again
To the same place ; and, which would make most mad,
She's robbed of all, yet knows not where she's robbed,
There's the dear precious mischief !

Vort. Is this practised ?

Hor. Too much, my lord, to be so little known ;
A springe to catch a maidenhead after sunset,
Clip it, and send it home again to the city,
There 'twill ne'er be perceived.

Vort. My raptures want expression : I conceit[2]
Enough to make me fortunate, and thee great.

Hor. I praise it then, my lord.—I knew 'twould take.
[*Aside.*]   [*Exeunt.*

[1] Summer-house.   [2] Conceive.

Mid. II.   z

SCENE II.

Grounds near the Palace.

Enter CASTIZA *with a book, and two* Ladies.

Cast. Methinks you live strange lives ; when I see it
    not,
It grieves me less ; you know how to ease me then :
If you but knew how well I loved your absence,
You would bestow't upon me without asking.

   1st Lady. Faith, for my part, were it no more for
ceremony than for love, you should walk long enough
without my attendance ; and so think all my fellows,
though they say nothing. Books in women's hands are
as much against the hair,[1] methinks, as to see men
wear stomachers, or night-rails.[2]—She that has the green-
sickness, and should follow her counsel, would die like
an ass, and go to the worms like a salad ; not I : so long as
such a creature as man is made, she is a fool that knows
not what he is good for.   [*Exeunt* Ladies.

   Cast. Though among life's elections, that of virgin
I did speak noblest of, yet it has pleased the king
To send me a contented blessedness
In that of marriage, which I ever doubted.

Enter VORTIGER *and* HORSUS *disguised.*

I see the king's affection was a true one ;
It lasts and holds out long, that's no mean virtue
In a commanding man ; though in great fear
At first I was enforced to venture on it.

   Vort. All's happy, clear, and safe.

   Hor. The rest comes gently on.

   Vort. Be sure you seize on her full sight at first,
For fear of my discovery.

    [1] Or, as we say, "against the grain."   [2] Night-gowns.

Hor. Now, fortune, and I am sped.

                   [*Seizes and blindfolds* CASTIZA.

Cast. Treason ! treason !

Hor. Sirrah, how stand you? prevent noise and clamour,
Or death shall end thy service.

    Vort. A sure cunning.   [*Aside.*

    Cast. O, rescue ! rescue !

    Hor. Dead her voice ! away, make speed !

    Cast. No help ? no succour ?

    Hor. Louder yet, extend
Your voice to the last rack ; you shall have leave now,
You're far from any pity.

    Cast. What's my sin ?

    Hor. Contempt of man ; and he's a noble creature,
And takes it in ill part to be despised.

    Cast. I never despised any.

    Hor. No ? you hold us
Unworthy to be loved ; what call you that ?

    Cast. I have a lord disproves you.

    Hor. Pish ! your lord ?
You're bound to love your lord, that's no thanks to you ;
You should love those you are not tied to love,
That's the right trial of a woman's charity.

    Cast. I know not what you are, nor what my fault is :
If it be life you seek, whate'er you be,
Use no immodest words, and take it from me ;
You kill me more in talking sinfully
Than acting cruelty : be so far pitiful,
To end me without words.

    Hor. Long may you live !
'Tis the wish of a good subject : 'tis not life
That I thirst after ; loyalty forbid
I should commit such treason : you mistake me,
I've no such bloody thought ; only your love
Shall content me.

Cast. What said you, sir ?

Hor. Thus plainly,
To strip my words as naked as my purpose,
I must and will enjoy thee. · [*She faints.*]—Gone
    already ?
Look to her, bear her up, she goes apace ;
I feared this still, and therefore came provided. ·
There's that will fetch life from a dying spark,
And make it spread a furnace ; she's well straight.
       [*Pours drops from a vial into* CASTIZA's *mouth.*
Pish, let her go ; she stands, upon my knowledge,
Or else she counterfeits ; I know the virtue.

Cast. Never did sorrows in afflicted woman
Meet with such cruelties, such hard-hearted ways
Human invention never found before :
To call back life to live, is but ill taken
By some departing souls ; then to force mine back
To an eternal act of death in lust,
What is it but most execrable ?

Hor. So, so :
But this is from my business. List to me :
Here you are now far from all hope of friendship,
Save what you make in me ; 'scape me you cannot,
Send your soul that assurance ; that resolved on,
You know not who I am, nor ever shall,
I need not fear you then ; but give consent,
Then with the faithfulness of a true friend
I'll open myself to you, fall your servant,
As I do now in hope, proud of submission,
And seal the deed up with eternal secrecy ;
Not death shall pluck't from me, much less the king's
Authority or torture.

Vort. I admire him.   [*Aside.*

Cast. O sir ! whate'er **you are**, I teach my knee
Thus to require you. be content to take   [*Kneels.*

Only my sight, as ransom for my honour,
And where you have but mocked my eyes with dark-
    ness,
Pluck them quite out ; all outward lights of body
I'll spare most willingly, but take not from me
That which must guide me to another world,
And leave me dark for ever ; fast without
That cursèd pleasure, which will make two souls
Endure a famine everlastingly.

    Hor. This almost moves.   [*Aside.*
    Vort. By this light he'll be taken !   [*Aside.*
    Hor. I'll wrestle down all pity.   [*Aside.*]—What ! will
      you consent ?
    Cast. I'll never be so guilty.
    Hor. Farewell words then !
You hear no more of me ; but thus I seize you.
    Cast. O, if a power above be reverenced by thee,
I bind thee by that name, by manhood, nobleness.
And all the charms of honour !

        [VORTIGER *snatches her up, and carries her off.*
    Hor. Ah, ha ! here's one caught
For an example : never was poor lady
So mocked into false terror ; with what anguish
She lies with her own lord ! now she could curse
All into barrenness, and beguile herself by't.
Conceit's a powerful thing, and is indeed
Placed as a palate to taste grief or love,
And as that relishes, so we approve ;
Hence comes it that our taste is so beguiled,
Changing pure blood for some that's mixed and soiled.

                    [*Exit.*

SCENE III.

A Chamber in a Castle.

Enter HENGIST.

Hen. A fair and fortunate constellation reigned
When we set foot here ; for from his first gift
(Which to a king's unbounded eyes seemed nothing),
The compass of a hide, I have erected
A strong and spacious castle, yet contained myself
Within my limits, without check or censure.
Thither, with all the observance of a subject,
The liveliest witness of a grateful mind,
I purpose to invite him and his queen,
And feast them nobly.
   Barber. [*Without.*] We will enter, sir ;
'Tis a state business, of a twelve-month long,
The choosing of a mayor.
   Hen. What noise is that ?
   Tailor. [*Without.*] Sir, we must speak with the good
      Earl of Kent :
Though we were ne'er brought up to keep a door,
We are as honest, sir, as some that do.

Enter a Gentleman.

   Hen. Now, sir, what's the occasion of their clamours ?
   Gent. Please you, my lord, a company of townsmen
Are bent, 'gainst all denials and resistance,
To have speech with your lordship ; and that you
Must end a difference, which none else can do.
   Hen. Why, then there's reason in their violence,
Which I ne'er looked for : first let in but one,
And as we relish him, the rest come on.
                    [*Exit* Gentleman.
'Tis no safe wisdom in a rising man

To slight off such as these ; nay, rather these
Are the foundations of a lofty work ;
We cannot build without them, and stand sure.
He that ascends first to a mountain's top
Must begin at the foot.

Re-enter Gentleman.

Now, sir, who comes ?
Gent. They cannot yet agree, my lord, of that :
They say 'tis worse now than it was before,
For where the difference was but between two,
Upon this coming first they're all at odds.
One says, he shall lose his place in the church by't ;
Another will not do his wife that wrong ;
And by their good wills they would all come first.
The strife continues in most heat, my lord,
Between a country barber and a tailor
Of the same town : and which your lordship names,
'Tis yielded by consent that he shall enter.
Heng. Here's no sweet coil ! I'm glad they are so
    reasonable.
Call in the barber; [*Exit* Gentleman.] if the tale be
    long,
He'll cut it short, I trust ; that's all the hope.

Re-enter Gentleman *with* Barber.

Now, sir, are you the barber ?
Barb. O, most barbarous ! a corrector of enormities
in hair, my lord ; a promoter of upper lips, or what your
lordship, in the neatness of your discretion, shall think
fit to call me.
Heng. Very good, I see you have this without book ;
but what's your business ?
Barb. Your lordship comes to a very high point
indeed ; the business, sir, lies about the head.

Heng. That's work for you.

Barb. No, my good lord, there is a corporation, a
body, a kind of body.

Heng. The barber is out at the body; let in the
tailor.   [*Exit* Gentleman.
This 'tis to reach beyond your own profession;
When you let go your head, you lose your memory:
You have no business with the body.

Barb. Yes, sir, I am a barber-chirurgeon; I have had
something to do with it in my time, my lord; and I was
never so out of the body as I have been of late: send
me good luck, I'll marry some whore but I'll get in
again.

Re-enter Gentleman *with* Tailor.

Heng. Now, sir, a good discovery come from you!

Tail. I will rip up the linings to your lordship,
And show what stuff 'tis made of: for the body
Or corporation—

Heng. There the barber left indeed.

Tail. 'Tis pieced up of two fashions.

Heng. A patched town the whilst.

Tail. Nor can we go through stitch, my noble lord,
The choler is so great in the one party:
And as in linsey-woolsey wove together,
One piece makes several suits, so, upright earl,
Our linsey-woolsey hearts make all this coil.

Heng. What's all this now? I'm ne'er the wiser yet.—
Call in the rest.
                [*Exit* Gentleman, *and re-enter with* Glover
                        and others.

Now, sirs,—what are you?

Glov. Sir-reverence[1] on your lordship, I am a glover.

Heng. What needs that then?

---

[1] A corruption of "save-reverence,' *salvâ reverentiâ.*

Glov. Sometimes I deal in dog's leather, sir-reverence the while.

Heng. Well, to the purpose, if there be any towards.[1]

Glov. I were an ass else, saving your lordship's presence.

We have a body, but our town wants a hand,
A hand of justice, a worshipful master mayor.

Heng. This is well handled yet ; a man may take some hold on it.—You want a mayor ?

Glov. Right, but there's two at fisty-cuffs about it ;
Sir, as I may say, at daggers drawing,—
But that I cannot say, because they have none,—
And you being Earl of Kent, our town does say,
Your lordship's voice shall part and end the fray.

Heng. This is strange work for me. Well, sir, what
be they ?

Glov. The one is a tanner.

Heng. Fie, I shall be too partial,
I owe too much affection to that trade
To put it to my voice. What is his name ?

Glov. Simon.

Heng. How, Simon too ?

Glov. Nay, 'tis but Simon once, sir ; the very same
Simon that sold your lordship a hide.

Heng. What sayest thou ?

Glov. That's all his glory, sir : he got his master's
widow by it presently, a rich tanner's wife : she has set
him up ; he was her foreman a long time in her other
husband's days.

Heng. Now let me perish in my first aspiring,
If the pretty simplicity of his fortune
Do not most highly take me : 'tis a presage, methinks,
Of bright succeeding happiness to mine,
When my fate's glow-worm casts forth such a shine.—
And what are those that do contend with him ?

[1] To hand.

Tail. Marry, my noble lord, a fustian-weaver.

Heng. How ! he offer to compare with Simon ? he a fit match for him !

Barb. Hark, hark, my lord ! here they come both in a pelting chafe from the town-house.

Enter SIMON *and* OLIVER.

Sim. How, before me ?   I scorn thee,
Thou wattle-faced singed pig.

Oliv. Pig ?   I defy thee ;
My uncle was a Jew, and scorned the motion.

Sim. I list not brook thy vaunts.   Compare with me,
Thou spindle of concupiscence ? 'tis well known
Thy first wife was a flax-wench.

Oliv. But such a flax-wench
Would I might never want at my need,
Nor any friend of mine : my neighbours knew her.
Thy wife was but a hempen halter to her.

Sim. Use better words, I'll hang thee in my year else,
Let who will choose thee afterwards.

Glov. Peace, for shame ;
Quench your great spirit : do not you see his lordship ?

Heng. What, Master Simonides ?

Sim. Simonides ? what a fair name hath he made of Simon ! then he's an ass that calls me Simon again ; I am quite out of love with it.

Heng. Give me thy hand ; I love thy fortunes, and like a man that thrives.

Sim. I took a widow, my lord, to be the best piece of ground to thrive on ; and by my faith, my lord, there's a young Simonides, like a green onion, peeping up already.

Heng. Thou'st a good lucky hand.

Sim. I have somewhat, sir.

Heng. But why to me is this election offered ?
The choosing of a mayor goes by most voices.

Sim. True, sir, but most of our townsmen are so hoarse with drinking, there's not a good voice among them all.

Heng. Are you content to put it to all these then ?
To whom I liberally resign my interest,
To prevent censures.

Sim. I speak first, my lord.

Oliv. Though I speak last, my lord, I am not least : if they will cast away a town-born child, they may ; it is but dying some forty years before my time.

Heng. I leave you to your choice a while.

All. Your good lordship.

                    [*Exeunt* HENGIST *and* Gentleman.

Sim. Look you, neighbours, before you be too hasty. Let Oliver the fustian-weaver stand as fair as I do, and the devil do him good on't.

Oliv. I do, thou upstart callymoocher,[1] I do; 'tis well known to the parish I have been twice ale-conner ;[2] thou mushroom, thou shot'st up in a night, by lying with thy mistress !

Sim. Faith, thou art such a spiny baldrib, all the mistresses in the town will never get thee up.

Oliv. I scorn to rise by a woman, as thou didst : my wife shall rise by me.

Glov. I pray leave your communication ; we can do nothing else.

Oliv. I gave that barber a fustian-suit, and twice redeemed his cittern :[3] he may remember me.

Sim. I fear no false measure but in that tailor ; the glover and the button-maker are both cock-sure ; that

---

[1] A term of reproach, probably connected with "micher."—*Halliwell.*

[2] An officer appointed in every court leet to look to the assize and goodness of bread, ale, and beer.—*Kersey.*

[3] A cittern or lute, formerly used to be part of the furniture of a barber's shop, and, as Sir John Hawkins observed, answered the end of a newspaper in amusing waiting customers.

collier's eye I like not ; now they consult, the matter is
in brewing : poor Gill, my wife, lies longing for the news ;
'twill make her a glad mother.

All. [*Except* OLIVER.] A Simon, a Simon !

Sim. Good people, I thank you all.

Oliv. Wretch that I am ! Tanner, thou hast curried
favour.

Sim. I curry ! I defy thy fustian fume.

Oliv. But I will prove a rebel all thy year,
And raise up the seven deadly sins against thee.   [*Exit.*

Sim. The deadly sins will scorn to rise by thee, if they
have any breeding, as commonly they are well brought
up : 'tis not for every scab to be acquainted with them :
but leaving the scab, to you, good neighbours, now I
bend my speech.   First, to say more than a man can say,
I hold it not fit to be spoken : but to say what a man
ought to say, there I leave you also.   I must confess
your loves have chosen a weak and unlearned man ; that
I can neither write nor read, you all can witness ; yet
not altogether so unlearned, but I can set my mark to a
bond, if I would be so simple ; an excellent token of
government.   Cheer you then, my hearts, you have done
you know not what : there's a full point ; there you must
all cough and hem.   [*They all cough and hem.*]   Now
touching our common adversary the fustian-weaver, who
threatens he will raise the deadly sins among us, let them
come ; our town is big enough to hold them, we will not
so much disgrace it ; besides, you know a deadly sin will
lie in a narrow hole : but when they think themselves
safest, and the web of their iniquity best woven, with the
horse-strength of my justice I will break through the loom
of their concupiscence, and make the weaver go seek his
shuttle : here you may cough and hem again, if you'll do
me the favour.   [*They cough and hem again.*]   Why, I
thank you all, and it shall not go unrewarded.   Now for

the deadly sins, pride, sloth, envy, wrath ; as for covetous-
ness and gluttony, I'll tell you more when I come out of
my office ; I shall have time to try what they are : I will
prove them soundly ; and if I find gluttony and covetous-
ness to be directly sins, I'll bury the one in the bottom
of a chest, and the other in the end of my garden. But,
sirs, for lechery, I'll tickle that home myself, I'll not leave
a whore in the town.

Barb. Some of your neighbours must seek their wives
in the country then.

Sim. Barber, be silent, I will cut thy comb else. To
conclude, I will learn the villany of all trades ; my own
I know already : if there be any knavery in the baker, I
will bolt it out ; if in the brewer, I will taste him
throughly, and piss out his iniquity at his own suckhole :
in a word, I will knock down all enormities like a butcher,
and send the hide to my fellow-tanners.

All. A Simonides, a true Simonides indeed !

Re-enter HENGIST *with* ROXENA.

Heng. How now ? how goes your choice ?

Tail. This is he, my lord.

Sim. To prove I am the man, I am bold to take
The upper hand of your lordship : I'll not lose
An inch of my honour.

Heng. Hold, sirs : there's some few crowns
To mend your feast, because I like your choice.

[*Gives money.*

Barb. Joy bless you, sir !
We'll drink your health with trumpets.

Sim. I with sackbuts,
That's the more solemn drinking for my state ;
No malt this year shall fume into my pate.

[*Exeunt all but* HENGIST *and* ROXENA.

Heng. Continues still that favour in his love ?

Rox. Nay, with increase, my lord, the flame grows
    greater ;
Though he has learned a better art of late
To set a screen before it.
    Heng. Speak lower.
            [*Retires to a seat and reads ; exit* ROXENA.

        Enter VORTIGER *and* HORSUS.

    Hor. Heard every word, my lord
    Vort. Plainly ?
    Hor. Distinctly.
The course I took was dangerous, but not failing,
For I conveyed myself behind the hangings
Even just before his entrance.
    Vort. 'Twas well ventured.
    Hor. I had such a woman's first and second longing
    in me
To hear how she would bear her mocked abuse
After she was returned to privacy,
I could have fasted out an ember-week,
And never thought of hunger, to have heard her ;
Then came your holy Lupus and Germanus—
    Vort. Two holy confessors.
    Hor. At whose first sight
I could perceive her fall upon her breast,
And cruelly afflict herself with sorrow
(I never heard a sigh till I heard hers) ;
Who, after her confession, pitying her,
Put her into a way of patience,
Which now she holds, to keep it hid from you :
There's all the pleasure that I took in't now ;
When I heard that, my pains was well remembered.
So, with applying comforts and relief,
They've brought it lower, to an easy grief ;
But yet the taste is not quite gone.

Vort. Still fortune
Sits bettering our inventions.
   Hor. Here she comes.

            Enter CASTIZA.

   Cast. Yonder's my lord ; O, I'll return again !
Methinks I should not dare to look on him.
                      [Aside, and exit.
   Hor. She's gone again.
   Vort. It works the kindlier, sir :
Go now and call her back. *[Exit* HORSUS.] She winds
    herself
Into the snare so prettily, 'tis a pleasure
To set toils for her.

    Re-enter CASTIZA *and* HORSUS.

   Cast. He may read my shame
Now in my blush.   *[Aside.*
   Vort. Come, you're so linked to holiness,
So taken with contemplative desires,
That the world has you, yet enjoys you not :
You have been weeping too.
   Cast. Not I, my lord.
   Vort. Trust me, I fear you have : you're much to
    blame
To yield so much to passion[1] without cause.
Is not some time enough for meditation ?
Must it lay title to your health and beauty,
And draw them into time's consumption too ?
'Tis too exacting for a holy faculty.—
My lord of Kent !—I prithee, wake him, captain ;
He reads himself asleep, sure.
   Hor. My lord !
   Vort. Nay,
              [1] Sorrow.

I'll take away your book, and bestow't here.

       [*Takes book from* HENGIST.

  Heng. Your pardon, sir.

  Vort. [*Giving book to* CASTIZA.] Lady, you that delight
   in virgins' stories,
And all chaste works, here's excellent reading for you :
Make of that book as made men do of favours,
Which they grow sick to part from.—And now, my lord,
You that have so conceitedly[1] gone beyond me,
And made so large use of a slender gift,
Which we ne'er minded,[2] I commend your thrift ;
And that your building may to all ages
Carry the stamp and impress of your wit,
It shall be called Thong Castle.

  Heng. How, my lord,
Thong Castle ! there your grace quits me kindly.

  Vort. 'Tis fit art should be known by its right name ;
You that can spread my gift, I'll spread your fame.

  Heng. I thank your grace for that.

  Vort. And, lovèd lord,
So well do we accept your invitation,
With all speed we'll set forwards.

  Heng. Your honour loves me.   [*Exeunt.*

    [1] Ingeniously.   [2] Intended.

ACT THE FOURTH.

SCENE I.

A Public Way near HENGIST'S *Castle.*

Enter SIMON *(a mace and sword before him), and all his brethren, meeting* VORTIGER, CASTIZA, HENGIST, ROXENA, HORSUS, *and two* Ladies.

 IM. Lo, I, the Mayor of Queenborough
          by name,
        With all my brethren, saving one
          that's lame,
        Are come as fast as fiery mill-horse
          gallops
To greet thy grace, thy queen, and her fair trollops.
For reason of our coming do not look ;
It must be done, I find it i' the town-book ;
And yet not I myself, I canno't read ;
I keep a clerk to do those jobs for need.
And now expect a rare conceit before Thong Castle see
    thee. —
Reach me the thing to give the king, the other too, I
    prithee. —
Now here they be, for queen and thee ; the gift all steel
    and leather,
But the conceit of mickle weight, and here they come
    together :

Mid. II.   2 A

To show two loves must join in one, our town presents
    by me
This gilded scabbard to the queen, this dagger unto thee.
                          [*Offers scabbard and dagger.*

Vort. Forbear your tedious and ridiculous duties ;
I hate them, as I do the riots of your
Inconstant rabble ; I have felt your fits :
Sheathe up your bounties with your iron wits.
                          [*Exit with his train.*

  im. Look, sirs, is his back turned?
  All. It is, it is.
  Sim. Then bless the good Earl of Kent, say I
I'll have this dagger turned into a pie,
And eaten up for anger, every bit on't :
And when this pie shall be cut up by some rare cunning
    pie-man,
They shall full lamentably sing, Put up thy dagger,
    Simon.   [*Exeunt.*

SCENE II.

A Hall in HENGIST'S *Castle. A feast set out.*

Enter VORTIGER, HENGIST, HORSUS, DEVONSHIRE,
    STAFFORD, CASTIZA, ROXENA, *two* Ladies, Guards,
    and Attendants.

  Heng. A welcome, mighty lord, may appear costlier,
More full of toil and talk, show and conceit ;
But one more stored with thankful love and truth
I forbid all the sons of men to boast of.
  Vort. Why, here's a fabric that implies eternity ;
The building plain, but most substantial ;
Methinks it looks as if it mocked all ruin,

Saving that master-piece of consummation,
The end of time, which must consume even ruin,
And eat that into cinders.

    Heng. There's no brass
Would pass your praise, my lord ; 'twould last beyond it,
And shame our durablest metal.

    Vort. Horsus !

    Hor. My lord.

    Vort. This is the time I've chosen; here's a full
        meeting,
And here will I disgrace her.

    Hor. 'Twill be sharp, my lord.

    Vort. O, 'twill be best.

    Hor. Why, here's the earl her father.

    Vort. Ay, and the lord her uncle ; that's the height
        of't ;
Invited both on purpose, to rise sick,
Full of shame's surfeit.

    Hor. And that's shrewd, by'r lady :
It ever sticks close to the ribs of honour,
Great men are never sound men after it ;
It leaves some ache or other in their names still,
Which their posterity feels at every weather.

    Vort. Mark but the least presentment of occasion,
As these times yield enough, and then mark me.

    Hor. My observance is all yours, you know't, my
        lord.—
What careful ways some take to abuse themselves !
But as there be assurers of men's goods
'Gainst storms or pirates, which gives adventurers courage,
So such there must be to make up man's theft,
Or there would be no woman-venturer left.
See, now they find their seats ! what a false knot
Of amity he ties about her arm,
Which rage must part ! In marriage 'tis no wonder.

Knots knit with kisses oft are broke with thunder. [*Music.*
Music? then I have done ; I always learn
To give my betters place.   [*Aside.*
    Vort. Where's Captain Horsus?
Sit, sit ; we'll have a health anon to all
Good services.
    Hor. They are poor in these days ;
They'd rather have the cup than the health.
He hears me not, and most great men are deaf
On that side.   [*Aside.*
    Vort. My lord of Kent, I thank you for this welcome ;
It came unthought of, in the sweetest language
That ever my soul relished.
    Heng. You are pleased, my lord,
To raise my happiness for slight deservings,
To show what power's in princes ; not in us
Aught worthy, 'tis in you that makes us thus.
I'm chiefly sad, my lord, your queen's not merry.
    Vort. So honour bless me, he has found the way
To my grief strangely.   Is there no delight——
    Cast. My lord, I wish not any, nor is't needful ;
I am as I was ever.
    Vort. That's not so.
    Cast. How? O, my fears !   [*Aside.*
    Vort. When she writ maid, my lord,
You knew her otherwise.
    Devon. To speak but truth,
I never knew her a great friend to mirth,
Nor taken much with any one delight ;
Though there be many seemly and honourable
To give content to ladies without taxing.
    Vort. My lord of Kent, this to thy full deserts,
Which intimates thy higher flow to honour. [*Drinking.*
    Heng. Which, like a river, shall return in service
To the great master-fountain.

Vort. Where's your lord?
I missed him not till now,—Lady, and yours?
No marvel then we were so out of the way
Of all pleasant discourse; they are the keys
Of human music; sure at their nativities
Great Nature signed a general patent to them
To take up all the mirth in a whole kingdom.
What's their employment now?

   1st Lady. May it please your grace,
We never are so far acquainted with them;
Nothing we know but what they cannot keep;
That's even the fashion of them all, my lord.

   Vort. It seems ye've great thought in their constancies,
And they in yours, you dare so trust each other.

   2nd Lady. Hope well we do, my lord; we've reason
     for it,
Because they say brown men are honestest;
But she's a fool will swear for any colour.

   Vort. They would for yours.

   2nd Lady. Truth, 'tis a doubtful question,
And I'd be loth to put mine to't, my lord.

   Vort. Faith, dare you swear for yourselves? that's a
     plain question..

   2nd Lady. My lord?

   Vort. You cannot deny that with honour;
And since 'tis urged, I'll put you to't in troth.

   1st Lady. May it please your grace—

   Vort. 'Twou d please me very well;
And here's a book, mine never goes without one;
              [*Taking book from* CASTIZA.
She's an example to you a.l for purity:
Come, swear (I've sworn you shall) that you ne'er knew
The will of any man besides your husband's.

   2nd Lady. I'll swear, my lord as for as my remem-
     brance—

Vort. How ! your remembrance ? that were strange.
1st Lady. Your grace
Hearing our just excuse, will not say so.
Vort. Well, what's your just excuse ? you're ne'er
without some.
1st Lady. I'm often taken with a sleep, my lord,
The loudest thunder cannot waken me,
Not if a cannon's burden be discharged
Close by my ear ; the more may be my wrong ;
There can be no infirmity, my lord,
More excusable in any woman.
2nd Lady. And I'm so troubled with the mother[1]
too,
I've often called in help, I know not whom ;
Three at once have been too weak to keep me down.
Vort. I perceive there's no fastening. [*Aside.*]—Well,
fair one, then,
That ne'er deceives faith's anchor of her hold,
Come at all seasons ; here, be thou the star
To guide those erring women, show the way
Which I will make them follow. Why dost start,
Draw back, and look so pale ?
Cast. My lord !
Vort. Come hither ;
Nothing but take that oath ; thou'lt take a thousand :
A thousand ! nay, a million, or as many
As there be angels registers of oaths.
Why, look thee, over-fearful chastity,
(That sinn'st in nothing but in too much niceness,)
I'll begin first and swear for thee myself :
I know thee a perfection so unstained,
So sure, so absolute, I will not pant on it,
But catch time greedily. But all those blessings
That blow truth into fruitfulness, and those curses

[1] **Hysterical fits.**

That with their barren breaths blast perjury,
Thou art as pure as sanctity's best shrine
From all man's mixture, save what's lawful, mine !
  Cast. O, Heaven forgive him, he has forsworn himself !
                                    [*Aside.*
  Vort. Come, 'tis but going now my way.
  Cast. That's bad enough.   [*Aside.*
  Vort. I've cleared all doubts, you see.
  Cast. Good my lord, spare me.
  Vort. How ! it grows later than so. For modesty's
    sake,
Make more speed this way.
  Cast. Pardon me, my lord,
I cannot.
  Vort. What ?
  Cast. I dare not.
  Vort. Fail all confidence
In thy weak kind for ever !
  Devon. Here's a storm
Able to wake all of our name inhumed,
And raise them from their sleeps of peace and fame,
To set the honours of their bloods right here,
 Hundred years after : a perpetual motion
Has their true glory been from seed to seed,
And cannot be choked now with a poor grain
Of dust and earth. Her uncle and myself,
Wild in this tempest,[1] as e'er robbed man's peace,
Will undertake, upon life's deprivation,
She shall accept this oath.
  Vort. You do but call me then
Into a world of more despair and horror ;
Yet since so wilfully you stand engaged
In high scorn to be touched, with expedition
Perfect your undertakings with your fames ;

        [1] Dyce suggests " In this wild tempest."

Or, by the issues of abused belief,
I'll take the forfeit of lives, lands, and honours,
And make one ruin serve our joys and yours.
   Cast. Why, here's a height of miseries never reached
      yet !
I lose myself and others
   Devon. You may see
How much we lay in balance with your goodness,
And had we more, it went; for we presume
You cannot be religious and so vile—
   Cast. As to forswear myself—'Tis truth, great sir,
The honour of your bed hath been abused.
   Vort. O, beyond patience !
   Cast. But give me hearing, sir,
'Twas far from my consent; I was surprised
By villains, and so raught.[1]
   Vort. Hear you that, sirs ?
O cunning texture to enclose adultery !
Mark but what subtle veil her sins puts on ;
Religion brings her to confession first,
Then steps in art to sanctify that lust.—
'Tis likely you could be surprised !
   Cast. My lord !
   Vort. I'll hear no more.—Our guard ! seize on those
      lords.
   Devon. We cannot perish now too fast ; make speed
To swift destruction. He breathes most accurst
That lives so long to see his name die first.
          [Exeunt DEVONSHIRE *and* STAFFORD, *guarded.*
   Hor. Here's no dear[2] villany !   *[Aside.*
   Heng. Let him entreat, sir,
That falls in saddest grief for this event,
Which ill begins the fortune of this building.
My lord !   *[Takes* VORTIGER *aside.*

      [1] Ravished.   [2] *i.e.* Precious.

Rox. What if he should cause me to swear, too,
   captain?
You know I am as far to seek in honesty
As the worst here can be; I should be shamed too.
   Hor. Why, fool, they swear by that we worship not;
So you may swear your heart out, and ne'er hurt
   yourself.
   Rox. That was well thought on; I'd quite lost myself
   else.
   Vort. You shall prevail in noble suits, my lord,
But this does shame the speaker.
   Hor. I'll step in now,
Though't shall be to no purpose.—Good my lord,
Think on your noble and most hopeful issue,
Lord Vortimer, the prince.
   Vort. A bastard, sir!
I would his life were in my fury now.
   Cast. That injury stirs my soul to speak the ...th
Of his conception.—Here I take the book, my lord:
By all the glorified rewards of virtue
And prepared punishments for consents in sin,
A queen's hard sorrow ne'er supplied a kingdom
With issue more legitimate than Vortimer.
   Vort. This takes not out the stain of present shame
Continuance crowns desert: she ne'er can go
For perfect honest that's not always so.—
Beshrew thy heart for urging this excuse;
Thou'st justified her somewhat.
   Hor. To small purpose.
   Vort. Among so many women, not one here
Dare swear a simple chastity! here's an age
To propagate virtue in! Since I've begun,
I'll shame you altogether, and so leave you.-
My lord of Kent!
   Heng. Your highness.

Vort. That's your daughter?

Heng. Yes, my good lord.

Vort. Though I'm your guest to-day,
And should be less austere to you or yours,
In this case pardon me ; I may not spare her.

Heng. Then her own goodness friend her !—she comes,
my lord.

Vort. The tender reputation of a maid
Makes your honour, or else nothing can :
The oath you take is not for truth to man,
But to your own white soul ; a mighty task :
What dare you do in this ?

Rox. My lord, as much
As chastity can put a woman to ;
I ask no favour.   And to approve the purity
Of what my habit and my time professeth,
As likewise to requite all courteous censure
Here I take oath I am as free from man
As truth from falsehood, or sanctity from stain.

Vort. O thou treasure that ravishes the possessor !
I know not where to speed so well again ;
I'll keep thee while I have thee : here's a fountain
To spring forth princes and the seeds of kingdoms !
Away with that infection of black honour,
And those her leprous pledges !—
Here will we store succession with true peace ;
And of pure virgins grace the poor increase.

[*Exeunt all but* HORSUS

Hor. Ha, ha!
He's well provided now : here struck my fortunes.
With what an impudent confidence she swore honest,
Having the advantage of the oath ! precious whore !
Methinks I should not hear from fortune next
Under an earldom now : she cannot spend
A night so idly, but to make a lord

With ease, methinks, and play. The Earl of Kent
Is calm and smooth, like a deep dangerous water ;
He has some secret way ; I know his blood ;
The grave's not greedier, nor hell's lord more proud.
Something will hap ; for this astonishing choice
Strikes pale the kingdom, at which I rejoice.   [*Exit.*

DUMB SHOW.

Enter LUPUS, GERMANUS, DEVONSHIRE, *and*
STAFFORD, *leading* VORTIMER, *whom they crown :*
VORTIGER *comes to them in passion ; they neglect
him.* *Enter* ROXENA *in fury, expressing discontent ; then they lead out* VORTIMER : ROXENA
gives two Villains *gold to murder him ; they swear
performance, and go with her :* VORTIGER *offers
to run on his sword,* HORSUS *prevents him, and
persuades him.* *The* Lords *bring in* VORTIMER
dead : VORTIGER *mourns, and submits to them :
they swear him, and crown him.* *Then enters*
HENGIST *with* Saxons : VORTIGER *draws,
threatens expulsion, and then sends a parley,
which* HENGIST *seems to grant by laying down
his weapons ; so all depart severally.*

Enter RAYNULPH.

Ray. Of Pagan blood a queen being chose,
Roxena hight, the Britons rose
For Vortimer, and crowned him king ;
But she soon poisoned that sweet spring.
Then unto rule they did restore
Vortiger ; and him they swore
Against the Saxons : they (constrained)

Begged peace, treaty, and obtained.
And now in numbers equally
Upon the plain near Salisbury,
A peaceful meeting they decreen,
Like men of love, no weapon seen.
But Hengist, that ambitious lord,
Full of guile, corrupts his word,
As the sequel too well proves : —
On that your eyes ; on us your loves.   [*Exit*.

SCENE III.

A Plain near Salisbury.

Enter HENGIST *with* Saxons.

Heng. If we let slip this opportuneful hour,
Take leave of fortune, certainty, or thought
Of ever fixing : we are loose at root,
And the least storm may rend us from the bosom
Of this land's hopes for ever.   But, dear Saxons,
Fasten we now, and our unshaken firmness
Will endure after-ages.
    1st Sax. We are resolved, my lord.
    Heng. Observe you not how Vortiger the king,
Base in submission, threatened our expulsion,
His arm held up against us ?   Is't not time
To make our best prevention ?   What should check me?
He has perfected that great work in our daughter,
And made her queen : she can ascend no higher.
Therefore be quick ; despatch.   Here, every man
Receive into the service of his vengeance
An instrument of steel, which will unseen
                              [*Distributing daggers.*

Lurk, like a snake under the innocent shade
Of a spread summer-leaf : there, fly you on.
Take heart, the commons love us ; those removed.
That are the nerves, our greatness stands improved.

1st Sax. Give us the word, my lord, and we are
perfect.

Heng. That's true ; the word,--I lose myself--"Nemp
your sexes : "[1]
It shall be that.

1st Sax. Enough, sir : then we strike.

Heng. But the king's mine : take heed you touch him
not.

1st Sax. We shall not be at leisure ; never fear it ;
We shall have work enough of our own, my lord.

Heng. Calm looks, but stormy souls possess you all !

Enter VORTIGER *and* British Lords.

Vort. We see you keep your words in all points firm.

Heng. No longer may we boast of so much breath
As goes to a word's making, than of care
In the preserving of it when 'tis made.

Vort. You're in a virtuous way, my lord of Kent :
And since both sides are met, like sons of peace,
All other arms laid by in signs of favour,
If our conditions be embraced—

---

[1] The appointment being agreed to on both sides, Hengist, with
a new design of villany in his head, ordered his soldiers to carry, .
every one of them, a long dagger under their garments ; and while
the conference should be held with the Britons, who would have no
suspicion of them, he would give them this word of command,
"Nemet oure saxas ; " at which moment they were all to be ready
to seize boldly every one his next man, and with his drawn dagger
stab him. Accordingly, at the time and place appointed, they all
met, and began to treat of peace ; and when a fit opportunity for
executing his villany served, Hengist cried out, "Nemet oure
saxas ;" and the same instant seized Vortegirn, and held him by
his cloak.—*Geoffrey of Monmouth.*

"Nemp your sexes" means "Take your daggers, or short
swords."

Heng. They are.

Vort. We'll use no other but these only here.

Heng. "Nemp your sexes."

British Lords. Treason! treason!

[*The* Saxons *stab the* British Lords.

Heng. Follow it to the heart, my trusty Saxons!
It is your liberty, your wealth, and honour.—
Soft, you are mine, my lord.   [*Seizing* VORTIGER.

Vort. Take me not basely, when all sense and
     strength
Lies bound up in amazement at this treachery.
What devil hath breathed this everlasting part
Of falsehood into thee?

Heng. Let it suffice
I have you, and will hold you prisoner,
As fast as death holds your best props in silence.
We know the hard conditions of our peace,
Slavery or diminution; which we hate
With a joint loathing.   May all perish thus,
That seek to subjugate or lessen us!

Vort. O, the strange nooks of guile or subtilty,
When man so cunningly lies hid from man!
Who could expect such treason from thy breast,
Such thunder from thy voice?   Or tak'st thou pride
To imitate the fair uncertainty
Of a bright day, that teems a sudden storm,
When the world least expects one? but of all,
I'll ne'er trust fair sky in a man again:
There's the deceitful weather.   Will you heap
More guilt upon you by detaining me,
Like a cup taken after a sore surfeit,
Even in contempt of health and Heaven together?
What seek you?

Heng. Ransom for your liberty,
As I shall like of, or you ne'er obtain it.

Vort. Here's a most headlong dangerous ambition !
Sow you the seeds of your aspiring hopes
In blood and treason, and must I pay for them ?
Heng. Have not I raised you to this height of pride ?
A work of my own merit, since you enforce it.
Vort. There's even the general thanks of all aspirers :
When they have all a kingdom can impart,
They write above it still their own desert.
Heng. I've writ mine true, my lord.
Vort. That's all their sayings.
Have not I raised thy daughter to a queen?
Heng. You have the harmony of your pleasure for it ;
You crown your own desires ; what's that to me ?
Vort. And what will crown yours, sir ?
Heng. Faith, things of reason :
I demand Kent.
Vort. Why, you've the earldom of it.
Heng. The kingdom of't, I mean, without control,
In full possession.
Vort. This is strange in you.
Heng. It seems you're not acquainted with my blood,
To call this strange.
Vort. Never was king of Kent,
But who was general king.
Heng. I'll be the first then :
Everything has beginning.
Vort. No less title ?
Heng. Not if you hope for liberty, my lord.
So dear a happiness would not be wronged
With slighting.
Vort. Very well : take it ; I resign it.
Heng. Why, I thank your grace.
Vort. Is your great thrist yet satisfied ?
Heng. Faith, my lord,
There's yet behind a pair of teeming sisters,
Norfolk and Suffolk, and I've done with you.

Vort. You've got a dangerous thirst of late, my lord,
Howe'er you came by't.

Heng. It behoves me then,
For my blood's health, to seek all means to quench it.

Vort. Them too?

Heng. There will nothing be abated, I assure you.

Vort. You have me at advantage : he whom fate
Does captivate, must yield to all. Take them.

Heng. And you your liberty and peace, my lord,
With our best love and wishes.—Here's an hour
Begins us, Saxons in wealth, fame, and power.

                           [*Exit with* Saxons.

Vort. Are these the noblest fruits and fair'st requitals
From works of our own raising?
Methinks, the murder of Constantius
Speaks to me in the voice of't, and the wrong
Of our late queen, slipt both into one organ.

                Enter HORSUS.

Ambition, hell, my own undoing lust,
And all the brood of plagues, conspire against me :
I have not a friend left me.

Hor. My lord, he dies
That says it, but yourself, were't that thief-king,
That has so boldly stolen his honours from you ;
A treason that wrings tears from honest manhood.

Vort. So rich am I now in thy love and pity,
I feel no loss at all : but we must part,
My queen and I to Cambria.

Hor. My lord, and I not named,
That have vowed lasting service to my life's
Extremest minute !

Vort. Is my sick fate blest with so pure a friend?

Hor. My lord, no space of earth, nor breadth of sea,
Shall divide me from you.

Vort. O faithful treasure !
All my lost happiness is made up in thee.   [*Exit.*
   Hor. I'll follow you through the world, to cuckold
       you ;
That's my way now.   Every one has his toy
While he lives here : some men delight in building,
A trick of Babel, which will ne'er be left ;
Some in consuming what was raised with toiling ;
Hengist in getting honour, I in spoiling.   [*Exit.*

ACT THE FIFTH.

SCENE I.

A Room in SIMON'S *House.*

Enter SIMON, Glover, Feltmonger, *and other of his brethren,* AMINADAB, *and Servants.*

SIM. Is not that rebel Oliver, that traitor to my year, 'prehended yet?

Amin. Not yet, so please your worship.

Sim. Not yet, sayest thou? how durst thou say, not yet, and see me present? thou malapert, thou art good for nothing but to write and read! Is his loom seized upon?

Amin. Yes, if it like your worship, and sixteen yards of fustian.

Sim. Good : let a yard be saved to mend me between the legs, the rest cut in pieces and given to the poor. 'Tis heretic fustian, and should be burnt indeed; but being worn threadbare, the shame will be as great : how think you, neighbours?

Glov. Greater, methinks, the longer it is wore ;
Where[1] being once burnt, it can be burnt no more.

Sim. True, wise and most senseless.—How now, sirrah?

---

[1] **Whereas.**

Enter a Footman.

What's he approaching here in dusty pumps?

Amin. A footman, sir, to the great King of Kent.

Sim. The King of Kent? shake him by the hand for
    me.
Thou'rt welcome, footman : lo, my deputy shakes thee !
Come when my year is out, I'll do't myself.
If 'twere a dog that came from the King of Kent,
I keep those officers would shake him, I trow.
And what's the news with thee, thou well-stewed foot-
    man ?

Foot. The king, my master—

Sim. Ha !

Foot. With a few Saxons,
Intends this night to make merry with you.

Sim. Merry with me ? I should be sorrow else, fellow,
And take it in ill part ; so tell Kent's king.
Why was I chosen, but that great men should make
Merry with me ? there is a jest indeed !
Tell him I looked for't ; and me much he wrongs,
If he forget Sim that cut out his thongs.

Foot. I'll run with your worship's answer.

Sim. Do, I prithee.   [*Exit* Footman.
That fellow will be roasted against supper ;
He's half enough already ; his brows baste him.
The King of Kent ! the King of Kirsendom[1]
Shall not be better welcome ;
For you must imagine now, neighbours, this is
The time when Kent stands out of Kirsendom,[2]
For he that's king here now was never kirsened.[3]
This for your more instruction I thought fit,

[1] A corruption of " Christendom."
[2] " In Kent and Christendom " was proverbial.
[3] Christened.

That when you're dead you may teach your children
    wit.—

Clerk !

    Amin. At your worship's elbow.

    Sim. I must turn
You from the hall to the kitchen to-night.
Give order that twelve pigs be roasted yellow,
Nine geese, and some three larks for piddling[1] meat,
And twenty woodcocks : I'll bid all my neighbours.
Give charge the mutton come in all blood-raw,
That's infidel's meat ; the King of Kent's a Pagan,
And must be servèd so. And let those officers
That seldom or never go to church bring it in,
'Twill be better taken. Run, run.   [*Exit* AMINADAB.
Come you hither now.
Take all my cushions down and thwack them soundly,
After my feast of millers ; for their buttocks
Have left a peck of flour in them : beat them carefully
Over a bolting-hutch,[2] there will be enough
For a pan-pudding, as your dame will handle it.
Then put fresh water into both the bough-pots,
And burn a little juniper in the hall-chimney :[3]
                        [*Exeunt* Servants.
Like a beast as I was, I pissed out the fire last night,
and never dreamt of the king's coming.

Re-enter AMINADAB.

How now, returned so quickly ?

    Amin. Please your worship, here are a certain com-
pany of players—

    Sim. Ha, players !

---

[1] Meat to trifle with. Pope has :—
    " Content on little I can *piddle* here
      On brocoli and mutton round the year."—*Bullen.*
[2] A trough into which meal is sifted.
[3] To sweeten the chamber.

Amin. Country comedians, interluders, sir, desire your worship's favour and leave to enact in the town-hall.

Sim. In the town-hall? 'tis ten to one I never grant them that. Call them before my worship. [*Exit* AMINADAB.]—If my house will not serve their turn, I would fain see the proudest he lend them a barn.

Re-enter AMINADAB *with* Players.

Now, sir, are you comedians?

2nd Play. We are, sir; comedians, tragedians, tragi-comedians, comi-tragedians, pastorists, humourists, clownists, satirists : we have them, sir, from the hug to the smile, from the smile to the laugh, from the laugh to the handkerchief.

Sim. You're very strong in the wrists, methinks. And must all these good parts be cast away upon pedlars and maltmen, ha?

1st Play. For want of better company, if it please your worship.

Sim. What think you of me, my masters? Hum ; have you audacity enough to play before so high a person as myself? Will not my countenance daunt you? for if you play before me, I shall often look on you ; I give you that warning beforehand. Take it not ill, my masters, I shall laugh at you, and truly when I am least offended with you : it is my humour · but be not you abashed.

1st Play. Sir, we have played before a lord ere now, Though we be country actors.

Sim. A lord? ha, ha !
Thou'lt find it a harder thing to please a mayor.

2nd Play. We have a play wherein we use a horse.

Sim. Fellows, you use no horse-play in my house ;
My rooms are rubbed : keep it for hackney-men.

1st Play. We'll not offer it to your worship.

Sim. Give me a play without a beast, I charge you.

2nd Play. That's hard; without a cuckold or a drunkard?

Sim. O, those beasts are often the best men in a parish, and must not be kept out. But which is your merriest play? that I would hearken after.

2nd Play. Your worship shall hear their names, and take your choice.

Sim. And that's plain dealing. Come, begin, sir.

2nd Play. The Whirligig, The Whibble, The Carwidgeon.

Sim. Hey-day! what names are these?

2nd Play. New names of late. *The Wildgoose Chase.*[1]

Sim. I understand thee now.

2nd Play. Gull upon Gull.

Sim. Why, this is somewhat yet.

1st Play. Woodcock of our side.

Sim. Get thee further off then.

2nd Play. The Cheater and the Clown.

Sim. Is that come up again.

That was a play when I was 'prentice first.

2nd Play. Ay, but the cheater has learned more tricks of late,

And gulls the clown with new additions.

Sim. Then is your clown a coxcomb; which is he?

1st Play. This is our clown, sir.

Sim. Fie, fie, your company must fall upon him and beat him: he's too fair, i'faith, to make the people laugh.

1st Play. Not as he may be dressed, sir.

Sim. Faith, dress him how you will, I'll give him that gift, he will never look half scurvily enough. O, the

---

[1] I is not necessary to look upon this as an allusion to Fletcher's come y.

clowns that I have seen in my time! The very peeping out of one of them would have made a young heir laugh, though his father lay a-dying; a man undone in law the day before (the saddest case that can be) might for his twopence have burst himself with laughing, and ended all his miseries. Here was a merry world, my masters!

Some talk of things of state, of puling stuff;
There's nothing in a.play to[1] a clown, if he
Have the grace to hit on't; that's the thing indeed :
The king shows well, but he sets off the king.
But not the King of Kent, I mean not so ;
The king is one, I mean, I do not know.

    2nd Play. Your worship speaks with safety, like a rich
        man ;
And for your finding fault, our hopes are greater,
Neither with him the clown, nor me the cheater.

    Sim. Away, then ; shift, clown, to thy motley crupper.
                            [*Exeunt* Players.
We'll see them first, the king shall after supper.

    Glov. I commend your worship's wisdom in that, master mayor.

    Sim. Nay, 'tis a point of justice, if it be well examined, not to offer the king worse than I'll see myself. For a play may be dangerous : I have known a great man poisoned in a play—

    Glov. What, have you, master mayor?

    Sim. But to what purpose many times, I know not.

    Felt. Methinks they should not destroy one another so.

    Sim. O, no, no ! he that's poisoned is always made privy to it; that's one good order they have among them.—[*A shout within.*] What joyful throat is that? Aminadab, what is the meaning of this cry?

                    [1] *i.e.* Compared to.

Amin. The rebel is taken.

Sim. Oliver the puritan?

Amin. Oliver, puritan, and fustian-weaver altogether.

Sim. Fates, I thank you for this victorious day!
Bonfires of peas-straw burn, let the bells ring!

Glov. There's two in mending, and you know they
cannot.

Sim. 'Las, the tenor's broken! ring out the treble!

Enter OLIVER, *brought in by* Officers.

I'm over-cloyed with joy.—Welcome, thou rebel!

Oliv. I scorn thy welcome, I.

Sim. Art thou yet so stout?
Wilt thou not stoop for grace? then get thee out.

Oliv. I was not born to stoop but to my loom:
That seized upon, my stooping days are done.
In plain terms, if thou hast anything to say to me, send
me away quickly, this is no biding-place; I understand
there are players in thy house; despatch me, I charge
thee, in the name of all the brethren.

Sim. Nay, now proud rebel, I will make thee stay;
And, to thy greater torment, see a play.

Oliv. O devil! I conjure thee by Amsterdam![1]

Sim. Our word is past;
Justice may wink a while, but see at last.
[*Trumpet sounds to announce the commencement of
the play.*
The play begins. Hold, stop him, stop him!

Oliv. O that profane trumpet! O, O!

Sim. Set him down there, I charge you, officers.

Oliv. I'll hide my ears and stop my eyes.

Sim. Down with his golls,[2] I charge you.

Oliv. O tyranny, tyranny! revenge it, tribulation!

---

[1] The city of refuge for dissenters from the established religion
of their country.

[2] Hands.

For rebels there are many deaths; but sure the only
    way
To execute a puritan, is seeing of a play.
O, I shall swound ![1]

Sim. Which if thou dost, to spite thee,
A player's boy shall bring thee aqua-vitæ.

Enter 1st Player *as* 1st Cheater.

Oliv. O, I'll not swound at all for't, though I die.

Sim. Peace, here's a rascal ! list and edify.

1st Play. I say still he's an ass that cannot live by his
wits.

Sim. What a bold rascal's this ! he calls us all asses
at first dash : sure none of us live by our wits, unless it
be Oliver the puritan.

Oliv. I scorn as much to live by my wits as the proudest
of you all.

Sim. Why, then you're an ass for company ; so hold
your prating.

Enter 2nd Player *as* 2nd Cheater.

1st Play. Fellow in arms, welcome! the news, the news ?

Sim. Fellow in arms, quoth he?   He may well call
him fellow in arms ; I'm sure they're both out at the
elbows.

2nd Play. Be lively, my heart, be lively ; the booty is at
hand.   He's but a fool of a yeoman's eldest son ; he's
balanced on both sides, bully ; he's going to buy household
stuff with one pocket, and to pay rent with the other.

1st Play. And if this be his last day, my chuck, he shall
forfeit his lease, quoth the one pocket, and eat his meat in
wooden platters, quoth the other.

Sim. Faith, then he's not so wise as he ought to be, to
let such tatterdemallions get the upper hand of him.

1st Play. He comes.

[1] Swoon.

Enter 3rd Player *as* Clown.

2nd Play. Ay, but smally to our comfort, with both his hands in his pockets. How is it possible to pick a lock, when the key is on the inside of the door?

Sim. O neighbours, here's the part now that carries away the play! if the clown miscarry, farewell my hopes for ever ; the play's spoiled.

3rd Play. They say say there is a foolish kind of thing called a cheater abroad, that will gull any yeoman's son of his purse, and laugh in his face like an Irishman. I would fain meet with some of these creatures : I am in as good state to be gulled now as ever I was in my life, for I have two purses at this time about me, and I would fain be acquainted with that rascal that would take one of them now.

Sim. Faith, thou mayest be acquainted with two or three, that will do their good wills, I warrant thee.

1st Play. That ways too plain, too easy, I'm afraid.

2nd Play. Come, sir, your most familiar cheats take best, They shew like natural things and least suspected.
Give me a round shilling quickly.

1st Play. It will fetch but one of his hands neither, if it take.

2nd Play. Thou art too covetous : let's have one out first, prithee ; there's time enough to fetch out the other after. Thou liest, 'tis lawful current money.   [*They draw.*

1st Play. I say 'tis copper in some countries.

3rd Play. Here is a fray towards ; but I will hold my hands, let who will part them.

2nd Play. Copper? I defy thee, and now I shall disprove thee. Look you, here's an honest yeoman's son of the country, a man of judgment.

3rd Play. Pray you be covered, sir ; I have eggs in my cap, and cannot put it off.

2nd Play. Will you be tried by him?

1st Play. I am content, sir.

Sim. They look rather as if they would be tried next
    sessions.

1st Play. Pray give your judgment of this piece of coin, sir.

3rd Play. Nay, if it be coin you strive about, let me see
it ; I love money.

1st Play. Look on it well, sir.   [*They pick his pocket.*

2nd Play. Let him do his worst, sir.

3rd Play. You'd both need wear cut clothes[1], you're so
choleric.

2nd Play. Nay, rub it, and spare not, sir.

3rd Play. Now by this silver, gentlemen, it is good
money ; would I had a hundred of them !

2nd Play. We hope well, sir.—The other pocket, and we
are made men.   [*Exeunt* 1st *and* 2nd Players.

Sim. O neighbours, I begin to be sick of this fool. to
see him thus cozened ! I would make his case my own.

3rd Play. Still would I meet with these things called
cheaters.

Sim. A whoreson coxcomb ; they have met with thee.
I can no longer endure him with patience.

3rd Play. O my rent ! my whole year's rent !

Sim. A murrain on you ! this makes us landlords stay
so long for our money.

3rd Play. The cheaters have been here.

Sim. A scurvy hobby-horse, that could not leave his
money with me, having such a charge about him ! A
pox on thee for an ass ! thou play a clown ! I will commit
thee for offering it.—Officers, away with him !

Glov. What means your worship ? why, you'll spoil the
    play, sir.

Sim. Before the King of Kent shall be thus served,
I'll play the clown myself.—Away with him !

                    [Officers *seize* 3rd Player.

---

[1] Openwork in linen, stamped or cut by hand (Nares) ; "cutter"
was a cant term for a swaggerer.

3rd Play. With me? if it please your worship, 'twas my part.

Sim. But 'twas a foolish part as ever thou playedst in thy life : I'll make thee smoke for it ; I'll teach thee to understand to play a clown ; thou shalt know every man is not born to it.—Away with him quickly ! He'll have the other pocket picked else ; I heard them say it with my own ears

Re-enter 2nd Player *as* 2nd Cheater.

See, he's come in another disguise to cheat thee again.
        [*Exit* 3rd Player *with* Officers.

2nd Play. Pish, whither goes he now?

Sim. Come on, sir, let us see what your knaveship can do at me now : you must not think you have a clown in hand. The fool I have committed too, for playing the part. [*Throws off his gown, discovering his doublet with a satin forepart, and a canvas back.*

2nd Play. What's here to do?

Glov. Fie, good sir, come away : will your worship base yourself to play a clown?

2nd Play. I beseech your worship let us have our own clown ; I know not how to go forwards else.

Sim. Knave, play out thy part with me, or I'll lay thee by the heels all the days of thy life.—Why, how now, my masters, who is that laughed at me? cannot a man of worship play the clown a little for his pleasure, but he must be laughed at? Do you know who I am? Is the king's deputy of no better account among you? Was I chosen to be laughed at?—Where's my clerk?

Amin. Here, if it please your worship.

Sim. Take a note of all those that laugh at me, that when I have done, I may commit them. Let me see who dare do it now.—And now to you once again, Sir Cheater : look you, here are my purse-strings ; I do defy thee.

2nd Play. Good sir, tempt me not; my part is so written, that I should cheat your worship if you were my father.

Sim. I should have much joy to have such a rascal to my son.

2nd Play. Therefore I beseech your worship pardon me; the part has more knavery in it than when your worship saw it at first : I assure you you'll be deceived in it, sir; the new additions will take any man's purse in Kent or Kirsendom.

Sim. If thou canst take my purse, I'll give it thee freely : And do thy worst, I charge thee, as thou'lt answer it.

2nd Play. I shall offend your worship.

Sim. Knave, do it quickly.

2nd Play. Say you so, ? then there's for you, and here is for me.

[*Throws meal in his face, takes his purse, and exit.*

Sim. O bless me ! neighbours, I am in a fog, A cheater's fog ; I can see nobody.

Glov. Run, follow him, officers.

Sim. Away ! let him go ; he will have all your purses, if he come back. A pox on your new additions ![1] they spoil all the plays that ever they come in : the old way had no such roguery in it. Call you this a merry comedy, when a man's eyes are put out in't ? Brother Honey-suckle——— [*Exit* AMINADAB.

Felt. What says your sweet worship ?

Sim. I make you deputy, to rule the town till I can see again, which will be within these nine days at farthest. Nothing grieves me now, but that I hear Oliver the rebel laugh at me. A pox on your puritan face ! this will make you in love with plays as long as you live ; we shall not keep you from them now.

---

[1] An allusion to the practice, common in Elizabethan times, of introducing additional matter into plays on the occasion of their revival.—*Bullen.*

Oliv. In sincerity, I was never better pleased at an exercise.[1] Ha, ha, ha!

Sim. Neighbours, what colour was the dust the rascal threw in my face?

Glov. 'Twas meal, if it please your worship.

Sim. Meal! 1 am glad of it; I'll hang the miller for selling it.

Glov. Nay, ten to one the cheater never bought it; he stole it certainly.

Sim. Why, then I'll hang the cheater for stealing it, and the miller for being out of the way when he did it.

Felt. Ay, but your worship was in the fault yourself; you bid him do his worst.

Sim. His worst? that's true; but the rascal hath done his best; for I know not how a villain could put out a man's eyes better, and leave them in his head, as he has done mine.

Re-enter AMINADAB.

Amin. Where is my master's worship?

Sim. How now, Aminadab? I hear thee, though I see thee not.

Amin. You are sure cozened, sir; they are all professed cheaters: they have stolen two silver spoons, and the clown took his heels with all celerity. They only take the name of country comedians to abuse simple people with a printed play or two, which they bought at Canterbury for sixpence; and what is worse, they speak but what they list of it, and fribble out the rest.

Sim. Here's no abuse to the commonwealth, if a man could see to look into it!

But mark the cunning of these cheating slaves,
First they make Justice blind, then play the knaves.

---

[1] The week-day sermons of the puritans were called exercises.

Heng. [*Without.*] Where's master mayor?

Glov. Od's precious, brother! the King of Kent is
newly alighted.

Sim. The King of Kent!
Where is he? that I should live to this day,
And yet not live to see to bid him welcome!

Enter HENGIST *attended.*

Heng. Where is Simonides, our friendly host?

Sim. Ah, blind as one that had been foxed[1] a seven-
night!

Heng. Why, how now, man?

Sim. Faith, practising a clown's part for your grace,
I have practised both my eyes out.

Heng. What need you practise that?

Sim. A man is never too old to learn; your grace will
say so, when you hear the jest of it: the truth is, my lord,
I meant to have been merry, and now it is my luck to
weep water and oatmeal; I shall see again at supper, I
make no doubt of it.

Heng. This is strange to me, sirs.

Enter a Gentleman.

Gent. Arm, arm, my lord!

Heng. What's that?

Gent. With swiftest speed,
If ever you'll behold the queen, your daughter,
Alive again.

Heng. Roxena?

Gent. They are besieged:
Aurelius Ambrose, and his brother Uther,
With numbers infinite of British forces,
Beset their castle, and they cannot 'scape
Without your speedy succour.

[1] **Drunk.**

Heng. For her safety
I'll forget food and rest ; away !
    Sim. I hope your worship will hear the jest ere
      you go.
    Heng. The jest ! torment me not.
    Sim. I'll follow you to Wales with a dog and a bell,
but I will tell it you.
    Heng. Unseasonable folly !   [*Exit with* Attendants.
    Sim. 'Tis sign of war when great men disagree.
Look to the rebel well, till I can see ;
And when my sight's recovered, I will have
His eyes pulled out for a fortnight.
    Oliv. My eyes ? hang thee !
A deadly sin or two shall pluck them out first ;
That is my resolution. Ha, ha, ha !   [*Exeunt.*

SCENE II.

Before a Castle in Wales.

Enter AURELIUS *and* UTHER, *and* Lords, *with* Soldiers.

    Uth. My lord, the castle is so fortified—
    Aur. Let wild-fire ruin it,
That his destruction may appear to him
In the figure of Heaven's wrath at the last day,
That murderer of our brother. Hence, away !
I'll send my heart no peace till't be consumed.
            [*Enter above* VORTIGER *and* HORSUS.
    Uth. There he appears again—behold, my lord !
    Aur. O that the zealous fire on my soul's altar,
To the high birth of virtue consecrated,

Would fit me with a lightning now to blast him,
Even as I look upon him !

Uth. Good my lord,
Your anger is too noble and too precious
To waste itself on guilt so foul as his :
Let ruin work her will.

Vort. Begirt all round ?

Hor. All, all, my lord ; 'tis folly to make doubt of't ·
You question things, that horror long ago
Resolved us on.

Vort. Give me leave, Horsus, though——

Hor. Do what you will, sir ; question them again ; I'll
tell them to you.

Vort. Not so, sir ; ·
I will not have them told again.

Hor. It rests then—

Vort. That's an ill word put in, when thy heart knows
There is no rest at all, but torment waking.

Hor. [*Aside.*] True ; my heart finds it, that sits
weeping blood now
For poor Roxena's safety.—You'll confess, my lord,
My love to you has brought me to this danger ?
I could have lived, like Hengist, King of Kent,
London, York, Lincoln, and Winchester,
Under the power of my command, the portion
Of my most just desert, enjoyèd now
By pettier deservers.

Vort. Say you so, sir ?
And you'll confess, since you began confession,
(A thing I should have died ere I had thought on),
You've marred the fashion of your affection utterly,
In your own wicked counsel, there you paid me :
You were bound in conscience to love me after ;
You were bound to't, as men in honesty,

Mid. II.   2 C

That vitiate virgins, to give dowries to them :
My faith was pure before to a faithful woman.

Hor. My lord, my counsel—

Vort. Why, I'll be judged by these
That knit death in their brows, and hold me now
Not worth the acception of a flattery ;
Most of whose faces smiled when I smiled once.
My lords '

Uth. Reply not, brother.

Vort. Seeds of scorn,
I mind you not ; I speak to them alone
Whose force makes yours a power, which else were none.
Show me the main food of your hate,
Which cannot be the murder of Constantius,
That crawls in your revenges, for your loves
Were violent long since that.

1st Lord. And had been still,
If from that Pagan wound thou'dst kept thee free ;
But when thou fled'st from Heaven, we fled from thee.

Vort. This was your counsel now.

Hor. Mine? 'twas the counsel
Of your own lust and blood ; your appetite knows it.

Vort. May thunder strike me from these walls, my
          lords,
And leave me many leagues off from your eyes,
If this be not the man whose Stygian soul
Breathed forth that counsel to me, and sole plotter
Of all those false injurious disgraces,
That have abused the virtuous patience
Of our religious queen.

Hor. A devil in madness !

Vort. Upon whose life I swear there sticks no stain
But what's most wrongful : and where now she thinks
A rape dwells on her honour, only I
Her ravisher was, and his the policy.

Aur. Inhuman practice !

Vort. Now you know the truth,
Will his death serve your fury ?

Hor. My death ?

Vort. Say, will it do it ?

Hor. Say they should say 'twould do't ?

Vort. Why, then it must.

Hor. It must ?

Vort. It shall.—
Speak but the word, it shall be yielded up.

Hor. Believe him not ; he cannot do it.

Vort. Cannot ?

Hor. 'Tis but a false and base insinuation
For his own life, and like his late submission.

Vort. O sting to honour ! Alive or dead, thou goest
For that word's rudeness only.   [*Stabs him.*

1st Lord. See, sin needs
No other destruction than it breeds
In its own bosom.

Vort. Such another brings him.

Hor. What ! has thy vile rage stamped a wound upon
    me ?
I'll send one to thy soul shall never heal for't

Vort. How, to my soul ?

Hor. It shall be thy master torment,
Both for the pain and the everlastingness.

Vort. Ha, ha, ha !

Hor. Dost laugh ? take leave of't : all eternity
Shall never see thee do so much again.
Know, thou'rt a cuckold.

Vort. What !

Hor. You change too soon, sir.
Roxena, whom thou'st raised to thy own ruin,
See was my whore in Germany.

Vort. Burst me open,
The violence of whirlwinds !

Hor. Hear me out first.
For her embrace, which my flesh yet sits warm in,
I was thy friend and follower.
        Vort. Defend me,
Thou most imperious noise that starts the world !
        Hor. And to serve both our lusts, I practised with thee
Against thy virtuous queen.
        Vort. Bane to all comforts !
        Hor. Whose faithful sweetness, too precious for thy
            blood,
I made thee change for love's hypocrisy.
        Vort. Insufferable !
        Hor. Only to make
My way to pleasure fearless, free, and fluent.
        Vort. Hell's trump is in that throat !
        Hor. It shall sound shriller.
        Vort. I'll dam it up with death first.
                [*They stab each other.   Enter* ROXENA *above.*
        Rox. O for succour !
Who's near me ? Help me, save me ! the flame follows me
'Tis in the figure of young Vortimer, the prince,
Whose life I took by poison.
        Hor. Hold out, breath,
And I shall find thee quickly.
        Vort. I will tug
Thy soul out here.
        Hor. Do, monster !
        Rox. Vortiger !
        Vort. Monster !
        Rox. My lord !
        Vort. Toad ! Pagan !
        Hor. Viper ! Christian !
        Rox. O hear me, O help me, my love, my lord ! 'tis
            here !
Horsus, look up, if not to succour me,

To see me yet consumed.   O what is love,
When life is not regarded !
   Vort. What strength's left
I'll fix upon thy throat.
     Hor. I have some force yet.
                  [*They stab each other,* HORSUS *falls.*
   Rox. No way to 'scape ? is this the end of glory ?
Doubly beset with enemies' wrath, and fire ?
It comes nearer—rivers and fountains, fall !—
It sucks away my breath ; I cannot give
A curse to sin, and hear't out while I live.
Help, help !   [*Falls.*
   Vort. Burn, burn !   Now I can tend thee.
Take time with her in torment, call her life
Afar off to thee, dry up her strumpet-blood,
And hardly parch the skin: let one heat strangle her,
Another fetch her to her sense again,
And the worse pain be only her reviving ;
Follow her eternally !   O mystical harlot,
Thou hast thy full due !   Whom lust crowned queen
    before,
Flames crown her now a most triumphant whore :
And that end crowns them all !   [*Falls.*
   Aur. Our peace is full
In yon usurper's fall ; nor have I known
A judgment meet the bad more fearfully.
Here, take this ring; deliver the good queen,
And those grave pledges of her murdered honour,
Her worthy father and her noble uncle.
           [*Exit* 2nd Lord *with ring.   Trumpets
              sound.*
How now ! the meaning of these sounds ?

Enter DEVONSHIRE, STAFFORD, *and* Soldiers, *with*
        HENGIST *prisoner.*

Hen. The consumer has been here ; she's gone, she's
    lost ;
In glowing cinders now lie all my joys :
The headlong fortune of my rash captivity
Strikes not so deep a wound into my hopes
As thy dear loss.
    Aur. Her father and her uncle !
    1st Lord. They are indeed, my lord.
    Aur. Part of my wishes.
What fortunate power has prevented[1] me,
And ere my love came, brought them victory ?
    1st Lord. My wonder sticks in Hengist, King of
    Kent.
    Devon. My lord, to make that plain which now I
    see
Fixed in astonishment ; the only name
Of your return and being, brought such gladness
To this distracted kingdom, that, to express
A thankfulness to Heaven, it grew great
In charitable actions ; from which goodness
We taste our liberty, who lived engaged
Upon the innocence of woman's honour,
(A kindness that even threatened to undo us) :
And having newly but enjoyed the benefit
And fruits of our enlargement, 'twas our happiness
To intercept this monstre of ambition,
Bred in these times of usurpation,
The rankness of whose insolence and treason
Grew to such height, 'twas armed to bid you battle ;
Whom, as our fame's redemption, on our knees
We present captive.
    Aur. Had it needed reason,
You richly came provided.   I understood
Not your deserts till now.—My honoured lords,

---

[1] Anticipated.

Is this that German Saxon, whose least thirst
Could not be satisfied under a province?

Heng. Had but my fate directed this bold arm
To thy life, the whole kingdom had been mine;
That was my hope's great aim: I have a thirst
Could never have been full quenched under all:
The whole must do't, or nothing.

Aur. A strange drought!
And what a little ground shall death now teach you
To be content withal!

Heng. Why let it then,
For none else can; you've named the only way
To limit my ambition; a full cure
For all my fading hopes and sickly fears;
Nor shall it be less welcome to me now,
Than a fresh acquisition would have been
Unto my new-built kingdoms. Life to me,
'Less it be glorious, is a misery.

Aur. That pleasure we will do you.—Lead him out:
And when we have inflicted our just doom
On his usurping head, it will become
Our pious care to see this realm secured
From the convulsions it hath long endured. ⌊*Exeunt.*

THE WIDOW.

ROM internal evidence *The Widow* is assigned by Mr. Bullen to about the same date (1608-9) as *A Mad World, My Masters*, and *A Trick to Catch the Old One*. It was acted at the Blackfriars Theatre with great applause; in 1660 it was one of the stock pieces belonging to the Red Bull Company, and it was revived at a later date; Langbaine writing in 1691 says "not many years ago." The play was printed in 1652 (by Gough, who had formerly been an actor of women's parts, and after the theatres were closed helped to organise surreptitious performances in noblemen's houses) as written by Jonson, Fletcher and Middleton, but it is now generally looked upon as almost solely the work of Middleton. Latrocinio, in the disguise of a quack doctor, seems to show Jonson's influence but not his hand. In a copy of the quarto, formerly in the possession of Mr. Dyce, the names of Jonson and Fletcher are drawn through with a pen, and the word "alone" written in an old hand after Middleton's name.

THE WIDOW

ACT THE FIRST.

SCENE I.

A Room in BRANDINO'S *House.*

MARTINO *seated at a writing-table.* *Enter* FRANCISCO.

RAN. Martino!

Mar. Signior Francisco? you're the luckiest gentleman to meet or see first in a morning: I never saw you yet but I was sure of money within less than half an hour.

Fran. I bring you the same luck still.

Mar. What, you do not? I hope, sir, you are not come for another warrant?

Fran. Yes, faith, for another warrant.

Mar. Why, there's my dream come out then. I never dreamed of a buttock but I was sure to have money for a warrant; it is the luckiest part of all the body to me: let every man speak as he finds. Now your usurer is of opinion that to dream of the devil is your wealthier dream; and I think if a man dream of

that part that brings many to the devil, 'tis as good, and
has all one smatch[1] indeed, for if one be the flesh, the
other's the broth : so 'tis in all his members, an we
mark it ; if gluttony be the meat, lechery is the porridge ;
they're both boiled together, and we clerks will have our
modicum too, though it conclude in the twopenny chop.
Why, sir, Signior Francisco !

Fran. 'Twas her voice sure,
Or my soul takes delight to think it was,
And makes a sound like hers.　　　　　　　　*[Aside.*

Mar. Sir, I beseech you—

Fran. It is the prettiest-contrived building this !
What posy's that, I prithee ?

Mar. Which, sir ? that
Under the great brass squirt ?

Fran. Ay, that, sir, that.

Mar. "From fire, from water, and all things amiss,
Deliver the house of an honest justice."

Fran. There's like to be a good house kept then
when fire and water's forbidden to come into the
kitchen.—
Not yet a sight of her ! this hour's unfortunate.— *[Aside.*
And what's that yonder, prithee ?—O love's famine,
There's no affliction like thee ! *[Aside.]*—Ay, I hear
you, sir.

Mar. You're quicker-eared than I, then ; you hear me
Before I heard myself.

Fran. A gift in friendship ;
Some call it an instinct.

Mar. It may be ;
The other's the sweeter phrase, though. Look you,
sir,
Mine own wit this, and 'tis as true as turtle :
"A goose-quill and a clerk, a constable and a lantern,

---

[1] Flavour.

PROLOGUE.

A sport only for Christmas is the play
This hour presents to you ; to make you gay[1]
Is all the ambition 't has, and fullest aim
Bent at your smiles, to win itself a name ;
And if your edge be not quite taken off,
Wearied with sports, I hope 'twill make you laugh

[1] "Merry" in the old ed.

BRANDINO, a justice.
MARTINO, his clerk.
FRANCISCO.
ATTILIO.
RICARDO.
Two Old Men, suitors to VALERIA.
LATROCINIO,
OCCULTO,
SILVIO,   } Thieves
STRATIO,
FIDUCIO,
SERVELLIO.
Officers, Servants.

VALERIA, a widow.
PHILIPPA, her sister, wife of BRANDINO.
MARTIA, daughter of one of VALERIA'S suitors, and disguised as ANSALDO.
VIOLETTA, waiting-maid to PHILIPPA.

SCENE—CAPO D'ISTRIA and the Neighbouring Country.

Brings many a bawd from coach to cart, and many a thief
    to one turn."

Fran. That one turn helped you well.

Mar. 'T has helped me to money indeed for many a
warrant. I am forty dollars the better for that one turn;
an 'twould come off quicker, 'twere ne'er a whit the
worse for me. But, indeed, when thieves are taken,
and break away twice or thrice one after another, there's
my gains; then goes out more warrants to fetch 'em
again. One fine nimble villain may be worth a man
ten dollars in and out a' that fashion: I love such a
one with my heart; ay, and will help him to 'scape too,
an I can: hear you me that: I'll have him in at all
times at a month's warning; nay, say I let him run like
a summer nag all the vacation—see you these blanks?
I'll send him but one of these bridles, and bring him
in at Michaelmas with a vengeance. Nothing kills my
heart but when one of 'em dies, sir; then there's no
hope of more money: I had rather lose at all times two
of my best kindred than an excellent thief, for he's a
gentleman I'm more beholding to.

Fran. You betray your mystery too much, sir.—Yet
    no comfort?
'Tis but her sight that I waste precious time for
For more I cannot hope for, she's so strict;
Yet that I cannot have.   *[Aside.*

Mar. I'm ready now, signior. Here are blank warrants of all dispositions; give me but the name and
nature of your malefactor, and I'll bestow him according
to his merits.

Fran. This only is the excuse that bears me out,
And keeps off impudence and suspicion
From my too frequent coming. What name now
Shall I think on, and not to wrong the house?
This coxcomb will be prating. *[Aside.]*—One Attilio,
His offence wilful murder.

Mar. Wilful murder ? O, I love a' life[1] to have such
a fellow come under my fingers ! like a beggar that's long
a-taking leave of a fat louse, I'm loth to part with him ; I
must look upon him over and over first.   Are you wilful ?
i'faith, I'll be as wilful as you then.   [*Writes.*

[PHILIPPA *and* VIOLETTA *appear above at a
window.*

Phil. Martino !

Mar. Mistress ?

Phil. Make haste, your master's going.

Mar. I'm but about a wilful murder, forsooth ;
I'll despatch that presently.[2]

Phil. Good morrow, sir.—O that I durst say more !

`[*Aside, and exit above with* VIOLETTA.

Fran.   'Tis   gone   again :   since   such   are   all   life's
pleasures,
No sooner known but lost, he that enjoys 'em
The length of life has but a longer dream,
He wakes to this i' the end, and sees all nothing.

[PHILIPPA *and* VIOLETTA *appear again above*

Phil. He cannot see me now ; I'll mark him better
Before I be too rash.   Sweetly composed he is ;
Now as he stands he's worth a woman's love
That loves only for shape, as most on's do ;
But I must have him wise as well as proper,[3]
He comes not in my books[4] else ; and indeed
I've thought upon a course to try his wit.   [*Aside.*
Violetta.

Vio. Mistress ?

Phil. Yonder's the gentleman again.

Vio. O sweet mistress,
Pray give me leave to see him !

---

[1] As my life.   [2] At once.   [3] Handsome.
[4] The phrase "in one's good books" still survives.

Phil. Nay, take heed,
Open not the window, an you love me.

Vio. No, I've the view of his whole body here, mistress,
At this poor little slit : O, enough, enough!
In troth, 'tis a fine outside.

Phil. I see that.

Vio. H'as curled his hair most judiciously well.

Phil. Ay, there's thy love now! it begins in barbarism. She buys a goose with feathers that loves a gentleman for's hair; she may be cozened to her face, wench. Away: he takes his leave. Reach me that letter hither; quick, quick, wench.

[VIOLETTA *brings a letter, which* PHILIPPA *presently throws down.*

Mar. [*Giving warrant to* FRANCISCO.] Nay, look upon't, and spare not: every one cannot get that kind of warrant from me, signior. Do you see this prick i' the bottom? it betokens 'power and speed; it is a privy mark that runs between the constables and my master: those that cannot read, when they see this, know 'tis for lechery or murder; and this being away, the warrant comes gelded and insufficient.

Fran. I thank you, sir.

Mar. Look you; all these are *nihils;*
They want the punction.

Fran. Yes, I see they do, sir
There's for thy pains [*Giving money*]:—mine must go unrewarded :
The better love, the worse by fate regarded. [*Aside and exit.*

Mar. Well, go thy ways for the sweetest customer that ever penman was blest withal! Now will he come for another to-morrow again: if he hold on this course, he will leave never a knave i' the town within this twelve-month: no matter, I shall be rich enough by that time.

Phil. Martino !

Mar. Say you, forsooth ?

Phil. What paper's that the gentleman let fall there ?

Mar. Paper !—'Tis the warrant, I hope ; if it be, I'll hide it, and make him pay for't again. No, pox ! 'tis not so happy. [*Aside.*

Phil. What is't, sirrah ?

Mar. 'Tis nothing but a letter, forsooth.

Phil. Is that nothing ?

Mar. Nothing in respect of a warrant, mistress.

Phil. A letter ! why, 't has been many a man's undoing, sir.

Mar. So has a warrant, an you go to that, mistress.

Phil. Read but the superscription, and away with't : Alas ! it may concern the gentleman nearly !

Mar. Why, mistress, this letter is at home already.

Phil. At home ! how mean you, sir ?

Mar. You shall hear, mistress [*Reads.*]:—"To the deservingest of all her sex, and most worthy of his best respect and love, Mistress Philippa Brandino."

Phil. How, sir, to me ?

Mar. To you, mistress.

Phil. Run, as thou lov'st my honour and thy life,
Call him again ; I'll not endure this injury ;—
But stay, stay, now I think on't, 'tis my credit ;
I'll have your master's counsel. Ah, base fellow,
To leave his loose lines thus ! 'tis even as much
As a poor honest gentlewoman's undoing,
Had I not a grave wise man to my husband :
And thou a vigilant varlet to admit
Thou car'st not whom !

Mar. 'Las, 'tis my office, mistress !
You know you have a kirtle every year,
And 'tis within two months of the time now ;
The velvet's coming over : pray, be milder.

A man that has a place must take money of anybody :
please you to throw me down but half a dollar, and I'll
make you a warrant for him now ; that's all I care for
him.

 Phil. Well, look you be clear now from this foul con-
  spiracy
Against mine honour ; or your master's love to you,
That makes you stout, shall not maintain you here ;
It shall not, trust to't. [*Exit above, with* VIOLETTA.
 Mar. This is strange to me now :
Dare she do this, and but eight weeks to new-year's tide ?
A man that had his blood as hot as hers now
Would fit her with French velvet : I'll go near it.

   Enter BRANDINO *and* PHILIPPA.

 Phil. If this be a wrong to modest reputation,
Be you the censurer, sir, that are the master
Both of your fame and mine.
 Bran. Signior Francisco !
I'll make him fly the land.
 Mar. That will be hard, sir :
I think he be not so well feathered, master ;
H'as spent the best part of his patrimony.
 Phil. Hark of his bold confederate !
 Bran. There thou'rt bitter ;
And I must chide thee now.
 Phil. What should I think, sir ?
He comes to your man for warrants.
 Bran. There it goes then.—
Come hither, knave : comes he to you for warrants ?
 Mar. Why, what of that, sir ?
You know I give no warrants to make cuckolds :
That comes by fortune and by nature, sir.
 Bran. True, that comes by fortune and by nature.—
  Wife,
Why dost thou wrong this man ?

Mar. He needs no warrant, master, that goes about
such business : a cuckold-maker carries always his warrant
about him.

Bran. La, has he answered well now, to the full ?
What cause hast thou to abuse him ?

Phil. Hear me out, I pray :
Through his admittance, h'as had opportunity
To come into the house, and court me boldly.

Bran. Sirrah, you're foul again, methinks.

Mar. Who, I, sir ?

Bran. You gave this man admittance into the house.

Mar. That's true, sir : you ne'er gave me any order
      yet
To write my warrants i' the street.

Bran. Why, sure thou tak'st delight
To wrong this fellow, wife, ha, 'cause I love him ?

Phil. Pray, see the fruits ; see what h'as left behind
      here :
Be angry where you should be : there's few wives
Would do as I do.

Bran. Nay, I'll say that for thee,
I ne'er found thee but honest

Phil. She's a beast
That ever was found otherways.

Bran. Read, Martino :
Mine eyes are sore already, and such business
Would put 'em out quite.

Mar. [*Reads letter.*] " Fair, dear, and incomparable
      mistress "——

Bran. O, every letter draws a tooth, methinks !

Mar. And it leads mine to watering.

Phil. Here's no villany ![1]

Mar. [*Reads.*] " My love being so violent, and the
opportunity so precious in your husband's absence to-

---

[1] The negative is often used ironically. — *Weber.*

night, who, as I understand, takes a journey this morning "——

    Bran. O plot of villany !

    Phil. Am I honest, think you, sir?

    Bran. Exactly honest, perfectly improved.[1]——
On, on, Martino.

    Mar. [*Reads.*] "I will make bold, dear mistress, though
your chastity has given me many a repulse, to wait the
sweet blessings of this long-desired opportunity at the
back gate, between nine and ten this night "——

    Bran. I feel this Inns-o'-court man in my temples !

    Mar. [*Reads.*] " Where, if your affection be pleased to
receive me, you receive the faithfullest that ever vowed
service to woman.—Francisco.

    Bran. I will make Francisco smart for't !

    Phil. Show him the letter, let him know you know
      him ;
That will torment him : all your other courses
Are nothing, sir, to that : that breaks his heart.

    Bran. The strings shall not hold long then.—Come,
      Martino.

    Phil. Now, if Francisco have any wit at all,
He comes at night : if not, he never shall.   [*Aside.*
                                  [*Exeunt.*

SCENE II.

The Country near FRANCISCO'S *House.*

Enter FRANCISCO, RICARDO, *and* ATTILIO.

    Ric. Nay, mark, mark it, Francisco ; it was the
naturallest courtesy that ever was ordained ; a young

                  [1] *i.e.* Proved.

gentleman being spent, to have a rich widow set him up again. To see how fortune has provided for all mortality's ruins! your college for your old-standing scholar, your hospital for your lame-creeping soldier, your bawd for your mangled roarer,[1] your open house for your beggar, and your widow for your gentleman;—ha, Francisco?

Fran. Ay, sir, you may be merry; you're in hope of a rich widow.

Ric. And why shouldst not thou be in hope of another, if there were any spirit in thee? thou art as likely a fellow as any is in the company. I'll be hanged now if I do not hit the true cause of thy sadness; and confess truly, i'faith; thou hast some land unsold yet, I hold my life.

Fran. Marry, I hope so, sir.

Ric. A pox on't, have I found it? 'Slight, away with't with all speed, man! I was never merry at heart while I had a foot. Why, man, fortune never minds us till we are left alone to ourselves; for what need she take care for them that do nothing but take care for themselves? Why, dost think if I had kept my lands still, I should ever have looked after a rich widow? alas! I should have married some poor young maid, got five and twenty children, and undone myself!

Fran. I protest, sir, I should not have the face, though, to come to a rich widow with nothing.

Ric. Why, art thou so simple as thou makest thyself? dost think, i'faith, I come to a rich widow with nothing.

Fran. I mean with state not answerable to hers.

Ric. Why, there's the fortune, man, that I talked on; She knows all this, and yet I am welcome to her.

Fran. Ay? that's strange, sir.

Ric. Nay more, to pierce thy hard heart,
And make thee sell thy land, if thou'st any grace,—

---

[1] Swaggering bully.

She has, 'mongst others, two substantial suitors ;
One, in good time be't spoke, I owe much money to ;
She knows this too, and yet I'm welcome to her,
Nor dares the unconscionable rascal trouble me ;
Sh'as told him thus,—those that profess love to her
Shall have the liberty to come and go,
Or else get him gone first ; she knows not yet
Where fortune may bestow her ; she's her gift,
Therefore to all will show a kind respect.
  Fran. Why, this is like a woman : I ha' no luck in't.
  Ric. And as at a sheriff's table,—O blest custom !—
A poor indebted gentleman may dine,
Feed well and without fear, and depart so,
So to her lips fearless I come and go.
  Fran. You may well boast, you're much the happier
    man, sir.
  Ric. So you would be, an you would sell your land,
    sir.
  Fran. I've heard the circumstance of your sweet
    fortunes :
Prithee, give ear to my unlucky tale now.
  Ric. That's an ill hearing ; but come on for once, sir.
  Fran. I never yet loved but one woman.
  Ric. Right,
I begun so too ; but I have loved a thousand since.
  Fran. Pray, hear me, sir : but this is a man's wife.
  Ric. So has five hundred of my thousand been.
  Fran. Nay, see an you'll regard me !
  Ric. No? you see I do ;
I bring you an example in for everything.
  Fran. This man's wife——
  Ric. So you said.
  Fran. Seems very strict.
  Ric. Ha, hum !
  Fran. Do you laugh at that ?

Ric. Seems very strict, you said ;
I hear you, man, i'faith ;· you are so jealous still !
Fran. But why should that make you laugh ?
Ric. Because she seems so : you're such another !
Fran. Nay, sir, I think she is.
Ric. You cannot tell then ?
Fran. I dare not ask the question, I protest,
For fear of a repulse ; which yet not having,
My mind's the quieter, and I live in hope still.
Ric. Ha, hum ! this 'tis to be a landed man.
Come, I perceive, I must show you a little of my fortune,
and instruct you.
Not ask the question ?
Fran. Methought still she frowned, sir
Ric. Why, that's the cause, fool, that she looked so
    scurvily.
Come, come, make me your woman ; you'll ne'er do't
    else ;
I'll show you her condition[1] presently.
I perceive you must begin like a young vaulter, and get
up at horse-tail before you get into the saddle : have you
the boldness to utter your mind to me now, being but in
hose and doublet ?   I think, if I should put on a farthin,
gale, thou wouldst never have the heart to do't.
Fran. Perhaps I should not then for laughing at you,
sir.
Ric. In the mean time I fear I shall laugh at thee with-
out one.
Fran. Nay, you must think, friend, I dare speak to a
    woman.
Ric. You shall pardon me for that, friend : I will not
think it till I see't.
Fran. Why, you shall, then : I shall be glad to learn
    too
Of one so deep as you are.

[1] Disposition.

Ric. So you may, sir.—
Now 'tis my best course to look mildly ; I shall put him
out at first else.

Fran. A word, sweet lady !

Ric. With me, sir ? say your pleasure.

Fran. Oh, Ricardo,
Thou art too good to be a woman long !

Ric. Do not find fault with this, for fear I prove
Too scornful ; be content when you're well used.

Fran. You say well, sir.—Lady, I've loved you long.

Ric. 'Tis a good hearing, sir.—If he be not out now,
I'll be hanged !

Fran. You play a scornful woman ![1] I perceive,
Ricardo, you have not been used to 'em : why, I'll come
in at my pleasure with you. Alas ! 'tis nothing for a man
to talk when a woman gives way to't ! one shall seldom
meet with a lady so kind as thou playedst her.

Ric. Not altogether, perhaps : he that draws their
pictures must flatter 'em a little ; they'll look he that
plays 'em should do't a great deal then.

Fran. Come, come, I'll play the woman that I'm used
to :
I see you ne'er wore shoe that pinched you yet ;
All your things come on easy.

Ric. Say you so, sir?
I'll try your ladyship, 'faith.—Lady, well met.

Fran. I do not think so, sir.

Ric. A scornful gom ![2] and at the first dash too !
My widow never gave me such an answer ;
I'll to you again, sir.—
Fairest of creatures, I do love thee infinitely !

Fran. There's nobody bids you, sir.

---

[1] A reference, perhaps, to Beaumont and Fletcher's *Scornful
Lady*, printed in 1616, but produced *circ.* 1612.—*Bullen.*

[2] " Gom " (Anglo-Saxon) means man, fellow.

Ric. Pox on thee, thou art the beastliest, crossest baggage that ever man met withal! but I'll see thee hanged, sweet lady, ere I be daunted with this.—Why, thou'rt too awkward, sirrah.

Fran. Hang thee, base fellow!

Ric. Now, by this light, he thinks he does't indeed! Nay, then, have at your plum-tree![1] faith, I'll not be foiled.—Though you seem to be careless, madam, as you have enough wherewithal to be, yet I do, must, and will love you.

Fran. Sir, if you begin to be rude, I'll call my woman.

Ric. What a pestilent quean's this! I shall have much ado with her, I see that.—Tell me, as you're a woman, lady, what serve kisses for but to stop all your mouths?

Fran. Hold, hold, Ricardo!

Ric. Disgrace me, widow?

Fran. Art mad? I'm Francisco.

Att. Signior Ricardo, up, up!

Ric. Who is't? Francisco?

Fran. Francisco, quotha! what, are you mad, sir?

Ric. A bots on thee, thou dost not know what injury thou hast done me; I was i' the fairest dream. This is your way now, an you can follow it.

Fran. 'Tis a strange way, methinks.

Ric. Learn you to play a woman not so scornfully then;

For I am like the actor that you spoke on:
I must have the part that overcomes the lady,
I never like the play else. Now your friendship,
But to assist a subtle trick I ha' thought on,
And the rich widow's mine within these three hours.

Att., Fran. We should be proud of that, sir.

Ric. List to me then.

---

[1] "Have at your plum-tree!" was a kind of proverbial expression. Plum-tree (see Cotgrave's Dict., under *Hoche-prunier*) was used to indicate the sexual parts of a woman.

I'll place you to,—I can do't handsomely,
I know the house so well,—to hear the conference
'Twixt her and I.   She's a most affable one,
Her words will give advantage and I'll urge 'em
To the kind proof, to catch her in a contract ;
Then shall you both step in as witnesses,
And take her in the snare.
    Fran But do you love her ?
And then 'twill prosper.
    Ric. By this hand, I do,
Not for her wealth, but for her person too.
    Fran. It shall be done then.
    Ric. But stay, stay, Francisco ;
Where shall we meet with thee some two hours hence
    now ?
    Fran. Why, hark you, sir.   [*Whispers.*
    Ric. Enough ; command my life :
Get me the widow, I'll get thee the wife.
                    [*Exeunt* RICARDO *and* ATTILIO.
    Fran. O, that's now with me past hope ! yet I must
    love her :
I would I could not do't !

            Enter BRANDINO *and* MARTINO.

    Mar. Yonder's the villan, master.
    Bran. Francisco ? I am happy.
    Mar. Let's both draw, master, for there's nobody with
    him :—
Stay, stay, master
Do not you draw till I be ready too ;
Let's draw just both together, and keep even.
    Bran. What an we killed him now, before he saw us ?
    Mar. No, then he'll hardly see to read the letter.
    Bran. That's true ; good counsel, marry.
    Mar. Marry, thus much, sir ; you may kill him law-

fully all the while he's a-reading on't ; as an Anabaptist
may lie with a brother's wife all the while he's asleep.

Bran. He turns, he looks.—Come on, sir ; you,
　　Francisco !

I loved your father well, but you're a villain ;
He loved me well too, but you love my wife, sir :
After whom take you that ?　I will not say
Your mother played false.

Fran. No, sir, you were not best.

Bran. But I will say in spite of thee, my wife's honest.

Mar. And I, my mistress.

Fran. You may, I'll give you leave.

Bran. Leave or leave not, there she defies you, sir.
　　　　　　　　　　　　　　　　　　　[Gives the letter.

Keep your adulterous sheet to wind you in
Or cover your forbidden parts at least,
For fear you want one : many a lecher may
That sins in cambric now.

Mar. And in lawn too, master.

Bran. Nay, read and tremble, sir.

Mar. Now shall I do't, master ?　I see a piece of an
open seam in his shirt ; shall I run him in there ? for my
sword has ne'er a point.

Bran. No ; let him foam a while.

Mar. If your sword be no better than mine, we shall
not kill him by daylight ; we had need have a lanthorn.

Bran. Talk not of lanthorns ; he's a sturdy lecher ;
He would make the horns fly about my ears.

Fran. I apprehend thee : admirable woman !
Which to love best I know not, thy wit or beauty. *[Aside.*

Bran. Now, sir, have you well viewed your bastard
　　　there,
Got of your lustful brain ? give you joy on't !

Fran. I thank you, sir : although you speak in jest,
I must confess I sent your wife this letter
And often courted her, tempted and urged her.

Bran. Did you so, sir? then first,
Before I kill thee, I forewarn thee my house.

Mar. And I, before I kill thee, forewarn thee my office:
die to-morrow next, thou never gettest warrant of me
more, for love or money.

Fran. Remember but again from whence I came, sir,
And then I know you cannot think amiss of me.

Bran. How's this?

Mar. Pray, hear him; it may grow to a peace: for,
master, though we have carried the business nobly, we are
not altogether so valiant as we should be.

 Bran. Peace! thou say'st true in that.—What is't
  you'd say, sir?

 Fran. Was not my father—quietness be with him!—
And you sworn brothers?

 Bran. Why, right: that's it urges me.

 Fran. And could you have a thought that I could
  wrong you,
As far as the deed goes?

 Bran. You took the course, sir.

 Fran. To make you happy, an you rightly weighed it.

 Mar. Troth, I'll put up[1] at all adventures, master:
It comes off very fair yet.

 Fran. You in years
Married a young maid: what does the world judge, think
  you?

 Mar. By'r lady, master, knavishly enough, I warrant
  you;
I should do so myself.

 Fran. Now, to damp slander,
And all her envious and suspicious brood,
I made this friendly trial of her constancy,
Being son to him you loved; that now confirmed,
I might advance my sword against the world
In her most fair defence, which joys my spirit.

    [1] Sheathe my sword.

Mar. O master, let me weep while you embrace him !

Bran. Francisco, is thy father's soul in thee?
Lives he here still? what, will he show himself
In his male seed to me? give me thy hand ;
Methinks it feels now like thy father's to me :
Prithee, forgive me !

Mar. And me too, prithee !

Bran. Come to my house ; thy father never missed it.

Mar. Fetch now as many warrants as you please, sir,
And welcome too.

Fran. To see how soon man's goodness
May be abused !

Bran. But now I know thy intent,
Welcome to all that I have !

Fran. Sir, I take it :
A gift so given, hang him who would forsake it ! [*Exit.*

Bran. Martino, I applaud my fortune and thy counsel.

Mar. You never have ill fortune when you follow it.
Here was things carried now in the true nature of a
quiet duello ; a great strife ended, without the rough
soldier or the——.[1] And now you may take your
journey.

Bran. Thou art my glee, Martino.   [*Exeunt.*

---

[1] There is a blank in the old ed.

ACT THE SECOND

SCENE I.

A Room in VALERIA'S *House.*

Enter VALERIA *and* SERVELLIO.

AL. Servellio !
    Ser. Mistress?
    Val. If that fellow come again,
Answer him without me ; I'll not
speak with him.
    Ser. He in the nutmeg-coloured
band, forsooth ?
  Val. Ay, that spiced coxcomb, sir : ne'er may I marry
    again,   [*Exit* SERVELLIO.
If his right worshipful idolatrous face
Be not most fearfully painted ; so hope comfort me.
I might perceive it peel in many places ;
And under 's eye lay a betraying foulness,
As maids sweep dust o' the house all to one corner ;
It showed me enough there, prodigious pride,
That cannot but fall scornfully. I'm a woman ;
Yet, I praise Heaven, I never had the ambition
To go about to mend a better workman :
She ever shames herself i' the end that does it.
He that likes me not now as Heaven made me,
I'll never hazard hell to do him a pleasure ;

Nor lie every night, like a woodcock, in paste[1]
To please some gaudy goose in the morning :
A wise man likes that best that is itself,
Not that which only seems, though it look fairer.
Heaven send me one that loves me, and I'm happy !
Of whom I'll make great trial ere I have him,
Though I speak all men fair, and promise sweetly :
I learn that of my suitors ; 'tis their own,
Therefore injustice 'twere to keep it from 'em.

Enter RICARDO, *followed by* FRANCISCO *and* ATTILIO,
who conceal themselves.

Ric. And so, as I said, sweet widow——

Val. Do you begin where you left, sir ?

Ric. I always desire, when I come to a widow, to begin
i' the middle of a sentence ; for I presume she has a bad
memory of a woman that cannot remember what goes
before.

Val. Stay, stay, sir ; let me look upon you well ;
Are not you painted too ?

Ric. How, painted, widow !

Val. Not painted widow : I do not use it, trust me, sir.

Ric. That makes me love thee.

Val. I mean painted gentleman,
Or, if you please to give him a greater style, sir,
Blame me not, sir ; it's a dangerous age, I tell you ;
Poor simple-dealing women had need look about 'em.

Ric. But is there such a fellow in the world, widow,
As you are pleased to talk on ?

Val. Nay, here lately, sir.

Ric. Here ! a pox, I think I smell him ; 'tis vermillion
sure ; ha, oil of ben ![2]   Do but show him me, widow, and
let me never hope for comfort, if I do not immediately
geld him, and grind his face upon one o' the stones.

---

[1] Almond paste, to whiten the skin.
[2] Or " been," any aromatic gum from the Levant.

Val. Suffices you've expressed me your love and
  valour,
And manly hate 'gainst that unmanly pride :
But, sir, I'll save you that labour ; he never comes
Within my door again.

Ric. I'll love your door the better while I know't, widow;
a pair of such brothers are fitter for posts without door
indeed, to make a show at a new-chosen magistrate's
gate,[1] than to be used in a woman's chamber. No, sweet
widow, having me, you've the truth of a man ; all that
you see of me is full mine own, and what you see, or not
see, shall be yours : I ever hated to be beholding to art,
or to borrow anything but money.

Val. True, and that you never use to pay again.

Ric. What matter is't? if you be pleased to do't for me,
I hold it as good.

Val. Oh, soft you, sir, I pray !

Ric. Why, i'faith, you may, an you will.

Val. I know that, sir.

Ric. Troth, and I would have my will then, if I were
as you : there's few women else but has.

Val. But since I cannot have it in all, signior,
I care not to have it in anything.

Ric. Why, you may have't in all, an you will, widow.

Val. Pish ! I'd have one that loves me for myself,
  sir,
Not for my wealth ; and that I cannot have.

Ric. What say you to him that does the thing you wish
  for?

Val. Why, here's my hand, I'll marry none but him
  then.

Ric. Your hand and faith ?

Val. My hand and faith.

---

[1] The posts that stood at sheriffs' and other magistrates' doors
were repainted when new magistrates entered into office.

Ric. 'Tis I, then.

Val. I shall be glad on't, trust me ; 'shrew my heart
else !

Ric. A match !

[FRANCISCO *and* ATTILIO *come forward.*

Fran. Give you joy, sweet widow !

Att. Joy to you both !

Val. How ?

Ric. Nay, there's no starting now, I have you fast,
widow.—
You're witness, gentlemen.

Fran., Att. We'll be deposed on't.

Val. Am I betrayed to this, then ? then I see
'Tis for my wealth : a woman's wealth's her traitor.

Ric. 'Tis for love chiefly, I protest, sweet widow ;
I count wealth but a fiddle to make us merry.

Val. Hence !

Ric. Why, thou'rt mine.

Val. I do renounce it utterly.

Ric. Have I not hand and faith ?

Val. Sir, take your course.

Ric. With all my heart ; ten courses, an you will,
widow.

Val. Sir, sir, I'm not so gamesome as you think me ;
I'll stand you out by law.

Ric. By law ! O cruel, merciless woman,
To talk of law, and know I have no money !

Val. I will consume myself to the last stamp,[1]
Before thou gett'st me.

Ric. 'Life, I'll be as wilful then, too ;
I'll rob all the carriers in Christendom,
But I'll have thee, and find my lawyers money.
I scorn to get thee under *forma pauperis ;*
I have too proud a heart and love thee better.

---

[1] Halfpenny.

Val. As for you, gentlemen, I'll take course against
   you :
You came into my house without my leave ;
Your practices are cunning and deceitful ;
I know you not, and I hope law will right me.
   Ric. It is sufficient that your husband knows 'em :
'Tis not your business to know every man ;
An honest wife contents herself with one.
   Val. You know what you shall trust to.   Pray depart,
      sir,
And take your rude confederates along with you,
Or I will send for those shall force your absence :
I'm glad I found your purpose out so soon.
How quickly may poor women be undone !
   Ric. Lose thee ! by this hand, I'll fee fifteen coun-
sellors first, though I undo a hundred poor men for 'em ;
and I'll make 'em yaul one another deaf, but I'll have
thee.
   Val. Me !
   Ric. Thee.
   Val. Ay, fret thy heart out.   [*Exit* RICARDO.
   Fran. Were I he now,
I'd see thee starve for man before I had thee.
   Val. Piay, counsel him to that, sir, and I'll pay you
      well.
   Fran. Pay me ! pay your next husband.
   Val. Do not scorn't, gallant ; a worse woman than I
Has paid a better man than you.
                    [*Exeunt* ATTILIO *and* FRANCISCO.

.   *Enter two* Suitors.

   1st Suit. Why, how now, sweet widow ?
   Val. O kind gentlemen, I'm so abused here !
   Both Suit. Abused !   [*Drawing their swords.*
   Val. What will you do, sirs ? put up your weapons.
   2nd Suit. Nay, they're not so easily drawn, that I must

tell you ; mine has not been out this three years ; marry,
in your cause, widow, 'twould not be long a-drawing.
Abused ! by whom, widow ?

Val. Nay, by a beggar.

2nd Suit. A beggar ! I'll have him whipped then, and
sent to the House of Correction.

Val. Ricardo, sir.

2nd Suit. Ricardo ! nay, by the mass, he's a gentleman-
beggar ; he'll be hanged before he be whipped. Why,
you'll give me leave to clap him up, I hope ?

Val. 'Tis too good for him ; that's the thing he would
have,
He would be clapped up, whether I would or no, me-
thinks ;
Placed two of his companions privately,
Unknown to me, on purpose to entrap me
In my kind answers, and at last stole from me
That which I fear will put me to some trouble,
A kind of verbal courtesy, which his witnesses
And he, forsooth, call by the name of contract.

1st Suit. O politic villain !

Val. But I'm resolved, gentlemen,
If the whole power of my estate can cast him,
He never shall obtain me.

2nd Suit. Hold you there, widow ;
Well fare your heart for that i'faith.

1st Suit. Stay, stay, stay ;
You broke no gold[1] between you ?

Val. We broke nothing, sir.

1st Suit. Nor drunk to one another?

Val. Not a drop, sir.

1st Suit. You're sure of this you speak ?

Val. Most certain, sir.

[1] A well-known token of affection in some parts of England.—
Weber.

1st Suit. Be of good comfort, wench : I'll undertake then,
At mine own charge, to overthrow him for thee.

Val. O, do but that, sir, and you bind me to you !
Here shall I try your goodness.   I'm but a woman,
And, alas ! ignorant in law businesses :
I'll bear the charge most willingly.

1st Suit. Not a penny ;
Thy love will reward me.

Val. And where love must be,
It is all but one purse, now I think on't.

1st Suit. All comes to one, sweet widow.

2nd Suit. Are you so forward ?   [*Aside.*

1st Suit. I know his mates, Attilio and Francisco ;
I'll get out process, and attach 'em all.
We'll begin first with them.

Val. I like that strangely.

1st Suit. I have a daughter run away, I thank her ;
I'll be a scourge to all youth for her sake :
Some of 'em has got her up.

Val. Your daughter ? what, sir, Martia ?

1st Suit. Ay, a shake[1] wed her !
I would have married her to a wealthy gentleman,
No older than myself ; she was like to be shrewdly hurt, widow.

Val. It was too happy for her.

1st Suit. I'm of thy mind.
Farewell, sweet widow ; I'll about this straight ;
I'll have 'em all three put into one writ,
And so save charges.

Val. How I love your providence !   [*Exit* 1st Suitor.

2nd Suit. Is my nose bored ! I'll cross ye both for this,
Although it cost me as much o' the other side :
I have enough, and I will have my humour.

---

[1] **Beggar.**

I may get out of her what may undo her too.—   [*Aside.*
Hark you, sweet widow, you must now take heed
You be of a sure ground, he'll o'erthrow you else.

Val. Marry, fair hope, forbid !

2nd Suit. That will he : marry, le' me see, le' me see ;
Pray how far passed it 'tween you and Ricardo ?

Val. Farther, sir,
Than I would now it had ; but I hope well yet.

2nd Suit. Pray, let me hear't ; I've a shrewd guess o'
the law.

Val. Faith, sir, I rashly gave ym hand and faith
To marry none but him.

2nd Suit. Indeed !

Val. Ay, trust me, sir.

2nd Suit. I'm very glad on't ; I'm another witness,
And he shall have you now.

Val. What said you, sir ?

2nd Suit. He shall not want money in an honest cause,
widow ;
I know I've enough, and I will have my humour.

Val. Are all the world betrayers ?

2nd Suit. Pish, pish, widow !
You've borne me in hand[1] this three months, and now
fobbed me :
I've known the time when I could please a woman.
I'll not be laughed at now ; when I'm crossed, I'm a
tiger :
I have enough, and I will have my humour.

Val. This only shows your malice to me,
The world knows you ha' small reason to help nim,
So much in your debt already.

2nd Suit. Therefore I do't,
I have no way but that to help myself ;
Though I lose you, I will not lose all, widow ;

---

[1] Kept me in ex cctation.

He marrying you, as I will follow't for him,
I'll make you pay his debts, or lie without him.
　Val. I looked for this from you.
　2nd Suit. I ha' not deceived you then: [*Exit* VALERIA.
Fret, vex, and chafe, I'm obstinate where I take.
I'll seek him out, and cheer him up against her :
I ha' no charge at all, no child of mine own,
But two I got once of a scouring-woman,
And they're both well provided for, they're i' the
　　Hospital.[1]
I have ten thousand pounds to bury me,
And I will have my humour.　　　　　　　　[*Exit.*

SCENE II.

A Street.

Enter FRANCISCO.

　Fran. A man must have a time to serve his pleasure,
As well as his dear friend : I'm forced to steal from 'em,
To get this night of sport for mine own use.
What says her amiable, witty letter here ?
[*Reads.*] " 'Twixt nine and ten,"—now 'tis 'twixt six and
　　seven ;
As fit as can be ; he that follows lechery
Leaves all at six and seven, and so do I, methinks :
Sun sets at eight, it's 'bove an hour high yet ;
Some fifteen mile have I before I reach her,
But I've an excellent horse ; and a good gallop
Helps man as much as a provoking banquet.

　　[1] *i.e.* Christ's Hospital, whither City foundlings were then sent
for maintenance and education.—*Dyce.*

Enter 1st Suitor *and* Officers.

1st Suit. Here's one of 'em ; begin with him first, officers.

1st Off. By virtue of this writ we attach your body, sir.
　　　　　　　　　　　　　　　　[Officers *seize* FRANCISCO.

Fran. My body ? 'life, for what ?

1st Suit. Hold him fast, officers.

1st Off. The least of us can do't, now his sword's off, sir ;
We have a trick of hanging upon gentlemen,
We never lose a man.

Fran. O treacherous fortune !—
Why, what's the cause ?

1st Suit. The widow's business, sir :
I hope you know me ?

Fran. For a busy coxcomb,
This fifteen year, I take it.

1st Suit. O, you're mad, sir ;
Simple though you make me, I stand for the widow.

Fran. She's simply stood for then : what's this to me, sir,
Or she, or you, or any of these flesh-hooks ?

1st Suit. You're like to find good bail before you leave us,
Or lie till the suit's tried.

Fran. O my love's misery !

1st Suit. I'm put in trust to follow't, and I'll do't
With all severity ; build upon that, sir.

Enter RICARDO *and* ATTILIO.

Fran. How I could curse myself !

Ric. Look, here's Francisco :
Will you believe me, now you see his qualities ?

Att. 'Tis strange to me.

Ric. I tell you 'tis his fashion :
He never stole away in's life from me,
But still I found him in such scurvy company.—
A pox on thee, Francisco ! wilt never leave
Thy old tricks ? are these lousy companions for thee ?
   Fran. Pish, pish, pish !
   1st Suit. Here they be all three now ; 'prehend 'em,
     officers.   [Officers *seize* RICARDO *and* ATTILIO.
   Ric. What's this ?
   Fran. I gave you warning enough to make away ;
I'm in for the widow's business, so are you now.
   Ric. What, all three in a noose ? this is like a widow's
     business indeed.
   1st Suit. Sh'as catched you, gentlemen, as you catched
     her.
The widow means now to begin with you, sir.
   Ric. I thank her heartily, sh'as taught me wit ; for had
I been any but an ass, I should ha' begun with her indeed.
By this light, the widow's a notable housewife ! she bestirs
herself. I have a greater mind to her now than e'er I
had : I cannot go to prison for one I love better, I protest ;
that's one good comfort.—
And what are you, I pray, sir, for a coxcomb ?
   1st Suit. It seems you know me by your anger, sir.
   Ric. I've a near guess at you, sir.
   1st Suit. Guess what you please, sir,
I'm he ordained to trounce you, and, indeed,
I am the man must carry her.
   Ric. Ay, to me ;
But I'll swear she's a beast, an she carry thee.
   1st Suit. Come, where's your bail, sir ? quickly, or
     away.
   Ric. Sir, I'm held wrongfully ; my bail's taken already.
   1st Suit. Where is't, sir, where ?
   Ric. Here they be both. Pox on you, they were taken

before I'd need of 'em.   An you be honest officers, let's
bail one another ; for, by this hand, I do not know who
will else.—

Enter 2nd Suitor.

'Ods light, is he come too ?   I'm in for midnight then ;
I shall never find the way out again : my debts, my debts !
I'm like to die i' the Hole[1] now.

1st Suit. We have him fast, old signior, and his con-
sorts ;
Now you may lay action on action on him.

2nd Suit. That may I, sir, i'faith.

1st Suit. And I'd not spare him, sir.

2nd Suit. Know you me, officers ?

1st Off. Your bounteous worship, sir.

Ric. I know the rascal so well, I dare not look upon
him.

2nd Suit. Upon my worth, deliver me that gentleman.

Fran. Which gentleman ?

2nd Suit. Not you, sir, you're too hasty ;
No, nor you neither, sir ; pray, stay your time.

Ric. There's all but I now, and I dare not think he
means me.

2nd Suit. Deliver me Ricardo.

Ric: O, sure he lies,
Or else I do not hear well.

1st Off. Signior Ricardo——

Ric. Well, what's the matter ?

1st Off. You may go ; who lets[2] you ?
It is his worship's pleasure, sir, to bail you.

Ric. Bail me ?

2nd Suit. Ay, will I, sir.   Look in my face, man ;
Thou'st a good cause ; thou'lt pay me when thou'rt able?

Ric. Ay, every penny, as I'm a gentleman.

---

[1] Where the poorest prisoners were confined.   [2] Hinders.

2nd Suit. No matter if thou dost not, then I'll make
 thee,
And that's as good at all times.
 1st Suit. But, I pray, sir,—
You go against the hair[1] there.
 2nd Suit. Against the widow, you mean, sir;
Why, 'tis my purpose truly, and 'gainst you too :
I saw your politic combination ;
I was thrust out between you.   Here stands one
Shall do as much for you, and he stands rightest,
His cause is strong and fair ; nor shall he want
Money, or means, or friends, but he shall have her :
I have enough, and I will have my humour.
 1st Suit. Hang thee ! I have a purse as good as thine.
 Ric. I think they're much alike, they're rich knaves
  both.—   *[Aside.*
Heart, an I take you railing at my patron, sir,
I'll cramp your joints !
 2nd Suit. Let him alone, sweet honey ;
I thank thee for thy love though.
 Ric. This is wonderful !
 Fran. O Ricardo,
'Tis seven struck in my pocket !   I lose time now.
 Ric. What say'st, Francisco ?
 Fran. I ha' mighty business
That I ne'er thought on ; get me bailed, I'm spoilt else.
 Ric. Why, you know, 'tis such a strange miraculous
  courtesy,
I dare not be too forward to ask more of him,
For fear he repent this, and turn me in again.
 Fran. Do somewhat, an you love me !
 Ric. I'll make trial, faith.—
May't please you, sir,—'life, if I should spoil all now !
 2nd Suit. What say'st, Ricardo ?

---

[1] Against the grain.

Ric. Only a thing by the way, sir ;
Use your own pleasure.

2nd Suit. That I like well from thee.

Ric. 'Twere good, an those two gentlemen were
bailed too ;
They're both my witnesses.

2nd Suit. They're well, they're well :
An they were bailed, we know not where to find 'em.
Let 'em go to prison ; they'll be forthcoming the better :
I have enough, and I will have my humour.

Ric. I knew there was no more good to be done upon
him :
Tis well I've this ; Heaven knows I never looked for't.

Fran. What plaguy luck had I to be ensnared thus !

1st Off. O, patience !

Fran. Pox o' your comfortable ignorance !

Enter BRANDINO *and* MARTINO.

Bran. Martino, we ride slow.

Mar. But we ride sure, sir ;
Your hasty riders often come short home, master.

Bran. Bless this fair company !

Fran. Here he's again too ;
I am both shamed and crossed.

Bran. Seest thou who's yonder, Martino?

Mar. We ride slow, I'll be sworn now, master.

Bran. How now, Francisco, art thou got before me?

Fran. Yes, thank my fortune, I am got before you.

Bran. What, no, in hold?

Ric. Ay, o' my troth, poor gentleman !
Your worship, sir, may do a good deed to bail him.

Bran. Why do not you do't then?

Mar. La you, sir, now, my master has that honesty,
He's loath to take a good deed from you, sir.

Ric. I'll tell you why ; I cannot, else I would, sir.

Fran. Luck, I beseech thee !
If he should be wrought to bail me now, to go to
His wife, 'twere happiness beyond expression.   [*Aside.*
    Bran. A matter but of controversy ?
    Ric. That's all, trust me, sir.
    Bran. Francisco shall ne'er lie for't ; he's my friend,
And I will bail him.
    Mar. He's your secret friend, master ;
Think upon that.
    Bran. Give him his liberty, officers ;
Upon my peril, he shall be forthcoming.
    Fran. How I am bound to you !
    1st Suit. Know you whom you cross, sir ?
'Tis at your sister's suit ; be well advised, sir.
    Bran. How, at my sister's suit ? take him again then.
    Fran. Why, sir, do you refuse me ?
    Bran. I'll not hear thee.
    Ric. This is unkindly done, sir.
    1st Suit. 'Tis wisely done, sir.
    2nd Suit. Well shot, foul malice !
    1st Suit. Flattery stinks worse, sir.
    Ric. You'll ne'er leave till I make you stink as bad, sir.
    Fran. O Martino, have I this for my late kindness ?
    Mar. Alas ! poor gentleman, dost complain to me ?
Thou shalt not fare the worse for't.—Hark you, master,
Your sister's suit, said you ?
    Bran. Ay, sir, my wife's sister.
    Mar. And shall that daunt you, master ? think again :
Why, were't your mother's suit,—your mother's suit,
Mark what I say,—the dearest suit of all suits,
You're bound in conscience, sir, to bail this gentleman.
    Bran. Yea, am I so ? how prov'st thou that, Martino ?
    Mar. Have you forgot so soon what he did lately ?
Has he not tried your wife to your hand, master,
To cut the throat of slander and suspicion ?

And can you do too much for such a man ?
Shall it be said, I serve an ingrateful master ?

Bran. Never, Martino ; I will bail him now,
An 'twere at my wife's suit.

Fran. 'Tis like to be so.   [*Aside.*

Mar. And I his friend, to follow your example, master.

Fran. Precious Martino !

1st Suit. You've done wondrous well, sir ;
Your sister shall give you thanks.

Ric. This makes him mad, sir.

2nd Suit. We'll follow't now to the proof.

1st Suit. Follow your humour out ;
The widow shall find friends.

2nd Suit. And so shall he, sir,
Money and means.

Ric. Hear you me that, old huddle ![1]

2nd Suit. Mind him not ; follow me, and I'll supply
          thee ;   [*Exeunt* 1st Suitor *and* Officers.
Thou shalt give all thy lawyers double fees :
I've buried money enough to bury me,
And I will have my humour.
                    [*Exit with* RICARDO *and* ATTILIO.

Bran. Fare thee well once again, my dear Francisco ;
I prithee, use my house.

Fran. It is my purpose, sir.

Bran. Nay, you must do't then ; though I'm old, I'm
          free.   [*Exit.*

Mar. And when you want a warrant come to me. [*Exit.*

Fran. That will be shortly now, within this few hours.
This fell out strangely happy.   Now to horse ;
I shall be nighted : but an hour or two
Never breaks square[2] in love ; he comes in time
That comes at all ; absence is all love's crime.   [*Exit.*

----

[1] A term of contempt for old decrepit persons.—*Nares.*
[2] Never gives offence.

ACT THE THIRD.

SCENE I.

The Country.

Enter OCCULTO, SILVIO, STRATIO, FIDUCIO, *and other*
Thieves.

CC. Come, come, let's watch the event
on yonder hill;
If he need help, we can relieve him
suddenly.

Sil. Ay, and with safety too, the
hill being watched, sir.

Occ. Have you the blue coats[1] and
the beards?

Sil. They're here, sir.

Occ. Come, come away, then; a fine cock-shoot[2]
evening. [*Exeunt.*

Enter LATROCINIO *and* MARTIA, *disguised as a man.*

Lat. [*Sings.*] Kuck before, and kuck behind, &c.

---

[1] To disguise themselves as serving-men.

[2] Properly cock-shut, and so termed from a large net which,
stretched across a glade, and suspended on poles in such a way as
to be easily drawn together, was employed to catch woodcocks when
the birds went forth to feed in the evening twilight. Hence the
phrases cock-shut time and cock-shut evening.

Martia. Troth, you're the merriest and delightfull'st
    company, sir,
That ever traveller was blest withal;
I praise my fortune that I overtook you, sir.
    Lat. Pish, I've a hundred of 'em.
    Martia. And believe me, sir,
I'm infinitely taken with such things.
    Lat. I see there's music in you; you kept time,
    methought,
Pretty and handsomely with your little hand there.
    Martia. It only shows desire, but, troth, no skill, sir.
    Lat. Well, while our horses walk down yonder hill,
    sir,
I'll have another for you.
    Martia. It rids way pleasantly.
    Lat. Le' me see now—one confounds another, sir—
You've heard this certainly, "Come, my dainty doxies"?[1]
    Martia. O, that is all the country over, sir!
There's scarce a gentlewoman but has that pricked.
    Lat. Well, here comes one I'm sure you never heard,
    then.

[*Sings.*] I keep my horse, I keep my whore,
    I take no rents, yet am not poor;
    I traverse all the land about,
    And yet was born to never a foot;
    With partridge plump, with woodcock fine,
    I do at midnight often dine;
    And if my whore be not in case,
    My hostess' daughter has her place:
    The maids sit up and watch their turns;
    If I stay long, the tapster mourns;
    The cookmaid has no mind to sin,
    Though tempted by the chamberlin:[2]

---

[1] A song given in Middleton's *More Dissemblers besides Women.*
[2] Head waiter.

But when I knock, O how they bustle!
The ostler yawns, the geldings justle;
If maid but sleep, O how they curse her!
And all this comes of—Deliver your purse, sir!

Martia. How, sir?

Lat. Few words: quickly, come, deliver your purse,
sir!

Martia. You're not that kind of gentleman, I hope,
sir,
To sing me out of my money?

Lat. 'Tis most fit
Art should be rewarded: you must pay your music,
sir,
Where'er you come.

Martia. But not at your own carving.

Lat. Nor am I common in't: come, come, your purse,
sir!

Martia. Say it should prove the undoing of a gentleman?

Lat. Why, sir, do you look for more conscience in us
than in usurers? young gentleman, you've small reason
for that, i'faith.

Martia. There 'tis, and all I have [*Gives purse*]; and,
so truth comfort me,
All I know where to have!

Lat. Sir, that's not written
In my belief yet; search—'tis a fine evening,
Your horse can take no harm—I must have more, sir.

Martia. May my hopes perish, if you have not all, sir!
And more, I know, than your compassionate charity
Would keep from me, if you but felt my wants.

Lat. Search, and that speedily: if I take you in
hand,
You'll find me rough; methinks men should be ruled,
When they're so kindly spoke to: fie upon't!

Mid. II.   2 F

Martia. [*Aside.*] Good fortune and my wit assist
    me then !
A thing I took in haste, and never thought on't.—
Look, sir, I've searched ; here's all that I can find,
                          [*Presents a pistol.*
And you're so covetous, you'll have all, you say,
And I'm content you shall, being kindly spoke to.
  Lat. A pox o' that young devil of a handful long,
That has frayed many a tall thief from a rich purchase![1]
  Martia. This and my money, sir, keeps company ;
Where one goes, the other must ; assure your soul
They vowed never to part.
  Lat. Hold, I beseech you, sir !
  Martia. You rob a prisoners' box[2] an you rob me,
    sir.
  Lat. There 'tis again.   [*Returns purse.*
  Martia. I knew 'twould never prosper with you ;
Fie, rob a younger brother ? O, take heed, sir !
'Tis against nature that : perhaps your father
Was one, sir, or your uncle ; it should seem so,
By the small means was left you, and less manners.
Go, keep you still before me ; and, do you hear me ?
To pass away the time to the next town,
I charge you, sir, sing all your songs for nothing.
  Lat. O, horrible punishment !   [*Sings.*

    Re-enter STRATIO, *disguised as a servant.*

  Stra. Honest gentleman——
  Martia. How now, what art thou ?
  Stra. Stand you in need of help ?
I made all haste I could, my master charged me,
A knight of worship ; he saw you first assaulted
From top of yonder hill.

  [1] Booty.
  [2] The begging-box suspended from the grate of a debtors' prison.

Martia. Thanks, honest friend.

Lat. I taste this trick already.   [*Aside and exit.*

Stra. Look, he's gone, sir;
Shall he be stopped? what is he?

Martia. Let him go, sir;
He can rejoice in nothing, that's the comfort.

Stra. You have your purse still then?

Martia. Ay, thanks fair fortune
And this grim handful!

Stra. We were all so 'fraid o' you;
How my good lady cried, O help the gentleman!
'Tis a good woman that. But you're too mild, sir
You should ha' marked him for a villain, faith,
Before h'ad gone, having so sound a means too.

Martia. Why, there's the jest, man; he had once my
        purse.

Stra. O villain! would you let him 'scape un-
        massacred?

Martia. Nay, hear me, sir, I made him yield it straight
        again,
And, so hope bless me, with an uncharged pistol.

Stra. Troth, I should laugh at that.

Martia. It was discharged, sir,
Before I meddled with't.

Stra. I'm glad to hear't.   [*Seizes her.*

Martia. Why, how now! whats your will?

Stra. Ho, Latrocinio,
Occulto, Silvio!

Re-enter LATROCINIO, OCCULTO, SILVIO, FIDUCIO, *and
other* Thieves.

Lat. What, are you caught, sir?

Stra. The pistol cannot speak.

Lat. He was too young.
I ever thought he could not; yet I feared him.

Martia. You've found out ways too merciless to
 betray,
Under the veil of friendship and of charity.
 Lat. Away, sirs, bear him into the next copse and
  strip him.
 Stra. Brandino's copse, the justice?
 Lat. Best of all, sir, a man of law; a spider lies un-
suspected in the corner of a buckram bag, man.
 Martia. What seek you, sirs? take all, and use no
  cruelty.
 Lat. You shall have songs enough.

· SONG.

By LATROCINIO *and the other* Thieves.

How round the world goes, and everything that's in it!
The tides of gold and silver ebb and flow in a minute:
From the usurer to his sons there's a current swiftly runs;
From the sons to queans in chief, from the gallant to
   the thief,
From the thief unto his host, from the host to husbandmen;
From the country to the court; and so it comes to us agen.
How round the world goes, and everything that's in it!
The tides of gold and silver ebb and flow in a minute.

Exeunt.

SCENE II.

Before BRANDINO'S *House.*

Enter PHILIPPA *and* VIOLETTA *above, at a window.*

 Phil. What time of night is't?
 Vio. Time of night do you call't?
It is so late, 'tis almost early, mistress.

Phil. Fie on him! there's no looking for him, then;
Why, sure this gentleman apprehends me not.
  Vio. 'Tis happy then you're rid of such a fool, mistress.
  Phil. Nay, sure, wench, if he find me not out in this,
Which were a beaten path to any wise man,
I'll never trust him with my reputation;
Therefore I made this trial of his wit:
If he cannot conceive what's good for himself,
He will worse understand what's good for me.
  Vio. But suppose, mistress, as it may be likely,
He never saw your letter?
  Phil. How thou pliest me
With suppositions! why, I tell thee, wench,
'Tis equally as impossible for my husband
To keep it from him as to be young again,
Or as his first wife knew him, which he brags on.
For bearing children by him.
  Vio. There's no remedy then;
I must conclude Francisco is an ass.
  Phil. I would my letter, wench, were here again!
I'd know him wiser ere I sent him one;
And travel some five year first.
  Vio. So h'ad need, methinks,
To understand the words; methinks the words
Themselves should make him do't, had he but the per-
        ceiverance [1]
Of a cock-sparrow, that will come at Philip,[2]
And can nor write nor read, poor fool! this coxcomb
He can do both, and your name's but Philippa;
And yet to see, if he can come when's called!
  Phil. He never shall be called again for me, sirrah.[3]
Well, as hard as the world goes, we'll have a song, wench,
We'll not sit up for nothing.

---

[1] Perception.
[2] Philip was a familiar name for a sparrow.
[3] This term was often applied to women.

Vio. That's poor comfort though.

Phil. Better than any's brought, for aught I see yet :
So set to your lute.   [*They sing.*
 Phil. If in this question I propound to thee
   Be any, any choice,
   Let me have thy voice.
 Vio. You shall most free.
 Phil. Which hadst thou rather be,
   If thou might choose thy life,
   A fool's, a fool's mistress,
   Or an old man's wife?
 Vio. The choice is hard, I know not which is best ;
   One ill you're bound to, and I think that's least.
 Phil. But being not bound, my dearest sweet,
   I could shake off the other.
 Vio. Then, as you lose your sport by one,
   You lose your name by t'other.
 Phil. You counsel well, but love refuses
   What good counsel often chooses. [*Exeunt above*

Enter MARTIA *in a shirt.*

Martia. I ha' got myself unbound yet ; merciless villain
I never felt such hardness since life dwelt in me ;
'Tis for my sins.   That light in yonder window,
That was my only comfort in the woods,
Which oft the trembling of a leaf would lose me,
Has brought me thus far ; yet I cannot hope
For succour in this plight, the world's so pitiless,
And every one will fear or doubt me now :
To knock will be too bold ; I'll to the gate,
And listen if I can hear any stirring.

Enter FRANCISCO.

Fran. Was ever man so crossed? no, 'tis but sweat,
 sure,

Or the dew dropping from the leaves above me;
I thought't had bled again. These wenching businesses
Are strange unlucky things and fatal fooleries;
No mar'l so many gallants die ere thirty;
'Tis able to vex out a man's heart in five year,
The crosses that belong to't: first, arrested,
That set me back two mangy hours at least;
Yet that's a thing my heat could have forgiven,
Because arresting, in what kind soever,
Is a most gentleman-like affliction;
But here, within a mile o' the town, forsooth,
And two mile off this place, when a man's oath
Might ha' been taken for his own security,
And his thoughts brisk and set upon the business,
To light upon a roguy flight of thieves!
Pox on 'em, here's the length of one of their whittles:[1]
But one of my dear rascals I pursued so,
The gaol has him, and he shall bring out's fellows.
Had ever young man's love such crooked fortune?
I'm glad I'm so near yet; the surgeon bade me too
Have a great care; I shall ne'er think of that now.
    Martia. One of the thieves come back again? I'll
        stand close;
He dares not wrong me now, so near the house,
And call in vain 'tis, till I see him offer't.
    Fran. 'Life, what should that be? a prodigious[2] thing
Stands just as I should enter, in that shape too
Which always appears terrible.
Whate'er it be, it is made strong against me
By my ill purpose; for 'tis man's own sin
That puts an armour upon all his evils,
And gives them strength to strike him: were it less
Than what it is, my guilt would make it serve:
A wicked man's own shadow has distracted him.
Were this a business now to save an honour,

---

[1] Knives.   [2] Portentous.

As 'tis to spoil one, I would pass this then,
Stuck all hell's horrors i' thee : now I dare not.
Why may't not be the spirit of my father,
That loved this man so well, whom I make haste
Now to abuse? and I've been crossed about it
Most fearfully hitherto, if I well think on't;
Scaped death but lately too, nay, most miraculously.
And what does fond man venture all these ills for,
That may so sweetly rest in honest peace?
For that which, being obtained, is as he was
To his own sense, but removed nearer still
To death eternal.   What delight has man
Now at this present for his pleasant sin
Of yesterday's committing? 'las, 'tis vanished,
And nothing but the sting remains within him!
The kind man bailed me too; I will not do't now
An 'twere but only that.   How blest were man
Might he but have his end appear still to him,
That he might read his actions i' the event!
'Twould make him write true, though he never meant.
Whose check soe'er thou art, father's, or friend's,
Or enemy's, I thank thee; peace requite thee!
Light, and the lighter mistress, both farewell!
He keeps his promise best that breaks with hell. [*Exit.*

    Martia. He's gone to call the rest, and makes all
        speed;
I'll knock, whate'er befalls, to please my fears,
For no compassion can be less than theirs.
                [*Knocks at the door.*

    Re-enter PHILIPPA *and* VIOLETTA *above.*

    Phil. He's come, he's come!—O, are you come at
        last, sir?
Make little noise.—Away, he'll knock again else.
            [*Exit above with* VIOLETTA.
    Martia. I should have been at Istria, by daybreak too :

Near to Valeria's house, the wealthy widow's;
There waits one purposely to do me good.
What will become of me?

Enter VIOLETTA.

Vio. O, you are a sweet gallant! this your hour?
Give me your hand; come, come, sir, follow me,
I'll bring you to light presently: softly, softly, sir.

[Exeunt.

SCENE III.

A Room in BRANDINO'S *House.*

Enter PHILIPPA.

Phil. I should ha' given him up to all my thoughts
The dullest young man, if he had not found it;
So short of apprehension and so worthless,
He were not fit for woman's fellowship;
I've been at cost too for a banquet for him:
Why, 'twould ha' killed my heart, and most especially
To think that man should ha' no more conceit;
I should ha' thought the worse on's wit for ever,
And blamed mine own for too much forwardness.

Enter VIOLETTA.

Vio. O mistress, mistress!
Phil. How now, what's the news?
Vio. O, I was out of my wits for a minute and a
half!
Phil. Hah!

Vic. They are scarce settled yet, mistress.

Phil. What's the matter?

Vio. Do you ask that seriously?
Did you not hear me squeak?

Phil. How? sure thou art
Out of thy wits indeed.

Vio. O, I'm well now
To what I was, mistress.

Phil. Why, where's the gentleman?

Vio. The gentleman's forthcoming, and a lovely one,
But not Francisco.

Phil. What say'st? not Francisco?

Vio. Pish, he's a coxcomb! think not on him, mistress.

Phil. What's all this?

Vio. I've often heard you say, ye'd rather have
A wise man in his shirt than a fool feathered;
And now fortune has sent you one, a sweet young
  gentleman,
Robbed even to nothing, but what first he brought with
  him:
The slaves had stripped him to the very shirt, mis-
  tress;
I think it was a shirt; I know not well,
For gallants wear both [1] now-a-days.

Phil. This is strange.

Vio. But for a face, a hand, and as much skin
As I durst look upon, he's a most sweet one;
Francisco is a child of Egypt [2] to him:
I could not but, in pity to the poor gentleman,
Fetch him down one of my old master's suits.

Phil. 'Twas charitably done.

Vio. You'd say, mistress, if you had seen him as I
did. Sweet youth! I'll be sworn, mistress, he's the
loveliest, properest [3] young gentleman, and so you'll say

Shirts and (the predecessors of chemises) smocks.
  [2] Gipsy.   [3] Handsomest.

yourself, if my master's clothes do not spoil him, that's
all the fear now; I would't had been your luck to have
seen him without 'em, but for scaring on you.

Phil. Go. prithee, fetch him in, whom thou commend'st
so.   [*Exit* VIOLETTA.
Since fortune sends him, surely we'll make much on
      him ;
And better he deserves our love and welcome
Than the respectless fellow 'twas prepared for :
Yet, if he please mine eye never so happily,
I will have trial of his wit and faith
Before I make him partner with my honour.
'Twas just Francisco's case, and he deceived me ,
I'll take more heed o' the next for't : perhaps now,
To furnish his distress, he will appear
Full of fair, promising courtship; but I'll prove him then
For a next meeting, when he needs me not,
And see what he performs then when the storm
Of his so rude misfortunes is blown over,
And he himself again.   A distressed man's flatteries
Are like vows made in drink, or bonds in prison ;
There's poor assurance in em : when he's from me,
And in's own power, then I shall see his love.
'Mass, here he comes.

Enter MARTIA *in* BRANDINO S *ciothes, and* VIOLETTA.

Martia. Never was star-crossed gentleman
More happy in a courteous virgin's love
Than I in yours.

Vio. I'm sorry they're no better for you ;
I wished 'em handsomer and more in fashion,
But truly, sir, our house affords it not :
There is a suit of our clerk's hangs i' the garret,
But that's far worse than this, if I may judge
With modesty of men's matters.

Martia. I deserve not this,
Dear and kind gentlewoman. Is yond your mistress?

Phil. Why, trust me, here's my husband young
again!—
It is no sin to welcome you, sweet gentleman.

Martia. I am so much indebted, courteous lady,
To the unmatchèd charity of your house,
My thanks are such poor things they would but shame
me.

Phil. Beshrew thy heart for bringing o' him! I fear
me
I have found wit enough already in him
If I could truly but resolve[1] myself
My husband was thus handsome at nineteen, .
Troth, I should think the better of him at fourscore
now.

Vio. Nay, mistress, what would he be, were he in
fashion—
A hempen curse on those that put him out on't!—
That now appears so handsome and so comely
In clothes able to make a man an unbeliever
And good for nothing but for shift, or so,
If a man chance to fall i' the ditch with better?
This is the best that ever I marked in 'em,—
A man may make him ready[2] in such clothes
Without a candle.

Phil. Ay, for shame of himself, wench.

Vio. My master does it oft in winter mornings,
And never sees himself till he be ready.

Phil. No, nor then neither, as he should do, wench.—
I'm sorry, gentle sir, we cannot show you
A courtesy in all points answerable
To your undoubted worth: your name, I crave, sir.

Martia. Ansaldo, lady.

[1] Satisfy.   [2] Dress himself.

Phil. 'Tis a noble name, sir.

Martia. The most unfortunate now !

Vio. So do I think truly,
As long as that suit's on.

Phil. The most unfitting
And unprovided'st, sir, of all our courtesies,
I do presume is that you've passed already ;
Your pardon but for that, and we're encouraged.

Martia. My faithful service, lady.

Phil. Please you, sir, to taste the next,
A poor slight banquet, for sure I think you were
Unluckily prevented of your supper, sir.

Martia. My fortune makes me more than amenas.
lady,
In your sweet kindness, which so nobly shown to me,
It makes me bold to speak my occasions to you :
I am this morning, that with clearness now
So cheerfully hastens me, to meet a friend
Upon my state's establishing, and the place
Ten mile from hence : O, I am forced unwillingly
To crave your leave for't, which done, I return
In service plentiful.

Phil. Is't so important?

Martia. If I should fail, as much as my undoing.

Phil. I think too well of you, t' undo you, sir,
Upon this small acquaintance.

Martia. My great happiness !

Phil. But when should I be sure of you here again,
sir ?

Martia. As fast as speea can possibly return me.

Phil. You will not fail?

Martia. May never wish go well with me then !

Phil. There's to bear charges, sir.   [*Gives purse.*

Martia. Courtesy dwells in you :
I brought my horse up with me from the woods,
That's all the good they left me, 'gainst their wills too.

May your kind breast never want comfort, lady,
But still supplied as liberally as you give!
    Phil. Farewell, sir, and be faithful.
    Martia. Time shall prove me.   [*Exit.*
    Phil. In my opinion, now, this young man's likeliest
To keep his word; he's modest, wise, and courteous,
He has the language of an honest soul in him;
A woman's reputation may lie safe there,
I'm much deceived else; h'as a faithful eye
If it be well observed.
    Vio. Good speed be with the
He puts him to't, i'faith.   [*Looking out.*
    Phil. Violetta.
    Vio. Mistress?
    Phil. Alas, what have we done, wench?
    Vio. What's the matter, mistress?
    Phil. Run, run, call him again; he must stay, tell him,
Though   be upon's undoing; we're undone else;
Your master's clothes, they're known the country over.
    Vio. Now, by this light, that's true, and well re-
        membered;
But there's no calling of him, he's out of sight now.
    Phil. O, what will people think?
    Vio. What can they think, mistress?
The gentleman has the worst on't: were I he now,
I'd make this ten mile forty mile about,
Before I'd ride through any market-town with 'em.
    Phil. Will he be careful, think'st?
    Vio. My life for yours, mistress.
    Phil. I shall long mightily to see him agen.
    Vio. And so shall I; I shall ne'er laugh till then.
                      [*Exeunt.*

ACT THE FOURTH.

SCENE I.

Near VALERIA'S *House.*

Enter RICARDO *and* 2nd Suitor *at one door, and* VALERIA *and* 1st Suitor *at the other.*

. It goes well hitherto, my sweet protector.

2nd Suit. Ay, and shall still to the end, to the end, my honey: Wherefore have I enough, but to have't go well, sir?

1st Suit. My whole state on't, thou overthrow'st him, widow.

Val. I hope well still, sir.

1st Suit. Hope? be certain, wench: I make no question now but thou art mine, As sure as if I had thee in thy night-gear.

Val. By'r lady, that I doubt, sir.

1st Suit. O, 'tis clear, wench, By one thing that I marked.

Val. What's that, good, sweet sir?

1st Suit. A thing that never failed me.

Val. Good sir, what?

1st Suit. I heard our counsellor speak a word of comfort,

Invita voluntate; ha, that's he, wench,
The word of words, the precious chief, i'faith !

Val. Invita voluntate; what's the meaning, sir?

1*st Suit.* Nay, there I leave you, but assure you thus
much,
I never heard him speak that word i' my life,
But the cause went on's side, that I marked ever.

2*nd Suit.* Do, do, and spare not: thou wouldst talk
with her?

Ric. Yes, with your leave and liking.

2*nd Suit.* Do, my adoption,
My chosen child ; an thou hold'st so obedient,
Sure thou wilt live and cozen all my kindred.

Ric. A child's part[1] in your love, that's my ambition, sir.

2*nd Suit.* Go, and deserve it then ; please me well now ;
I love wrangling a' life,[2] boy, there's my delight ;
I have no other venery but vexation,
That's all, my honey, now : smartly now to her ;
I have enough, and I will have my humour.

Ric. This need not ha' been, widow.

Val. You say right, sir ;
No, nor your treachery, your close conspiracy
Against me for my wealth, need not ha' been neither.

Ric. I had you fairly ; I scorn treachery
To your woman that I never meant to marry,
Much more to you, whom I reserved for wife.

Val. How? wife !

Ric. Ay, wife, wife, widow ; be not ashamed on't,
It's the best calling ever woman came to,
And all your grace indeed, brag as you list.

2*nd Suit.* Ha, ha !

Val. I grant you, sir, but not to be your wife

1*st Suit.* O, O !

---

[1] Thus Heywood speaks of "a child's part or a daughter's
portion."

[2] As my life, excessively.

Ric. Not mine? I think 'tis the best bargain
That e'er thou mad'st i' thy life, or ever shall again,
When my head's laid, but that's not yet this threescore
    year;
Let's talk of nearer matters.
  Val. You're as near, sir,
As e'er you're like to be, if law can right me.
  Ric. Now, before conscience, you're a wilful housewife.
  Val. How?
  Ric. Ay, and I fear you spend my goods lavishly.
  Val. Your goods?
  Ric. I shall miss much, I doubt me,
When I come to look over the inventory.
  Val. I'll give you my word you shall, sir.
  Ric. Look to't, widow;
A night may come will call you to account for't.
  Val. O, if you had me now, sir, in this heat,
I do but think how you'd be revenged on me!
  Ric. Ay, may I perish else, if I would not get
Three children at a birth, an I could, o' thee!
  1st Suit. Take off your youngster there.
  2nd Suit. Take off your widow first;
He shall have the last word, I pay for't dearly.-
To her again, sweet boy, that side's the weaker:
I have enough, and I will have my humour.

      Enter BRANDINO *and* MARTINO.

  Val. O brother, see I'm up to the ears in law here!
Look, copy upon copy.[1]
  Bran. 'Twere grief enough.
If a man did but hear on't, but I am
In pain to see it.
  Val. What, sore eyes still, brother?
  Bran. Worse and worse, sister; the old woman's water
Does me no good.

        [1] Law-papers.

Val. Why, 't'as helped many, sir.

Bran. It helps not me, I'm sure.

Mar. O, O!

Val. What ails Martino, too?

Mar. O, O, the toothache, the toothache!

Bran. Ah, poor worm! this he endures for me now:
There beats not a more mutual pulse of passion
In a kind husband when his wife breeds child
Than in Martino; I ha' marked it ever;
He breeds all my pains in's teeth still, and to quit[1]
    me,
It is his eye-tooth too.

Mar. Ay, ay, ay, ay.

Val. Where did I hear late of a skilful fellow,
Good for all kind of maladies? true, true, sir;
His flag[2] hangs out in town here i' the Cross Inn,
With admirable cures of all conditions;
It shows him a great travelling and learned empiric.

Bran. We'll both to him, Martino.

Val. Hark you, brother;
Perhaps you may prevail, as one indifferent.

1st Suit. Ay, about that, sweet widow.

Val. True; speak low, sir.

Bran. Well, what's the business? say, say.

Val. Marry, this, brother;
Call the young man aside from the old wolf there,
And whisper in his ear a thousand dollars,
If he will vanish and let fall the suit,
And never put's to no more cost and trouble.

1st Suit. Say me those words, good sir, I'll make
    'em wort'ı
A chain of gold to you at your sister's wedding.

Bran. I shall do much for that.

---

[1] Be even with.

[2] It was usual for quacks to hang out a flag when they took up
their quarters in a town.

Enter VIOLETTA

Val. Welcome, sweetheart,
Thou com'st most happily; I'm bold to send for thee
To make a purpose good.
  Vio. I take delight, forsooth,
In any such employment.
  1st Suit. Good wench, trust me.
  Ric. How, sir, let fall the suit? 'life, I'll go naked
first.
  Bran. A thousand dollars, sir; think upon them.
  Ric. Why, they're but a thousand dollars, when they're
thought on.
  Bran. A good round sum.
  Ric. A good round widow's better;
There's meat and money too. I have been bought
Out of my lands and yielded; but, sir, scorn
To be bought out of my affection.
  Bran. Why, here's even just my university spirit;
I prized a piece of red deer above gold then.
  Ric. My patron would be mad, an he should hear
on't.
  Mar. I pray, what's good, sir, for a wicked tooth?
  Ric. Hanged, drawn, and quartering: is't a hollow
one?
  Mar. Ay, 'tis a hollow one.
  Ric. Then take the powder
Of a burnt warrant, mixed with oil of felon
  Mar. Why, sure you mock me.
  Ric. Troth, I think I do, sir.
  2nd Suit. Come hither, honey; what's the news? in
whispers.
  Bran. He will not be bought out.
  Val. No? that's strange, brother:
Pray take a little pains about this project then
And try what that effects.

Bran. I like this better.—
Look you, sweet gentles, see what I produce here
For amity's sake and peace, to end all controversy;
This gentlewoman, my charge, left by her friends,
Whom for her person and her portion
I could bestow most richly, but in pity
To her affection, which lies bent at you, sir
I am content to yield to her desire.

Ric. At me!

Bran. But for this jar, 't had ne'er been offered.
I bring you flesh and money, a rich heir,
And a maid too, and that's a thing worth thanks, sir;
Nay, one that has rid fifteen mile this morning
For your love only.

2nd Suit. Honey, hearken after her;
Being rich, I can have all my money there;
Ease my purse well, and never wage law further:
I have enough, yet I will have my humour.

Ric. Do you love me, forsooth?

Vio. O, infinitely!

Ric. I do not ask thee, that I meant to have thee,
But only to know what came in thy head to love me.

Vio. My time was come, sir; that's all I can say.

Ric. 'Las, poor soul! where did thou love me first,
   prithee?

Vio. In happy hour be't spoke, out at a window, sir.

Ric. A window? prithee, clap't to, and call it in again:
What was I doing then, should make thee love me?

Vio. Twirling your band-string, which, methought,
   became you
So generously well.

Ric. 'Twas a good quality to choose a husband for:
that love was likely to be tied in matrimony that begun
in a band-string; yet I ha' known as much come to pass
ere now upon a tassel. Fare you well, sister; I may be
cozened in a maid, I cannot in a widow.

2nd Suit. Art thou come home again? stick'st thou
    there still?
I will defend thee still, then.
   1st Suit. Sir, your malice
Will have enough on't.
   2nd Suit. I will have my humour.
   1st Suit. Beggary will prove the spong
   2nd Suit. Sponge i' thy gascoyns,
Thy gally-gascoyns[1] there!
   Ric. Ha, brave protector!
   Bran. I thought 'twould come to open wars again:
Let 'em agree as they will, two testy fops!
I'll have a care of mine eyes.
   Mar. I of my chops.   [*Exeunt.*

SCENE II.

A Room in the Cross Inn.

Enter LATROCINIO *disguised as an empiric, and* OCCULTO
as his man.

   Lat. Away, out with the banner! send's good luck
   to-day!
   Occ. I warrant you; your name's spread, sir, for an em-
   piric: [*Hanging up a banner of cures and diseases.*
There's an old mason troubled with the stone
Has sent to you this morning for your counsel;
He would have ease fain.
   Lat. Marry, I cannot blame him, sir;
But how he will come by't, there lies the question.
   Occ. You must do somewhat, sir; for he's swoln most
   piteously;
Has urine in him now was brewed last March.

                [1] See note *ante,* p. 103.

Lat. 'Twill be rich gear for dyers.

Occ. I would 'twere come to that, sir

Lat. Le' me see,

I'll send him a whole musket-charge of gunpowder.

Occ. Gunpowder!

What, sir, to break the stone?

Lat. Ay, by my faith, sir,

It is the likeliest thing I know to do't;

I'm sure it breaks stone walls and castles down

I see no reason but't should break the stone.

Occ. Nay, use your pleasure, sir.

Lat. Troth, if that do not,

I ha' nothing else that will

Occ. I know that too.

Lat. Why, then, thou'rt a coxcomb to make question on't.

Go call in all the rest, I've employment for them.

　　　　　　　　　　　　　　　[Exit OCCULTO.

When the highways grow thin with travellers,

And few portmanteaus stirring, as all trades

Have their dead time we see, thievery poor takings,

And lechery cold doings, and so forwards still;

Then do I take my inn, and those curmudgeons

Whose purses I can never get abroad,

I take 'em at more ease here i' my chamber,

And make 'em come to me; it's more state-like too

Hang him that has but one way to his trade!

He's like a mouth that eats but on one side,

And half-cozens his belly, 'specially if he dine 'mong

　　　　shavers

And both-handed feeders.—Stratio, Silvio, and Fiducio!

Enter SILVIO, STRATIO, *and* FIDUCIO.

I will have none left out, there's parts for you.

Sil. For us? pray let us have 'em.

Lat. Change yourselves

With all speed possible into several shapes,
Far from your own: as, you a farmer, sir;
A grazier you; and you may be a miller.
    Fid. O no, a miller comes too near a thief;
That may spoil all again.
    Lat. Some country tailor then.
    Fid. That's near enough, by'r lady, yet I'll venture
      that;
The miller's a white devil; he wears his theft
Like innocence in badges most apparently
Upon his nose, sometimes between his lips;
The tailor modestly between his legs.
    Lat. Why, pray, do you 'present that modest thief,
      then;
And hark you, for the purpose.
    Sil. 'Twill improve you, sir.
    Lat. 'Twill get believers, believe that, my masters,
Repute and confidence, and make all things clearer;
When you see any come, repair you to me,
As samples of my skill : there are few arts
But have their shadows, sirs, to set 'em off;
Then where the art itself is but a shadow,
What need is there, my friends! Make haste, away,
    sirs.   [*Exeunt* SILVIO, STRATIO, *and* FIDUCIO

Re-enter OCCULTO.

    Occ. Where are you, sir?
    Lat. Not far, man; what's the news?
    Occ. The old justice, sir, whom we robbed once by
      moonlight,
And bound his man and he in haycock time,
With a rope made of horse meat, and in pity
Left their mares by 'em, which, I think, ere midnight
Did eat their hay-bound masters both at liberty——
    Lat. 'Life, what of him, man?
    Occ. He's inquiring earnestly

For the great man of art, indeed for you, sir :
Therefore withdraw, sweet sir ; make yourself dainty now,
And that's three parts of any profession.
    Lat. I have enough on't.   [*Exit.*

       Enter MARTIA *in* BRANDINO'S *clothes.*

    Occ. [*Aside.*] How now, what thing's this?
Now, by this light, the second part o' the justice
Newly revived, with never a hair on's face.
It should be the first rather by his smoothness,
But I ha' known the first part written last : [1]
'Tis he, or let me perish, the young gentleman
We robbed and stripped; but I am far from knowledge
    now.
    Martia. One word, I pray, sir.
    Occ. With me, gentle sir?
    Martia. Was there not lately seen about these parts,
    sir,
A knot of fellows, whose conditions
Are privily suspected?
    Occ. Why do you ask, sir?
    Martia. There was a poor young gentleman robbed
    last night.
    Occ. Robbed?
    Martia. Stripped of all, i'faith.
    Occ. O beastly rascals !
'Las, what was he?
    Martia. Look o' me, and know him, sir.
    Occ. Hard-hearted villains ! strip? troth, when I saw
    you,
Methought those clothes were never made for you, sir.

---

   [1] This alludes to the first and second parts of historical plays and
tragedies, which had been so much in fashion. It has been ascertained,
in more than one instance, that the first part of a successful play was
written after the second had met with applause. —*Collier.*

Martia. Want made me glad o' 'em.

Occ. Send you better fortunes, sir!—

That we may have a bout with you once again. [*Aside.*

Martia. I thank you for your wish of love, kind sir.

Occ. 'Tis with my heart, i'faith; now store of coin
And better clothes be with you i

Martia. There's some honest yet,
And charitably-minded. How, what's here to do?

[*Reads on the banner.*

     " Here within this place is cured
       All the griefs that were ever endured."

Nay, there thou liest; I endured one last night
Thou canst not cure this morning; a strange promiser!

[*Reads.*] " Palsy, gout, hydropic humour,
       Breath that stinks beyond perfumer,
       Fistula in ano, ulcer, megrim,
       Or what disease soe'er beleaguer 'em,
       Stone, rupture, squinancy,[1] imposthume
       Yet too dear it shall not cost 'em."

That's consci, ably said, i'faith.

[*Reads.*] " In brief, you cannot, I assure you,
       Be unsound so fast as I can cure you."

By'r lady, you shall pardon me, I'll not try't, sir.

      Enter BRANDINO *and* MARTINO.

Bran. Martino, is not yond my hinder parts?

Mar. Yes, and your fore parts too, sir.

Bran. I trow so;
I never saw my hind parts in my life else,
No, nor my fore ones neither.—What are you, sir?
Are you a justice, pray?

Martia. A justice? no, truly.

Bran. How came this suit to you, then?

      [1] Quinsey.

Martia. How this suit?
Why, must he needs be a justice, sir, that wears it?
   Bran. You'll find it so ; 'twas made for nobody else:
I paid for't.
   Martia. O strange fortune ! I have undone
The charitable woman.   [*Aside.*
   Bran. He'll be gone.
Martino, hold him fast, I'll call for aid.
   Martia. Hold me ?   O curse of fate !
                         [*Strikes* MARTINO.
   Mar. O master, master !
   Bran. What ails Martino?
   Mar. In my conscience,
H'as beat out the wrong tooth ; I feel it now
Three degrees off.
   Bran. O slave, spoiled a fine penman !
   Martia. He lacked good manners, though ; lay hands
      o' me !
I scorn all the deserts that belong to it.

            Re-enter LATROCINIO.

   Lat. Why, how now? what's the broil?
   Bran. The man of art,
I take you, sir, to be.
   Lat. I'm the professor
Of those slight cures you read of in the banner.
   Bran. Our business was to you, most skilful sir ;
But in the way to you, right worshipful,
I met a thief.
   Lat. A thief!
   Bran. With my clothes on, sir :
Let but the hose be searched, I'll pawn my life
There's yet the tailor's bill in one o' the pockets,
And a white thimble that I found i' moonlight—
Thou saw'st me when I put it in, Martino?

Mar. Oy, oy :

Bran. O, h'as spoiled
The worthiest clerk that e'er drew warrant here !

Lat. Sir, you're a stranger, but I must deal plain with
you ;
That suit of clothes must needs come oddly to you.

Martia. I dare not say which way, that's my affliction.   [*Aside.*

Lat. Is not your worship's name Signior Brandino, sir?

Bran. It has been so these threescore years and
upwards.

Lat. I heard there was a robbery done last night
Near to your house.

Martia. You heard a truth then, sir,
And I the man was robbed.

Lat. Ah, that's too gross !—
Send him away for fear of farther mischief ;
I do not like him, he's a cunning knave.

Bran. I want but aid.

Lat. Within there !

Enter Servants.

Bran. Seize upon
That impudent thief.

Martia. Then hear me speak.

Bran. Away !
I'll neither hear thee speak, nor wear those clothes
again.—
To prison with the varlet !

Martia. How am I punished !

Bran. I'll make thee bring out all before I leave thee.
[*Exeunt* Servants *with* MARTIA.

Lat. You've took an excellent course with this bold
villain, sir.

Bran. I'm sworn for service to the commonwealth, sir.

Enter Silvio, Stratio, *and* Fiducio *disguised.*

What are these, learnèd sir?
  Lat. O, they're my patients.—
Good morrow, gout, rupture, and palsy.
  Stra. 'Tis farewell gout almost, I thank your wor-
    ship.
  Lat. What, no, you cannot part so soon, I hope?
You came but lately to me.
  Stra. But most happily;
I can go near to leap, sir.   [*Leaps.*
  Lat. What, you cannot?
Away, I say! take heed, be not too vent'rous though;
I've had you but three days, remember that.
  Stra. Those three are better than three hundred, sir.
                                               [*Leaps.*
  Lat. Yet again!
  Stra. Ease takes pleasure to be known, sir.
  Lat. You with the rupture there, *hernia in scrotum,*
Pray let me see your space this morning; walk, sir,
I'll take your distance straight; 'twas F. O. yesterday:
Ah, sirrah, here's a simple alteration!
Secundo gradu, ye F. U. already;
Here's a most happy change. Be of good comfort,
    sir;
Your knees are come within three inches now
Of one another; by to-morrow noon,
I'll make 'em kiss and jostle.
  Sil. Bless your worship!
  Bran. You've a hundred prayers in a morning, sir.
  Lat. Faith, we have a few to pass away the day
    with.—
Tailor, you had a stitch?
  Fid. O, good your worship,
I have had none since Easter: were I rid
But of this whoreson palsy, I were happy;
I cannot thread my needle.

Lat. No? that's hard;
I never marked so much.

Fid. It comes by fits, sir.

Lat. Alas, poor man!—What would your worship say
now
To see me help this fellow at an instant?

Bran. And make him firm from shaking

Lat. As a steeple,
From the disease on't.

Bran. 'Tis to me miraculous.

Lat. You with your whoremaster disease, come hither;
Here, take me this round glass, and hold it steadfast;
    [*Gives glass.*
Yet more, sir; yet, I say; so.

Bran. Admirable!

Lat. Go, live, and thread thy needle.

Bran. Here, Martino:—
Alas, poor fool, his mouth is full of praises,
And cannot utter 'em.

Lat. No? what's the malady?

Bran. The fury of a tooth.

Lat. A tooth? ha, ha!
I thought 't had been some gangrene, fistula,
Canker, or ramex.

Bran. No, it's enough as 'tis, sir.

Lat. My man shall ease that straight.—Sit you down
    there, sir.—   [MARTINO *seats himself.*
Take the tooth, sirrah, daintily, insensibly—
But what's your worship's malady? that's for me, sir.

Bran. Marry, pray, look you, sir; your worship's
    counsel
About mine eyes.

Lat. Sore eyes? that's nothing too, sir.

Bran. By'r lady, I that feel it think it somewhat.

Lat. Have you no convulsions, pricking aches, sir,
Ruptures, or apostemates?

Bran. No, by my faith, sir,
Nor do I desire to have 'em.

Lat. Those are cures ;
There do I win my fame, sir.—Quickly, sirrah,
Reach me the eye-cup hither.

> [OCCULTO *gives him the eye-cup.*
> Do you make water well, sir?

Bran. I'm all well there.

Lat. You feel no grief i' the kidney ?

Bran. Sound, sound, sound, sir.

Lat. O, here's a breath, sir, I must talk withal,
One of these mornings.

Bran. There I think, i'faith,
I am to blame indeed, and my wife's words
Are come to pass, sir.

Mar. O, O ! 'tis not that, 'tis not that !

> [*While* OCCULTO *gives a pull at one of his teeth.*

It is the next beyond it ; there, there, there !

Occ. The best have their mistakings : now I'll fit you, sir.

Bran. What's that, sweet sir, that comforts with his
coolness ?

Lat. O, sovereign gear : wink hard, and keep it in,
sir.

> [*While he applies the eye-cup to* BRANDINO, *he picks
> his pocket.*

Mar. O, O, O !

Occ. Nay, here he goes ; one twitch more, and he
comes, sir.

> [*While he draws one of* MARTINO'S *teeth, he picks
> his pocket.*

Mar. Auh, ho !

Occ. Spit out ; I told you he was gone, sir.

Bran. How cheers Martino ?

Mar. O, I can answer you now, master ;
I feel great ease, sir.

Bran. So do I, Martino.

Mar. I'm rid of a sore burden, for my part, master,
Of a scald[1] little one.

Lat. Please but your worship now
To take three drops of the rich water with you,
I'll undertake your man shall cure you, sir,
At twice i' your chamber.

Bran. Shall he so, sir?

Lat. I will uphold him in't.

Mar. Then will I do't, sir.

Lat. How lively your man's now!

Mar. O, I'm so light, methinks,
Over I was![2]

Bran. What is't contents your worship?

Lat. Even what your worship please; I'm not mercenary.

Bran. My purse is gone, Martino!

Lat. How, your purse, sir!

Bran. 'Tis gone, i'faith; I've been among some rascals.

Mar. And that's a thing
I ever gave you warning of, master; you care not
What company you run into.

Bran. Lend me some money; chide me anon, I
prithee.
A pox on 'em for vipers! they ha' sucked blood o' me.

Mar. O master!

Bran. How now, man?

Mar. My purse is gone too!

Bran. How?
I'll ne'er take warning more of thee while I live then:
Thou art an hypocrite, and art not fit
To give good counsel to thy master, that
Canst not keep from ill company thyself.

Lat. This is most strange, sir; both your purses gone!

Mar. Sir, I'd my hand on mine when I came in.

Lat. Are you but sure of that? O, would you were!

[1] Scabby.   [2] *i.e.* Beyond that I was.

Mar. As I'm of ease.

Lat. Then they're both gone one way,
Be that your comfort.

Bran. Ay, but what way's that, sir?

Lat. That close knave in your clothes has got 'em both :
'Tis well you've clapped him fast.

Bran. Why, that's impossible.

Lat. O, tell not me, sir! I ha' known purses gone,
And the thief stand and look one full i' the face,
As I may do your worship and your man now.

Mar. Nay, that's most certain, master.

Bran. I will make
That rascal in my clothes answer all this then,
And all the robberies that have been done
Since the moon changed.—Get you home first, Martino,
And know if any of my wife's things are missing,
Or any more of mine : tell her he's taken,
And by that token he has took both our purses.

Mar. That's an ill token, master.

Bran. That's all one, sir,
She must have that or nothing : for I'm sure
The rascal has left nothing else for a token.
Begone!
Make haste again, and meet me part o' the way.

Mar. I'll hang the villain,
An 'twere for nothing but the souse[1] he gave me. [*Exit.*

Bran. Sir, I depart ashamed of my requital,
And leave this seal-ring with you as a pledge
Of further thankfulness.   [*Gives ring.*

Lat. No, I beseech you, sir.

Bran. Indeed you shall, sir.

Lat. O, your worship's word, sir

Bran. You shall have my word too, for a rare gentleman
As e'er I met withal.

Lat. Clear sight be with you, sir,— [*Exit* BRANDINO.

_____
[1] Blow.

If conduit-water, and my hostess' milk,
That comes with the ninth child now, may afford it!—
Life, I feared none but thee, my villanous tooth-drawer.

Occ. There was no fear of me; I've often told you
I was bound prentice to a barber once,
But ran away i' the second year.

Lat. Ay, marry,
That made thee give a pull at the wrong tooth,
And me afraid of thee. What have we there, sirs?

Occ. Some threescore dollars i' the master's purse,
And sixteen in the clerk's, a silver seal,
Two or three amber beads, and four blank warrants.

Lat. Warrants! where be they? the best news came yet:
'Mass, here's his hand, and here's his seal; I thank him:
This comes most luckily; one of our fellows
Was took last night, we'll set him first at liberty,
And other good boys after him; and if he
In the old justice's suit, whom we robbed lately,
Will come off roundly,[1] we'll set him free too.

Occ. That were a good deed, faith; we may, in pity.

Lat. There's nothing done merely for pity now-a-days,
Money or ware must help too.

SONG.

In parts, by LATROCINIO *and the rest*

Give me fortune, give me health,
Give me freedom, I'll get wealth:
Who complains his fate's amiss,
When he has the wide world his?
He that has the devil in fee
Can have but all, and so have we.
Give us fortune, give us health,
Give us freedom, we'll get wealth:
In every hamlet, town, and city.
He has lands that was born witty.　　[*Exeun*

[1] *i.e.* Pay handsomely.

Vid. II.　　　　　　　　　　　　2 H

ACT THE FIFTH.

SCENE I.

A Room in BRANDINO'S *House.*

Enter PHILIPPA *and* VIOLETTA.

PHIL. How well this gentleman keeps
    his promise too!
Sure there's no trust in man.
    Vio. They're all Franciscos,
That's my opinion, mistress; fools or
    false ones.
He might have had the honesty yet,
    i'faith,
To send my master's clothes home.
    Phil. Ay, those clothes!
    Vio. Colliers come by the door every day, mistress—
Nay, this is market-day too, poulterers, butchers;
They would have lain most daintily in a pannier,
And kept veal from the wind.
    Phil. Those clothes much trouble me.
    Vio. Faith, an he were a gentleman, as he seemed
To be, they would trouble him too, I think;
Methinks he should have small desire to keep 'em.
    Phil. Faith, and less pride to wear 'em, I should
    think, wench.

Unless he kept 'em as a testimony
For after-times, to show what misery
He passed in his young days, and then weep over 'em.

Vio. Weep, mistress!
Nay, sure, methinks he should not weep for laughing.

Enter MARTINO.

Phil. Martino!—O, we're spoiled, wench! are they
  come, then?

Mar. Mistress, be of good cheer, I've excellent news
  for you;
Comfort your heart.   What have you to breakfast, mistress?
You shall have all again, I warrant you.

Phil. What says he, wench?

Vio. I'm loth to understand him.

Mar. Give me a note of all your things, sweet mis-
  tress;
You shall not lose a hair, take't of my word;
We have him safe enough.

Phil. O, 'las, sweet wench,
This man talks fearfully

Vio. And I know not what yet ·
That's the worst, mistress.

Mar. Can you ell me, pray,
Whether the rascal has broke ope my desk or no?
There's a fine little barrel of pome-citrons
Would have served me this seven year: O, and my fig-
  cheese,—
The fig [1] of everlasting obloquy
Go with him, if he have eat it!   I'll make haste;
He cannot eat it all yet.   He was taken, mistress,
Grossly and beastly; how do you think, 'faith?

---

[1] To make (or give) the fig was to thrust the thumb between two
fingers as a mark of derision.

Phil. I know not, sir.

Mar. Troth, in my master's clothes :
Would any thief but a beast been taken so ?

Phil. Wench, wench !

Vio. I have grief enough of my mine own to tend,
mistress.

Phil. Did he confess the robbery ?

Mar. O no, no, mistress ;
He's a young cunning rascal, he confessed nothing ;
While we were examining on him, he took away
My master's purse and mine, but confessed nothing
still.

Phil. That's but some slanderous injury raised against
him.—   [*Aside to* VIOLETTA.
Came not your master with you ?

Mar. No, sweet mistress :
I must make haste and meet him ; pray, despatch me,
then.

Phil. I've looked o'er all with special heedfulness ;
There's nothing missed, I can assure you, sir,
But that suit of your master's.

Mar. I'm right glad on't :
That suit would hang him, yet I would not have
Him hanged in that suit though ; it will disgrace
My master's fashion for ever, and make it as hateful
As yellow bands.[1]   [*Exit.*

Phil. O, what shall's do, wench ?

Vio. 'Tis no marvel, mistress,
The poor young gentleman could not keep his promise.

Phil. Alas, sweet man, h'as confessed nothing yet,
wench !

---

[1] Bands dyed with yellow starch, once very fashionable, and said
to have been introduced by Mrs. Turner, executed 1615, for com-
plicity in the murder of Sir Thomas Overbury. She wore a ruff of
her favourite colour at the gallows, and the hangman's bands and
cuffs were also yellow —*Dyce.*

Vio. That shows his constancy and love to you,
    mistress :
But you must do't of force, there is no help for't,
The truth can neither shame nor hurt you much ;
Let 'em make what they can on't. 'Twere sin and pity,
    i'faith,
To cast away so sweet a gentleman
For such a pair of infidel hose and doublet ;
I'd not hang a Jew for a whole wardrobe on 'em.
    Phil. Thou say'st true, wench.

Enter MARTIA, *disguised as before.*

    Vio. O, O, they're come again, mistress !
    Phil. Signior Ansaldo?
    Martia. The same ; mightily crossed, lady,
But, past hope, freed again by a doctor's means,
A man of art, I know not justly what indeed ;
But pity, and the fortunate gold you gave me,
Wrought my release between 'em.
    Phil. Met you not
My husband's man?
    Martia. I took such strange ways, lady,
I hardly met a creature.
    Phil. O, most welcome !
    Vio. But how shall we bestow him now we have him,
    mistress?
    Phil. Alas, that's true !
    Vio. Martino may come back again.
    Phil. Step you into that little chamber speedily, sir,
And dress him up in one of my gowns and headtires,
His youth will well endure it.
    Vio. That will be admirable.
    Phil. Nay, do't, do't quickly then, and cut that suit
Into a hundred pieces, that it may never
Be known again.

Vio. A hundred! nay, ten thousand at the least,
mistress; for if there be a piece of that suit left as
big as my nail, the deed will come out: 'tis worse than
a murder: I fear 'twill never be hid.

Phil. Away, do your endeavour, and despatch, wench.
                              [*Exeunt* VIOLETTA *and* MARTIA.
I've thought upon a way of certain safety,
And I may keep him while I have him too,
Without suspicion now; I've heard o' the like:
A gentleman, that for a lady's love
Was thought six months her woman, tended on her
In her own garments, and, she being a widow,
Lay night by night with her in way of comfort:
Marry, in conclusion, match they did together: [1]
Would I'd a copy of the same conclusion!

Enter BRANDINO *with a writing.*

He's come himself now.   If thou be'st a happy wench,
Be fortunate in thy speed!   I'll delay time
With all the means I can.—O, welcome, sir!

Bran. I'll speak to you anon, wife, and kiss you
          shortly;
I'm very busy yet: [*Reads.*] "Cocksey-down, Memberry,
Her manor-house at Well-dun."

Phil. What's that, good sir?

Bran. The widow's, your sweet sister's deed of gift:
Sh'as made all her estate over to me, wench;
She'll be too hard for 'em all: and now come buss
          me,
Good luck after thieves' handsel.

Phil. O, 'tis happy, sir.
You have him fast!

---

[1] This occurrence, which seems to have been well known, probably suggested Bold's attempt on the widow in Field's *Amends for
Ladies.*

Bran. I ha' laid him safe enough, wench.

Phil. I was so lost in joy at the report on't,
I quite forgot one thing to tell Martino.

Bran. What's that, sweet blood?

Phil. He and his villains, sir,
Robbed a sweet gentlewoman last night.

Bran. A gentlewoman?

Phil. Nay, most uncivilly and basely stripped her, sir.

Bran. O barbarous slaves!

Phil. I was even fain, for womanhood's sake,
Alas, and charity's, to receive her in,
And clothe her poor wants in a suit of mine.

Bran. 'Twas most religiously done; I long for her.
Who have I brought to see thee, think'st thou, woman?

Phil. Nay, sir, I know not.

Bran. Guess, I prithee, heartily ;
An enemy of thine.

Phil. That I hope you have not, sir.

Bran. But all was done in jest : he cries thee mercy ;
Francisco, sirrah.[1]

Phil. O, I think not on him!

Bran. That letter was but writ to try thy constancy ;
He confessed all to me.

Phil. Joy on him, sir!

Enter FRANCISCO.

So far am I from malice, look you, sir——
Welcome, sweet signior ;· but I'll ne'er trust you, sir.

Bran. Faith, I'm beholding to thee, wife, for this.

Fran. [*Aside.*] Methinks I enter now this house with
joy,
Sweet peace, and quietness of conscience ;
I wear no guilty blush upon my cheek
For a sin stamped last midnight : I can talk now,

---

[1] See note *ante*, p. 437.

With that kind man, and not abuse him inwardly
With any scornful thought made of his shame :
What a sweet being is an honest mind !
It speaks peace to itself and all mankind.

Re-enter MARTINO.

Bran. Martino !
Mar. Master ?
Bran. There's another robbery done, sirrah,
By the same party.
 Mar. What ! your worship mocks,
Under correction.
 Phil. I forgot to tell thee ;
He robbed a lovely gentlewoman
 Mar. O pagan !
This fellow will be stoned to death with pipkins
Your women in the suburbs will so maul him
With broken cruises and pitchers without ears,
He'll never die alive, that's my opinion.

Re-enter MARTIA *dressed as a woman, and* VIOLETTA.

 Phil. Look you, your judgments, gentlemen ;—yours
  especially,
Signior Francisco, whose mere [1] object now
Is woman at these years ; that's the eye-saint, I know,
Amongst young gallants :—husband, you've a glimpse
  too :
You offer half an eye, as old you are.
 Bran. By'r lady ; better, wench ; an eye and a half, I
  trow ;
I should be sorry else.
 Phil. What think you now, sirs,
Is't not a goodly, manly gentlewoman ?

     [1] Whole.

Bran. Beshrew my heart else, wife.—
Pray, soft a little, signior ; you're but my guest, rememver ;
I'm master of the house, I'll have the first buss.

Phil. But, husband, 'tis the courtesy of all places
To give a stranger ever the first bit.

Bran. In woodcock or so ; but there's no heed to be
taken in mutton ; we commonly fall so roundly to that,
we forget ourselves.—
I'm sorry for thy fortune, but thou'rt welcome, lady.

[*Kisses* MARTIA.

Mar. My master kisses as I've heard a hackney-man
Cheer up his mare,—chap, chap !   [*Aside.*

Bran. I have him fast, lady,
And he shall lie by't close.

Martia. You cannot do me
A greater pleasure, sir.

Bran. I'm happily glad on't.

Fran. Methinks there's somewhat whispers in my soul,
This is the hour I must begin my acquaintance
With honest love, and banish all loose thoughts ;
My fate speaks to me from the modest eye
Of yon sweet gentlewoman.   *Aside.*

Phil. Wench, wench !

Vio. Pish, hold in your breath, mistress ;
If you be seen to laugh, you spoil all presently :
I keep it in with all the might I have—puh !

Martia. Pray, what young gentleman's that, sir

Bran. An honest boy, i'faith,
And came of a good kind ; dost like him, lady ?
I would thou hadst him, an thou be'st not promised :
He's worth ten thousand dollars.

Vio. By this light, mistress,
My master will go near to make a match anon .
Methinks I dream of admirable sport, mistress.

Phil. Peace ! thou'rt a drab.

Bran. Come hither now. Francisco :

I've known the time I've had a better stomach;
Now I can dine with looking upon meat.

 Fran. [*Kissing* MARTIA.] That face deserved a better
  fortune, lady,
Than last night's rudeness showed.

 Martia. We cannot be
Our choosers, sir, in our own destiny.

 Fran. I return better pleased than when I went.
             |*Aside.*

 Mar. And could that beastly imp rob you, forsooth?

 Martia. Most true, forsooth.
I will not altogether, sir, disgrace you,
Because you look half like a gentleman.

 Mar. And that's the mother's half.

 Martia. There's my hand for you.

 Mar. I swear you could not give me anything
I love better, a hand gets me my living:
O sweet lemon-peel!   [*Kisses* MARTIA'S *hand.*

 Fran. May I request a modest word or two,
Lady, in private with you?

 Martia. With me, sir?

 Fran. To make it sure from all suspect of injury
Or unbeseeming privacy, which Heaven knows
Is not my aim now, I'll entreat this gentleman
For an ear-witness unto all our conference.

 Martia. Why, so, I am content, sir.

 Bran. So am I, lady.
     [*Exeunt* MARTIA *and* FRANCISCO.

 Mar. O master, here is a rare bedfellow
For my mistress to-night! for you know we must
Both out of town again.

 Bran. That's true, Martino.

 Mar. I do but think how they'll lie telling of tales
  together,
The prettiest!

 Bran. The prettiest indeed.

Mar. Their tongues will never lin[1] wagging, master.
Bran. Never,
Martino, never.

[*Exeunt* BRANDINO *and* MARTINO *severally.*

Phil. Take heed you be not heard.
Vio. I fear you most, mistress.
Phil. Me, fool! ha, ha!
Vio. Why, look you, mistress, faith, you're faulty;
ha, ha!
Phil. Well said, i'faith: where lies the fault now,
gossip?
Vio. O for a husband! I shall burst with laughing
else;
This house is able to spoil any maid.
Phil. I'll be revenged now soundly of Francisco,
For failing me when time was.
Vio. Are you there, mistress? I thought you would
not forget that, however: a good turn disappointed is
ever the last thing that a woman forgives; she'll scarce
do't when she's speechless; nay, though she hold up her
whole hand for all other injuries, she'll forgive that but
with one finger.
Phil. I'll vex his heart as much as he mocked mine.
Vio. But that may mar your hopes too, if our gentle-
woman
Be known to be a man.
Phil. Not as I'll work it;
I would not lose this sweet revenge, methinks,
For a whole fortnight of the old man's absence,
Which is the sweetest benefit next to this.—

Re-enter MARTIA.

Why, how now, sir? what course take you for laughing?
We are undone for one.
Martia. Faith, with great pain

¹ Cease.

Stifle it, and keep it in ; I ha' no receipt for't.
But, pray, in sadness,[1] say, what is the gentleman
I never knew his like for tedious urgings,
He will receive no answer.

    Phil. Would he would not, sir !

    Martia. Says I'm ordained for him, merely for him,
And that his wiving fate speaks in me to him ;
Will force on me a jointure speedily
Of some seven thousand dollars.

    Phil. Would thou hadst 'em, sir !
I know he can an he will.

    Martia. For wonder's pity,
What is this gentleman ?

    Phil. Faith, shall I tell you, sir ?
One that would make an excellent, honest husband,
For her that's a just maid at one and twenty ;
For, on my conscience, he has his maidenhead yet.

    Martia. Fie, out upon him, beast !

    Phil. Sir, if you love me,
Give way but to one thing I shall request of you.

    Martia. Your courtesies, you know, may lay commands on me.

    Phil. Then, at his next solicitings, let a consent
Seem to come from you ; 'twill make noble sport, sir
We'll get jointure and all ; but you must bear
Yourself most affable to all his purposes.

    Martia. I can do that.

    Phil. Ay, and take heed of laughing.

    Martia. I've bide the worst of that already, lady.

    Phil. Peace, set your countenance then, for here h
comes.

Re-enter FRANCISCO.

    Fran. There is no middle continent in his passion :
I feel it, since it must be love or death.

Seriousness.

It was ordained for óne.   [*Aside.*

   Phil. Signior Francisco,
I'm sorry 'twas your fortune in my house, sir,
To have so violent a stroke come to you;
The gentlewoman's a stranger; pray, be counselled,
    sir,
Till you hear further of her friends and portion.
   Fran. 'Tis only but her love that I desire;
She comes most rich in that.
   Phil. But be advised, though;
I think she's a rich heir, but see the proof, sir,
Before you make her such a generous jointure.
   Fran. 'Tis mine, and I will do't.
   Phil. She shall be yours too,
If I may rule her then.
   Fran. You speak all sweetness.
   Phil. She likes your person well; I tell you so
    much,
But take no note I said so.
   Fran. Not a word.
   Phil. Come, lady, come, the gentleman's desert-
    ful,
And, o' my conscience, honest.
   Martia. Blame me not;
I am a maid, and fearful.
   Fran. Never truth
Came perfecter from man.
   Phil. Give her a lip-taste,
That she herself may praise it.
      [FRANCISCO *kisses* MARTIA, *and then exit with*
        her, PHILIPPA, *and* VIOLETTA.

        Re-enter BRANDINO.

   Bran. Yea, a match, i'faith!
My house is lucky for 'em.—

Re-enter MARTINO.

Now, Martino?

Mar. Master, the widow has the day.

Bran. The day?

Mar. Sh'as overthrown my youngster.

Bran. Precious tidings!
Clap down four woodcocks more.

Mar. They're all at hand, sir.

Bran. What, both her adversaries too?

Mar. They're come, sir.

Bran. Go, bid the cook serve in two geese in a dish.

Mar. I like your conceit, master, beyond utterance.

[*Exit.*

Enter VALERIA, RICARDO, *and two* Suitors.

Bran. Welcome, sweet sister! which is the man must
have you?
I'd welcome nobody else.

1st Suit. Come to me then, sir.

Bran. Are you he, faith, my chain of gold? I'm
glad on't.

Val. I wonder you can have the face to follow me,
That have so prosecuted things against me.
But I ha' resolved [1] myself 'tis done to spite me.

Ric. O dearth of truth!

2nd Suit. Nay, do not spoil thy hair;
Hold, hold, I say; I'll get thee a widow somewhere.

Ric. If hand and faith be nothing for a contract,
What shall man hope?

2nd Suit. 'Twas wont to be enough, honey,
When there was honest meaning amongst widows:
But since your bribes came in, 'tis not allowed
A contract without gifts to bind it fast:

---

[1] Convinced.

Everything now must have a feeling first.—
Do I come near you, widow?

Val. No, indeed, sir,
Nor ever shall, I hope:—and for your comfort, sir,
That sought all means to entrap me for my wealth,
Had law unfortunately put you upon me,
You'd lost your labour, all your aim and hopes, sir;
Here stands the honest gentleman, my brother,
To whom I've made a deed of gift of all.

Bran. Ay, that she has, i'faith; I thank her, gentlemen;
Look you here, sirs.   [*Shows writing.*

Val. I must not look for pleasures,
That give more grief if they prove false, or fail us,
Than ever they gave joy.

1st Suit. Ha' you served me so, widow?

2nd Suit. I'm glad thou hast her not.—Laugh at him,
honey; ha, ha!

Val. I must take one that loves me for myself;
Here's an old gentleman looks not after wealth,
But virtue, manners, and conditions.[1]

1st Suit. Yes, by my faith, I must have lordships too,
widow.

Val. How, sir?

1st Suit. Your manners, virtue, and conditions,
widow,
Are pretty things within doors, I like well on 'em;
But I must have somewhat without, lying or being
In the tenure or occupation of master such a one, ha!
Those are fine things indeed.

Val. Why, sir, you swore to me it was for love.

1st Suit. True; but there's two words to a bargain
ever,
All the world over; and, if love be one,

---

[1] Disposition.

I'm sure money's the other; 'tis no bargain else:
Pardon me, I must dine as well as sup, widow.

Val. Cry mercy, I mistook you all this while, sir;
It was this ancient gentleman indeed,
Whom I crave pardon on.

2nd Suit. What of me, widow?

Val. Alas, I've wronged you, sir! 'twas you that swore
You loved me for myself.

2nd Suit. By my troth, but I did not;
Come, father not your lies upon me, widow:
I love you for yourself!—Spit at me, gentlemen,
If ever I'd such a thought.—Fetch me in, widow!
You'll find your reach too short.

Val. Why, you've enough, you say.

2nd Suit. Ay, but I'll have
My humour too; you never think of that;
They're coach-horses, they go together still.

Val. Whom should a widow trust? I'll swear 'twas
one of you
That made me believe so.—Mass, think 'twas you, sir,
Now I remember me.

Ric. I swore too much,
To be believed so little.

Val. Was it you then?
Beshrew my heart for wronging of you!

Ric. Welcome blessing!
Are you mine faithfully now?

Val. As love can make one.

1st Suit. Why, this fills the commonwealth, so full
of beggars,
Marrying for love, which none of mine shall do.

Val. But, now I think on't, we must part again, sir.

Ric. Again!

Val. You're in debt, and I, in doubt of all,
Left myself nothing too; we must not hold;
Want on both sides makes all affection cold.

I shall not keep you from that gentleman ;
You'll be his more than mine ; and, when he list,
He'll make you lie from me in some sour prison ;
Then let him take you now for altogether, sir,
For he that's mine shall be all mine, nor nothing.
   Ric. I never felt the evil of my debts
Till this afflicting minute.
   2nd Suit. I'll be mad
Once in my days : I have enough to cure me,
And I will have my humour ; they are now
But desperate debts again, I ne'er look for 'em :
And ever since I knew what malice was,
I always held it sweeter to sow mischief
Than to receive money ; 'tis the finer pleasure.
I'll give him in his bonds, as 'twere in pity,
To make the match, and bring 'em both to beggary :
Then will they ne'er agree, that's a sure point ;
He'll give her a black eye within these three days,
Beat half her teeth out by All-hallowtide,
And break the little household stuff they have
With throwing at one another : O sweet sport !—
                                      [Aside.
Come, widow, come, I'll try your honesty :
Here to my honey you've made many proffers,
I fear they're all but tricks.—Here are his debts, gentle-
      men ;   *[Shows bonds.*
How I came by 'em I know best myself.—
Take him before us faithfully for your husband,
And he shall tear 'em all before your face, widow.
   Val. Else may all faith refuse me !
   2nd Suit. Tear 'em, honey ;
'Tis firm in law, a consideration given :
                *[*RICARDO *tears the bonds.*
What, with thy teeth ? thou'lt shortly tear her so,
That's all my hope, thou'dst never had 'em else :
I have enough, and I will have my humour.
   M id. II.   2 I

Ric. I'm now at liberty, widow.

Val. I'll be so too,
And then I come to thee.—Give me this from you,
    brother.   [*Takes the writing.*

Bran. Hold, sister, sister !

Val. Look you, the deed of gift, sir ; I'm as free :
He that has me has all, and thou art he.

Both Suit. How's that?

Val. You're bobbed ;[1] 'twas but a deed in trust,—
And all to prove thee, whom I've found most just.

Bran. I'm bobbed among the rest too ; I'd have
    sworn
'T had been a thing for me and my heirs for ever ;
If I'd but got it up to the black box above,
It had been past redemption.

1st Suit. How am I cheated !

2nd Suit. I hope you'll have the conscience now to
    pay me, sir.

Ric. O wicked man, sower of strife and envy,
Open not thy lips !

2nd Suit. How, how's this ?

Ric. Thou hast no charge at all, no child of thine own,
But two thou gott'st once of a scouring-woman,
And they're both well provided for, they're i' the Hos-
    pital :
Thou hast ten thousand pound to bury thee ;
Hang thyself when thou wilt, a slave go with thee :

2nd Suit. I'm gone, my goodness comes all out to-
    gether :
I have enough, but I have not my humour.   [*Exit.*

Re-enter VIOLETTA.

Vio. O master, gentlemen, and you, sweet widow,—
I think you are no forwarder, yet I know not,—

           [1] Cheated.

If ever you be sure to laugh again
Now is the time!
   Val. Why, what's the matter, wench?
   Vio. Ha, ha, ha!
   Bran. Speak, speak.
   Vio. Ha!—a marriage,
A marriage; I cannot tell't for laughing—ha, ha!
   Bran. A marriage? do you make that a laughing
    matter?
   Vio. Ha!—ay, and you'll make it so when you
    know all.
Here they come, here they come, one man married to
    another![1]
   Val. How! man to man!
   Vio. Ay, man to man, i'faith;
There'll be good sport at night to bring 'em both to bed:

     Re-enter MARTIA, PHILIPPA, *and* FRANCISCO.

Do you see 'em now? ha, ha, ha!
   1st Suit. My daughter Martia!
   Martia. O my father! your love and pardon, sir
   Val. 'Tis she indeed, gentlemen.
   Martia. I have been disobedient, I confess,
Unto your mind, and Heaven has punished me
With much affliction since I fled your sight;
But finding reconcilement from above
In peace of heart, the next I hope's your love.
   1st Suit. I cannot but forgive thee now I see thee.
Thou fled'st a happy fortune of an old man.
But Francisco's of a noble family,
Though he be somewhat spent.
   Fran. I loved her not, sir,
As she was yours, for I protest I knew't not,

---

[1] Gifford observes that there is a similar incident in Jonson s *New Inn*, v. 1.

But for herself, sir, and her own deservings,
Which, had you been as foul as you've been spiteful,
I should have loved in her.

 1st Suit. Well, hold your prating, sir;
You are not like to lose by't.

 Phil. O Violetta,
Who shall laugh at us now?

 Vio. The child unborn, mistress.

 Martia. Be good.

 Fran. Be honest.

 Martia. Heaven will not let you sin, an you'd be
  careful.

 Fran. What means it sends to help you, think, and
  mend,
You're as much bound as we to praise that friend.

 Phil. I am so, and I will so.

 Martia. Marry you speedily;
Children tame you, you'll die like a wild beast else.

 Vio. Ay, by my troth, should I.   I've much ado
To forbear laughing now, more's my hard fortune.

Re-enter MARTINO.

 Mar. O master, mistress, and you gentles all,
To horse, to horse, presently,[1] if you mean to do
Your country any service!

 Bran. Art not ashamed, Martino, to talk of horsing
So openly before young married couples thus?

 Mar. It does concern the common wealth, and me,
And you, master, and all: the thieves are taken.

 Martia. What say'st, Martino?

 Mar. La, here's commonwealth's-men!
The man of art, master, that cupped your eyes
Is proved an arrant rascal; and his man,
That drew my tooth, an excellent purse-drawer—

---

[1] Immediately.

I felt no pain in that, it went insensibly—
Such notable villanies confessed !——

   Bran. Stop there, sir ;
We will have time for them.—Come, gentlefolks,
Take a slight meal with us : but the best cheer
Is perfect joy, and that we wish all here.

   Ric. Stay, stay, sir; I'm as hungry of my widow
As you can be upon your maid, believe it ;
But we must come to our desires in order ;
There's duties to be paid ere we go further.—

                  [*Speaking the rest as an Epilogue.*
He that without your likings leaves this place,
Is like one falls to meat and forgets grace ;
And that's not handsome, trust me, no :
Our rights being paid, and your loves understood,
My widow and my meat then does me good.—
I ha' no money, wench, I told thee true,—
For my report, pray let her hear't from you. [*Exeunt.*